HITLER'S

SILENT

PARTNERS

ALSO BY ISABEL VINCENT

*See No Evil: The Strange Case of Christine Lamont
and David Spencer*

Hammersfeld Family Tree

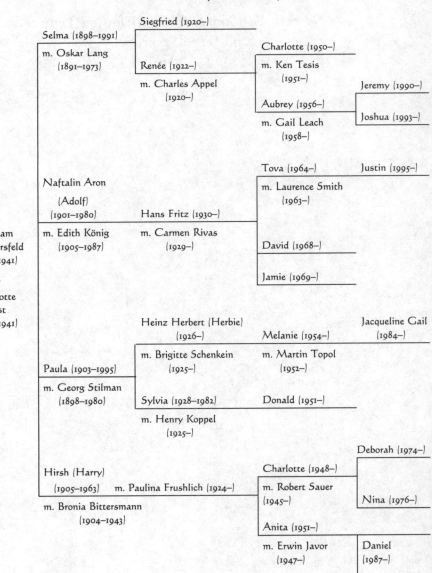

Abraham Hammersfeld (1874–1941) m. Charlotte Faust (1876–1941)

Selma (1898–1991) m. Oskar Lang (1891–1973)

Siegfried (1920–)

Renée (1922–) m. Charles Appel (1920–)

Charlotte (1950–) m. Ken Tesis (1951–)

Aubrey (1956–) m. Gail Leach (1958–)

Jeremy (1990–)

Joshua (1993–)

Naftalin Aron (Adolf) (1901–1980) m. Edith König (1905–1987)

Hans Fritz (1930–) m. Carmen Rivas (1929–)

Tova (1964–) m. Laurence Smith (1963–)

Justin (1995–)

David (1968–)

Jamie (1969–)

Paula (1903–1995) m. Georg Stilman (1898–1980)

Heinz Herbert (Herbie) (1926–) m. Brigitte Schenkein (1925–)

Melanie (1954–) m. Martin Topol (1952–)

Jacqueline Gail (1984–)

Donald (1951–)

Sylvia (1928–1982) m. Henry Koppel (1925–)

Hirsh (Harry) (1905–1963)   m. Paulina Frushlich (1924–)

m. Bronia Bittersmann (1904–1943)

Charlotte (1948–) m. Robert Sauer (1945–)

Deborah (1974–)

Nina (1976–)

Anita (1951–) m. Erwin Javor (1947–)

Daniel (1987–)

HITLER'S

Swiss Banks, Nazi Gold,

SILENT

and the Pursuit of Justice

PARTNERS

Isabel Vincent

William Morrow and Company, Inc. | New York

Library of Congress Cataloging-in-Publication Data

Vincent, Isabel, 1965–
    Hitler's silent partners : Swiss banks, Nazi gold, and the pursuit
of justice / Isabel Vincent.—1st ed.
        p.   cm.
    ISBN 0-688-15425-5 (alk. paper)
    1. World War, 1939–1945—Destruction and pillage—Europe.
2. World War, 1939–1945—Confiscations and contributions—Europe.
3. Banks and banking—Switzerland.   4. Gold.   5. World War,
1939–1945—Economic aspects—Germany.   6. World War, 1939–1945—
Reparations.   I. Title.
D810.D6V56   1997
940.53'1—dc21   97-23518
                                                                        CIP

Printed in the United States of America

First Edition

1 2 3 4 5 6 7 8 9 10

BOOK DESIGN BY CHRIS WELCH

IN MEMORY OF

ABRAHAM HAMMERSFELD

ACKNOWLEDGMENTS

This book was written while I was on a Southam Research Fellowship at Massey College in the University of Toronto. I am grateful to Southam Corporation for their generous support, and particularly to Conrad Black, who is a tremendous supporter of young journalists. I continue to be overwhelmed by his efforts on my behalf, and am very grateful for his flexibility and unwavering confidence in my abilities.

People spread over three continents gave their support to this project. In the United States, I must thank Claire Wachtel, my editor at William Morrow, who had enough confidence in me to suggest I write this book in the first place. I am grateful for her encouragement, her guidance, and, most of all, for dragging me to a bookstore in Manhattan in high summer to show me the best of contemporary nonfiction. I am also hugely indebted to Kate Fillion and Rick Hornung, who have been strong supporters of my work and great friends.

In Canada, I want to thank my indefatigable agent, Anne

McDermid, who believed in me from the very beginning; my editor, David Kilgour, who never complained as he nursed a broken leg while doing his usual magic on the manuscript, and Ken Whyte at *Saturday Night,* who was a constant source of support and inspiration. Rick Cash at the *Globe and Mail* library was a great researcher, and Louise Dennys at Knopf Canada was a most particular and exacting editor. Thank you to Dietlinde Frey for her insights into Swiss banking, and to my translators, Eva Cooper, Monica Krueger-Bandy, and Frank Gabriel, who worked against the clock to translate piles of faded and difficult-to-read correspondence and official documents. Manuel Prutschi, executive director of the Canadian Jewish Congress, sprang into action whenever I needed a letter of introduction or contacts in Jewish communities throughout Europe. Rabbi Jordan Pearlson was always generous with his time and patient with me when I asked him to explain rather obscure biblical references. Gloria Torem Goodis at Temple Sinai was equally generous and attentive. Moses Wuggenig, John Bentley Mays, and Deirdre Kelly were pillars of strength during the last trying days of completing the manuscript in Toronto. I want to thank the staff of Massey College and my Southam colleagues, who so generously and unflinchingly took up some of my duties during the academic year so that I could have the time to write this book. I also want to acknowledge James Cooper, who photocopied articles, checked historical and legal references, and was very supportive and encouraging of my work in the initial phase of this project.

I am indebted to my editors at the *Globe and Mail,* who gave me the freedom I needed to write this book, and then the time off to recover.

Although I have never met them personally, I would like to acknowledge historians Raul Hilberg and Arthur L. Smith, Jr., for their groundbreaking works on the Holocaust and the Nazi plunder of gold, respectively. Smith's *Hitler's Gold: The Story of the Nazi War Loot* is undoubtedly the most complete and readable account of the Nazi looting of national treasuries during the war. Hilberg's *Destruction of the European Jews* is an exacting and thorough overview of the mechanics of genocide. I would also like to acknowledge writer Nicholas Faith, whose *Safety in Numbers: The Mysterious World of Swiss Banking* is an excellent primer on Swiss banks. Historian Gertrude Schneider, whom I have interviewed, gave me some very interesting insights into pre-Anschluss and postwar Vienna, which were supplemented by her excellent book *Exile and Destruction: The Fate of Austrian Jews, 1938–1945*.

In Austria, I am grateful to Hans Peter Martin of *Der Spiegel* and Suzanne Martin for their generous hospitality and insights into Austrian politics and history. I am also indebted to Dr. Steiner and the staff at the State Archives in Vienna for helping me search out documents. Thank you also to Elfie Rometsch, who helped me with translation, and Kurt Fraser, whose insights into wartime Riga were invaluable.

In England, I must thank Martin Dowle and Fabricio Jorge da Silva for their hospitality and for helping me to set up interviews on such short notice. I am also grateful to Andrew Nurnberg and his staff for their support of this project.

In Switzerland, I want to thank my researcher Jessica Hottinger, who clipped articles, set up interviews and offered piercing insights into the Swiss character. Thanks also to Alessandro Delprete of the Swiss parliament in Bern, Daniel Guggenheim for clearing up questions of international banking law, and Hans Baer of the Bank Julius Baer for his candor and illuminating insights into Swiss banking. There are a number of Swiss journalists who were very generous with information and contacts, including Beat Brenner of the *Neue Zürcher Zeitung*, Antoine Maurice of the *Journal de Genève*, and Ueli Haldimann of the *SonntagsZeitung*. I also owe gratitude to a long list of Swiss government officials and bankers, whom unfortunately I cannot mention by name here.

In Latvia, I must extend thanks to Margers Vestermanis, chief of the Museum of Documentation "Jews in Latvia," and the staff of the Latvian National Archives who responded to my requests for information quickly and with great professionalism.

In Argentina, I am indebted to my longtime friend and researcher

Monica de Escardo, and to Ruben Beraja of the World Jewish Congress, whose great integrity and candor are much appreciated and admired.

I am grateful to the Hamersfeld, Appel, and Stilman families without whose openness and patience it would not have been possible to write this book. I also want to thank Sergio Karas and his family for allowing me to pry into painful parts of their family history that they would probably have preferred to have left forgotten. Thanks are due also to my wonderful parents, Afonso Costa Vicente and Irene Ferreira Vicente, for their constant support, strength, and encouragement; to my sister-in-law Franklynne Vincent for her wisdom and support, and to my brother George Vincent, a remarkable orthopedic surgeon, who fixed my Canadian editor's leg when he broke it last winter.

CONTENTS

HITLER'S

SILENT

PARTNERS

INTRODUCTION

O ne afternoon in the fall of 1938, a twelve-year-old boy sat cross-legged on his parents' bed in a well-appointed flat in the center of Vienna, and watched with rapt attention as his mother carefully rolled a pair of heavy silver candlesticks in two plush towels and placed them in the upper drawers of an old-fashioned wooden trunk in preparation for a journey. The candlesticks, adorned with garlands of exquisitely engraved flowers at their bases, were a gift from the boy's grandfather, a well-to-do Viennese textile exporter named Abraham Hammersfeld. In better times, they had stood in a prominent place on the mantel in the family's living room, and every Friday night, for as long as the boy could remember, his mother, following Jewish tradition, had lit them to welcome the Sabbath.

Like the other items that were stacked on the bed waiting to be packed for the journey—his sister's teddy bear, clothing, a toothbrush—the candlesticks were an essential part of their lives, and his mother had said fiercely that she would not give them up, even though the Nazis had already taken just about everything else.

The next day the family waited in line at the Vienna airport while a group of Gestapo agents rifled through their carefully packed trunk. The boy watched his mother hold her breath as the inspectors unraveled the towels containing the candlesticks. An inspector picked up one of the heavy candlesticks, lifted it to the light, and then tossed it carelessly back into the drawer and closed the trunk. Another Gestapo agent examined their passports, each of which had been stamped with a large red "J" for "Jew" on the opening page, and motioned the family to a waiting room. They took their place in line with several other Jewish refugees who were lucky enough to be leaving Austria with a few cherished possessions—and their lives. Over the next three years, as war raged across Europe and Adolf Hitler prepared to exterminate the region's Jews, the boy's family would make a long, perilous journey that eventually landed them in New York. At every customs inspection in every country they passed through—Sweden, the Soviet Union, Japan—the boy would watch his mother hold her breath whenever an official rifled through the family trunk and unraveled the towels.

Today, nearly sixty years later, the same candlesticks are tarnished and scratched, but nevertheless occupy a place of distinction on a living-room mantel in a high-rise apartment in Queens, New York. The twelve-year-old boy who fled Vienna so many years ago is now over seventy, and the candlesticks are almost all that remain of a brutally interrupted childhood in Austria and of a very special grandfather.

"I now know why they were so important to my mother," says the elderly, white-haired Herbie Stilman, who arrived in the United States in 1941. "They are the only things we have left from Grandfather Hammersfeld, the only things we have left from our life in Vienna."

The candlesticks, so lovingly transported over several continents during wartime, were passed on to Herbie by his mother when she died several years ago. And they will be passed on after his own death, in remembrance of a grandfather who taught him Hebrew, prepared him for his bar mitzvah, and then disappeared forever in the conflagration that consumed six million Jewish souls.

When civilizations are brutally wiped out, it's their inanimate objects—household utensils, heirlooms, and keepsakes—that endure as silent witnesses to their existence. Archaeologists and art historians study objects to gain certain insights into the past, but they can never record the sentimental value the objects had for their owners. What would the experts make of Abraham Hammersfeld's candlesticks? That they were forged by Austrian silversmiths in the nineteenth century, certainly. But they could never know that to a man living in a high rise in Queens they are almost his only links to the past—the only things his family managed to safeguard from a marauding group of Nazi thugs who ruthlessly expropriated their businesses and homes and murdered some of them.

Today, Herbie says he is one of the luckiest members of the surviving Hammersfeld family because whenever he looks at the candlesticks he can relive his happy childhood in Vienna and draw strength from his Jewish heritage. But when his wife lights the candlesticks on special occasions, their dancing flames also remind him of a distant genocide whose scope and horror are still unimaginable to him. And when he remembers his beloved grandfather, the crushing sorrow of that genocide overwhelms him, and he can barely speak.

"They are the only things I have from Grandfather," he says again, contemplating the candlesticks. "The only things."

UNLIKE HER COUSIN in Queens, one of the only surviving granddaughters of Abraham Hammersfeld has no candlesticks or family heirlooms on her living-room mantel. If archaeologists were to examine her suburban bungalow in north Toronto, they would find no physical reminders of her upper-middle-class childhood in Vienna or the horrors of her incarceration in a Nazi death camp. In many ways, the granddaughter has deliberately tried to keep the painful past firmly behind her. Most of her possessions—her carefully polished dining-room table and matching chairs, the objets d'art that adorn her living-room shelves—reflect a pleasant, prosperous North American domesticity.

"When I arrived in North America, I left Europe behind for good and I didn't want anything to remind me of the past," says Renée Appel, who, like Herbie, is now in her seventies.

Still, it is impossible for her to keep the past behind her. Only her family knows about the silver menorah that she keeps tightly sealed in a Ziploc bag tucked in the back of one of her kitchen cabinets. The antique menorah, which she recently had cleaned and restored, was a gift from Herbie's mother and used to belong to her grandfather. She only removes it from its hiding place once a year, at Hanukkah, when her family gathers in her dining room every night for a week to light a candle and contemplate the past. "When I light the candles, I realize that I can never forget," says Renée. "I can never forget about the murder of a million children. I can never forget what they did to me, what they did to my grandfather."

IN LATE OCTOBER 1996, art historians, collectors, and the curious crowded the lobby of the Museum of Applied Arts (MAK) in Vienna to look upon the last remaining, unclaimed possessions of Austria's prewar Jewish community, part of an entire culture that had been violently and indiscriminately obliterated by Nazi terror. With the hushed whispers of mourners at a funeral, the crowd wandered through the high-ceilinged salons of the museum, awkwardly paying their respects to people they never knew, whose mundane household furnishings and cherished objects were now only testaments to genocide.

The viewers' awkwardness was understandable, for it was difficult to know just how to react to this exhibition and auction of mostly nineteenth-century paintings, objets d'art, books, and coins—in all, some eight thousand items—that had been looted from Jewish homes in Austria by Nazi storm troopers between 1938 and 1945, then gathered up by the Allied forces after the war, and stored at various collection points throughout the country. In 1955, the Allies handed over the unclaimed property to the Austrian authorities on condition that they try to find the original owners or their heirs. But only a handful of items reverted to their rightful heirs. Most gathered mold and dust in their final collection point at Mauerbach, a fourteenth-century Carthusian monastery just north of Vienna. At last, following intense lobbying by Austrian Jewish leaders for more than three decades, the Austrian Parliament unanimously voted to transfer legal ownership of the collection to the Federation of Jewish Communities of Austria in July 1995, on the condition that they auction it all off for the benefit of victims of the Holocaust.

The organizers of the Mauerbach auction, as the event came to be known, had really no idea what to expect when they advertised this unusual exhibition and sale. Who would attend? What would they buy? Unlike most contemporary auctions, where objects are prized for historic provenance and artistic merit, the most striking items at the Mauerbach sale were often of questionable artistic merit and of no discernible provenance. There were few Old Master paintings, little valuable sculpture. Rather, the objects were remarkable for their sentimentality—the keepsakes and *tchotchkes* (trinkets) of Vienna's prewar, mostly middle-class, highly assimilated Jewish community.

Professional curators from Washington's Holocaust Museum and Jerusalem's Yad Vashem picked through broken china, tarnished silver, faded tapestries, damaged paintings, and worn books, hoping to find things that were somehow reflective of Austria's flourishing prewar Jewish heritage. Surprisingly, these were few at Mauerbach—no silver menorahs or ceremonial kiddush cups used to sanctify wine on the Sabbath, no Hebrew books or silken prayer shawls. There was only one painting that depicted a rather sentimentalized view of an eastern European *shtetl,* or Jewish settlement, and as such it became one of the most sought-after items at the auction.

Most of the Mauerbach collection consisted of nineteenth-century landscape paintings and Christian religious art, which had a lot of the Jewish collectors and curators at the sale frankly baffled. Why would Austrian Jews have collected paintings of Benedictine monks, Christ, and the Madonna? they murmured, incredulously. The Viennese art experts called it an indication of the bourgeois art collecting style of the 1920s and '30s, when Christian religious painting and sculpture were quite popular among connoisseurs in Europe. Others viewed it as a sign of the cultural assimilation of many Jews in Vienna just before the Second World War.

"Why should anyone be surprised by the type of art collected?" said one prominent Viennese Jew. "Jewish collectors were no different from their non-Jewish counterparts when it came to artistic tastes. The Viennese Jewish community at that time was quite assimilated, which I think makes the horror of what happened to most of them that much worse."

Most of the items at the auction fetched exponentially more than their listed prices. Fran Laufer, a seventy-year-old Polish-born interior decorator and survivor of the Bergen-Belsen concentration camp, had traveled all the way from her home in New York to bid on the shtetl oil painting, by Ludwig Knaus. "It would give me the greatest joy to have that painting," she said. "It is the only painting here that has a tremendous Jewish feeling about it."

But after the first day of bidding, as she saw prices rise far beyond their original estimates, Mrs. Laufer gave up. The shtetl painting, which depicts an old Jewish man surrounded by children on the busy main street of a village, fetched almost ten times its lowest estimate of $47,000.*

In addition to the art dealers, museum curators, and private collectors who called in their bids from around the world or came to Vienna from as far away as Indonesia with large acquisitions budgets to spend, many who lined up outside the MAK on that first blustery auction morning in midautumn had more modest goals in mind. They came for the smaller items, which were ultimately the most heartbreaking relics because they were the kinds of things anyone might

*All dollar figures are in U.S. 1997 dollars, unless otherwise noted.

find in his or her grandmother's dining room: the Japanese teapot, cups, and saucers, preserved in their original gift box, or the mismatched collection of glassware, valued at $33 by the auctioneers.

"It's hard," said a middle-aged Viennese woman, carefully examining several dusty volumes of the collected works of Goethe, stacked on a large table amid a sprawl of old books, Romanesque seals, and maps, yellowed and brittle with age. The elegant woman, who wore a gold Magen David ring set with a tiny pearl, identified herself only as Suzanne. She said that her grandparents had perished in a concentration camp during the war, and she was searching among the books and the paintings at the MAK for things that might have belonged to her family.

"I just want to find something to remember them by," said Suzanne, dabbing at tears with a damp Kleenex as she prepared to sort through another pile of books. (Although Suzanne was not able to identify any family heirlooms at the Mauerbach sale, a handful of others were luckier. At least eleven works of art were withdrawn from the auction by Christie's International, the auction house that supervised the sale on a nonprofit basis, when they were successfully identified by Holocaust survivors or their heirs.)

Annette Landers, a plucky biochemist from Sydney, was also looking for a remnant of her family history. She had made the trip to Vienna determined to recover the oil painting that used to hang in her great-grandfather's central Vienna law office before the war. Nobody had ever found out what had happened to the elderly Jewish lawyer, who, unlike the rest of his family, decided to remain in Vienna after the Nazis annexed Austria in 1938. Armed with a faded black-and-white photograph of the oil painting and an address scribbled on a worn piece of paper, Landers knocked on doors, asking the bewildered present-day occupants of her great-grandfather's office and flat what had happened to the cherished painting. She scoured the items in the Mauerbach catalog, but could not find the painting. Still, she was undaunted, and attended the two-day auction, hoping to make contact with someone who might be able to get her a step closer to her family treasure, which may or may not have been a priceless work of art, but whose sentimental value is far more important to her.

"I'm getting a little bit tired," Landers confessed, distractedly flipping through her glossy catalog on the second day of the auction. "It's really hard to look at all of these things here. To imagine who they belonged to."

But, wandering among the Mauerbach treasures at the MAK, it was difficult not to imagine the plight of the desperate families who were forced to give up their treasures. Where did the worn Florentine tapestries displayed in a room off the MAK's main lobby last hang, and who owned the ceramic bunny, now missing an ear? Who avidly collected the leather-bound adventure books, one of them detailing a German expedition to Antarctica in 1938–1939, its pages speckled with tiny termite holes and its title page bearing the cheerful German inscription "In remembrance of our time in Vienna," signed simply "Hans Friedrich." And what had become of the owners of lot 672, a German cast-iron strongbox whose broken locks—described as "distressed" in the auction catalog—appeared to have been smashed open with an axe, or maybe the butt end of a storm trooper's bayonet?

"I have no idea what actually happened, but I can only imagine that this was the strongbox in a household and the SS came in and smashed the thing open to look for money and jewels," said Stephen Lash, vice chair of Christie's International. "This goes beyond being an auction of works of art. One has the experience of walking into that room and looking at those objects and of suddenly having a shiver go down your spine because what you start thinking is that if these objects could speak, what stories would they tell?"

Wilhelm Becker, a sixty-six-year-old retired schoolteacher from Vienna, wandered through the lobby of the MAK, pondering that same question. "I really can't tell you why I'm here. I just felt that I had to see this," said Becker, a non-Jew, who taught for much of his career at a largely Jewish high school in Vienna. "Terrible things happened during that war that we as Austrians denied for so long. I feel sad as an Austrian looking at these paintings. This was a huge wrong, and we cannot ever right what's happened."

The "wrong" Becker was referring to was not only the systematic murder of six million Jews by the Nazis, but the well-organized and, in many cases, "legal" plunder of Jewish property throughout Europe. The confiscation of Jewish property, sometimes referred to as "Aryanization," was part of a complex legal process that encompassed the gradual erosion of Jewish citizenship, which formally began in Germany in 1935 with the introduction of the so-called Nuremberg Laws. (In practice, however, Jews had already been excluded from the civil service and other professions in Germany as early as 1933, the first year of the Third Reich.)

A few months after the German Army marched into Austria on March 12, 1938, Jews were forced by law to register their property with the Gestapo, the secret state police, which worked under the auspices of the SS, the most powerful organization within the Nazi party. Jews were also encouraged to leave the country as per the Nazis' Jewish emigration policy. However, they could do so only by buying their way out and selling all of their valuables and property at cut-rate prices to various government agencies. A year later, when the war started, confiscation by the SS was commonplace in countries occupied by the Nazis, who seemed to thumb their noses at Article 46 of the 1907 Hague Convention on the Rules of Land Warfare, which states that "the honor and rights of families, the lives and private property of citizens, as well as religious convictions and practices will be respected. Private property will not be confiscated."

Although Jewish organizations have been successful in seeking compensation for the victims of Nazism in Germany, other countries that were under Nazi rule during the war have been slow to deal publicly with the issues of restitution and compensation, or to come to grips with their own historical complicity in the murder of millions.

In Austria, the Mauerbach sale became one of the most vivid symbols in the reexamination of modern society's response to the Holocaust—a topic that many had found either too painful or too politically awkward to address before. Although a year earlier the Austrian government had set up a fund for the victims of Nazism, promising to pay some $7,000 to each surviving Austrian victim of the Holocaust, Mauerbach took the issues of compensation and restitution one step further. Mauerbach was not only about recovering a few art objects, it was about reexamining the past, and recovering the truth.

For years Austrians had glossed over the fact that the majority of them had enthusiastically embraced the Anschluss that integrated the country into Nazi Germany. They preferred to adopt as official history their role as Nazism's first victim—a revisionist innocence that many now realize was more indicative of geopolitical expediency than of truth. With postwar Austria occupied partly by the Soviets, the Allies had understood the Cold War necessity of keeping Austria onside. Fifty-one years later, at a memorial ceremony officially opening the Mauerbach auction, then Austrian Chancellor Franz Vranitsky, the first Austrian leader in history to acknowledge that Austrians had been willing servants of Nazism, was full of contrition for his country's role during the war.

"We know that we Austrians were members of the SS, of the Sturmband, of the Wehrmacht, that we were Nazi party members," Vranitsky said in an address to Jewish community leaders on the night before the auction. "We know their crimes were possible because we supported the system which made the Holocaust possible."

Mauerbach also took place against a backdrop of intense scrutiny outside Austria under which popular World War II myths were exploding like so many cluster bombs, sparking incendiary debates far and wide. More than a half century after the unconditional German surrender, the Second World War was again on the front pages of newspapers around the world. History, or rather the reexamination of history, became news.

In the United States, a young Harvard historian named Daniel Jonah Goldhagen alleged in his powerful book, *Hitler's Willing Executioners,* that many ordinary Germans had assisted the SS in the murder of thousands of Jews.

In Italy, the trial of former Nazi SS Captain Erich Priebke had plunged the entire country into a serious reexamination of its wartime role. Priebke had been extradited from Argentina in December 1995 to face trial for his role in the execution of 335 Italian civilians at the Ardeatine Caves outside Rome in 1944.

In France, allegations that some prominent Parisians were living in luxury rent-controlled flats that had been built on lands expropriated from Jews by the Vichy government, led to a national scandal. Paris Mayor Jean Tiberi ordered a deed search on buildings being sold off by the city after it was alleged that hundreds of flats in up to five hundred buildings in the Marais district had been expropriated from Jews killed in Nazi death camps. The search was ordered when a journalist discovered that President Jacques Chirac's brother-in-law was living in a municipally owned flat built on land that had belonged to a Jewish antique dealer who was killed at Auschwitz in 1944. In another stunning revelation in France, government officials publicly admitted in the spring of 1997 that the French government is still holding on to 987 paintings, drawings, and sculptures looted by Nazi occupation forces from Jewish collectors. The artworks, retained by the French government immediately after the war, have not been reclaimed by their original owners or their heirs. Critics said that the French government had not done enough to find the original owners of the works, which include oils and drawings by Gauguin, Degas, Seurat, Renoir, Monet, Cézanne, and Picasso. Much of the looted art is on permanent display at the country's most important museums, including the Louvre, the d'Orsay Museum, and the Georges Pompidou Center.

In Britain, journalists discovered that more than four hundred former SS soldiers, Nazi collaborators, and those suspected of being involved in war crimes were being paid more than $2 million per year in German government pensions, although they were now living in England. The German government insisted that no foreigner could claim a war pension if guilty of crimes against humanity, but the Nazi Investigation Center noted that men and women receiving pensions had never been systematically checked against records of war criminals.

Government-sponsored investigations into events now more than half a century old were becoming de rigueur in many European countries. Following a meeting of the World Jewish Congress in Oslo, Norway, in November 1996, Prime Minister Thorbjorn Jagland promised to compensate the country's Jewish population for property stolen by the government of Vidkun Quisling during the war. Half of Norway's estimated two thousand Jews had fled to neutral Sweden. Of the 736 shipped to Nazi concentration camps, all but 26 died. The Liquidation Board for Confiscated Jewish Property seized all their valuables. A great deal of the loot went to Norwegian Nazis; the rest just vanished.

For years the World Jewish Congress and the World Jewish Restitution Organization had been pressing for compensation for Jewish victims of expropriation. Their efforts had been given huge boosts following the fall of the Berlin Wall in 1989. Unfettered by the strict dictates of Soviet rule, victims of Nazism in many former Eastern Bloc countries began to clamor for the return of their expropriated property, and for justice. And for the first time in more than five decades, previously classified government records in former Iron Curtain countries were made available for public perusal. In Poland, the government also ordered an investigation into property and other assets expropriated from Polish victims of the Holocaust.

Other countries that had been neutral during the war found themselves for the first time in the international spotlight for their wartime dealings with Nazi Germany. Portugal, which had profited handsomely during the war from the sale of wolfram and other goods to Germany, was allegedly paid with gold bullion looted from occupied countries. Some of the gold may even have come from victims of the Holocaust. Several Portuguese historians say that when the Nazis lost the war, Portugal secretly sold off some of the gold to Indonesia, the Philippines, and China. In addition, Lisbon was used as an important base for the transfer of Nazi gold to Latin America. The Portuguese government promised to declassify its wartime central bank records to clarify the allegations.

The raging debates were not just restricted to Europe. Thousands of miles away in Argentina, Jewish groups intensified the pressure on the government of Carlos Saul Menem to open further the country's so-called Nazi archives to shed light on how the government of Juan Domingo Perón had offered a safe haven for Nazi war criminals in the years immediately following the Second World War. Did the Nazis launder war booty through Argentina? asked a new generation of historians and journalists. In Brazil, Jewish groups were asking the same questions, and demanding that the government of Fernando Henrique Cardoso open up the country's central bank archives to ascertain whether Reichsbank gold had found its way to Brazil.

The biggest explosion by far took place in Switzerland. The headlines said it all: SWISS BANKING SECRECY. SOMETHING NASTY IN THE VAULT? (*The Economist,* May 11, 1996); SECRET BANKERS FOR THE NAZIS (*Newsweek,* June 24, 1996); and SWISS DEALERS WERE THE "FENCES" OF THE HOLOCAUST (*SonntagsZeitung,* September 15, 1996). In a flood of articles that followed the declassification of some U.S. intelligence documents in the spring of 1996, the World Jewish Congress (WJC) attacked Swiss bankers for cynically profiting from the Holocaust by, among other things, holding on to money that had been deposited by desperate Jews fleeing Nazi tyranny before the Second World War.

"This is the last unfinished business of the Holocaust," said Israel Singer, the WJC's secretary general, and the son of Viennese Jews who fled from Austria. "It is time to draw a black line at the bottom and finalize these accounts."

By then, the WJC had enlisted the assistance of Republican Senator Alfonse D'Amato, a powerful U.S. legislator, who helped shine the international spotlight on Switzerland by convening a series of Senate hearings in Washington, designed to condemn Swiss banks for their wartime role. D'Amato and the World Jewish Congress argued that there could be billions of dollars in dormant accounts belonging to Jewish victims of Nazi aggression. They demanded that justice be served. The money should either be returned to the survivors and their heirs, or given to Jewish charitable organizations around the world, they said.

D'Amato's efforts opened up a Pandora's box: They laid open to question Swiss dealings with the Axis powers during the war, and exploded the time-honored myth of Swiss neutrality. In addition to holding on to Jewish assets, the Swiss were accused of being Hitler's silent partners during the war. They were also accused of retaining huge quantities of gold looted from countries under Nazi occupation and wrenched from the mouths and fingers of victims of the Holocaust. One historian accused Switzerland of using the unclaimed accounts of victims of the Holocaust to ease Switzerland's postwar compensation disputes with Poland and Hungary.

No Swiss institution was spared. A U.S. intelligence report from 1945, now declassified fifty years later, accused the International Committee of the Red Cross of smuggling Nazi assets and valuables across Europe in diplomatic pouches. Another intelligence report accused Switzerland's Bally shoe company of taking over the management of Jewish companies seized by the Nazis.

It didn't matter that much of this so-called "new" information had been known to historians for years. The secrecy that surrounded the Swiss banks—the most powerful in the world—became a focal point for anger in a new era of openness in which the wealth and power and secrecy of the banks had often drawn the ire of ordinary citizens throughout the Western world. D'Amato and the World Jewish Congress marshaled all the evidence they could find to pressure Switzerland into compensating those victims of Nazism who had put their trust in Swiss banks.

The Swiss had a political time bomb on their hands. For the first time, their quiet, unassuming country, known for its reluctance to enter the international arena under any circumstances, was forced to air its dirty laundry before the eyes of the world. Their country's reputation at stake, Swiss authorities quickly agreed to throw their World War II archives open to international examination. Swiss parliamentarians unanimously voted to lift the veil of banking secrecy for five years in order to conduct a proper investigation into the dormant wartime accounts.

At the same time, there was internal pressure from Swiss historians forcing the country to reexamine its past. If Switzerland was neutral during the war, why had Swiss authorities turned back some thirty thousand Jewish refugees after 1938? A generation of Swiss baby boomers had grown up being taught that their country's strong army and impregnable geographical features had saved them from Nazi tyranny. Now they were finding out that Switzerland had probably escaped German aggression only because its bankers had agreed to continue their business relationships with the Nazis, profiting from both the war and the Holocaust.

"This is classic psychoanalysis on a national level," said Verena Grendelmeier, the first Swiss parliamentarian to lobby vigorously for the lifting of banking secrecy before the international outcry began in 1995. "As with an individual patient, a country cannot live with a lie, so we're going to do a proper investigation, and we're going to find the truth. This is cathartic. And it hurts."

While many Europeans took to the newspapers, the airwaves, and the Internet to engage in this collective psychoanalysis, Holocaust victims and their heirs from around the world were clamoring to settle Israel Singer's "unfinished business." They wanted a sense of closure. If more than fifty years after the war the Austrians could give back the Mauerbach treasures, then the Swiss would have to give back the money and other assets that were languishing in their bank vaults. The WJC took this one step further—perhaps even one step too far, according to its critics—by demanding that the Swiss government start to make amends now by offering a financial "gesture" for aging Holocaust survivors, who, the WJC argued, would not be able to wait for the Swiss to finish what might turn into a lengthy investigation.

In Switzerland, the WJC's demands sparked controversy. Outgoing Swiss President Jean-Pascal Delamuraz called the demands "blackmail" in an interview with a Geneva newspaper in December 1996. The comment drew a flurry of protests from Jewish groups, including an official protest from Israel and threats by Israel's Jewish Agency and the WJC to begin boycotts and class-action suits against Swiss banks.

Perhaps Grendelmeier was right to note that the cathartic process was not going to be easy. In the years that it will take to resolve these issues, there will probably be more diplomatic rows, more disagreements, and more apologies. But one thing is certain: There is no turning back. "If we don't face the past, how will we ever face the future in an honorable manner?" asked the Swiss parliamentarian.

Into this global minefield stepped people like Annette Landers, infused with the hope that maybe, just maybe, even more than half a century later, they could retrieve some of what the Nazis and their collaborators had so thoroughly and ruthlessly taken from them—not just an oil painting or money in a long-forgotten bank account, but the memory of a family, a small sense of justice, a part of themselves.

The grandchildren of Abraham Hammersfeld are also struggling to recover a part of themselves. Before the outbreak of war, most of the Hammersfeld family assets in Vienna were expropriated by the Nazis. Everything was taken from the family except for two silver candlesticks and a menorah spirited across several continents, and a bank account in Switzerland, opened by a caring grandfather who wanted to protect part of his legacy and ensure a secure future for his children and grandchildren in increasingly insecure times.

In 1997, the Hammersfeld family is still searching for that elusive bank account. It is a search fraught with legal and bureaucratic obstacles and a torturous journey into a past that is marked by brutal expropriation—of assets, of memory, of lives.

Stories like those of Annette Landers and the Hammersfelds moved me to write this book. I had first become aware of Switzerland's financial relationship with the Nazi regime in, of all places, Buenos Aires. In 1992, while the Latin America correspondent for Canada's *Globe and Mail,* I covered the opening of the Argentine government's "Nazi archives," which contained official documents showing how hundreds of Nazis had escaped to the South American country in the immediate postwar period with the aid of Argentine leader Juan Domingo Perón. While the information was not unknown, the archival material clearly and definitively demonstrated how high-ranking Argentine officials had helped the members of the

Nazi regime after the war. Before the opening of the archives, the Argentine government had officially denied its postwar collusion with escaping Nazis. Among the dusty boxes of press reports and government memos at the National Archives in downtown Buenos Aires, there were a few curious reports of financial transfers from Swiss financial institutions to German banks in Argentina.

The story behind those curious transactions began to unfold only three years later, after the fiftieth anniversary of the end of the Second World War. In the United States, the government marked the occasion by declassifying many of its intelligence reports on the Nazi regime's wartime financial transactions. Some of those reports, supplemented by interviews with historians in Europe and North America, finally helped me to make sense of the Argentine records.

However, this book is not so much about deciphering old reports as it is about people. As I read the avalanche of press reports that followed in the wake of the World Jewish Congress's campaign against Swiss banks, I was moved, as it is impossible not to be, by the riveting stories of Holocaust survivors and their families, and their struggle against Nazi persecution during the war. But I was also deeply affected by the inescapable fact that, fifty years later, they are still struggling—this time against Swiss bureaucracy.

I met the heirs of Abraham Hammersfeld through their lawyer in Toronto. As I began to piece together their family history through old correspondence, Nazi records, and long interviews with family members in the United States, Canada, and Austria, the relentless efficiency of the Holocaust hit me as never before. I studied the minute details of the gradual Nazi expropriation of the family's assets in Austria, and read with horror letters in which family members persisted in their beliefs that nothing could happen to them because they were citizens of what was among the most civilized countries in the world.

Much has already been written about the Nazi confiscation of the grand art collections and other holdings of prominent Jewish families, such as the Rothschilds and the Warburgs, but scant attention has been paid to the *effects* of expropriation of artwork, businesses, and bank deposits by the Nazis and their collaborators from middle- and working-class Jews. The Hammersfelds are one of those typical Jewish families so vividly recalled in every object at Mauerbach. The Florentine tapestries could easily have hung in their living room, the leather-bound works of Goethe and Schiller once had a place of honor in their library. All that the descendants of Abraham Hammersfeld know for certain is that the sole tangible parts of their grandfather's legacy survive in the tarnished silver candlesticks in a high rise in Queens and an antique menorah carefully preserved in plastic in a kitchen cabinet in Toronto. The rest of it was locked up in a bank vault somewhere in Switzerland. Perhaps it is still there.

—ISABEL VINCENT
Toronto, Canada
June 1997

ONE

"FILE CLOSED"

Abraham Hammersfeld could have started preparing for the worst in the summer of 1934.

It's not that the year was particularly out of the ordinary for the Hammersfelds or any other well-to-do Viennese Jewish family. As was his custom every summer, the sixty-year-old patriarch closed down his textile business in downtown Vienna and headed with his wife, Charlotte, whom he affectionately called Lotte, to their pastoral retreat in Voslau, a small, quiet town, south of the Austrian capital, where many middle-class Viennese families whiled away the summer months, hiking along forest trails and visiting with friends. Abraham was looking forward to doing what he liked to do best on quiet days deep in midsummer: reading, dozing in his garden, and surrounding himself with his four children and five grandchildren at Villa Charlotte, the stately, two-story summer home he had named after his wife.

But one dramatic event shattered the summer stillness. Although, for most Austrians, the news came and went with the unexpected ferocity of a freak downpour on a lazy summer afternoon, it left many astute political observers imagining bigger and blacker storm clouds on the horizon.

In the early evening of July 25, as Abraham relaxed with his family at the Voslau summer house, he turned on the radio to find out about the day's news and was horrified by what he heard. The voice of the reporter was breathless and sometimes difficult to make out over the static as he described how a group of more than 150 members of the National Socialist party, which was outlawed in Austria at the time, had broken into the federal chancellery in Vienna and shot Austrian Chancellor Engelbert Dollfuss in the throat at point-blank range. Over the static, Abraham heard that the Nazis had been dressed in the uniforms of the Austrian Army. Later that day Dollfuss died of his wounds, but by that time the poorly organized Nazi putsch had already failed. Austrian government forces, led by Austria's then minister of justice, Kurt von Schuschnigg, quickly took control of the situation. They arrested the rebels and later condemned thirteen of them to hang. In the days that followed the violent outburst, peace was restored, and Dr. Schuschnigg, a cultivated gentleman with impeccable Old World manners, was sworn in as Austria's new chancellor.

The events of the summer of 1934 had not come without warning. For months before the Dollfuss assassination, Austrian Nazis had terrorized the country in order to unseat Dollfuss, a fascist dictator, who had come to power amid economic instability and political turmoil in 1932. When Dollfuss took office, Austria had not yet fully recovered from its crushing defeat in the First World War, which culminated in the breakup of the Austro-Hungarian Empire and unleashed economic chaos, high inflation, and violent political confrontations among Communists, Christian Socialists, and later National Socialists or Nazis.

To keep the country together, Dollfuss, a Christian Socialist, ruthlessly cracked down on any opposition, particularly the rapidly growing Austrian Nazi party, whose members violently clamored for a

political and economic union with Germany. With weapons and dynamite supplied by the ruling Nazi party in Germany, the Austrian
Nazis, whose membership grew from about three hundred members
to more than forty thousand in the space of three years, had blown
up railways, power stations, and government buildings in their battle
against the ruling Christian Socialists. The Austrian government had
responded by stamping out democratic political freedoms and dealing
harshly with dissidents. Under the clerical-conservative dictatorship
of Dollfuss, both Nazis and Socialist workers did not escape sometimes brutal repression. For instance, in February 1934, the government targeted the Austrian Social Democrats and sent seventeen
thousand government troops to fire on workers' lodgings in Vienna,
killing a thousand people, many of them women and children, and
wounding some four thousand others.

Although Abraham Hammersfeld was a sophisticated man who
must have been acutely aware of everything that was going on around
him, he had little time for politics. He tended to immerse himself in
his daily life, dividing his time among his textile export business, his
family, and the affairs of the small Orthodox synagogue of which he
was president. But the news in the summer of 1934 must have given
him pause.

"For some reason, the shooting of Dollfuss stayed in my head,"
says Renée, Abraham's eldest granddaughter, who was eleven years
old at the time of the assassination. "It didn't mean that much to
me, of course. I was a young girl on summer holidays. But I remember my grandfather constantly listening to the news on the radio, and
I remember that summer as the beginning of a time when things
started to get worse in Austria."

On the evening of July 25, as darkness descended and a welcome
breeze tossed the embroidered curtains in the sitting room at Villa
Charlotte, Abraham may have sat in his favorite chair as usual, lit a
cigar, and, mulling over the day's events, made the connection with
a similar putsch that had occurred while he and his son Adolf were
on a business trip in Munich eleven years earlier. On the evening of
November 8, 1923, a band of Nazi thugs led by a diminutive, rather

comical-looking Austrian with a Charlie Chaplin mustache launched a daring attempt to take over the Bavarian government by ambushing Bavarian State Commissioner Gustav von Kahr at the Munich beer hall where von Kahr was scheduled to speak. The Beer Hall Putsch, as it came to be known, was a resounding failure that resulted in the outlawing of the Nazi party and the imprisonment of its rabble-rousing leader. Within a decade, that charismatic leader and his band of toughs held supreme power in Germany.

In 1933, Adolf Hitler was sworn in as chancellor of Germany, and his expansionist plans to restore the German nation to its former Teutonic glory were known to anyone who had bothered to read the first page of *Mein Kampf*, Hitler's ranting memoir-cum-political treatise, which after his inauguration as chancellor became a best-seller in Germany. In the first paragraph, Hitler wrote that the reunion of Austria and Germany was a "task to be furthered with every means our lives long."

Hitler officially distanced himself from the assassination of Dollfuss, calling it an internal Austrian affair. Nonetheless, it was cause for concern in Austria, foreshadowing what was to take place just four years later when German troops marched into Vienna, making Austria part of the German Reich and unleashing a campaign of terror against the country's Jews.

If they saw the storm clouds gathering as early as 1934, few well-to-do Austrian Jews of the stature of Abraham Hammersfeld started to panic. They may have thought about diversifying their financial assets, perhaps looking at investment opportunities abroad or stashing part of their savings in a foreign bank in a stable country like Switzerland. Just in case. But mostly they went about their daily lives, content in the knowledge that they were upstanding, hard-working citizens, living in one of the most civilized countries in the world.

WITH HIS RESPECT for religion and secular learning, Abraham Hammersfeld was the very model of the modern, enlightened

Jewish gentleman. Even in his sixties, he was a handsome, broad-shouldered man, with an immaculately cropped salt-and-pepper mustache, which he trimmed every day with the aid of a foul-smelling sulfur shaving cream and a razor fashioned from a sharp wooden stick. In keeping with strict Orthodox observance, Abraham did not believe in taking a blade to his face. So every morning before the workday began, he could be found in the small washroom of his sixth-floor office on Vienna's bustling Wipplingerstrasse, lathering his face with the sulfur cream, which loosened his beard, so that he could shave with the wooden stick. Lotte would not allow him to shave at home because she would have had to air out the flat for hours to get rid of the sulfur smell.

Abraham did not move in elegant social circles, but he did appreciate the finer things in life, which was why he insisted that Hammersfeld family portraits be taken by S. Weitzmann, Vienna's foremost portrait photographer, who had once worked for the Austrian royal court before the dissolution of the monarchy in 1918. In town Abraham was rarely seen without an immaculately pressed, dark, three-piece suit, silk tie, and the gold Schaffhausen pocket watch—his most prized possession—tucked into the pocket of his vest. A successful businessman who ran his own textile company, he was also a profoundly religious man and a scholar, with a great passion for knowledge.

"He spoke perfect German and had a great love for the German classics," recalls his grandson Hans, Herbie and Renée's cousin. "I remember he was constantly correcting my German when I was a little boy. When I wrote him letters he was always pointing out my spelling mistakes."

Like many educated and assimilated Austrian Jews of his age, Abraham Hammersfeld, who grew up in a family of textile merchants, was the product of a high German education. He was born on December 24, 1874, in Galicia, the region in southeast Poland and northwest Ukraine that had been annexed to Austria after the first partition of Poland in 1772. Like many of the Jewish students studying at the Gymnasium in the Galician city of Tarnow, where Abraham settled as a young man, he undoubtedly looked toward Germany as the great symbol of modernity and progress. But while he read Goethe and Schiller at school, Abraham remained a deeply religious Orthodox Jew at home.

For many Jews, the desire to balance the secular and the sacred grew out of the Enlightenment, the eighteenth-century philosophy that stressed reason and individualism over tradition and had what some hoped would be its greatest manifestation in the French Revolution of 1789. That same year, Emperor Joseph II of Austria tried to improve the condition of Jews living in the Austro-Hungarian Empire by assimilating them completely. Traditionally, Jews lived in segregated communities throughout the empire, from which they were also periodically expelled by local authorities. Joseph II was much more tolerant of the Jews than previous rulers, who had frequently passed anti-Jewish laws restricting Jewish religious practices and their social and professional mobility. But in his desire to assimilate Jews into the broader society, Joseph II abolished the self-government of the Jewish community and of the rabbinical court, causing huge rifts between Jews who wished to assimilate and those who wanted to maintain their autonomy.

Nowhere were these conflicts more apparent than in the thriving and largely prosperous Jewish community of Galicia, where there were often tense relations between the Orthodox traditionalists, the Hasidim, the adherents of the *Haskalah,* and later the Zionist factions. An established Hasidic center, Galicia had also become a cradle for the Haskalah, a Jewish movement that had its roots in the Enlightenment and that endorsed assimilation. Unlike the followers of Hasidism, who focused on strong, patriarchal religious leaders, stressed a fundamentalist interpretation of the Torah and discouraged secular studies, the first followers of Haskalah (the term means enlightenment in Hebrew), or Maskilim, argued that secular studies should be pursued as an important part of the curriculum of a Jew. At its core, Haskalah, one of the earliest precursors to the Reform movement in modern Judaism, was structured around the belief that the essential values of Judaism could not be adversely affected by knowledge of the secular world. In fact, worldly knowledge came to be seen as an important ingredient in religious thought. The Maskilim also professed loyalty to the centralized state. For this reason, many Maskilim identified themselves first as Germans or as Austrians rather than as Jews.

In Galicia, many followers of Haskalah looked to Germany for inspiration and guidance. After all, the man considered to be the father of Haskalah was an eighteenth-century German Jewish philosopher named Moses Mendelssohn, who taught among other things that Yiddish, a language that evolved from a German dialect laced with Hebrew words and spoken by the shtetl-dwelling Jews of Central and Eastern Europe, was a cause of moral corruption. Educated and assimilated Jews must use the language of their countries of origin, he argued. In the nineteenth century, German literature, arts, and ideas were the only Western culture accessible to Jews in Galicia and Hungary who wanted to assimilate, argues historian Steven Beller. In his book *Vienna and the Jews,* Beller notes that "the reactionary style of the Poles and the backwardness of the Ruthenian peasantry meant that most assimilating Jews who followed the dictates of the Enlightenment had to do so through German." He goes on to say that what the Eastern European Jews felt for German culture

> was not something which could be rationally explained away as the attempt to get on in the world, to fit in. They were not escaping their Jewish fate so much as entering, crossing over, into a promised land of freedom. Historical circumstance was such that for a vast number of Jews in Germany and outside, this promised land happened to be Germany. It came to sum up, to symbolize, all their great desires and came, like liberalism, to be desired in itself.[1]

Although legal oppression of Jews had virtually disappeared by the late nineteenth century, hatred of Jews was still very much alive, especially in Central Europe. Galicia was wracked by instability, and so Polish anti-Semitism increased just as Zionism, or the political manifestation of Jewish nationalism, was gaining ground. The Zionists, in turn, clashed with the Jews wishing for quiet assimilation. Violence erupted on a regular basis. Between 1881 and 1910, more than 230,000 Jews, out of a total population of 800,000, left Galicia, bound for points west or for Palestine. Among them was Abraham Hammersfeld, now an established textile merchant, and his wife, Charlotte (née Faust), who headed with their four young children to seek their fortune in pre–World War I Vienna, which was still the seat of the Austro-Hungarian Empire and one of the most sophisticated cultural and intellectual centers in Europe.

For Jews like Abraham, brought up in the spirit of the German Jewish Enlightenment, who wanted to free themselves from the confining traditions of the Eastern European shtetl or ghetto, Vienna at the beginning of the twentieth century must have seemed like a paradise. Indeed, a decade after arriving in Vienna, Abraham Hammersfeld had become a successful merchant and businessman whose industrial linens were exported to some of the finest hotels, pensions, and restaurants throughout Europe.

Other enterprising young Jewish intellectuals and professionals arrived in the city from the farthest reaches of the Austro-Hungarian Empire, and congregated at smoky coffeehouses, such as the Café Griensteidl or the Café Central, to argue politics and philosophy. Writers such as Joseph Roth and Siegfried Lipiner moved to the city to escape their strict Jewish upbringing in Galicia. Theodor Herzl, the Hungarian-born father of modern Zionism and the founder of the World Zionist Organization, also made his way to Vienna, where he worked as a journalist.

"Viennese Judaism was unique," says the Austrian historian Gertrude Schneider, who grew up in an affluent Jewish household in pre–World War II Vienna. "It was a combination of Orthodoxy and modernity."

Although the Jewish community in turn-of-the-century Vienna was in itself varied and stratified in socio-economic background and degree of religious observance, most Jews were quite assimilated. According to Steven Beller, "whereas other towns had a tradition of a

Jewish community, and hence a ghetto, Vienna had virtually none.
. . . The result was . . . that Jewish individuals felt much more free
and easy than they had in ghettos . . . both with regard to the non-
Jewish society and culture and their own Jewish traditions. The distance from the patriarchal regimentation of the ghetto led to a
large-scale secularization."

While wide-eyed Jews from the provinces may have thought they
had assimilated into a great culture, the truth was something different. Viennese society was anything but progressive when it came to
Jews. For those Jews who aspired to be part of Austria's cultural elite,
religious conversion became de rigueur. Austria was a Catholic country, and the Hapsburg monarchy was determined to keep it that way.
Although Jews had gained full rights by 1867, they were still virtually
banned from the army and the diplomatic and civil services. Composer and conductor Gustav Mahler had to be baptized into the
Catholic faith in order to secure his position as director of the Vienna
Court Opera in 1897. Many Jews had difficulties securing places at
universities.

However, many people battled the restrictions: Although both
Herzl and Viennese psychiatrist Sigmund Freud experienced similar
problems in their respective careers because they were Jewish, neither converted to Christianity. Instead, Herzl abandoned his assi-
milationist tendencies altogether. His 1895 treatise Der Judenstaat
was grounded in Jewish nationalism and was written as a direct response to Herzl's disillusionment with increasing anti-Semitism
throughout Europe. Freud was not a practicing Jew, but he never
disavowed his religion.

Despite anti-Semitism, historians credit Austrian Jews with trans-
forming turn-of-the-century Vienna into Europe's leading intellectual
and cultural hub. According to Beller, "the greater intellectuality of
Viennese culture during this era can be explained largely by the Jewish tradition of respect for the mind and learning. . . . The Jewish
element . . . provided the leading ideas and principles of modernism
in Vienna."

Jews comprised nearly 10 percent of Vienna's population of more than two million people. Although Jews lived throughout the city, the majority of the new immigrants who came from the eastern provinces of Austria-Hungary before the First World War settled in the collection of narrow, cobblestone streets on the banks of the Danube Canal known as the Second District. The neighborhood, with its talmudic schools, kosher shops, and synagogues, was the city's most visible Jewish quarter.

When they arrived in Vienna on the eve of the First World War in 1914, Abraham and Lotte Hammersfeld settled with their four young children in a cramped flat in the heart of the Second District. Although their Viennese accommodations, which had running water and electricity, must have appeared modern by Galician standards, their flat, like many others built in the nineteenth century, did not have its own private washroom, and the Hammersfeld family had to share a communal toilet with the other families who lived on the same floor of their building. But for the Hammersfelds, who eagerly began their new life in Vienna, this was hardly an inconvenience in a modern city that seemed bursting with opportunity.

In those first years, Abraham worked around the clock to establish his own business. But he never sacrificed his religious principles, and as hard as he worked he always seemed to have time to attend to his religious obligations. Every Friday night, he walked to Levias-Chaim, one of the small Orthodox synagogues in his neighborhood, for Sabbath services. Although he was not a rabbi, he immersed himself in religious studies, and family members recall that he was periodically called into the synagogue to debate issues of *Halachah*, Jewish law. He was also a talented Hebrew scribe, often charged with inscribing the Yahrzeit plaques or memorials that are used in the Jewish religion to mark the anniversary of a loved one's death. The stiff linen squares that bore Abraham's intricate handiwork were prominently displayed on a wall of the tiny Orthodox synagogue on Hollandstrasse.

By the 1920s, Abraham's textile firm, A. Hammersfeld, Wien, was prospering. When his sons Harry and Adolf were still in their teens, he took them on international business trips, in an effort to teach them his trade and prepare them to take over the Hammersfeld firm. Only Harry decided to stay on, traveling throughout Europe as his father's most trusted representative.

By the mid-1930s, all of Abraham and Lotte's children were in their thirties and thriving. Selma, the oldest of the Hammersfeld children, had married a successful Polish-born businessman named Oskar Lang, and had two children, a teenager named Siegfried and his younger sister by two years, Renée. Paula, who was a few years younger than her sister Selma, had married a successful Austrian textile merchant named Georg Stilman, and had two children, an adolescent named Heinz Herbert and a younger child named Sylvia. Adolf, who owned a successful dry-goods store in Vienna, married a beautiful Viennese girl named Edith König and had a young son named Hans Fritz. Harry, the youngest of the Hammersfeld children, was the closest to his father, even though the elder Hammersfeld sometimes despaired of Harry's penchant for gambling and womanizing. Abraham worried that Harry was too much of a *bon vivant* to settle down, so he must have breathed a happy sigh of relief in 1928 when he presided at the wedding of his youngest son to Bronia Bittersmann in a summer ceremony in Baden, a small town just outside of Vienna.

Nothing pleased Abraham more than celebrating Passover and the Jewish high holidays surrounded by his closely knit family and special friends. For even though his children were scattered across the city, Abraham insisted that they congregate at Levias-Chaim on Jewish festive days.

"He was so proud of that little synagogue, and we would all get together there for special occasions," says Renée, whose mother, Selma, insisted that the family walk from their home in the Eighth District to Abraham's synagogue in the Second so that the family could be together for holiday services. "But, you know, while he was really proud of his religion, he was never a fanatic. He used to laugh at people who were fanatical about their religion."

Following religious services, family and friends would then return to Abraham and Lotte's flat on Negerlegasse, a small, quiet street tucked into a corner of the Second District, a short walk from the Danube Canal. Depending on the occasion, the family would sit down to a hearty meal and then retire to the sitting room, where family members would take turns playing the piano, which was Grandmother Lotte's favorite pastime. On Passover, Heinz Herbert, Abraham's oldest grandson, would occupy the place of honor beside his grandfather at the family's long, mahogany, dining-room table. Heinz, who was the only grandson studying Hebrew in the mid-1930s, would be charged with reading The Four Questions, which Abraham referred to as the "Ma Nischtanes." On Purim, a Jewish festival day and a favorite family holiday because the Jewish calendar date often coincided with Grandmother Lotte's birthday, the grandchildren hid sweets under their grandparents' bed so that they could take them away to their homes when the celebration was over.

True to his own upbringing in Galicia, Abraham stressed secular learning, yet tried to ensure that his children and grandchildren developed a strong Jewish identity and took pride, as he still did, in their Galician roots. But although his children all benefited from a solid German education, they did not seem to share their father's passion for Judaism. Unlike him, they did not follow strict dietary laws or attend synagogue on a regular basis. They barely spoke Hebrew. By the time the next generation—the grandchildren—were born, the sense of Jewish identity that burned in the souls of the grandparents had become markedly diluted in the younger generation. In fact, later the grandchildren were hard-pressed to recall a time when they felt conscious of their Judaism or were victims of overt anti-Semitism while they were growing up in Vienna before 1938.

"I had Jewish friends and non-Jewish friends," says Renée, recalling that she also went to school on Saturdays. "It didn't matter that I was Jewish. I never really thought about it. The only time being Jewish became an issue was after the Anschluss in 1938."

In the winter of 1937–1938, Renée Lang, a bright, pretty fifteen year-old brunette, was attending the exclusive Albert Gymnasium, a private girls' school, in Vienna's Eighth District. One of her closest friends, a non-Jew named Ruth Langer, boasted that she had just joined a great after-school youth group. Teenage members went hiking and skiing, sang songs and organized debates. But there were a few problems with the group, confessed Ruth. First of all, it was secret, and second, you couldn't join if you were Jewish.

The words "Hitler Youth" meant little to Renée, who was somewhat bewildered by Ruth's obsession with the group. However, Renée took it in stride, and went on with her daily life. Six days a week, she spent her mornings at school, and in the afternoons she would do her homework, meet her friends or go to the museum, accompanied by the Langs' housekeeper. On the occasions when she scored a particularly high mark on an essay, which happened often, she would take the tram to her grandfather's office on Wipplingerstrasse in the heart of the First District. Abraham, who took great pride in Renée's academic success, stopped whatever he was doing to read her schoolwork aloud. Renée, who had been named after her great-grandmother, was the self-confessed favorite grandchild. On Sunday afternoons, she, her brother Siegfried, and her parents would gather with her grandparents at the Café Sweden, a short walk from the grandparents' flat, to play cards, read the newspapers, and feast on delicious Sacher torte or strudel.

The Hammersfelds' world came crashing down around them on Saturday, March 12, 1938. The night before, the beginning of the Sabbath, the older members of the family had uncharacteristically interrupted the preparations for the festive meal to gather around the radio in the sitting room of the Negerlegasse flat. Above the radio's crackle came the noise of triumphant Nazi mobs clamoring in the street below. The Hammersfelds strained to hear Chancellor Schuschnigg's moving farewell broadcast to the nation:

The German government today handed to President [Wilhelm] Miklas an ultimatum, with a time limit, ordering him to nominate as Chancellor a person designated by the German government . . . otherwise German troops would invade Austria. . . . I declare before the world that the reports launched in Germany concerning disorders by the workers, the shedding of streams of blood and the creation of a situation beyond the control of the Austrian government are lies from A to Z. President Miklas has asked me to tell the people of Austria that we have yielded to force since we are not prepared even in this terrible hour to shed blood. We have decided to order the troops to offer no resistance. So I take leave of the Austrian people with a German word of farewell, uttered from the depth of my heart: God protect Austria![2]

Since the Dollfuss assassination in 1934, Schuschnigg had consistently made concessions to Hitler, believing that this was the best way to preserve Austrian independence. In secret negotiations, Schuschnigg had agreed to give amnesty to Nazi political prisoners and to appoint Nazi representatives to positions in the Austrian government. Throughout 1937, the Nazis had infiltrated the Austrian police and the military, and spread dissension among the population, invoking the threat of a Communist putsch. On February 11, 1938, Hitler had summoned the Austrian chancellor to his retreat at Berchtesgaden in Germany and began the last phase of the process to destroy Austrian independence. Under the threat of a German invasion of Austria, Hitler demanded that the Austrian ban against the Nazi party be lifted completely and that the pro-Nazi Viennese lawyer Arthur Seyss-Inquart be made minister of the interior with authority over the Austrian police and security. Schuschnigg knew that this meant "nothing else but the complete end of the independence of the Austrian government."[3] He must have also realized that to stand up to Hitler would prove foolhardy, especially since he couldn't count on the governments of France and Britain to come to Austria's defense. Both governments had remained passive in the face of Hitler's increasing aggression, and had watched in official silence in 1936 as his troops boldly marched into the Rhineland in flagrant violation of the 1919 Treaty of Versailles.

Under extreme duress, Schuschnigg capitulated during the Berchtesgaden meeting, but he told Hitler that only the president of the Austrian Republic, who was head of state, could constitutionally agree to his demands. Although Austrian President Wilhelm Miklas initially balked at Hitler's demands, he eventually gave in as Austrian Nazis, under orders from Berlin, stepped up massive demonstrations throughout the country, designed to provoke civil unrest and plunge Austria farther into chaos. In one last-ditch effort to save Austrian independence, Schuschnigg decided to hold a plebiscite on March 13, asking the people of Austria whether they wanted a "free, independent, social, Christian, and united Austria." The announcement of the plebiscite threw Hitler into a rage, and he ordered an immediate military invasion of Austria even though the German Army was, at that point, ill-equipped for the task. On March 11, Nazi Field Marshal Hermann Goering was on the phone to Vienna demanding Schuschnigg's immediate resignation and the appointment of Seyss-Inquart as chancellor. Fearing a bloody conflict, Schuschnigg called off the plebiscite and resigned. A Nazi-drafted telegram was sent by Seyss-Inquart to Berlin requesting German military intervention to reestablish law and order. At dawn the following day, German troops marched into the country. Overnight, Austrian independence disappeared and the country became a province of the German Reich.

In the early morning of Saturday, March 12, triumphant Nazi troops rolled into Adolf Hitler's hometown of Linz, where crowds were already gathering on the main streets in anticipation of the Führer's arrival later in the afternoon. In Vienna, Renée Lang, her satchel strapped to her back, walked the few blocks to school, gingerly stepping over shattered glass and other debris left over from the wild Nazi rampage of the night before. When she reached the Albert Gymnasium, school administrators barred her entrance and told her to go home. Jews were no longer welcome, they said.

Renée's secure, upper-middle-class world had vanished. For Renée, "everything ended in 1938"—the skiing and skating in the winters, the outings to the theater and the opera, the summers at Voslau, and the Sunday afternoon strudels at the Café Sweden with her family. Within a few months, the Langs were forced to leave their fashionable flat in the Eighth District. Renée, her brother Siegfried, and her parents squeezed into Abraham and Lotte's small Negerlegasse flat. The Second District, which already had the highest concentration of Jews in Vienna, was transformed into an informal Jewish ghetto by Nazi officials, who wished to contain the city's 180,000 Jews in a single area.

"Within an hour after the Anschluss, there was a total change," says Renée. "Jews had to give up everything. A lot of people we knew committed suicide, or did everything they could to leave the country."

DRAWING ON NEARLY five years of experience in disenfranchising the Jews in Germany, the Nazis turned their well-honed campaign of terror and legalized plunder against the Jews of Austria, which Hermann Goering, second in command after Hitler, promised to make *Judenrein* (free of Jews) by 1942. The campaign against Austria's Jews was marked by staggering brutality and brilliant efficiency. In many ways the Austrian process was much harsher and swifter than that against Jews in Germany.

In the early days of the Anschluss, as high-ranking Nazi officials and the Führer himself arrived to celebrate the German annexation with wild shopping sprees and sumptuous meals in Vienna's finest restaurants, a wave of anti-Jewish terror swept the city that was much more ruthless and sadistic than anything that had taken place in Germany. U.S. foreign correspondent William Shirer, who was stationed in the city at the time, wrote:

For the first few weeks the behavior of the Vienna Nazis was worse than anything I had seen in Germany. There was an orgy of sadism. . . . Hundreds of Jews, men and women, were picked off the streets and put to work cleaning public latrines and the toilets of the barracks where the SA [*Sturmabteilungen*, storm troopers] and SS [*Schutzstaffel*, Hitler's special protection squads] were quartered. Tens of thousands more were jailed. Their worldly possessions were confiscated or stolen. I myself, from our apartment in the Plosslgasse, watched squads of SS men carting off silver, tapestries, paintings and other loot from the Rothschild palace next door.[4]

In addition to the looters, German entrepreneurs arrived en masse in Vienna to buy up Jewish property and businesses at rock-bottom prices. In some cases, as with the looting of the Rothschild palace, property was confiscated outright. Albert Sternfeld, an affluent Jew living in Vienna in 1938, recalls that Nazis took over his family's summer home, just outside the city, to use as a training camp for Hitler Youth. When he returned after the war, the house was in complete disrepair. "When I walked into the houses of my neighbors to ask what had happened, I noticed they had taken things from the house that belonged to my parents—tapestries, books, furniture," he says. "The gardener had taken my father's books. We never recovered anything."

In the week after the Anschluss, Adolf Hammersfeld and his brother-in-law Georg Stilman were roughed up by Nazi thugs who looted their textile stores and forced them to clean the streets. Twenty-four-year-old sales clerk Aloisia Celnar watched in horror as Adolf and Georg were handed old toothbrushes and pails of boiling-hot water, and forced by a crowd of jeering Nazis to scrub away pro-Schuschnigg graffiti on building walls and sidewalks. Stilman was then handed a broom and forced to sweep the Mariahilferstrasse, the broad main thoroughfare around the corner from his store. Adolf's young son Hans, who was then eight years old, remembers that his father returned home that night with severe burns on his hands and arms.

Hans didn't know what to make of his father's humiliation by the SS, the most powerful organization within the Nazi state, which started out as a group of 200 black-shirted personal bodyguards for Hitler, and grew to about 52,000 members under the rule of Nazi Heinrich Himmler. The SS would eventually become its own empire within the Nazi regime, and would oversee state terrorism of opponents of the regime and the systematic murder of Jews. But in the innocent world of childhood, the SS were kindly officers who were nice to little boys. A few months before the harassment of his father, Hans had gone to the park with his Christian nanny and her brother, a farmer from a small town in the Austrian interior. Anna's brother, a tall, athletic youth with a ruddy complexion from working outdoors, had just become a member of the SS, and to celebrate he took his sister and Hans to the park, bought the boy an ice-cream cone, and stuck a swastika emblem on his chest. Why, Hans wondered, were these nice people being so mean to his father?

Throughout the city, high-profile Jews endured similar humiliations. "I was given a bucket of boiling water," recalled Moritz Fleischmann, a senior representative of the Jewish community of Vienna, "and I was told to clean the steps. I lay down on my stomach and began to clean the pavement. It turned out that the bucket was half-full of acid and this burned my hands . . . the SS sentries threw out the chief rabbi Dr. Taglicht, a man of seventy, and he, like myself, was ordered to brush these pavements. In order that he should feel the full force of the degradation and the humility of it, he was thrown out wearing his gown, and with his prayer shawl on."[5]

The Austrian Nazis spared no one. Jewish women as well as men were publicly humiliated. According to one Austrian historian who witnessed the public humiliation of Jews after the Anschluss, Jewish matrons were forced to clean the streets with their coats and Orthodox women were forced to clean the sidewalks with their wigs. As the women bent to their tasks, they were repeatedly kicked and beaten by Austrian Nazi thugs. "Even the newly arrived German soldiers could not get over the ferocity of these anti-Semitic Austrians and the treatment they meted out to their momentary captives. In some cases, it was the Germans who stopped these mindless cruelties and saw to it that the Jews were no longer molested by sending them home," writes historian Gertrude Schneider.[6]

"People were let loose when the Nazis arrived in Vienna," says Aloisia Celnar, whose eyes still well up with tears when she speaks about how the Nazis treated her employer. "It was awful. They [the Jews] had no rights at all."

Indeed, in a few years Adolf Hitler had managed to undo a century of Jewish emancipation. By the time his troops took over Austria in 1938, Jewish people were completely outlawed from German society. In 1935, Hitler had decreed a set of laws inspired by his belief in racial superiority. The so-called Nuremberg Laws of September 15, 1935, were designed to exclude Jews, whom Hitler likened to "chaff" polluting the noble Aryan master race. The first Nuremberg Law—"the Law Respecting Reich Citizenship"—stripped Jews of their German citizenship by decreeing that only persons "of German or related blood" could be citizens of the German Reich. "The Law for the Protection of German Blood and German Honor" prohibited Jews and Aryans from intermarrying or having sexual relations with each other. Jews were also forbidden from employing German domestic servants under thirty-five years of age.

To complete the disenfranchisement process, Hitler sought to remove Jews from the German economy. As early as 1933, Jews were gradually being removed from the marketplace, public and private. When Hitler took power in January of that year, many Jews started to be excluded from the civil service, journalism, farming, and all professions in the arts. In 1934, they were kicked out of the stock exchanges. On June 14, 1938, the Reich Interior Ministry produced a decree that required all private-sector firms to fire Jewish directors and managers; Jews were also prohibited from practicing medicine or law. The Nazis then focused on small businesses, which struck at the very heart of the Jewish community in Germany, where 60 percent of the Jewish population of some 500,000 earned its livelihood from small or midsized business enterprises, often family owned and operated. Independent stores and other businesses were to be taken over by German owners in a process called *Arisierung,* or "Aryanization." The Interior Ministry also ordered all Jews to register with the state any property in excess of 5,000 Reichsmarks (about $18,000 in 1997).

Although voluntary Aryanization, whereby a Jew could freely sell his firm to an Aryan, had been going on in Germany since January 1933, the practice became mandatory after 1938, when the concepts of free negotiations and market value no longer existed. By 1938, the longer a Jew waited to sell his business, the greater the pressure to do so and the lower the price. The Nazis added to the pressure by organizing official boycotts of Jewish businesses and products.

When the Nuremberg Laws and Aryanization requirements were introduced by decree in Austria on May 20, 1938, Abraham retreated to his library, where he spent several hours at a time typing letters to business associates in Czechoslovakia, Sweden, and Latvia, desperately trying to collect on outstanding debts and to expand his business connections abroad. In Austria, Nazi-led boycotts were making it difficult for him to sell his industrial linens for hotels and restaurants to his regular customers. Looking up from his work, his eyes might have rested on the well-thumbed volumes of Goethe and Schiller, crowded onto wooden shelves that sagged under the weight of so many books. For Abraham, a product of the Enlightenment and a deeply religious man with a tremendous respect for the law (both religious and secular), the chaos that surrounded him must have been difficult to comprehend.

Which is probably why Abraham and so many others tried to work at first within the Nazi legal system. In letters to his sons, who were traveling around Europe drumming up business connections and looking for safer places to live, Abraham reassured them that if he just followed the rules maybe everything would be all right, that he and his family would be left alone to continue with their lives in Vienna. The Nazi disturbances, the lootings, the attacks against Jews would probably pass, he wrote to his son Harry, who was on the road trying to tap prominent business associates in Czechoslovakia and Scandinavia for work. But, just in case, would Harry and his wife, Bronia, mind writing in subsequent correspondence "some details about the Jewish life in Prague. How about Finland? Is there a Jewish community and is there a possibility for ritual meals? I ask you please to inform me about everything."[7]

Confident in his belief that law and order would prevail, Abraham set out on July 13, 1938, to comply with the newly implemented regulations for Jews living in Austria. He arrived at the *Vermogensverkehrstelle,* or Reich Main Security Office, the Nazi ministry set up by the Gestapo to register Jewish property, and duly listed his assets and outstanding debts in his tightly restrained Old World script. He filled in his name on an official form stamped with the number

10024, which began: "I am a Jew and have German citizenship. Since I am a Jew with German citizenship, I have listed all my assets in this country and abroad and I have stated their value." For the next several pages, Abraham carefully enumerated his half ownership in an apartment building on Haupstrasse in the Third District, his textile wholesale operation on Wipplingerstrasse, and other assets, including an Austrian Worker's Bond, worth 66,50 Reichsmarks, and his beloved Schaffhausen watch, which he declared to be worth 200 Reichsmarks. Perhaps he held back a few things, wasn't entirely honest with the German authorities, but he could not have avoided seeing the concise warning at the beginning of the form which clearly stated that withholding information or lying about assets was punishable by imprisonment.[8]

The formal registry of Jewish property with the Gestapo was a clever way for Nazi authorities to compile an inventory of assets and valuables belonging to wealthy Jews. In the summer of 1938, the Nazis brought to Austria a policy that they had informally encouraged in Germany since 1933: forced emigration of Jews from the Third Reich. Jews who had enough money were forced to emigrate and, in some cases, to subsidize the emigration of poorer Jews. In order to emigrate, Jews had to surrender all their previously registered property, which was bought up by various government agencies at deep discounts.

In the months following the Anschluss, the Nazis continued to pressure the Jews to leave the country. In an official memorandum entitled "The Jewish Situation" sent to the U.S. State Department in the summer of 1938, the American consul general in Vienna, John C. Wiley, described the Nazis' forced emigration campaign:

In respect of Jewish activities in general, there seems to be no relaxation whatsoever in the pressure which is being applied by the authorities. Wholesale arrests continue on an ever increasing scale. There is, moreover, a new wave of Jew-baiting in various sections of Vienna, as well as in several of the provincial cities of Austria. There are innumerable cases where individuals are given the choice of leaving Austria within a given period, varying between two and eight weeks, or of being sent to Dachau [in 1938, a labor camp]. In many of these cases the individuals are supplied with police certificates attesting to the fact that there is nothing against them. This innovation is interesting in that the German authorities are expelling German citizens and in many cases are forcing would-be migrants to the United States to leave the country before a quota number can be made available to them. . . . A section of the population that is in particular distress are the Mischlings or part Jews. I know one case of a distinguished composer whose property was sequestered and who is now seriously ill. He was refused admission to the Jewish hospital on the grounds that he was not a Jew. The municipal hospital refused him admission because he was. He is now at the home of a friend living on private charity. He is 59 years old; despite the fact that he is a former officer, three times wounded in the War, he was sent to forced labor in Styria where three days of work in the flooded areas brought on his illness. I cite this case as typical of the treatment meted out to Jews.[9]

The terror campaign was all part of a brilliant plan devised in Germany and perfected in Austria by a young SS officer named Adolf Eichmann. This workaholic Nazi bureaucrat was to do such a good job in forcing Jews to emigrate from Austria that by the end of 1939 he was promoted to the Reich Main Security Office in Berlin, where he would eventually become the architect of the "Final Solution" to wipe out European Jews.

A failed engineering student and former salesman for Vienna's Vacuum Oil Company, Adolf Eichmann was only thirty-two when he was put in charge of the Central Office of Jewish Emigration in Vienna in August 1938. Possessed of a steely determination and a ruthless efficiency, Eichmann had earned his credentials earlier in the 1930s as a bureaucrat in the Security Service (the *Sicherheitsdienst*, or SD), the intelligence branch of the SS that watched over members of the Nazi party. By 1935, he was the SD official responsible for "Jewish questions," specializing in the Zionist movement. Considered an expert on Jewish affairs, he studied Hebrew and Yiddish, and even visited Palestine in 1937 to explore the possibility of Jewish emigration from Germany to the region.

Eichmann's plan, which was first implemented in Vienna, was developed by a Dutch lawyer named Erich Rajakowitsch, whom Eichmann employed "for the handling of legal questions in the central offices for Jewish emigration in Vienna, Prague and Berlin."[10] In *Eichmann in Jerusalem,* her groundbreaking study of Eichmann's career, Hannah Arendt describes how the Rajakowitsch-Eichmann plan worked in practice after Jews had been disenfranchised of their property, and were technically without sufficient funds to emigrate:

> Jews could not be left "without any money," for the simple reason that without it no country at this date would have taken them. They needed, and were given, their *Vorzeigegeld,* the amount they had to show in order to obtain their visas and to pass the immigration controls of the recipient country. For this amount, they needed foreign currency, which the Reich had no intention of wasting on its Jews. These needs could not be met by Jewish accounts in foreign countries, which in any event, were difficult to get at because they had been illegal for many years; Eichmann therefore sent Jewish functionaries abroad to solicit funds from the great Jewish organizations, and these funds were then sold by the Jewish community to the prospective emigrants at a considerable profit—one dollar, for instance, was sold for 10 or 20 marks when its market value was 4.20 marks. It was chiefly in this way that the community acquired not only the money necessary for poor Jews and people without accounts abroad, but also the funds it needed for its own hugely expanded activities.[11]

Eichmann's biggest coup, however, lay in delegating much of the responsibility for the running of the emigration scheme to Jewish organizations in Austria. In Vienna, the *Israelitische Kultusgemeinde,* or Jewish community organization, was largely responsible for administering the emigration program, under the menacing supervision of Nazi guards stationed in its offices. Under duress, these Jewish organizations were transformed from autonomous community groups to the vehicles by which the Nazis expelled Austrian Jews.

Centralizing the registration and emigration process through one agency made for greater efficiency. In Berlin, Eichmann's boss, Reinhard Heydrich, boasted that between April and November 1938 Austria had expelled fifty thousand Jews, while Germany had only expelled nineteen thousand in the same period. In one year, Eichmann's office forced the emigration of 100,000 Jews, says Nora Levin in her book *The Holocaust: The Destruction of European Jewry, 1933–1945*. She notes that Eichmann's Austrian operation was so successful that it was adopted in Germany in 1939 to replace a cumbersome bureaucracy that forced Jews to visit several different offices to gather the necessary documents for emigration: "In Germany, every prospective emigrant had to acquire more than a dozen official papers certifying his health, good conduct, property holdings or disposition, tax payments, emigration opportunities and other details. Many offices were involved in this processing and slowed down the exodus of Jews. Eichmann suggested the idea of uniting the numerous administrative offices in a single Gestapo department to speed up emigration."[12]

Despite Eichmann's bureaucratic streamlining, the process by which Jews disposed of their property and left the country was still marked by violence and corruption. The Aryanization or expropriation of Adolf Hammersfeld's Viennese textile store, for instance, was probably the biggest indication for the family, and especially for Abraham, that the high German precepts of law and order were definitely things of the past.

Following his humiliating treatment by Nazi mobs in the days after the Anschluss, Adolf Hammersfeld, a shrewd businessman, set about putting his business affairs in order so that he could emigrate with his young family as quickly as possible. Unlike his father, Abraham, who busied himself with synagogue affairs or shuttered himself in his office writing copious letters to his business associates abroad inquiring about immigration formalities and living conditions for Jews, Adolf snapped into action and immediately began to comply with Nazi regulations to Aryanize his retail operation on Reindorfgasse so that he, his wife, Edith, and eight-year-old Hans could leave the country. Adolf's brother Harry, who was doing business in Stockholm, had managed to secure Swedish immigration visas for Adolf's family, as well as for their sister Paula and her husband, Georg Stilman, and their children, Heinz Herbert and Sylvia. Sweden, a neutral country where the Hammersfelds had good business connections, seemed like an ideal place for them to settle in 1938.

So that summer, Adolf decided to Aryanize his store to Johann Greisinger, an employee. Adolf trusted Greisinger completely and treated him more like a son than an employee. Greisinger had been fourteen years old when he arrived at the store to apprentice with Adolf in 1929. The shy, awkward boy who had first entered the store, uncomfortably dressed in a crisp white shirt and spit-polish black shoes on a cold day in January so many years ago, had grown under Adolf's guidance into a mature, hardworking manager. Adolf knew that Greisinger would take good care of the business until it was safe enough for the Hammersfelds to return to Vienna.

For Johann Greisinger, who was then twenty-three years old and engaged to be married, the temporary acquisition of the store was a dream come true—something that would bring financial security to a young couple in what were increasingly difficult economic times. Handsome, ambitious, he was head over heels in love with Aloisia Celnar. He had first met the tall brunette with twinkling brown eyes and a captivating smile when he was eighteen years old. She had just been hired as a clerk at the dry-goods store that Adolf Hammersfeld ran with Georg Stilman before the two split their business operations. On her first day at work, a flustered Aloisia, who was folding underwear in the storeroom, took several minutes to realize that the attractive young man had stopped his stock taking to fix her with an intense stare. It was, as Aloisia recalls happily more than sixty years later, love at first sight when she finally looked up, blushed crimson, and smiled at Johann. He courted her for the next five years, even after Stilman opened a separate store across town and took Aloisia to work for him there. The two wanted to get married soon, but were worried about their financial security.

When Adolf Hammersfeld proposed that Johann Aryanize the store, the former apprentice must have felt as if he'd just won the lottery. Aloisia remembers how touched she and Johann were by Adolf's words: "Rather than give my store to anybody else, I will give it to you."

There were conditions, of course. Johann Greisinger would have to raise 5,000 Reichsmarks (about $18,000 today) to take over the business. Aloisia's father, who worked for the Vienna Bridge and Iron Construction Company, managed to get an advance on his pay in order to lend his daughter and future son-in-law the money to buy the Hammersfeld operation. Johann Greisinger and his fiancée were ecstatic. In his letter to the *Vermogensverkehrstelle* applying to purchase the Hammersfeld business, an earnest Johann set out to curry as much favor as possible with the Nazi authorities:

I was born on September 29, 1914, in Vienna and I am of the Roman Catholic faith and single. I have primary education and I began to apprentice at the Adolf Hammersfeld textile business on January 7, 1929. During the three years of my apprenticeship I also attended the technical school for the textile industry. Since then all my working life has been spent in this store. During the last years I have managed the store on my own. . . . Miss Aloisia Celnar, my fiancée, who also apprenticed with Adolf Hammersfeld, has worked for Georg Stilman, another textile store, for the last six years. We intend to marry in the near future and this store will be the basis for our future life together. I and my bride are of certifiable Aryan descent and members of the DAP [German Workers' Party] and also NSDAP [National Socialist German Workers' Party]. In addition, I am also a musician and member of Musical Detachment 94 of the NSKK [National Socialist Motorized Vehicle Corps] of the city [streetcar] transportation department.[13]

In a subsequent letter sent to the authorities and signed by his lawyer, Walter Mardetschlager, Johann Greisinger reemphasized his racial purity: "I am enclosing a sworn declaration by the above mentioned lawyer in regard to my racial purity and also the two required applications. Adolf Hammersfeld and I therefore put the plea before you to approve the purchase."[14]

On August 31, 1938, Johann Greisinger handed his employer the 5,000 Reichsmarks which he had borrowed from his future father-in-law, and took over the Hammersfeld shop. As part of the transaction, Adolf had arranged for the future Greisingers to look after Josef and Theresa König, his elderly in-laws, by providing them with a small monthly stipend. As everything appeared to be in order, Adolf and his family packed their bags and boarded a plane for Sweden along with the Stilmans, whose dry-goods store had also been Aryanized, in early September.

Abraham's German ideal of rational law and order and justice began to fall apart just as Adolf and Georg were preparing to leave for Sweden. In the late summer of 1938, Abraham had lost his business and part of his family. His textile operation had been taken over by the Nazis, and he was now relegated to his library, frantically writing desperate letters to his business associates abroad.

Still, the prospect of leaving Austria was a difficult one for Abraham. That summer, in letters to Harry, who was in Sweden on business and attempting to obtain visas for the family, he had dithered about details:

What are you suggesting we do with the furniture? Mother wants to take everything, but I am against that. . . . Even if we and the children take a larger place, there won't be much space anyway, so that I shouldn't fill the whole apartment with my furniture. . . . That's why I think one should sell at least the dining room and kitchen (with the exception of the piano). Do you agree with me? Unfortunately, the way things are here, you can get hardly anything for furniture. Everybody is running around selling it and you can't imagine how low the prices are.[15]

His fifteen-year-old granddaughter, Renée, had also been growing increasingly desperate that summer. At the end of one of her grandfather's letters to her beloved uncle Harry, who had bought her her first pair of high heels, she pleaded with him to find her a job and some way to leave Vienna: "Please ask [Heinrich] Klinger if he could use me [in Czechoslovakia]. I have perfect English, I speak some French. I have some stenography, typewriting, and book-keeping skills. I could help with correspondence."[16]

But by the autumn of 1938, while Abraham fussed about details, the family's options for refuge were diminishing almost daily. Czechoslovakia, where he had good business connections with businessman Heinrich Klinger, was no longer a possibility after September, when Hitler's aggressive actions in the Sudetenland very nearly brought the Western Powers and the Third Reich to war. And—in a bitter irony—Adolf, Harry, and their families, who had only just recently landed in the relative safety of Sweden, fell victim to that aggression.

Just before Hitler took over the Sudetenland, Adolf, his wife, Edith, and young Hans, along with Harry and his wife, Bronia, foolishly left their refuge in Sweden to make a business trip to Heinrich Klinger's factory to view the season's new line of industrial linens. Adolf and Harry, hoping to represent the Klinger company in Scandinavia, embarked on the trip to his factory in Zwittau, a major city in the Sudetenland, despite repeated warnings from Georg and Paula, who wisely remained in Stockholm with their two children. Adolf and Harry and their families had only made it as far as Riga, Latvia, across the Baltic Sea, when Hitler made his move on the Sudetenland. Prohibited from traveling to Czechoslovakia or from going back to Sweden, which had immediately closed its borders to refugees, the two families were stuck in Riga. Marooned there, they desperately applied for visas to the United States.

In Vienna, Abraham grew increasingly embittered when he realized that the political situation in Europe was tearing his family apart. To save himself and his family, he was being faced with some agonizing choices. In a letter to Georg and Paula, he outlined plans to divide up the family should they obtain visas to go to the United States, where he had a sister:

I received a letter from my sister in the United States, who says that they have found two guarantors for two families, but things will get more difficult for Dolfi [Adolf] and his family and Georg's family . . . Only when I explained this [that Georg's family could enter the United States by other means and therefore the U.S. guarantor should sponsor Harry and his wife, who had no other means of getting a visa] to her over the phone did she agree with my point of view and replace Georg's family with Harry and his wife, with pleasure, in fact, because there are only two people for Harry instead of Georg's four. Now, dear Georg! You are going to have to agree that this is the right thing to do.[17]

Life became a daily struggle for the remaining Hammersfelds, crowded into Abraham and Lotte's flat. Ration cards issued to Jews did not meet the family's needs. It became increasingly difficult to buy kosher products, and Abraham was forced to set aside his religious scruples and buy food on Vienna's thriving black market. One day, in particularly desperate times, he bought a ham for his family, but true to his religious convictions, he would not allow the meat to be placed on any of the family dishes. Instead, he took a piece of paper that was wrapped around the ham and carefully cut off strips of the meat, grasping each of them in the paper so that his hands never touched the ham. Still using the paper, he picked up the strips and deposited them directly into the mouths of his grandchildren.

"He was a very religious man, but also a modern man," says Renée about her grandfather. "He bought the ham because he was afraid we weren't getting enough protein."

The Hammersfelds' desperation increased on the night of November 9, 1938, when roving bands of thugs waged an all-out war against Jews and their property. The pogrom, which came to be known as *Kristallnacht,* "the night of broken glass," was launched throughout the Third Reich after a Jewish youth named Herschel Grunspan walked into the German embassy in Paris on November 7 and coolly shot a German consular official at point-blank range to protest Nazi treatment of the Jews. When Ernst vom Rath, the German official, died two days later on the afternoon of November 9, the Nazis used the incident as a provocation to go after all Jews living in the Third Reich.

In Vienna, marauding crowds of Nazis, who wore civilian clothes as per a party directive, looted Jewish stores and destroyed synagogues. An official report of a Vienna SD unit, dated November 10, stated that operations were completed "thoroughly and rapidly." The official went on to write that "it is natural that the operation made a deep impression on the Jews. The events paralyzed the Jews to such an extent that they could not even exhibit the customary outbursts of despair. It may be stated with certainty that after today's events the Jews have lost every vestige of desire to carry on." Indeed, on November 10, just as the rioting stopped, 680 Jewish men and women committed suicide in Vienna.[18]

Historian Gertrude Schneider, daughter of an affluent Viennese couple, wrote about her own family's experiences the day after Kristallnacht:

Five men, wearing the brown uniforms of the SA came to our apartment between 10 and 11 A.M. Among them was Rudolf Randa, the son of our grocery's proprietors. He proudly wore the insignia of the "illegal" party member and convinced his cohorts not to smash our valuables, but rather to pack them into two large oval laundry baskets standing in the foyer in preparation for the monthly wash day. They took paintings from the wall, among them two lovely oils by Pettenkofen, they took the Augarten porcelain statue of Prince Eugen on his horse, . . . they took crystal and silver, money and jewelry, going systematically through every drawer. When they got to my father's desk, they found his sword, his father's bayonet, and a valuable, engraved, seventeenth-century scimitar. Accusing him of being an assassin who was going to murder Aryans with these antiquated weapons, brandishing handcuffs, and screaming obscenities, they wanted to arrest him immediately. It was Randa who convinced them that arresting my father was really not necessary. "Let s just take the weapons, and go," he said, "we have still other calls to make."[19]

The looting and violence were particularly pronounced in the Second District. Residents watched in horror as an angry mob burned down the neighborhood's biggest Orthodox synagogue, locally known as the Schiffshul after the name of the street—the Grosse Schiffegasse—on which it was built in 1864.

For Abraham, Kristallnacht was a turning point in his life. It was a broken man who watched the flames of the burning synagogue from his living-room window. If he had any faith left in law and order, it was consumed in the fires that destroyed Jewish homes and businesses on that chilly night in November.

"After Kristallnacht, everything was sort of expected," says Renée. "We were no longer surprised at what they could do to Jews. Now we knew that everything was possible and we did everything we could to get out."

Renée's mother, who had been allowed to work in Georg Stilman's store after it had been Aryanized, was unceremoniously kicked out by a group of thugs. In one letter Georg notes, "Selma writes me that she's not allowed in the store anymore, but I don't understand. I don't know who has taken over the store. But it's probably a criminal like all of the others We Jews take no revenge but the Heavenly Father will reckon with them. You can be convinced of that. My brother-in-law said that many of our acquaintances have been locked up, all because they are Jews."[20]

A few days after Kristallnacht, an angry mob dragged Abraham Hammersfeld from his third-floor flat onto the street below, where they took turns kicking him. Abraham, whose face was covered in blood, tried to gain his composure long enough to convince his tormentors that as an exporter, a businessman who sold his hotel and restaurant linens across Europe, he was bringing much-needed foreign capital into Austria, and therefore should not be made to suffer such indignities. His comments seemed to have an effect on the SS officer leading the rabble, who ordered them to stop. Dabbing at the blood on his face with a starched linen handkerchief, Abraham watched his tormentors round the corner of the tiny cobbled street before he made his way unsteadily into the foyer of his apartment building.

Following that violent incident, Abraham furiously made plans to leave Vienna. Renée, who would turn sixteen on December 23, 1938, with no prospects for leaving the country, grew restless and irritable. Not only could she not attend school, but curfews prevented her from being out on the streets after dark. In a letter to her cousin Sylvia in Stockholm, written three weeks before her sixteenth birthday, Renée described a typical day:

. . . And now I'll write you about what I do all day: I get up around 8 o'clock, wash and dress, have breakfast, and air the beds. Then we usually argue for a little bit and then I go shopping with Grandmother or stay home and clean up. Then there's usually something to peel and so the time passes until dinnertime. Afterwards, the dishes get done quickly and then I get dressed and go to Trude's. Every day we take walks along the Hauptallee [the main commercial avenue]. At 5 o'clock we come home to Trude's place and grab a snack and pass the time somehow. Around 8 o'clock I go home or sometimes I spend the night there and the next day begins the same all over again. That's the way it is, day in, day out, and it's only altered by breaking the rules. Interesting, huh? I can't go to the cinema or theater anymore either.[21]

Going to the theater and the cinema were the least of the elder Hammersfelds' concerns in December 1938. The Hammersfelds were being assaulted on all fronts. Nearly two months after the Aryanization of Adolf's store, things went awry, adding to the Hammersfelds' long list of woes. Adolf, who had now settled with his family in Riga, wrote: "I am getting terrible news from Vienna. [Johann Greisinger] tells me that they smashed my glass sign as well as those of other Jews and also held boycott days. So it's always bad news. God will have mercy."[22]

There was no such thing as mercy in Vienna, not even for good, hardworking Aryans like the Greisingers. "Eight days before Christmas, around noon, like a thunderbolt from a blue sky, the district administrator closed the store in a surprise attack," wrote Aloisia's father, Franz Celnar, in a letter of complaint to Josef Burckel, the Reich governor of Austria.[23] The store was taken over by Hans Allnoch, a businessman and member of the Nazi party, who had better connections with the party than either the Greisingers or the Celnars. Hans Allnoch, who had already Aryanized another Jewish textile store in Vienna, had been a member of the Nazi party when it was still an underground movement in Austria prior to 1938.

This flagrant takeover of the Hammersfeld store and the seizure of their inventory not only shattered the lives of the young couple, who had to abandon their marriage plans, but also impoverished their extended families. In letter after letter to Nazi officials, Aloisia's father, Franz, implored them to uphold that great hallmark of German society—the law:

I ask you, is it possible that in a country with justice, decent countrymen can be robbed of their duly acquired possessions, without any official sanction or judicial order, out of purely personal interests and egotistical desires. I ask you, is it really possible in a cultured country with the highest civilization, with a new and ideal leadership, that rightfully and duly purchased possessions can be confiscated in an entirely arbitrary manner and without due process of the law. . . . Through the expulsion of Jews from businesses my children were losing their jobs and they had to abandon their plan to get married. To spare my child unemployment and no hope of a marriage, I decided after serious consideration—"a nation helps itself"—to buy, with cash and by legal means, that is, with a lawyer and a sales contract, the business of Adolf Hammersfeld . . . and provide a living for the couple. . . . As a faithful German, I cannot imagine that this kind of behavior is indicative

of the NSDAP [the National Socialist German Workers' Party].
Heil Hitler.[24]

The Greisingers and the Celnars were not the only ones left destitute. The elderly Königs were now faced with the horrible realization that their main source of support would be immediately cut off.
Under the terms of the agreement that their son-in-law Adolf had
hammered out with Greisinger, the latter was to pay them 60 Reichsmarks (about $215 today) a month to supplement their pensions. In
a desperate letter to the Nazi agency that had overseen the business
transaction, Josef König wrote:

> My son-in-law was in no position to provide us with any support
> before he left and this arrangement was to shield us from the worst
> needs. . . . We are two old people. I am seventy-eight and my wife
> is seventy-one years old and nearly blind and we cannot expect
> anything from our children. One lives as an emigrant and the other
> is destitute and will soon have to leave the country. Since it is
> documented that there was an extensive warehouse left behind
> which the Vermogensverkehrstelle has in its possession and can
> therefore realize, we ask you, please consider our hopeless situation
> and spare us distress and misery by making a positive decision.[25]

Despite their protestations, the Königs were not given a penny,
and eventually they were sent to a concentration camp.

Abraham, who was accountable by law for his children's debts,
was now drawn into the sad expropriation when a destitute Johann
Greisinger turned to him to help him pay the store's debts, which he
now owed to the rapacious Hans Allnoch. Abraham was devastated
when he realized, like Aloisia Celnar's father, that in this "cultured
country with the highest civilization" there was no more respect for
due process, there was no law to protect him anymore. Abraham had
no choice but to pay the debts with some of the money that he had
managed to keep hidden from the Nazis after they Aryanized his
textile firm.

Abraham continued to behave like a cornered animal. To his son Adolf, he wrote long, complaining missives about how he, Adolf, had run off to Sweden, leaving a great deal of unfinished business. He wrote of the disaster of the Greisinger Aryanization and expressed a great deal of resentment that he had to pay the debts to the new Nazi owner. He also bemoaned his wife's failing health. Lotte, who was nervous by nature, could not deal with the fact that the family business had been Aryanized and the future was increasingly grim and uncertain.

In the winter of 1938–1939, the Hammersfelds, now scattered in various European countries, were still trying to get visas to the United States. Selma and Renée, and Renée's older brother, Siegfried, were still living at the flat on Negerlegasse, unable to leave the country because they did not have Austrian citizenship and could not easily acquire a passport. (When Oskar Lang, Renée's father, had immigrated to Austria from Poland just before the First World War, he had neglected to take out Austrian citizenship. In order to remedy the situation, Oskar, who was still a Polish citizen, returned to his native country in 1938 to volunteer for the Polish Army. Polish authorities in Austria had told him that by volunteering for a few months of military service in Poland, he could acquire Polish passports for his family. That would turn out to be a terrible mistake: When the Second World War broke out in September 1939, Oscar was stuck. By 1940, the Nazis had prohibited Polish Jews and stateless Jews of Polish origin living in the Reich from leaving German territory.)

Then things improved, at least for the elderly Hammersfelds, in early 1939 when Harry's wife, Bronia, managed to obtain visas for Abraham and Lotte to join them in Riga, in neutral Latvia. Abraham instructed Renée to help him with preparations for the move. In order to comply with Nazi regulations for emigration, Abraham paid off Johann Greisinger's debts from the sabotaged Aryanization of Adolf's store, and prepared to dispose of the last of the Hammersfeld family heirlooms. Renée helped him pack the silver, a chandelier, the good china, her grandmother's jewelry, and her grandfather's beloved Swiss pocket watch. Abraham bundled Renée and the family treasures into a taxi, and instructed the driver to take her to the Dorotheum, an elegant auction house that had been converted under the Nazis into the Public Purchasing Institute, which bought up Jewish valuables. Dorotheum officials severely undervalued the goods. They also charged a 10 percent commission for their services.

Renée then made her way to Gestapo headquarters, which was a few blocks away from the Dorotheum in the palace that had been confiscated from the Rothschild family. She had been sent by her grandfather to register a mortgage he had in Poland. Renée waited nervously in line to speak to the Gestapo agent who was responsible for Jewish property. Without looking up at her, the agent motioned Renée into his office in one of the palace's sitting rooms where Renaissance frescoes covered the ceilings. The agent must have been struck by this tall, beautiful teenager who sat in front of him, for as soon as he looked up at her, he uttered a startled "You can't be Jewish?! You certainly don't look Jewish."

Indeed, Renée knew that she could easily "pass" for an Aryan. Just after the Anschluss, she had gone to a photo studio down the street from her grandfather's office on Wipplingerstrasse to have her picture taken for visa applications. A few days later, she was startled to find that the photographer, in a fit of patriotic fervor, was displaying her portrait in the window as a tribute to "The perfect Austrian woman." The portrait mounted above hers in the display case was none other than that of a triumphant Adolf Hitler, with the inscription "Our glorious Führer."

Now Renée sat bolt upright in her chair in front of the Gestapo agent's desk. She was surprised by her own boldness: "Not only am I a Jew, but I'm an eastern Jew," she said in her perfect private-school German, emphasizing that her family was made up of Eastern European Jews, who were despised the most by the Nazi party.

The agent, somewhat embarrassed by this outburst, busied himself with Abraham Hammersfeld's file. "Ah, well. We like Jews," he said matter-of-factly, without looking up. "Especially dead Jews."

If she was shaken by the comment, Renée didn't show it. She had more important concerns in that spring of 1939. In a few days her grandmother and grandfather would leave Vienna bound for Riga, and Renée and her mother would be alone in Vienna. Renée's brother Siegfried had managed to obtain a visa to travel to England with other Austrian Jewish youths, but although Abraham had tried every means possible to get his remaining daughter and grandchild out of the country after his son-in-law disappeared in Poland, there was nothing he could do to help them. He promised them he would write and send regular food parcels from Riga. Somehow he would arrange for American visas for them through his sister in New York. He told them to be strong, to trust in God, not to worry.

Just before his departure for Riga, Abraham Hammersfeld summoned Renée to his library, now stripped of much of the family furniture and books. He tried his best to reassure his favorite granddaughter, whose eyes were welling up with tears.

That was when he told her about the bank account in Switzerland. He had kept it a close-guarded secret from the Nazi authorities, since it was illegal for Jews living in the Third Reich to have undeclared assets abroad. In calm, measured tones, Abraham explained to Renée that if anything happened to him, she was to make contact with his Swiss bank. She thinks he gave her the name of the bank, an account number, or the address of a business associate or trustee. But in the grief of that final embrace, Renée did not pay much attention. She was worried about his survival, about how she was going to buy food on the black market, about how she and her mother were going to get out of Vienna.

On April 21, 1939, Abraham Hammersfeld became a Nazi statistic. At Gestapo headquarters inside the once sumptuous Rothschild palace, where the valuable Persian carpets and period furniture had long been replaced with military-issue typewriters and wooden desks, a Nazi bureaucrat carefully affixed a bold piece of red tape to file number 10024, which indicated that Abraham Hammersfeld, a Jew, had formally emigrated to a foreign country. "File Closed" was stamped in a heavy medieval Germanic script at the top of the document. No detail was too small for the Nazi bureaucrat, who noted in a tight, efficient script: "Property at time of move: one piano."

VEIT WYLER SAYS that the first calls came from Germany sometime in 1935. The voices on the other end of the crackling phone line were almost always hesitant, sometimes a little desperate. It was that hint of fear in the distant voices that sent a shiver through Wyler and made him sit up straighter in his chair as he reached for his fountain pen and a stray piece of paper on his cluttered desk.

A young Jewish lawyer in Zürich, barely three years out of law school, Wyler had already mastered the art of discretion and secrecy. He knew better than to conduct business over the telephone, especially when the voices at the other end sounded so nervous. Wyler tried as best he could to reassure them. He often knew without asking that the callers were Jewish, that they had found his phone number through a friend of a friend or a business associate and that they were calling about—yes, it was almost always phrased the same way—"a very delicate matter."

Wyler would sometimes arrange to meet these would-be clients at his office in Zürich; but usually they preferred to meet somewhere else in the city in order not to attract too much attention. Sometimes they met in a park, the lobby of a hotel, or one of the crowded cafés off the bustling Bahnhofstrasse, Zürich's financial center. Most of them didn't have big fortunes. They were middle- and upper-middle-class businessmen who had means—men very much like Abraham Hammersfeld, who were concerned about the political instability and growing anti-Semitism in the Third Reich. Sometimes they would bring cash and try to convert it into Swiss francs; more often, they would bring gold ingots, bonds, jewelry, wills, or deeds to property.

Wyler sympathized with these victims of anti-Semitism, and willingly helped them to safeguard their assets. Although he had lived a fairly sheltered Orthodox Jewish life in Baden, a small town northwest of Zürich, where his father was the leader of the local Jewish community organization, he had been the victim of anti-Semitism when he enlisted in the Swiss Army for his obligatory training. Everyday for the few months of his military training, his mother would arrive at the barracks, bearing a hot kosher meal for her son. Wyler's Orthodox lifestyle soon became the object of a great deal of derision among his fellow recruits. He hated being the butt of anti-Semitic jokes, and even though he had the opportunity to become an officer, he declined, deciding instead to pursue a career in law.

The bitter memories of Wyler's days in the Swiss Army almost always came rushing back to him when he met one of his distraught foreign clients, who recounted terrible stories of the violent anti-Semitism that was sweeping the German Reich. So it was not unusual that after a ten-minute conversation, lawyer and client had formed a silent bond. An outside observer might have been struck by the ease with which these hard-nosed businessmen would find themselves voluntarily entrusting their assets to Wyler, sometimes without so much as a written guarantee or even a receipt—just a firm handshake and the young lawyer's word that he would deposit the assets in a numbered account or under his own name in a Swiss bank. When clients could not travel to Switzerland to meet personally with the young lawyer, they would often send whatever assets they could—usually bonds and securities, in some cases gold ingots—via trusted couriers.

A Communist with a sterling reputation for professionalism and honesty, Wyler became one of an informal network of legal and financial experts who helped Jews hide assets in Swiss banks. These men and women would eventually work with clients fleeing Nazi aggression all over Europe.

The calls to Wyler's office increased in 1936 when Hitler promulgated very strict exchange-control laws that made foreign holdings illegal. This was nothing new in German economic policy, which had been dominated by strict exchange controls since the 1920s, when Hjalmar Schacht, Reich currency commissioner for the Weimar Republic, tried to stem the hyperinflation that was destabilizing Germany's economy. Under the controls, tight restrictions were placed on German citizens who took money outside the country. Wyler, who was going to school in Wiesbaden, Germany, at the time, recalls that he was often approached by desperate Germans on the train who wanted to exchange their Reichsmarks for Swiss francs.

"What they were doing at the time was illegal," says Wyler, who would exchange the hundred Swiss francs his father gave him for school expenses on the train to Germany. "If the Germans got caught trading money, they could go to jail back then."

By December 1936, the stakes were higher. Hitler's law against what the Nazis called "economic sabotage" was punishable by death. The law, which extended to German citizens living outside the Reich, stated in part that "any German national who knowingly and having as a motive vulgar self-interest and other low motives acts against the law in transferring assets abroad, or keeps them abroad and thereby damages the German economy, is punished with death."[26] The law was aimed partly at encouraging Germans to repatriate their foreign holdings. Those prepared to admit that they had foreign assets could repatriate a third of them after they had delivered two thirds to the Reichsbank.

BEFORE SWITZERLAND BECAME a center of European banking in the 1930s, it had been generally regarded as a small, politically stable, mostly pastoral nation of hardworking, no-nonsense dairy farmers, merchants, and skilled craftsmen who produced the world's finest watches and chocolate. The alpine country, with its snow-capped mountains and crystalline lakes, is a collection of twenty-five federated states of which nineteen are called cantons and six, half cantons. Because of its geographic location in the center of Europe, surrounded by Italy, Austria, Germany, and France, Switzerland's history has been dominated by a series of local incursions and regional power plays by its powerful neighbors. Originally inhabitants of the Roman province of Helvetia, the Swiss obtained independence from the Holy Roman Empire in the fifteenth century, and their cantons were joined under a federal constitution in 1848, with large powers of local control retained by each canton. The constitution, which was further amended in 1874, fostered national unity in a country made up of several different ethnic groups (German, French, Italian, Romansch) and religious convictions.

The staunch, conservative Swiss, a small nation of six million people, organized in their largely autonomous cantons ruled by small, powerful oligarchies, remained largely aloof from regional skirmishes. As a trading nation, Switzerland profited handsomely from the neutrality that it had practically invented during the Thirty Years' War in the seventeenth century. Historically, neutrality became such an important principle in Switzerland that the Swiss confederacy would only admit cantons after they made a pledge of strict neutrality in the event of disputes between confederate states. The international community formally recognized Switzerland's "perpetual neutrality" in the 1815 Congress of Vienna, which enlarged Switzerland to its present size and recognized the country as crucial to the balance of power in Europe. Neutrality contributed to stability, allowing the local Swiss oligarchies to concentrate on building up the country's economic base and the region's strongest currency.

As a result of a booming economy, advances in science, art, and political thought flourished in Switzerland, making the country an important European intellectual center. It was the birthplace of influential eighteenth-century philosopher Jean-Jacques Rousseau and nineteenth-century educational reformer Johann Heinrich Pestalozzi, whose groundbreaking pedagogical method stressed love and understanding of a child's world rather than the teaching methods of the day, which stressed strict discipline and memorization. Switzerland also attracted a host of intellectuals—writers, philosophers, and revolutionaries—from neighboring countries. Goethe and Rilke wrote in Zürich, the country's German-speaking intellectual capital, and Russian revolutionary Vladimir Ilyich Lenin had a favorite table at the city's smoky Café Odeon and a card for the Zürich municipal library.

Although Switzerland was poor in natural resources, its economy prospered at the turn of the century through the export of manufactured goods—textiles, machinery, watches, and chemicals—to its European trading partners, which were mainly Germany, France, and Italy. Switzerland's economic prosperity spawned a small but highly professional cadre of bankers who had an international reputation for discretion and integrity, and as a result began to attract a growing clientele of foreign investors.

Still, not much had changed in Switzerland at the beginning of the twentieth century. It remained a quiet, pastoral enclave, known for its chocolate, breathtaking alpine vistas, and the professionalism of its banks. But it was not a banking capital until the mid-1930s, when it became a financial safe haven for Reich citizens trying to circumvent the law, often dependent for their lives on the banks' secrecy and confidentiality.

Although banking secrecy would be reinforced with a 1934 law that strictly penalized bankers for not abiding by it, the Swiss concept of secrecy in banking was more than three hundred years old. Contrary to the popular myth that the secrecy laws came into effect to protect Jewish assets after Hitler came to power, Switzerland actually became the premier discreet destination for European flight capital in the seventeenth century, when French Protestant Huguenots fled to Switzerland to escape religious and political persecution and the confiscation of their property by French Catholic kings. About a century later, France's royal house of Bourbon followed suit, using Switzerland as a quiet haven when the victors of the French Revolution tried to confiscate royal property.

The origins of banking secrecy are enshrined in Swiss democratic and legal principles. Swiss law protects the rights of every individual and business entity in a "sphere of secrecy," known in German as *Geheimsphäre*. An individual's sphere of secrecy, or sphere of privacy, could include issues of health, family life, and financial affairs. In the United States, on the other hand, the constitutional right to privacy extends only to those matters that the Supreme Court considers fundamental. In the Swiss civil law tradition, the right to privacy is inviolable. In the financial sector, secrecy prohibits bank officials from disclosing any information they obtain about their clients in the course of business.

In 1932, Swiss lawmakers sought to strengthen banking secrecy by codifying it into an umbrella legislation to regulate the banking sector. The immediate impetus for the secrecy provisions of the law was a huge French tax scandal, which broke in the autumn of that year and exposed Swiss bankers. In October, French police raided the Paris branch of the Basler Handelsbank to crack down on a tax-evasion racket involving a number of influential Parisians who were using the Swiss bank to hide their assets. In a separate but related incident, Socialist federal deputy Fabien Albertin released a list of prominent French citizens, including government ministers, senior military officials, and clergymen, who maintained secret Swiss bank accounts to evade withholding and income taxes, contrary to French law. Albertin's list had reportedly been leaked to him by Swiss bankers living in Paris, who were later arrested by French police. In both cases, French law-enforcement authorities demanded that the Swiss bankers assist them in their prosecution efforts. The French police wanted to view the records of all French clients of the Basler Handelsbank, and to know who had leaked the list of prominent tax-evading citizens to Albertin. Swiss authorities were scandalized, and the events caused a diplomatic row between the two countries. Switzerland's Federal Council refused to cooperate with the French, and Swiss lawmakers set about drafting a law that would ensure that the privacy of Switzerland's bank clients could not be violated under any circumstances.

The Federal Law Relating to Banks and Savings Banks, passed on November 8, 1934, severely penalized bankers for breaching secrecy. According to Article 47(b):

Anyone who in his capacity as an officer or employee of a bank, or as an auditor of his employee,

or as a member of the banking commission or an officer or employee of its bureau intentionally

violates his duty to observe silence or his professional rule of secrecy or anyone who induces or

attempts to induce a person to commit any such offense, shall be liable to a fine of up to 20,000

francs or imprisonment of up to six months, or both.[27]

The banking law of 1934 also sought to centralize regulation in a sector that had never been federally supervised, and as a result had suffered several crises and closures after the First World War. The 1934 law created the Federal Banking Commission, which supervised and implemented the legislation, regulated auditing procedures, and oversaw the reorganization of banks. Members of the Federal Banking Commission were elected by the Swiss Federal Council, to whom they also reported.

The tough new banking law appealed to Jews who needed guarantees that their assets could never be traced. In the years immediately preceding the war, many Jews sought out lawyers, accountants, and other trustees or agents in Switzerland to help them hide their assets. In opening a Swiss bank account to shield some of his assets, Abraham Hammersfeld may have tapped into this informal network of Jewish professionals in Zürich or any of the other German-speaking banking centers of Switzerland. Although it would have been tricky for Jews to travel out of Austria after the 1938 Anschluss for a short trip to Switzerland, Abraham, with his myriad European textile customers, could easily have asked one of his clients to deposit the amount owed his textile firm into a numbered Swiss account that may or may not have been opened by him directly. He is certainly known to have opened at least one account outside Austria: He had one at a branch of the Enskilda Bank in Stockholm, where his firm's Swedish clients deposited the money they owed him for the wares his company shipped to Sweden. According to the Stilmans, who accessed the Swedish account during the war, Abraham had accumulated more than 30,000 Swedish kronor by 1939 (about $75,000 in 1997) at the Enskilda Bank—a substantial amount of money during the war.

The nature of the secrecy laws made it such that a depositor was often closer to his Swiss trustee with regard to financial matters than he was to his own family. If the depositor left his assets in the name of a scrupulous trustee, such as Wyler, he would undoubtedly receive his deposit back—with interest—if he survived the war. The more unscrupulous professionals often kept the money—or accepted Nazi

funds. "All kinds of people were wandering around Switzerland looking for trustees or lawyers to open an account for them," said Wyler.
"I tried as best I could to check up on my clients, and as far as I
know, not one penny of Nazi money went through my hands."

There are no available estimates of how many Jews and non-Jews
put money in Swiss banks to escape Nazi persecution after the Swiss
Parliament enshrined banking secrecy in 1934. At first, most of the
Jewish money going into Switzerland came from Germany after the
Nazi regime had enacted the Nuremberg Laws. A few years later, as
the Nazi menace spread across Europe, bringing its discriminatory
legislation against Jews to the occupied countries, Jews from Austria,
Czechoslovakia, France, Belgium, Holland, and Eastern Europe began to look to Swiss banks to hide their assets from the Nazis.

In one of the most ingenious and daring attempts to safeguard
Jewish funds from Nazi invaders, agents of the *maquis*, the French
underground resistance movement against the Nazis, tapped into
Swiss neutrality and the Red Cross's reputation for compassion.
Many maquis agents entered Switzerland, posing as refugees and
carrying suitcases full of gold and other valuables belonging to French
and Belgian Jews. The maquis agents often took young Jewish children on their journey to ensure that they were allowed entry into
Switzerland. In the early 1940s, the International Committee of the
Red Cross had a policy not to turn away refugee children. The maquis agents could accomplish two tasks in one: They ensured a safe
haven for Jewish children who would otherwise be sent to Nazi concentration camps, and they passed on Jewish valuables to banking
contacts in Switzerland for safekeeping during the war.

Switzerland's humanitarian tradition was born more than one hundred years ago when a wealthy Genevan named Jean-Henri Dunant
gathered together a small group of fellow Swiss notables in 1863,
forming the centerpiece of what was to become the International
Committee of the Red Cross (ICRC), the world's most recognizable
humanitarian agency, whose symbol, a red cross on a white background, is the inverse of the Swiss flag. Deeply troubled by his 1859
journey through the battlefields of northern Italy, Dunant sought to

gather support for an international convention that would allow an impartial group of civilian volunteers to care for the wounded in wartime. The result in 1864 was the Geneva Convention, one of the world's most comprehensive humanitarian charters, which set out the rules of "civilized" warfare, upheld the protection of civilians in wartime, and established the principle that enemy soldiers had the same right to medical treatment as those of one's own country.

As a result of Switzerland's international humanitarian reputation, many members of the maquis put their trust in Swiss institutions. Willy Halpert, a French Jew, whose wealthy father was a member of the Resistance, says that in 1942 his parents gathered the family gold and silver at their home in Antwerp and melted everything down. They then wrapped gold and silver pieces in skeins of wool and packed them in suitcases for the journey to Switzerland. Halpert, who is now sixty-three and lives in Israel, says that his two younger sisters accompanied a maquis agent on a harrowing journey to Switzerland that could only be made under cover of darkness. The agents spirited the young girls through dense forests. They ate what they could find on the journey and slept in cemeteries as they made their way to the Swiss border. When they finally reached Switzerland after several days of travel, Halpert's exhausted and emaciated sisters, Solange and Lillianne, were placed with a Swiss family outside Lausanne by the ICRC for the duration of the war.

Upon arrival in Switzerland, the maquis agents contacted underground members of their group, many of whom were Swiss professionals, with good contacts with clerks and other minor officials at the leading Swiss banks. In many cases, the Swiss maquis affiliates would deposit the gold and silver, and other assets brought across the border, using their own names in numbered accounts. In these cases, it is not clear how the agents kept track of what assets belonged to whom, and whether the Swiss affiliates of the group later pocketed the assets when the beneficial owners did not return to claim them after the war. In many cases, the maquis bribed minor bank officials in order to open accounts, using identity documents of comrades who had not been able to cross the border but had surrendered their documentation to the maquis couriers, who then spirited their assets to Switzerland. In other instances, the couriers simply deposited the assets in existing bank accounts opened by the beneficial owners before the beginning of the war. The whole operation was indeed risky, but for people desperate to salvage their assets from the marauding Nazis, there was no other choice, says Willy Halpert.

Following a pogrom in Antwerp in 1942, Willy Halpert's father told his son the location of the family's assets in Switzerland. "My father told me not to worry, that he had managed to take eighty thousand pounds sterling to Switzerland," says Halpert. "When he disappeared and I was sent to an orphanage, I recited the information he gave me every day like a catechism. But I eventually forgot the name of the bank and any other information I had about the bank account. After the war I tried to forget everything about that time."

Halpert survived the war, safe in a cloister in rural Belgium. But his parents died in Auschwitz. He says he has been trying for more than twenty years to find his father's bank account.

DESPITE SWISS NEUTRALITY and banking secrecy, Jewish money was not always safe in Swiss bank vaults. As economic sanctions against Jews living in the Third Reich became more stringent, the Swiss holdings of Jews became targets for the Nazi expropriation machine. It was not unusual for Gestapo agents to travel to Switzerland, posing as individuals they suspected of being account holders, in order to ferret out information about Swiss bank accounts. Sometimes, they would bribe bank officials for information. As early as the mid-1930s, Swiss banks regularly received visits from members of the Gestapo, sometimes posing as customs agents or business agents, armed with forged powers of attorney or accompanying nervous account holders in person. The Nazis' Foreign Intelligence Service of the Armed Forces (*Oberkommando der Wehrmacht*) and the SS Security Service (*Sicherheitsdienst*) operated special agents through the German legation in Bern and German consulates spread throughout Switzerland. (The Nazis also used Germans resident in Switzerland for espionage purposes, although the penalty for such treason in Switzerland was quite severe. In 1942 and 1943, numerous trials for treason took place in Switzerland, where several of the accused, who included Swiss Army officers, were found guilty of betraying military secrets to Germany. Nineteen people were sentenced to death and thirty-three to life imprisonment.[28])

In 1934, Gestapo agent Georg Hannes Thomae settled in Zürich for the express purpose of ferreting out the Swiss bank accounts of German citizens—Jewish and otherwise. Thomae, who had apprenticed in a bank as a young man in Germany, posed as a vacationing *rentier* and proceeded to blend in with the approximately 200,000 German nationals living in Switzerland at the time. Armed with a list of suspected German and Jewish account holders, Thomae opened accounts in several large Swiss banks and made it a point to meet as many minor employees as he could to verify his information. Bribery was the most effective means of acquiring what must have seemed to most bank clerks as fairly innocuous information about their clients. Thomae also developed other clever tactics. According to writer T. R. Fehrenbach, who recounts Thomae's adventures in Switzerland,

> He [Thomae] began to approach banks with a respectable sum of money, trying to deposit it to the account of certain names. In 1934 neither Switzerland nor its banks were prepared for the Gestapo agent and his bag of tricks. Everything depended upon the immediate judgment of counter clerks and minor bank officials when confronted with this situation—and some, tragically guessed wrong. . . .[29]

Fehrenbach recounts an instance in which Thomae entered the Swiss Bank Corporation in Zürich to deposit the then equivalent of $5,000 in the name of Anton Fabricius of Hannover, Germany. Thomae explained to the bank clerk that he had carried the money over the border for Fabricius, since it was impossible for Fabricius to leave

Germany. The clerk conferred with another bank official, who established the fact that Anton Fabricius of Hannover did indeed have an account at the bank.

It no longer mattered whether the bank now accepted the money or turned it back—Agent Thomae had been told all he needed to know. The bank would never have given any information in the face of a direct demand; no Swiss bank would. But the situation for German depositors in Swiss banks—of which there were thousands—had become chaotic. Every means of electronic communication between Switzerland and Germany and the mails were watched. Communication had broken down. In this situation, it was not always possible for banks to follow strictly customers' instructions made years before. Almost all German customers were now using third parties or Swiss agents to handle their business. Thomae's offered deposit might very well have been a legitimate one, and it might seriously inconvenience Fabricius if the bank failed to take it. The bank took the money.[30]

Two hours after Thomae communicated the results of his mission to his superiors in Berlin, Anton Fabricius disappeared. Three days later, the Swiss Bank Corporation received a cable from Fabricius requesting the repatriation of his assets. According to Fehrenbach, German records do not reveal what was done to Fabricius to force him to cooperate with German officials.

In other attempts to track down Jewish assets in Switzerland, Nazi Germany placed "French-speaking ardent Nazis in the leading Swiss banks," U.S. intelligence records show. In one case in the late 1930s, Nazi officials arrested Henry Lowinger, a wealthy Viennese Jew who owned and operated a major laundry business in Vienna, but allowed him to buy his way out of jail by surrendering his Swiss bank holdings to the Gestapo. According to the documents, "the Gestapo knew exactly how much Lowinger had on deposit and where it was held." In exchange for his foreign assets, the Nazis allowed Lowinger and his wife to escape to Switzerland.[31]

But some Swiss banks were prepared for the onslaught of Nazi espionage and, by the late 1930s, had counterespionage experts on hand. British journalist Nicholas Faith recounts the adventures of Dr. Max Homberger, a non-Jewish lawyer employed by the Swiss Bank Corporation (SBC) in the mid-1930s, who eventually became the bank's fearless expert on counterespionage and a leader in the fight against fascism. In the late 1930s, Homberger was sent to Germany to find out why a high-school teacher who had an account at the SBC had sent a letter asking his banker to hand over all his assets—about 45,000 Swiss francs worth—to the *Deutsche Winterhelfe,* a well-known Nazi fund controlled by Hermann Goering. Homberger tracked down the frightened teacher, who fearfully confessed that he had been pressured by Nazi thugs to make his request to the bank. As a result of the experience, the SBC's legal department devised a series of responses "to implausible requests for funds to be repatriated to Germany, or for information about an account held by a German." Whenever the bank received a suspicious request, it sent out a form letter invoking Clause 47(b) of the Banking Law, declaring that the bank could neither admit nor deny the existence of an account or give out specific information about an account holder. As Gestapo espionage activities increased just before the war, Homberger helped devise other ways to outwit the Nazis. According to Nicholas Faith, "Homberger remembers one client called Weiss: if the bank received any letter in which he had left the dot off the 'I' in his name then the bank would ignore any instructions it contained. Another client gave the bank half a torn card: if anyone arrived claiming a power of attorney without the other half then the bank was to refuse payment."[32]

For his part, Veit Wyler says he never revealed or even officially recorded the names of clients who entrusted him with their assets. "I had to keep the name in my memory," says Wyler, who is now eighty-eight years old and has had a distinguished sixty-five year legal career in Switzerland. Wyler, who can no longer remember how many clients entrusted their assets to him, says that he kept information about deposits in a ledger, which he hid among the legal volumes in the library of his home in Zürich.

In his comfortable sitting room, lined with shelves full of those same Swiss legal volumes that once contained so many secrets, ancient Hebrew texts, and a collection of silver kiddush cups, Wyler, dressed in a faded pin-striped suit, sits upright in a worn armchair, painfully recalling his most difficult moment as a trustee for Jews trying to safeguard their assets from Nazi expropriation. Just after the outset of the war in 1939, Wyler received a visit from a Gestapo agent, accompanied by one of his former law-school colleagues—"an earnest, blond chap with glasses, who was well known in Zürich as a fervent Nazi." The Gestapo agent came armed with a power of attorney signed by one of Wyler's clients, who had just been arrested for contravening German law by smuggling his assets to Switzerland. Wyler examined the power of attorney, which appeared to be in order, and accompanied his former classmate and the Gestapo agent to the Bank Julius Baer, the most prominent Jewish bank in Switzerland at the time. Wyler, a loyal Julius Baer customer, had deposited all of his clients' assets at the bank. The Gestapo agent instructed Wyler to withdraw his client's assets. The young Jewish lawyer faced a terrible dilemma: If Wyler complied with the Gestapo agent, his client might have a good chance of "buying his freedom" and getting out of jail; however, if Wyler chose not to cooperate, his client might be killed. As he walked into the small bank's main reception area, Wyler shuddered to think what kind of torture the Gestapo had used to pry information from his client, a wealthy German Jewish businessman.

Carl Kuenzler, the bank's chief executive officer, was returning from lunch when he saw Wyler accompanied by the two men. In the 1930s, Bank Julius Baer was a relatively small operation, and its employees personally knew most of the bank's clients. For Kuenzler, a keen observer and a Christian, something was not quite right about the scene he saw before him in the lobby of the bank: the young Wyler, escorted by two tall, rather imposing gentlemen, one of them a well-known Nazi sympathizer in Zürich legal circles. Perhaps he noted that Wyler looked ill at ease. Kuenzler, a shrewd forty-eight-year-old financial expert who had worked as a grain trader before joining the bank nearly twenty years before, could tell a shady situation when he saw one. Kuenzler, whose stocky build and wiry features reminded Wyler of a boxer, boldly approached the young lawyer, who surrendered the power-of-attorney documents and asked for Kuenzler's advice. Kuenzler took one look at the documents and made it plain that the Bank Julius Baer would not be pressured to cooperate with Nazis.

"We don't give money to Nazis," said the white-haired Kuenzler, handing the power-of-attorney documents back to the Gestapo agent, and showing him the door. "Not one penny."

Wyler, who remembers being both horrified and relieved by Kuenzler's actions, worried for years about the fate of his German Jewish client. Yet, somehow the client survived, and returned to Switzerland soon after the war to collect his assets. "He was one of the lucky ones," says Wyler. "Others never came back. They were not so fortunate."

TRANSFERS

In her desperation to flee Nazi persecution in Vienna, Renée Lang considered a daring escape across the Swiss border under cover of darkness. But it was only a fleeting thought, lodging itself in her mind only when her grandfather told her about his Swiss bank account. She had quickly dismissed Switzerland as a safe haven for Jews. A few months after the Anschluss, some university students she knew had made a dangerous and ill-fated attempt to find refuge there. A week after setting out for the Swiss border, they were back in Vienna recounting their sad exploits to anyone who would listen. The students had been flatly denied entrance into the neutral country by Swiss border officials, who sent them back into the Third Reich.

"We soon found out Switzerland was neutral, all right, but only on the German side," says Renée, who was still living in her grandparents' bare flat on Negerlegasse.

The historian Gertrude Schneider, who lived in Vienna with her family until they were deported to Riga in February 1942, had already learned firsthand that Swiss neutrality was a myth if you were Jewish. Schneider recalls that in July 1938, her father, a wealthy Viennese merchant, sent his youngest daughter, Rita, aged seven, to Canton Appenzell in the Swiss Alps as part of a summer youth program organized by Vienna's Jewish community center. At ten years old, says Schneider, she was too old to qualify for the youth program. Although the center, which sent one hundred children to Switzerland in the summer of 1938, did not advertise the excursion as a humanitarian effort to spirit Jewish children out of Austria, most of the Viennese Jewish families who registered their children for the trip planned to use the youth program to go to Switzerland, under the pretext of visiting their vacationing children, and once in Switzerland both parents and children would claim refugee status. They did not think the Swiss would turn them back, especially since their children were already in Switzerland. However, only three weeks after Gertrude Schneider's sister was sent to Canton Appenzell, Swiss authorities sent her and many of the other Austrian Jewish children back to Vienna. The Swiss, who had arrested the parents of some of the children who had tried to claim refugee status, sent back the children in August as a warning to Austrian Jews that they were not welcome as refugees.

"We were very surprised," says Schneider, a professor at New York's City University. "We did not think the Swiss would turn the children back. But they did."

No matter what their financial background had been before the Anschluss, an estimated ninety thousand Viennese Jews—half Vienna's pre-Anschluss Jewish population—crowded into the Second District during the summer of 1939, where they endured a bleak existence. Renée's grandparents' old neighborhood, which had always been associated with happy occasions—with birthday parties, Jewish holidays, and long Sunday afternoons at the Café Sweden—was now overrun with desperate Jews. Walking through the cobbled streets of the Second District, once the center of Jewish life in Vienna with bustling kosher butcher shops and Hebrew schools, was like visiting a ruin from another era. Like most of Renée's family, many middle-class Jews had already left Vienna, purchasing their freedom to emigrate by handing over everything they owned to the Nazi authorities. The ones who remained were desperate to get out. The faces of the women who made their way to the black market to barter family heirlooms for food were lined with worry and fear. Jews were restricted from visiting non-Jewish shops except between the hours of 11:00 A.M. and 4:00 P.M. As anti-Semitism worsened, they had to queue up in front of special shops for Jews to purchase defective goods and rotting vegetables that had been rejected by the regular stores. After her daily forays to the market, Renée kept her head down, avoiding eye contact, and walked quickly home past the abandoned shops and the blasted neighborhood synagogues, their crumbling walls crowded with anti-Jewish graffiti. Although Renée still met with one or two of her friends, she barely left her mother's side.

"We faced the realization that we had no friends," she says, recalling the nearly four years she spent in the Second District after her grandparents left for Riga. "Everyone was out for themselves. There was no such thing as friendship or help. I never experienced any sort of help from my fellow Jews, not even in the Second District."

When Germany invaded Poland on September 1, 1939, and war began to rage across Europe, Renée and Selma became even more isolated and miserable. The outbreak of war worsened their daily lives, making food even scarcer for everyone—non-Jews as well as Jews—in Vienna, and communications with other Hammersfeld family members in Riga and Stockholm much more difficult. Besides a general mobilization of Austrian troops, the war with Poland resulted in a crackdown against Polish-born Jews in Vienna. A week after the war started, the Gestapo began to arrest Polish citizens, many of whom had lived most of their lives in Austria. Gestapo agents were merciless, invading orphanages and old-age homes to weed out these new enemy aliens and deport them to the Dachau and Buchenwald work camps. According to historian Raul Hilberg, more than six thousand Jews were sent from Vienna to the *Generalgouvernement*, as the

Nazi-controlled region of Poland was now known, before the onset of the Final Solution. Although Renée's father, Oskar Lang, a Polish citizen, had left Austria several months before the outbreak of war, Renée and her mother feared that because they were not officially Austrian citizens, they could easily be rounded up and mistaken for Poles because of their relationship to him.

By the time she celebrated her seventeenth birthday in late December, Renée carried the burdens of somebody twice her age. She was preoccupied with finding a way to leave the country, with having enough to eat. Confined almost all the time to the Second District and forced into close quarters with her mother, Renée lost her carefree spirit and became increasingly nervous and distant. "I worry about my little Renée," wrote Selma in a letter to her sister. "It hurts me to see her so nervous, and she doesn't look well." The two women were still pinning their hopes on obtaining immigration visas for the United States. But a full-fledged war was now raging in Europe, and the waiting list for visas at the U.S. consulate in Vienna was long. The United States still had quotas on emigrants from Europe, and candidates had to make a substantial deposit if they wanted to be considered for entry into the country.

Even though life was becoming desperate, mother and daughter tried to make the best of things in Vienna. Selma, who was an excellent cook, opened up a makeshift restaurant in her father's flat, serving lunches concocted of whatever vegetables and meat they could find to fellow ghetto dwellers who could afford to pay. Renée enrolled in a dressmaking course to learn a trade in the event that she would have to start a new life in another country. On weekends she sometimes accompanied her mother to a small café in the Third District, where she would sit daydreaming about life in America while her mother gossiped and exchanged recipes with some of her friends who had remained in Vienna.

Selma spent much of her spare time locked away in her father's old library, writing letters to family members, which because of the war sometimes took months to reach their destination. From time to time, Selma reminded her family not to forget to address packages destined for her and Renée to "Sara" Lang. All Jews in the Third Reich were forced by law to adopt the additional names of Sara, for women, and Israel, for men.

In a letter to her sister Paula Stilman in Stockholm, Selma wrote:

Unfortunately the possibilities to leave have momentarily fallen into the water. Apparently you can travel through Russia but you need 750 Reichsmarks and a ship-passage for Japan to America, which costs $200. And who is going to send this to us? We're afraid people will stop sending welfare assistance, so we can't put anything aside for leaving the country. There may be another possibility for travel, we hope, through Spain, but we have to wait and hope. . . . Paula Fish would perhaps do it but she can't afford it, and Rosenbluth does have a lot of money but little heart. That's why we have so little hope. As things stand, we will have to stay for the winter and I'm already starting to make preparations, and have preserved some eggs and even prepared some carrots and barley. . . . I even hope to store coal in this way, too."[1]

In addition to food shortages, the violence against Jews was growing worse by the day. By February of 1940, the deportations of Jews to the "east," a euphemism for forced resettlement or transport to labor camps in Eastern Europe, were escalating in Vienna. The few Jewish-owned businesses that were still left standing in the city were regularly vandalized by Nazi hoods. Jews were forbidden from attending most cultural events and had to abide by strict curfews. Gertrude Schneider tells the story of her thirteen-year-old friend Lili Brender, who boldly decided to go to the cinema. But that evening, the local police entered the movie house, checked everyone's identity card, and arrested Lili, whose card had a big "J" on it. She was taken into custody, and her mother, Laura, was called into the jail. Two months later mother and daughter were shipped to a work camp in Poland. Schneider found out later that the mother had died of typhoid fever several months after their arrival at the camp, and Lili was sent on to a death camp.

"Well, what else is there to say?" wrote Selma in a letter to Paula that summer. "We don't see many nice things, and I don't want to write about the bad. . . ."[2]

To make matters worse, the Langs heard that Renée's older brother, Siegfried, who had received a work permit to live in England, had suffered a debilitating nervous breakdown during the savage Nazi blitzkrieg of London in the autumn of 1940. There was nothing family members could do for the young man, who was interned in a London hospital for the duration of the war. Moreover, it had been almost a year since Selma had had any news from her husband, Oskar, in Poland.

By the following year, life in Vienna had become almost unbearable for the Langs, who had now rented out two rooms in the Negerlegasse flat to five other Viennese Jews in order to make ends meet. "Now everything requires a lot of patience and endurance, but my nerves aren't worth much anymore," wrote Selma in January 1941. "There are now seven people living in the flat. If you close both eyes you can take it. How could life get any worse?"[3]

But life did get progressively worse for the Jews of Europe. By September 1, 1941, all Jews in the Third Reich from the age of six were further humiliated by having to wear the infamous six-pointed yellow star affixed to the left sides of their chests as identification badges at all times. (The star had been introduced two years earlier in Poland.) If Jews were found without the star, they risked a long jail sentence and deportation to a labor camp. Schneider describes what it was like to wear the star, which identified Jews as "Jude" in pseudo-Hebrew lettering: "On the very first day of our wearing the yellow star, my sister Rita and I were accosted and beaten up at the corner of Hollandstrasse and Sperlgasse by a bunch of rowdy boys our age. There were seven of them. It was the lady in charge of the Anker Bakery who came out of the store, chased them away, and consoled us. Other adults just passed by and did not interfere."[4]

Anti-Semitism increased dramatically after Jews were forced to wear the yellow star and thus became immediately identifiable. They were not allowed to travel on public transportation on the weekends, they were excluded from libraries as well as public and private schools, and they were prohibited from owning their own telephones or using public telephone boxes. Even the most minute aspects of daily life were strictly regulated by the Nazis: ". . . the post office, publishing firms and newsagents were ordered to cease delivering newspapers, journals and official gazettes to Jewish houses. Jews were forced to part with their pets. No Jew was allowed to have his hair cut by a non-Jewish barber. Jews were not allowed to use honorary academic titles."[5]

As deportations to the "east" increased, Jews in Vienna had no reason not to believe the Nazi propaganda that the deportations were resettlement schemes in other parts of the Reich. For Viennese Jewry, deportations were not yet synonymous with death, although they were dreaded nonetheless. Rumors of the brutality with which Nazi officials treated deportees, seizing their belongings and housing them in filthy detention centers, known as *Kommissionierung,* or collecting points, near the Viennese train stations were widespread and enough to distress the Jews who remained in Vienna.

The Nazis themselves did not actually begin their mass extermination of the Jews until 1942. However, by the summer of 1941, preparations were well under way for Hitler's Final Solution. Reinhard Heydrich, director of the Reich Main Security Office and the Nazi bureaucrat responsible for coordinating the mass murder of European Jews, ordered the able Adolf Eichmann to prepare the system of convoys that would take European Jews to their deaths. By the fall of 1941, the Nazis were already gassing inmates of the Auschwitz concentration camp in Poland, and building other death camps at Chelmno, Belzec, and Majdanek. Hitler's plan called for the removal of the Jews of Central and Western Europe to death camps in the east. Eichmann, who had proven himself to be such a ruthlessly efficient organizer of forced emigrations from Austria in the late 1930s, was quickly promoted through the SS ranks. In November 1941, he was made lieutenant colonel of the SS, and was put in charge of overseeing Hitler's grand plan to rid Europe of Jews.

A YEAR BEFORE Eichmann and his team began to busy themselves with preparations for genocide, Abraham Hammersfeld paced the sitting room of his tiny flat in Riga, worrying about the fate of his daughter and granddaughter trapped in Vienna, his son-in-law in Poland, and his distraught grandson in a London psychiatric ward. Abraham and Lotte shared their apartment in the Latvian capital with their sons Harry and Adolf, their wives, and Adolf's ten-year-old son, Hans. Abraham, now approaching sixty-seven, tried as best he could to reestablish some semblance of a normal life. He joined a small synagogue in Riga, wrote copious letters to his daughter Paula, who was still in Stockholm, and taught his grandson Hebrew at the kitchen table.

Although the Hammersfelds were forced to live in more frugal circumstances in Riga, they still lived much better than most other Jewish refugees scattered throughout Europe, partly because the Stilmans were able to send regular cash infusions from Abraham's bank account in Stockholm. Adolf and Harry worked in Mitau, a town thirty miles away, where they represented a successful building-supply firm. On weekends, the family would frequent a local café, and in the summer months they rented a small house on the Baltic Sea.

In 1940, just before Passover, Abraham wrote to his son-in-law Georg Stilman of his longing to see the family together once again, especially for the Jewish holidays:

It would be wonderful for us all if we could finally be together again. Will I experience this in my lifetime; do you believe I will? Oh, how nice it would be . . . to celebrate our Seder evening together again and [hear] my [grandson] Heinz—how I remember now with a tear-stained face—recite the "Ma Nischtanes." Were there ever better moments for the Jews? Oh, probably not. And if we should experience this again, these "Ma Nischtanes" will be asked in a completely different sense and with even more enthusiasm. God grant that I experience this again..... [6]

But try as hard as they could, they were not able to recapture the placid normalcy of their life in Vienna. The strain of living at such close quarters during increasingly uncertain times seems to have got on everybody's nerves and contributed to family discord. In letter after letter to Paula and Georg, Abraham complained about Riga, his family, and the lack of respect his son Dolfi (Adolf) was showing for his mother, Lotte, who was growing quite old and sick:

When we came here . . . Harry still got along with us and had the courtesy to speak a few nice words to his very sick mother. Dolfi, on the other hand, who imagines that he isn't Polish anymore and has learned all the Viennese customs and conventions from [his wife] Edith and his colleagues, wants to be considered a ruler. And because he can't rule over others he takes it out with a vengeance on your sick mother. It doesn't matter, he says, if an elderly mother peels the potatoes for all seven people by herself, and washes the dishes three times a day; young women, like Edith, have to go out after dinner with their painted nails. [7]

Most of the family considered Riga merely a transit point on their way to the United States, and waited impatiently for their visas in the windswept Baltic port capital. But although he feared for the safety of his family, Abraham was still not convinced that the United States was the best option for them. In a letter to Paula written in March 1940, he worried about being able to keep the whole family together and exhibited a little bit of the European disdain for things American:

About whether you should send your two children ahead of you, I must (and everyone agrees with me) unfortunately firmly refuse to agree. First of all, you can't let children go on such a long journey of three to four months alone, as you said yourself. Not even adults decide so easily with this war to travel by ship. . . . Secondly, you seem to really believe that America is just waiting for you and doesn't know who to give its many dollars to. I can only tell you that roasted pigeons don't fly into your mouth. There is a great deal of unemployment there and you have to work hard to earn every dollar. We have a very good chance to get there but I still don't know if we would quickly decide to go if we had half an opportunity to find another place in Europe.[8]

Two months later, Abraham had made the decision that he was not going to accompany his family to the United States. He could not face the stress of uprooting his life yet again. He and Lotte would stay in Riga, where he was comfortable now and had even made friends with one of the local rabbis. "In my advanced years, I'd rather stay here because the Jews here are visible and they honor me," he wrote on May 31, 1940. "It's enough to say that the rabbi often invites me to visit him and even wants to go for walks with me on nice days. Now I'm supposed to be poured into that big American kettle, even though I really need peace and quiet."[9] Abraham's obstinacy and his anti-American attitude would come back to haunt him. A few days after he posted that letter to his daughter, the Soviet Army marched into Latvia and the other two Baltic states, Estonia and Lithuania. By late June 1940, the Soviets had dissolved the Latvian government, legalized the Latvian Communist party, and outlawed all other opposition parties. Political undesirables and bourgeois industrialists were rounded up by the Soviet Army and either shot or thrown into Soviet labor camps in Siberia. The Soviets set about turning the country into a dictatorship of the proletariat, and they let nobody get in their way.

Foreign residents were encouraged to move out of the major cities. All the Hammersfelds in Riga, uprooted yet again, packed their bags for Mitau. In Mitau, known as Jelgava in Latvian, 25 percent of the population of 35,000 was Jewish. The Hammersfelds settled into their new flat amid the chaos of marauding Soviet soldiers, who arrested wealthy businessmen and landowners, collectivized farms and industry, and brutally repressed their opponents. Harry and his brother Adolf, already working for their Mitau-based firm before the Soviet takeover of the company, were now kept on by the new owners, who needed their entrepreneurial expertise to keep the company going.

With war raging across Europe, the Soviets easily took over the Baltics. Moreover, just before the German invasion of Poland, the Germans had signed a convenient nonaggression pact with the Soviet Union. The Molotov–Von Ribbentrop pact, signed August 23, 1939, by Vyacheslav Molotov, foreign commissar of the Soviet Union, and Joachim von Ribbentrop, minister of foreign affairs in the Third Reich, included two secret protocols that essentially sanctioned the Soviet occupation of the three Baltic countries and Germany's expansionist designs on Poland, which provoked the beginning of the European war in September 1939.

The bilateral nonaggression treaty was short-lived. After Hitler's armies conquered France, Belgium, The Netherlands, Luxembourg, Denmark, and Norway, they set their sights on the vast region of the Eastern Front. In keeping with Hitler's policy to acquire *Lebensraum,* or living space, for Reich citizens, to rid the world of eastern Jews and what he called the "subhuman" Slavic populations, and, most importantly, to crush Communism, the German armies launched Operation Barbarossa. The ruthless German attack that would nearly destroy the Soviet Union came on June 22, 1941.

The Soviets were furious with the German double cross and the flagrant violation of the bilateral pact. The Nazis, in turn, claimed that they had abided loyally by the agreement and were forced to attack the Soviet Union because it had practiced "sabotage, terrorism, and espionage" against Germany. Journalist William Shirer wrote that the German excuse "was a familiar declaration strewn with all the shop-worn lies and fabrications at which Hitler and Ribbentrop had become so expert and which they had concocted so often before to justify each fresh act of unprovoked aggression."[10]

Hitler had taken control of Latvia in the first week of July 1941. The Hammersfelds, who had fled to Latvia two years earlier largely because of the country's neutrality and substantial German-speaking population, were now caught in the middle of an ugly war. At the outbreak of the German-Russian war, Harry decided to abandon his plans to wait for an American visa, and escape with his wife, Bronia, to Russia. Hans, who was staying with his grandparents, aunt, and uncle at the family flat in Mitau while his parents, Adolf and Edith, conducted business in Riga, went with them. The three hopped a cattle train bound for Moscow, leaving the feeble and frightened older Hammersfelds alone in the tiny flat.

The occupying Germans moved fast, annexing the Baltic states into a new German province that Hitler named the Ostland. Along with the invading troops, Hitler sent special SS killing squads to eliminate all Jews in the region. The *Einsatzgruppen* (Task Forces), which were responsible for organizing local collaborators into special lynching squads to murder Jews, set to work almost immediately in Latvia. As in other occupied territories, the Nazis stripped the Jews of all of their legal rights and herded them into ghettos in the most run-down parts of cities and towns. As historian Martin Gilbert noted,

On August 15 Hinrich Lohse, the Reich Commissar for the newly designated Eastern Territories of the Ostland region, covering what had earlier been Lithuania, Latvia, Estonia and White Russia, issued a directive ordering all Jews to be registered; to wear two yellow badges, one on the chest, one on the back; not to walk on the pavements, not to use public transport, not to visit parks, playgrounds, theaters, cinemas, libraries or museums; not to own cars or radio sets. All Jewish property outside the designated ghetto area was to be confiscated. The ghetto was to be cut off physically from the rest of the town, its food supplies to be restricted to food that was "surplus" to local needs. All able-bodied Jews were to be subject to forced labor.[11]

In the Baltic region, the Nazi persecution and murder of Jews were marked by a savage brutality that was unlike anything that went on in the German Reich. Members of the Einsatzgruppen unleashed deeply ingrained anti-Semitic tendencies when they employed local thugs to do their bidding. In Riga, a city of 360,000 where about 10 percent of the population was Jewish, it was not difficult to conscript local hoodlums to beat up Jews. Paul Salitter, a captain with a German police battalion who accompanied a trainload of German Jews being deported to Latvia, noted that the locals "do not like the Bolsheviks, since almost every family suffered a bloody loss at the hands of the Soviets. They especially hate Jews, this being the reason they took such an intensive part in the annihilation of these parasites since the Liberation."[12] In Riga, the locals often equated Bolshevism with Judaism because of their mistaken belief that the Soviets had put many Jews in positions of power after their invasion of Latvia in the spring of 1940.

Although Harry had implored his parents to accompany them on the journey to Russia, the elder Hammersfelds couldn't face being uprooted a third time. By the summer of 1941, Abraham, once the handsome, revered Viennese patriarch, was a broken man. In one of the last letters he would send to his daughter Paula, he wrote: "If you are surprised at my using the expression 'Godforsaken' don't think that I'm being *meschuge* [crazy]. I'll briefly tell you in the strictest confidence that had I not learned so much tolerance, I would have already taken my life long ago. . . . But I can't help it. You can only hold out for so long."[13]

Abraham had reached his limit. It was a bitter, deeply disillusioned man who watched the enlightened German ideal of his youth reduced to a mob of violent, well-armed thugs. In his last letter to Paula, he wrote:

Who could have predicted that at such a time progress would lead us astray of our goal, that people would beat people for no other reason than because they have entered the world and live within a tradition that they do not need to be ashamed of? It has got so out of hand today that the ancient inner bestiality will not allow itself to be subordinated, but rather searches for opportunities to break free. Base forces that lay under the restraints of culture and civilization have broken free and have destroyed what so many generations have worked so hard to achieve. In the end, they have won the upper hand over empathy, honor, shame, consideration. Today, he who is strong has rights and the weaker has no rights. He who can beat someone has every right to do so, and he who cannot defend himself has lost his rights. . . . We stand here betrayed as people treat us worse than animals.[14]

On August 5, 1941, in Mitau, where the elder Hammersfelds had remained after the outbreak of war, the officer in charge of the Einsatzgruppen filed a report stating that "the 1,550 Jews who still remained" had been "removed" from the population, "without any exception."[15]

IN VIENNA, RENÉE and Selma had finally found a way to go to the United States. They booked tickets on a boat bound for Cuba, which, in the early years of the war, served as an informal base for refugees seeking entry into the United States. But the Langs' preparations for their trip came to nothing when Japanese bombers attacked Pearl Harbor on December 7, 1941, forcing the United States into what was now a full-scale world war. As a result, the United States severely reduced its immigration quotas, especially for those living in enemy territory. Moreover, with a war being waged in just about every corner of the globe, civilian travel anywhere was extremely restricted. To make matters worse, by the end of the year the Nazis had outlawed all Jewish emigration from German-controlled areas: Emigration was soon to be replaced by extermination. Renée and Selma could no longer leave Austria by legal means.

Several thousand miles away, safe in the United States, Georg Stilman, who had now changed his name to the more American-sounding "George," sat in a Manhattan law office preparing to sue Atlantic Tours, Inc., the American tour company that was supposed to have arranged for Selma and Renée's passage to Cuba. War or no war, George, a hard-nosed businessman in the process of setting up a new dry-goods store, was determined to get back the $1,150 (about $10,000 in 1997) he had paid to bring the two women to safety.

"My father spent almost all the money we had on those passages and in bribes to Cuban diplomats to arrange for transit visas," recalls Heinz Herbert Stilman, then fifteen, who, like his father, had also changed his first name to the more American "Herbie." "When he bought those tickets to bring Renée and her mother to safety, I remember that we only had eighteen dollars left in our bank account."

The entire Stilman family had contributed to the purchase of the Cuban passages. Herbie, then enrolled at Abraham Lincoln High School in the Bronx, got a job after school in the stockroom at Royal Leather Goods, where he made $12 a week. George began to moonlight as a presser, Paula began to do piecework at home, and even Sylvia contributed babysitting fees.

The Stilman family had arrived in New York without a great deal of money because they had used most of the Hammersfelds' Swedish bank account to pay their living expenses in Sweden, to support the other Hammersfeld family members in Latvia, and to buy their own passages to the United States. After receiving their coveted U.S. visas, they had left their temporary home in Stockholm in February 1941, boarded the Trans-Siberian Express to Vladivostock, made their way to the Japanese port of Yokohama, and sailed to Seattle, where they boarded a train bound for New York City in late April. The long, rather circuitous route was necessary to avoid a direct Atlantic crossing, which would have exposed them to a great deal of danger on the European front of the war. They settled on Grant Avenue in the Bronx, around the corner from Abraham's sister, who was known to her grandniece and nephew simply as Great-aunt Snow White.

Despite their feelings of relief after arriving in the United States, they were worried about family members in Latvia and Austria. Paula hadn't heard from her father or her brothers Harry and Adolf. How was her elderly mother faring in Latvia? How was her young nephew Hans managing to get an education? How were Selma and Renée?

With the United States joining the war effort on the Allied side, there was no way to communicate with the family or to send them packages of food. For the next several years, there was only silence as Paula and George tried not to think about the horrors their family could be facing in Europe. In 1944, fate dealt them a cruel blow when their son Herbie, who had just turned eighteen, was conscripted into the U.S. armed forces and sent back to Europe to fight against Germany. Perhaps they tried not to read the news reports or listen to the radio broadcasts about the war too closely. As they launched themselves vigorously into building new lives, George and Paula tried to convince themselves that Herbie and their family were safe, that they were resourceful, and that they would be all right.

Selma and Renée were not so convinced, especially with Jewish deportations to concentration camps growing at an alarming rate by the beginning of 1943. The Nazi system for deporting Jews varied. Some people received deportation orders by mail, in the form of an official notice commanding them to show up at local schools or houses, which functioned as collecting points for Jews, who were sometimes held in these makeshift detention centers for several weeks at a time until a transport could be organized. Other Jews were picked up at their homes by the Austrian police or taken directly to the train station from the jails where many were being held on minor infractions, mostly for being caught without their yellow stars.

Gertrude Schneider describes how many Jews were rounded up for deportations:

Still others were "collected" en masse. In that case, police, supported by SS, simply closed off a street at both ends. After that, certain employees of the *Kultusgemeinde*, called *Ordners*, fanned out into the houses on both sides of the street, telling the Jews living in specified apartments to pack one suitcase each and be ready in an hour. After this all-too-short time had passed, a cursory check by an SS official took place and everyone had to assemble downstairs and the trek to the school began, watched over carefully by the police and the SS. Upon arrival at the school, people were

registered, their names were entered on lists, and they were assigned to former classrooms, where mattresses were lying around
helter-skelter. Chaos reigned until everyone found himself or herself a space, the mattress surrounded by the suitcase and hand-
luggage brought from home. It was, and I am sure it was meant
to be, a dismal experience. Personal hygiene was almost impossible, facilities at the school were hopelessly inadequate for so many
people at once, food was scarce, people were perched either on
their mattresses or luggage, looking extremely uncomfortable and
unhappy. In a way, one had a foretaste of what was yet to come."[16]

As Schneider notes, Jewish community center officials in Vienna
were actively involved in seizing Jews, a procedure that was no doubt
inspired by Eichmann's management of forced emigration after the
Anschluss in which he forced members of the Kultusgemeinde to do
much of his work. According to Raul Hilberg, Viennese Jewish officials would

> swarm into a Jewish apartment, stationing themselves at the door,
> while an SS man and the chief of the Jewish Kommando would
> seat themselves at a table to inquire about family members and to
> make sure of property declarations. The SS man might then depart,
> leaving the Jewish raiders with the victims, allowing them to help
> with the packing but admonishing them to prevent escapees. At
> the collecting points, service by the Jewish guards was to be ar-
> ranged in such a way that flight by the inmates would be impos-
> sible. For each person missing from the premises [director of the
> Jewish community center Dr. Josef] Lowenherz was told, two Jew-
> ish guards would be deported instead.[17]

Renée and Selma had seen too many Jews taken away from the
Second District in this manner, and they were not about to wait until
a Nazi bureaucrat got around to sending them a deportation notice
in the mail, or until SS agents raided their flat and forced them to
leave. Stateless Jews, like themselves, had been among the first to

be deported. In desperation, mother and daughter abandoned the Negerlegasse flat, sold off some of their remaining belongings, and went into hiding rather than risk the regular Nazi roundups that were now happening almost daily in the Second District. Through a non-Jewish friend, Selma found a place to hide on the top floor of an old tenement building in the First District. For several weeks, mother and daughter disappeared, becoming what the Austrians quaintly dubbed *U-Boote,* German for "submarines." In Vienna, the term referred to Jews who were in hiding or had gone "underground." According to C. Gwyn Moser, who studied the U-Boote phenomenon, the key to being a successful U-Boot was to find a trustworthy Aryan protector:

> Successful hiding required finding lodging in someone's apartment, home, or summer house, or possibly in a shop, cellar, or attic. A few [U-Boote] wandered from place to place, living in ruins and cemeteries. Many tried hiding by wandering the streets during the day and sleeping in train stations or closed shops at night, but these people were usually caught and deported. Living unregistered without ration cards for food made it impossible for these Jews to support themselves. Hunger drove them back to the Jewish ghetto and its periodic roundups. Thus, successful hiding required self-imposed incarceration in a benefactor's home. Almost one half of the U-Boote stayed at only one address.[18]

Only about six hundred U-Boote survived the war in Vienna by living underground. The Nazis severely punished anyone caught helping Jews, but in the war-ravaged economy of Austria it seemed possible to find a few "good-hearted" Aryans who would take the risk if the price was right.

Renée and Selma were successful for a while. In addition to the meager revenue she had earned from renting out rooms in the Negerlegasse flat and running an informal soup kitchen, Selma had also relied on the money that Abraham left her before setting out for Riga. But the money her father had left her was dwindling, and Selma knew that they could not survive the war hiding in Vienna. Through an acquaintance, Selma hooked into the underground network of "human smugglers," who for a hefty fee arranged to take Jews across the border into Hungary.

"At the time Hungary was the only safe country to go to," says Renée. "There was still no war going on there and we heard that the Hungarians were not turning back Jewish refugees."

So, in late April 1943, mother and daughter sold the rest of their paltry possessions and boarded a bus to the Hungarian border. They took nothing with them so as not to attract the suspicions of Nazi officials, who would surely check documents at the main bus station in Vienna to crack down on Jewish refugees. Renée says she wore three dresses, "one on top of the other," to make the journey to Hungary. Once they reached the Hungarian border, Selma and Renée waited by the roadside until nightfall, when they were met by a guide who made his living spiriting Jews out of Austria. They set out to cross the Hungarian border at night, their shoes and ankles caked in mud from trudging through wet fields. In the darkness of a dense forest, Renée, Selma, and their guide lost their way, and were so disoriented that they did not even realize that they had already crossed the border into Hungary. As they rested in the woods, a unit of Hungarian police, armed with flashlights and attack dogs straining at their leashes, invaded their retreat and promptly arrested them. Renée and her mother were immediately interned.

They spent more than a year in a series of Hungarian jails and internment camps. "I know every jail from the Austrian border to Budapest," says Renée, whose recollection of her incarceration in Hungary is peppered with happy memories of the kindness of her fellow prisoners. In one jail near the Austrian border, Renée and her mother shared a cell with prostitutes, who would share food from the parcels they received from their families. At an internment camp near Budapest, prisoners were even allowed to spend several hours in the capital city every two weeks. Renée took advantage of these occasions to visit museums and other cultural centers.

"I used to say to my mother that if we could stay in Hungary until the war is over, we have won because then we wouldn't have to go to a concentration camp. At that time in Hungary there were no Nazis, no concentration camps."

Indeed, as late as 1943, a Jewish refugee from Poland remarked in a letter:

How amazed we were to see Jews, dressed in holiday clothes—crowds of them—praying undisturbed. This was a sight we had long forgotten. . . . In Dohany Street, where the great synagogue is, Hungarian policemen in white gloves were directing the traffic. Our feeling was that the war had not yet reached Hungary and the people, including the Jews, did not even want to know about it. . . . [19]

Renée and Selma's year-long sojourn in Hungary eventually came to an end. That it lasted as long as it did was a testament not so much to the Hungarian government's respect for human rights, but rather to diplomatic tensions between Hungary and Germany over how to handle Hungary's nearly one million Jews. Although Hungary was on Hitler's side in the war against the Soviet Union, the Hungarians fiercely guarded their sovereignty, especially when it came to internal political matters. During the regime of the pro-German prime minister, Laszlo Bardossy, the Hungarians had cooperated somewhat with the Germans on the Final Solution, at least when it came to non-Hungarian Jews. In August 1941 the Hungarians had rounded up some eighteen thousand Jews who had escaped to Hungary from Galicia and sent them back over the border, where they were killed by German execution squads. In January 1942, Hungarian Army units had killed thousands of Jews and Serbs in Novi Sad, a city in Yugoslav territory that had been given to Hungary. However, when Bardossy was replaced by nationalist Miklos Kallay in the spring of that year, the Germans no longer knew where they stood on the Hungarian Jewish question. Although Kallay admitted to the Germans that he wished to rid Hungary of Jews, he warned them that the issue was a "purely internal matter,"[20] and made it clear that he was not ready to do Germany's bidding. Besides, with more than 800,000 Jews out of a population of 14 million in Hungary, deportations on a mass scale would not be easy to accomplish.

Although Kallay told the expansionist Germans that he would allow them to deport Jews who had escaped to Hungary from the German Reich, Hungarian Jews would stay in Hungary. Adolf Eichmann, however, was not interested in this proposal since "it was a mere 'partial action' affecting only Jews who had illegally fled to Hungary," wrote historian Christopher Browning. "Deportation of these Jews would require just as much preparation and effort as the evacuation of all Hungarian Jews. He [Eichmann] would consider it 'inexpedient' to set in motion the 'entire evacuation apparatus' on this basis. It would be better to wait until Hungary was ready to include all Jews in these measures."[21]

Then on March 19, 1944, the Germans occupied Hungary, set up a Nazi puppet regime, and every Jew living in Hungary became fair game. Less than a month following the German occupation, Adolf Eichmann was dispatching Jewish deportees to concentration camps. Renée and Selma were finally brutally rounded up with several thousand others and herded onto the second Hungarian transport of Jews to Auschwitz.

"We were forced into a cattle car," says Renée. "It was full of desperate people. There was no place to sit. There was no place to go to the toilet, so people just did everything they had to do standing up."

Mother and daughter arrived at Auschwitz with thousands of other Jews from Hungary at the beginning of May 1944. As they stepped weakly off the cattle car, shielding their eyes from the harsh glare of the station lights, they heard the booming voice of an SS officer echoing throughout the train station, which seemed to be enveloped in a thick haze. Renée, exhausted and nearly dehydrated from the journey, strained to understand what he was saying. In clear, precise German, the tall, youthful officer who paced the damp station platform informed the trainload of Jews that those who were too weak and tired should move to one side of the platform, where Red Cross trucks were waiting to give them food, water, and medical assistance. For a split second Renée was tempted to take him up on his offer, but there was something in that smug voice that put her on her guard. And something was not right about the scene she saw before her. Elderly Jews, doubled over from hunger and exhaustion, moved in the direction of the SS officer's voice. A group of prisoners, clad in what looked like striped, threadbare pajamas and ill-fitting clogs, scurried up and down the station platform grabbing suitcases, coats, purses—anything that the weary Jews had set down as they got off the train. Through a remarkable force of will, Renée straightened herself up, grabbed her mother by the hand, and boldly walked through the crowd of frightened Jews in the direction of the menacing voice.

"We're healthy," said Renée as she approached the tall, thirty-three-year-old officer, whom she would later find out was Dr. Josef Mengele, one of the most sadistic Nazi murderers, whose specialties included performing macabre medical experiments on young twins. "We don't need medical help. We can walk."

With those few words, uttered in her best German, Renée saved her life as well as her mother's. As she stood waiting in a lineup of women to register at one of the camp's offices, Renée casually asked what had happened to the other Jews who had been too weak to accompany them. One of the camp officials pointed to billows of smoke and what looked like ash spewing from a nearby chimney stack. "They're burning," she said, without any emotion. It took a few seconds for Renée to grasp the meaning of what had been said to her.

And then the terror, exhaustion, and stress came pouring out of her all at once, and she laughed uncontrollably.

THE COMPLEX OF concentration camps known collectively as Auschwitz began operating in 1940 as a detention center for Poles and then for Soviet POWs. A former Austro-Hungarian artillery barracks of the First World War, the camp was located in the Polish town of Oswiecim (Auschwitz in German) in the damp, marshy region of East Upper Silesia. By 1941, work had begun on a separate camp on the moor of Brzezinka (Birkerau in German), where two old peasant houses were remodeled with airtight doors and special ventilation systems, which would serve as gas chambers.

Unlike at other concentration camps in the Reich, where carbon monoxide was used to kill prisoners, officials at Auschwitz were the first to experiment with a revolutionary new gas known by its commercial name, Zyklon B. The hydrogen cyanide gas was a fast-working lethal agent, solidified into pellets and shaken into the gas chambers through shafts. In the gas chamber, the substance immediately passed into its gaseous state and was effective within minutes. Camp administrators required only 1 milligram of the substance per kilogram of body fat to kill. As Raul Hilberg noted,

The gassing was a short process in Auschwitz. As soon as the victims were trapped in the "shower-room" they recognised in a flash the whole pattern of the destruction process. The imitation shower facilities did not work. Outside, a central switch was thrown to turn off the lights. A Red Cross car drove up with the Zyklon, and a masked SS man lifted the glass shutters over the lattice, emptying one can after another into the gas chamber. Untersturmführer [SS Lieutenant] Graebner, political chief of the camp, stood steady with stop watch in hand. As the first pellets sublimated on the floor of the chamber, the law of the jungle took over. To escape from the rapidly rising gas, the stronger knocked down the weaker, stepping on the prostrate victims in order to prolong their own life by reaching the gas-free layers of air. The agony lasted for about two minutes; then the shrieking subsided, the dying slumping over. Within four minutes everybody in the chamber was dead.[22]

At first, the bodies of the people killed in the gas chambers were buried in mass graves, but by the summer of 1942 a survivor reported a "black, evil-smelling mass oozed out and polluted the groundwater in the vicinity."[23] As a result, the decomposing bodies had to be disinterred and burned in pits. The camp hierarchy, which was controlled by the SS, decided to rectify the problem by building ovens to burn the bodies. By 1943, Auschwitz housed four major crematoria, several gas chambers, and a collection of cremation pits in the Birkenau section of the camp.

Using such technological innovations and logistical readaptations, the SS transformed Auschwitz into the largest and most efficient death center the world had ever seen. According to Raul Hilberg, more than 1 million Jews and other Nazi "undesirables" from Germany, Hungary, Slovakia, and other German-occupied countries were killed at Auschwitz between December 1941 and October 1944, the period during which the Nazis' plan of mass extermination was in full force. Two million more were killed at the smaller death camps, such as Treblinka, Belzec, Sobibor, and Kulmhof. Millions more died in concentration and labor camps, in open-air shootings, and from general privation in ghettos. By Eichmann's own estimation, more than four million Jews were killed in the extermination camps, and a further two million died at the hands of the Einsatzgruppen, the-mobile killing units.

The death camps were models of military precision, efficiency, and conservation. Jews who were too weak or too old to work in the main slave-labor factories at Auschwitz were immediately gassed upon arrival. The Nazis believed in saving everything from their hapless victims, and recycling them and their remaining possessions back into the German war effort. As soon as a trainload of Jews disembarked at Auschwitz, a group of inmates was deployed to sort through the luggage on the freight cars. Before women went into the gas chamber their hair was cut off to be used in the manufacture of felt slippers for German submarine personnel. Even the human fat escaping from the burning bodies, thrown into the crematoria after they were gassed, was poured back onto the flames to speed cremations. One doctor reported that she witnessed the bleeding of seven hundred young Jewish women in Auschwitz. Despite the Nazi obsession with racial purity, the blood was reportedly used for wounded German soldiers in the last frenzied year of the war.[24]

Other items confiscated from Jews at the concentration camps were distributed to German charity organizations or used in the German war effort. Textiles were converted for use in the manufacture of SS uniforms; men's underwear and clothing were to be handed over to the *Volksdeutsche Mittelstelle*, the welfare organization for ethnic Germans. Women's silk underwear were used in the manufacture of parachutes. One SS bureaucrat collected watches and fountain pens expropriated from Jews to give as Christmas gifts to the *Waffen*-SS and the U-Boot command. In a report written on May 13, 1943, the SS bureaucrat mentioned receipt of "Jewish stolen goods," including 94,000 men's watches, 33,000 women's watches, and 25,000 fountain pens for distribution to German soldiers in recognition of their brave service to the Reich.[25] On November 6, 1943, another SS official wrote to SS chief Heinrich Himmler,

> stating that he intended to make gifts of watches and fountain pens to SS units, and asked whether the gifts should be made in Himmler's name. Himmler approved Pohl's generous plan and added that 15,000 ladies' watches should be distributed to Germans coming from Russia for resettlement. Pohl thought it would be a generous gesture to distribute 3,000 clocks which had been repaired to guards at the concentration camps and to Berlin inhabitants who had been bombed. As an afterthought, he suggested to Himmler that 16 extra-fine gold precision wrist watches, valued at 300 Reichsmarks each, which had been repaired, be distributed among commanders of technical units.[26]

Their first day at Auschwitz, Selma and Renée Lang stripped off their clothes and surrendered all of their valuables to the inmate commandos who hovered over them in a damp cell block. Selma, forty-six, tried in vain to stand in front of her naked twenty-one-year-old daughter to shield her from the leering SS officers who walked in and out of the block.

"I've got nothing to be embarrassed about," Renée told her nervous mother. And then she pointed her gaze at the glaring SS officers across the room and aimed her words in their direction. "They're the ones who should be embarrassed."

Renée's boldness and sheer determination gave her the strength to endure at Auschwitz. For instance, when she discovered that her mother was on a list of prisoners to be gassed, Renée boldly approached the SS officer in charge, whom she had found out was also from Vienna, and asked him to please remove her mother from the list. "I figured I had nothing to lose," says Renée, who found out her mother had been saved from the gas chambers the following day. "But you know I probably had a lot of luck on my side because two days after I asked that officer to save my mother, I saw him shoot two girls who tried to escape."

During the year that they spent at Auschwitz, mother and daughter, who were now known by the neatly tattooed numbers on their forearms (81005 and 81006, respectively), were assigned to the night shift at the Union Werke munitions factory, a slave-labor operation owned by the German arms manufacturer Krupp. The factory was guarded by female SS officers, who paced the shop floor barking orders to workers who were moving too slowly. If a worker got a finger accidentally caught in a machine, production would grind to a halt, and the worker would be severely punished. One of the SS officers would drag her away to have her hair shaved off.

Selma and Renée tried to be as unobtrusive as possible. Twice a day they showed up for roll call, and they worked silently at their posts at the Krupp factory. Because she spoke fluent German, Renée was in charge of reporting on worker schedules and progress to the factory manager. She was conscientious about her work, but she did nothing to interfere with a group of Polish girls who operated a smuggling ring within the factory. Every day, she watched in silence as about twenty girls ferreted out handfuls of gunpowder or wrapped explosive devices and sticks of dynamite in the flimsy folds of their prison-issue rags. Fully aware of what was going on at the factory, she simply chose not to report it. Not even after the October 7, 1944, explosion that shook the barracks of Birkenau and engulfed one of the four Auschwitz crematoria in flames. For while she tried not to get involved with her fellow prisoners, Renée secretly admired her fearless co-workers who spearheaded the most dramatic prisoner uprising at Auschwitz-Birkenau by smuggling materials out of the factory.

Led by a twenty-three-year-old Zionist named Roza Robota, the twenty or so young women at the Krupp factory "carried out the little wheels of dynamite, which looked like buttons in small matchboxes which they hid in their bosoms or in special pockets they had sewn into the hems of their dresses"[27] and gave them to members of the Auschwitz underground and the *Sonderkommando*, male Jewish inmates who had been promised their lives and adequate food in exchange for their labor, to build homemade bombs. Their plan was to destroy the gas chambers and crematorium installations at the camp.

The revolt, which took place ahead of the rebels' own schedule, began at Crematorium IV when members of the Sonderkommando found out they were marked for liquidation. (Although members of the Sonderkommando were promised their lives in exchange for performing the most ghastly deeds at the concentration camps, they were periodically marked for death by the SS, which did not want any witnesses alive to report on their procedures.) According to Salmen Lewental, the Sonderkommando who coordinated the plans for the campwide uprising, during the noon roll call a group of Sonderkommandos attacked their SS guards with axes, picks, and crowbars, and set fire to the straw mattresses in their barracks. The fire soon spread to the wooden roof of Crematorium IV. "Our men," noted Lewental in a small notebook that he buried in a jar under the earth in his barracks, "seeing they were brought to destruction, wanted to set fire to Crematorium IV at the last moment and perish in battle, fall on the spot under the hail of bullets. And in this way, the whole crematorium went up in flames."[28]

The blaze at the crematorium was seen by the Sonderkommando of Crematorium II, who took it as a sign that the camp-wide revolt was beginning, but before they could snap into action, their well-laid plans were foiled by a group of Russian prisoners of war. When the Russians, who were also working at Crematorium II, saw a group of SS officers running in their direction, they panicked and began to revolt. The Jews joined them, killing three SS corporals and wounding several others before launching a daring breakout through a hole in the barbed wire fence that encircled the camp. "Within minutes of the breakout through the wire near Crematorium II, the alarm siren had sounded. Almost immediately, SS men with dogs drove up in trucks and surrounded the whole area of the break-out."[29] Nearly five hundred prisoners who tried to escape were shot by the SS.

The SS began systematically to interrogate and torture prisoners to find out who had led the revolt and collected the explosives. A few days later they arrested four women from the Krupp factory and took them to the dreaded Block 11 for questioning. According to eyewitnesses, none of the women broke under torture that lasted for several weeks. Roza Robota, the fearless twenty-three-year-old organizer, refused to crack under even the most sadistic pressure, even though "her hair was matted, her face puffed up and bruised beyond recognition, her clothes torn [and] she could not walk and had to be dragged by two women."[30] Roza Robota managed to smuggle out a message to her comrades. She said she had taken all of the blame for the revolt upon herself: "You have nothing to fear. I shall not talk," she wrote on a torn scrap of paper that was handed to a comrade who had managed to sneak into her cell.[31]

The four women were hanged two at a time on January 6, 1945, so that each shift at the armaments factory could get a good look at how the Nazis dealt with rebellious prisoners. Renée, who was preparing to take over her shift when the hangings were announced, looked away just as Roza Robota and one of her accomplices were led to the gallows.

"I tried to turn my head away. I didn't want to look, but the SS woman standing at my side told me to look, or I would be next."

Renée bit her bottom lip. Her face expressionless, she stared in silence as the lifeless bodies of her co-workers lolled back and forth on their ropes. The SS guards who supervised operations at the factory ordered the women back to work and led them in a chorus of a popular German military song. Through her tears, Renée sang as loudly as she could.

Although Renée and her mother were largely confined to their barracks and the Krupp factory, they knew from the other inmates about the horrible things that the Nazis did to prisoners at Auschwitz every day. They were told about Dr. Mengele's macabre experiments on twins, and the mutilation of corpses after they were removed from the gas chambers.

One of the grisliest operations at Auschwitz involved removing the gold fillings and other valuables that Jews managed to hide on and in their bodies when they were led to the gas chambers. The ghastly process was conducted by members of the Sonderkommando. Wearing rubber boots and gas masks and armed with hoses, they stepped gingerly into the gas chambers to pry apart the bodies of the victims who, in their desperate attempt to escape the deadly gas, had mauled and clawed their fellow prisoners and, as one observer put it, died "piled up in one blue clammy blood-spattered pyramid." The first task was "to remove the blood and defecations before dragging the clawing dead apart with nooses and hooks, the prelude to the ghastly search for gold and the removal of teeth and hair which were regarded by the Germans as strategic materials."[32] In addition to prying out gold fillings, the Sonderkommando also "retrieved any jewels or coins that the prisoners might have managed to conceal in anatomical cavities, and piled up the corpses in the crematoria."[33]

Clothing, jewelry, cash, and other valuables were meticulously sorted and sent to either the Reichsbank or to the Economic and Administrative Main Office of the SS (known by its German acronym WVHA), which covered all works projects for concentration camp inmates. The office was initially set up to devise ways of deriving as much profit as possible from slave labor operations for the SS. Oswald Pohl was the chief of the WVHA and responsible for making sure that all valuables seized from murdered Jewish inmates were sent back to Germany to finance SS operations. In his affidavit, which was used as evidence at the Nuremberg Trials, Pohl outlined the workings of the WVHA:

> It was in the year 1941 or 1942, when large quantities of articles of value, such as jewelry, gold rings, gold fillings, spectacles, gold watches, and such had been collected in the extermination camps. These valuables came packed in cases to the WVHA in Berlin. [SS Chief Heinrich] Himmler had ordered us to deliver these things to the Reichsbank. I remember that Himmler explained to me that negotiations concerning this matter had been conducted with the Reichsbank, that is, Herr [Walther] Funk [president of the Reichsbank]. As a result of an agreement which my chief had made, I discussed with the Reichsbank director, Emil Puhl, the manner of delivery. In this conversation no doubt remained that the objects to be delivered were the jewelry and valuables of concentration camp inmates, especially of Jews, who had been killed in extermination camps. The objects in question were rings, watches, eyeglasses, ingots of gold, wedding rings, brooches, pins, frames of glasses, foreign currency and other valuables. . . . It was an enormous quantity of valuables, since there was a steady flow of deliveries for months and years.[34]

Pohl went on to describe how in 1943 he learned that "gold teeth and crowns of inmates of concentration camps were broken out of their mouths after liquidation. This gold was melted down and delivered to the Reichsbank."[35]

Gold, foreign currency, and precious metals were supposed to be secretly delivered by truck to the Reichsbank under the supervision of Hauptsturmführer Bruno Melmer, chief of WVHA A-II (finance and payroll). Although Melmer wore civilian clothes, the shipments to the bank between 1941 and 1944 (seventy-seven truckloads in all) were guarded by a few SS guards in uniform, and the murky origins of their contents did not remain a secret for long. Much of the "Melmer" loot was identified with a rubber stamp denoting "Auschwitz" or "Lublin," which even Reichsbank officials in faraway Berlin knew to be the sites of major concentration camps. By November 1942, Reichsbank officials started to notice a great quantity of dental gold arriving at the Reichsbank vaults as part of the Melmer operation. Albert Thoms, chief of the Precious Metals Division at the Reichsbank and one of the bureaucrats responsible for overseeing the Melmer shipments testified at the Nuremberg trials that "deliveries were increasing and . . . apart from gold and silver coins they contained particularly a great deal of jewelry, gold rings, wedding rings, gold and silver fragments, dental gold and all sorts of gold and silver articles . . . [O]n one occasion something like 12 kilograms of pearls had been collected. . . . I had never before seen such an unusual amount in all my life."[36]

The loot was scattered on a table in a storeroom of the Reichsbank and about four or five bank employees, who were sworn to secrecy, sorted it. Most of it was then placed in a special part of one of the main safes. The gold teeth were sent to the Prussian State Mint for melting, and "the gold was then refined and the fine gold was returned to the Reichsbank" as gold bars, according to Thoms.[37] Jewelry was delivered to the Berlin Pawnshop, where it was sold to German citizens. Some of the jewelry and foreign currency ended up in Switzerland, according to Rudolf Höss, who wrote in his 1958 autobiography *Kommandant in Auschwitz*, that "the jewelry and foreign currency were sold in Switzerland; in fact, they swamped the whole Swiss jewel market."[38] According to a recent U.S. government report, some of the jewelry, which made its way to Switzerland by diplomatic pouch, was sent to the German legation in Bern for pickup by German agents, who then traded the jewelry for industrial diamonds and other materials critical to the German war effort.[39] All the proceeds from the disposal of concentration camp valuables were credited to the SS-controlled account under the cover name of "Max Heiliger."

With so many shipments arriving from concentration camps throughout the Third Reich, the bureaucrats at the Reichsbank couldn't work fast enough. In the last desperate days of the war, Reichsbank officials ran out of time to sort through Jewish concentration camp loot. Albert Thoms stated that just before the German defeat, 207 containers filled with gold, currency, and other valuables were sent to the Kaiseroda Mine, an abandoned potassium mine at Merkers, a village in western Thuringia, where the shipment remained until it was discovered by American troops.[40]

Where did the Reichsbank gold looted from murdered camp inmates end up? At least some of it—the gold fillings wrenched from the mouths of the dead, the wedding bands and rings from their fingers—was resmelted into gold bars at the Prussian mint, stamped with the Reichsbank symbol, and shipped off to Switzerland as part of a stream of gold that flowed steadily into the country from Reichsbank vaults.

In addition to acting as a safe haven for individual depositors—Jewish and non-Jewish alike—Switzerland offered a number of financial services that benefited the Axis war effort in direct contravention of international law governing neutral countries in wartime. Throughout the war, in addition to gold stolen from the Jews, most of the gold looted from the federal treasuries of countries occupied by the Nazis made its way to the Swiss National Bank and the Bank for International Settlements (BIS), a "neutral" international bank based in Basel.

The BIS is, in essence, a world bank and as such has unique financial powers, such as, for example, keeping gold for central banks. A joint creation of the world's central banks, the BIS was established by international charter in 1930 to further the cooperation among central banks to sort out World War I reparations payments. In effect, the BIS acted as a clearinghouse for these payments. A convention signed by Germany, Belgium, France, Great Britain, Northern Ireland, Italy, Japan, and Switzerland, guaranteed the BIS had an untouchable status. The bank's charter safeguarded all of the bank's assets and deposits in times of peace and of war.

But the BIS was not a bank in the conventional sense. There were no tellers or counters, and it was not open to the public. All transactions were secret, and soon after the bank opened for business, it ceased to handle reparations payments, even though that had been one of the principal reasons for its creation. Instead, the BIS concentrated on trying to save the gold standard and on facilitating gold transactions among central banks by setting up gold accounts at its Basel headquarters for the world's central banks. This ensured that there would be no need physically to ship gold from central bank to central bank; gold transactions would simply be a matter of bookkeeping.

The Nazi regime soon began to see great potential in the unique facilities of the BIS. Before the outbreak of hostilities, the Nazis would use the bookkeeping facilities of the BIS to seize Czechoslovakia's gold with no opposition from the BIS board of directors. By the outbreak of the Second World War, the bank was completely under Hitler's control, with some of his closest financial collaborators on the BIS board. In addition to Reichsbank officials Walther Funk and Emil Puhl, Hitler's personal appointees, BIS directors included Hermann Schmitz, head of the Nazi industrial trust I. G. Farben, and Baron Kurt von Schröder, director of the J. H. Stein Bank of Cologne and a leading financier of the Gestapo. The director of the BIS from 1940 to 1946 was an American Nazi sympathizer named Thomas Harrington McKittrick, a blue-blooded Harvard graduate and international financier from St. Louis.

Since the Germans needed foreign currency in order to finance their war effort and to pay for imports of essential goods from neutral countries, the gold would then be sold to the Swiss National Bank in exchange for Swiss francs, at the time the strongest currency in Europe.

The Reichsbank had actually been hiding gold since 1933, in flagrant violation of the 1919 Treaty of Versailles. In order to facilitate Germany's rearmament, Hitler secretly appointed Hjalmar Schacht as plenipotentiary general for the war economy. Schacht, a former finance minister in the Weimar government, was ordered to keep two sets of books for the Nazi regime in order to plan secretly for a war economy.

When Germany ran out of its own gold reserves in the early days of the war, the Nazis brazenly broke international law again by seizing those of the countries they occupied. Under the Hague Convention of 1907 with respect to warfare on land, occupying powers can take publicly held property for the administration of the occupation only, but not to finance their war effort. When the Nazis looted a treasury, the gold reserves of the occupied country would be transferred via armed convoy to the Reichsbank in Berlin, where, like some of the gold from the camps, they would be resmelted into gold bars bearing the Reichsbank symbol. However, the Nazis were faced with a problem: How would they launder the stolen gold? In his testimony at the Nuremberg Trials, Walther Funk, president of the Reichsbank, noted that Switzerland was one of the only neutral countries willing to buy looted gold: ". . . The other countries with which we still had business relations introduced gold embargoes. Sweden refused to accept gold at all. Only in Switzerland could we still do business through changing gold into foreign currency."[41]

Estimates vary as to the precise amount of looted gold that passed through Switzerland. Historian Arthur L. Smith, Jr., estimates that in the course of the war the Nazis looted a total of $621,847,038 ($6 billion in 1977) in gold from the countries they occupied,[42] and it is believed that much of that amount was laundered through Switzerland. Moreover, Smith estimates that just before the beginning of the war, Germany possessed gold reserves of $150 million ($1.4 billion). Add to this the total amount of the gold that the Nazis stole from the treasuries of occupied countries, and it means that Hitler had more than $770 million of gold ($7.5 billion) at his disposal to fight the war.

However, a recently declassified 1946 U.S. intelligence document suggests that Swiss banks might have made as much as $6 billion (in 1997 figures) worth of financial transactions for Germany during the war. This figure is based not only on the looted gold that was sold to the Swiss, but on the profits from currency speculation and industrial concerns confiscated by the Nazis from occupied countries. The U.S. report cites an interview with Dr. Landwehr, a former head of the foreign exchange department of the Reich Economics Ministry. According to the intelligence officer who conducted the interview,

During the conversation, I learned to my surprise that the estimates on the total of the transactions which took place through
Switzerland were really far from the Swiss estimates and closer to
the Allied point of view. Dr. Landwehr estimated that all in all the
sum of German assets which passed into Switzerland amounted to
at least 15 billions RM. Landwehr dismissed with an ironic smile
the Swiss Verrechnungsstelle's estimate of 1 billion RM. I could
not conceal my astonishment. . . . [43]

The main beneficiary of looted gold from Europe's national treasuries was the Swiss National Bank; the country's central bank, which
acted as a clearinghouse for the Third Reich by purchasing its gold
reserves in exchange for foreign currency. The Swiss National Bank
bought the gold from the Reichsbank at a discount, charged an additional commission (0.5 percent of the value of the gold) for the
clearinghouse service, and sold the gold to other neutral European
central banks at higher prices. According to a recent U.S. State Department report, the Swiss National Bank in Bern knowingly took in
$400 million ($3.9 billion in 1997) in looted gold from the Nazis
between January 1939 and June 30, 1945, in outright violation of
international law, which prohibits banks from fencing stolen goods.
On the 0.5 percent commission alone, the bank made more than $20
million (about $200 million today). In his May 1997 report on the
Nazi gold issue, Stuart E. Eizenstat, an undersecretary of commerce
for international trade and a special envoy of the State Department,
noted that "the amount of Germany's gold reserves before the war
was well known. Clearly, the evidence . . . is incontrovertible: the
Swiss National Bank . . . knew as the war progressed that the Reichsbank's own coffers had been depleted, and that the Swiss were handling vast sums of looted gold."[44]

The Nazi looting of gold reserves began with the liquidation of the
reserves in the Austrian central bank a day before the Anschluss on
March 11, 1938. The Reichsbank received 91,256 kilograms of gold
from the Austrian National Bank and transferred most of it to its
account at the BIS.

The Nazis employed bizarre legal fictions and creative accounting techniques to legitimize their looting of the central banks of Europe. For example, in an attempt to play along with the Hague Convention rules for belligerent occupation, which prevent occupying forces from plundering national treasuries, the Reichsbank would open accounts in its Berlin headquarters for an occupied country and make entries in its ledgers to legitimate the theft of that country's central bank gold reserves. When the Nazis looted a total of $193 million worth of gold (about $1.9 billion in 1997) from the Netherlands after the Dutch surrendered in May 1940, the Reichsbank directors opened an account for the Dutch in Berlin in order to disguise the theft. According to the fiction, the Dutch were participating in the war against communism and making monthly payments to the Reich to aid its own war efforts against the Soviet Union.

Gold looted from Czechoslovakia in 1939 is another example of creative accounting and the Nazi penchant for "legal" expropriation. In this instance, the BIS was instrumental in facilitating the Nazi acquisition of Czech gold reserves. When Hitler's troops marched into Prague on March 15, 1939, they were accompanied by top Reichsbank officials, who immediately ordered that the estimated $44 million worth of gold (about $440 million) that represented the country's national treasury be transferred to the Reichsbank. However, some of the Czech gold reserves (about $26 million worth, or about $260 million today) had been deposited in the BIS account at the Bank of England for safekeeping. In order to release the gold to the Nazis, Czech officials would have to make a formal request to the Bank of England. Five days after the Nazi invasion, officials at the Czech National Bank were forced at gunpoint to send a telegram to the BIS instructing it to transfer into a Reichsbank account the gold being held for Czechoslovakia in the Bank of England's BIS account. Since this gold was held in the BIS account in London, the order entailed transferring the gold to the German account with the Bank of England. Bank of England governor Montagu Norman, himself a Nazi sympathizer and member of the BIS directorate, simply authorized the BIS to deduct the Czech gold from the Bank of England's BIS account. Predictably, there was a great public outcry in Britain when news of this transfer reached the British public, who denounced England's central bank for assisting in Nazi looting. But because the British government controlled neither the BIS nor the Bank of England, there was conveniently little for Montagu Norman to account for. And on May 5, 1939, a sum equivalent to that held in the Bank of England for Czechoslovakia was deposited in the Reichsbank in Berlin in the name of the National Bank of Bohemia and Moravia. The Germans, who wanted to preserve the appearance of legality, had not liquidated the Czechoslovakian National Bank or merged it with the Reichsbank as they had in the case of Austria. Instead, the Czech bank was reorganized into the National Bank of Bohemia and Moravia, "which gave the outward impression that it was autonomous as an institution in the new protectorate."[45]

By far the single biggest Nazi haul of gold sent to the Prussian mint for resmelting was the shipment taken from the Belgian treasury, which was valued at $223 million (about $2.2 billion in 1997). Officials at the Belgian central bank attempted to stop the German capture of their gold by placing their reserves with the Bank of France in anticipation of a Nazi invasion. The French, in turn, shipped the Belgian gold to their colony in Senegal for safekeeping. The Germans foiled this plan, however, by insisting that the gold sent to Dakar by France before the French collapse in 1940 be returned for use by the Reichsbank. The Germans arranged for the signing of a formal agreement in October 1940 to get the gold back. Over the next two years, 4,854 cases of Belgian gold with a weight of more than 240 tons underwent an incredible journey. The valuable cargo was transported through northwest Africa by light truck, by riverboat along the Niger, by camel through the Sahara, and by train to Algiers, where it was airlifted to Marseilles and then sent by truck to Berlin. By the summer of 1942, all the gold had reached the Reichsbank, where it was resmelted for sale to banks in Switzerland and Portugal. Recently declassified intelligence records show that Sweden's central bank refused to take much of the gold from Germany, which bank officials suspected was looted. However, the Swiss

National Bank readily accepted it. "How can the Swiss claim they acted in good faith when this gold was acquired at the time . . . when they knew it had been refused by the Swedes?" says a 1946 U.S. intelligence document.[46] Of the Belgian gold that ended up in Portugal, much of it was used to purchase materials for the production of armaments.[47]

Portugal, a neutral country whose fascist regime had strong Nazi sympathies, was the largest importer of Nazi gold after Switzerland. Allied records show that nearly one hundred tons of Nazi gold ended up in Portugal after first being laundered through Swiss banks. Gold was shipped several hundred miles by truck from Bern to Lisbon from the fall of 1941 until 1944. The Nazis also used looted gold to buy Portuguese wolfram, an ore that is essential in the hardening of steel, and of vital importance to their war economy. "We have just received information," wrote an official at the British embassy in Washington to an official of the U.S. Treasury Department in 1942,

> from a most reliable source that over the period from the end of October to the beginning of December 1941, more than 21 tons of gold passed through Basel, Switzerland en route to Berlin from Bern and escorted by Reichsbank officials. This movement supports the theory that it is German gold which is being sold from time to time by the Banque Nationale Suisse [Swiss National Bank] to the Banco de Portugal, the counter value usually being in escudos credited to Banque Nationale Suisse, although sometimes the Banco de Portugal's Swiss bank account is debited. . . . The Banque Nationale Suisse are noted as having informed the Banco de Portugal that they might be able to assign at least 1000 kilos (1 ton) twice monthly, presumably from Bern to Lisbon.[48]

The Swiss National Bank recently acknowledged that it did in fact ship Nazi gold to both Portugal and Spain during the war—but, claimed Jean-Pierre Roth, a Swiss National Bank board member, the bank functioned solely as a clearinghouse in order to facilitate trade among Germany, Portugal, and Spain, which was also neutral during the war. "Portugal and Spain exported goods to Germany during the war and were paid in gold," he said. "The payments took place in Bern. The Reichsbank made the payments to the two central banks in accounts they held there at the Swiss National Bank."[49]

Although the Nazis moved stolen gold through the banks of neutral countries, Germany's main gold-laundering efforts took place in Switzerland. In essence, Switzerland's official banks not only aided in the creation of Germany's war machine, but they also facilitated the Nazi looting of occupied countries. A telegram from the U.S. Department of State just after the war confirmed that "the German Reichsbank maintained an important depot of gold in the Swiss National Bank throughout the war; the major part of all German gold shipments abroad during the war were destined for the Swiss National Bank; approximately $123,000,000 worth of the Belgian gold [about $1.2 billion in 1997] stolen by the Germans . . . was, after resmelting, sent to the Swiss National Bank; and part of the gold looted by Germany during the war was sent to the Bank for International Settlements."[50]

In addition to the Swiss National Bank and the BIS, the Nazis used a myriad of smaller commercial banks to defy strict European currency controls. In one instance, the Eizenstat report outlines how Germany bought gold coin on the French black market, used diplomatic pouches to spirit it into Switzerland, where it was converted to bullion and shipped to South America to purchase gasoline and other supplies. The Nazis also used smaller commercial banks to deposit ransoms from Jews and others who wanted to emigrate from occupied territories. According to the Eizenstat report,

> German authorities . . . obtained large sums of foreign exchange by extorting ransom. . . . This practice of extortion was particularly prevalent in the Netherlands, where the large sums of money that were demanded appeared to be readily procurable. According to the US legation in Bern, the amounts demanded were as high as $30,000 per person. Reports of much higher ransoms were also

reaching the State Department. The victims, or their friends and relatives abroad, were instructed to pay the ransom into accounts in Swiss . . . banks.[51]

However, Swiss banks were not merely depositories for the Nazis. For Swiss banks,

the circumstances varied wildly; if Gestapo agents were bribed to stop the transport of the Jewish population of Slovakia to Poland, then the money required was deposited in the Union Bank; if the Reichsbank wanted to get funds to a German agent in Dublin, another neutral capital, then the Swiss Volksbank and the Swiss Bank Corporation obliged by transmitting money to one "William Greene."[52]

In fact, "no deal was too convoluted . . . and no client too disreputable. . . ."[53]

Why did the Swiss collaborate?

For one thing, Swiss bankers who aided the Nazis also made huge profits, especially with the network of combines, trusts, and cartels owned by German companies in Switzerland. Swiss firms were used as "shelf companies" by the Germans, who were able to hide their role in international business operations. The complexity of Swiss law aided in this coverup. Swiss company law is so convoluted that it was almost impossible for Allied investigators to uncover the web of corporate structures set up to evade the control of Germany's enemies. With banking secrecy provisions and trust arrangements conducted through Swiss lawyers, Switzerland became a convenient shield under which many German businessmen did international business. In some instances, the German government would provide a Swiss firm with a license to sell German technology or a product to the British in complete contravention of the British blockade of Germany, and have the Swiss company receive, in exchange, other material from the British to support German industry.

Moreover, U.S. intelligence reports suggest that many Swiss bankers were not only compliant but corruptible during the war, and would often bend strict banking regulations if the price was right. The false valorization of bearer shares, looted by Nazis from France, Holland, and Belgium during the years of Nazi occupation, is a case in point. A year after the end of the war, an American intelligence officer outlined how many Swiss bankers participated in legal fictions to overvalue looted shares. In much the same way that the Nazis resmelted looted gold and stamped the new bars with pre–1939 markers, a number of Swiss bankers participated in the fraudulent predating of looted shares on behalf of unscrupulous clients, and shared in the profits:

Due to the tremendous premium paid for shares continually owned from 1938, a scheme was often used by purchasers after 1938 to circumvent paying premiums. In carrying out this scheme, financial agents in Switzerland locate owners of safe deposit boxes in Swiss banks who have either not opened their boxes since 1938 or preferably have not been in Switzerland since 1938 and approach them concerning a deal which works as follows: (1) Box owners come to Switzerland and by bribing some bank official get shares in question put secretly in their safe deposit boxes; (2) Later they appear with a notary public and along with high ranking official of the bank either show by their passports that they have not been in Switzerland since 1938 or sign affidavit to effect they have not opened their safe deposit boxes since 1938, whichever the case may be; (3) The box is then opened before notary, bank officials and other witnesses, and all sign affidavit that shares in question have been in box since 1938. Thus when the deal is completed the profits are either two or three hundred percent and ample rewards are given to the bankers, employees and witnesses concerned in the transaction.[54]

Switzerland's financial services to the Nazis continued virtually unchecked throughout the war. Even after the Inter-Allied Declaration Against the Acts of Dispossession Committed in Territories Under

Enemy Occupation came into effect on January 5, 1943, strictly prohibiting the looting and laundering of the national treasuries of occupied countries, the gold shipments from Germany not only continued, they increased. In 1943 alone, U.S. investigators estimated that the Nazis sent more than $120 million worth of looted gold (about $1.2 billion in 1997) to Switzerland. In fact, as late as April 1945, one month before Germany's unconditional surrender, the Reichsbank vice president, Emil Puhl, managed to convince the Swiss National Bank's president, Ernst Weber, to purchase three more tons of looted gold. The Swiss National Bank's acceptance of the gold was in direct violation of an agreement that the Swiss government had made in March 1945 with the Allies to stop all commerce with Germany and freeze all German assets in Switzerland. The Swiss had also agreed to return any "identifiable" gold to its rightful owners.

Switzerland's wartime banking assistance to Germany became so widespread that Allied intelligence agents began to track Germany's financial dealings with the country's banks, and froze Swiss assets in U.S. banks in June 1941 as a precautionary measure, although they were not considered enemy assets until 1943, when the American Treasury Department became well aware of Switzerland's financial collaboration with the Nazis. In 1944, the Allies officially created "Operation Safehaven," an intelligence-gathering operation, just to monitor the activities of the neutrals' financial sector, which the Allies accused of conducting "economic warfare." Safehaven was a cooperative effort between the U.S. and Britain to prevent Germany from laundering money through various neutral countries in the final phase of the war. Although Safehaven examined German financial activities in neutral countries such as Sweden, Portugal, Spain, and Turkey, its main focus was on Switzerland, by far the largest money launderer. An American intelligence document notes that ". . . it should be pointed out that their [the Swiss] aid to the enemy in the banking field was clearly beyond the obligations under which a neutral must continue to trade with a belligerent, and dictated solely by the profit motive of the Swiss banks. The Swiss should make up for this undue amount of aid given to the enemy, which we have not interfered with up to the present time."[55]

Although many within the U.S. Treasury Department had worked diligently since 1942 gathering financial data on Swiss-German financial collaboration, Operation Safehaven was largely marked by intra-governmental squabbling in the United States and by inter-Allied bickering over how strongly it should be enforced with respect to Switzerland. As a result, intelligence gathering under Safehaven was not as widespread as it could have been. The British, who wanted to build their shattered economy after the war, knew that they would have to count on Swiss banks for favorable terms on loans, and they did not want to anger the Swiss by paying too much attention to Safehaven. The Americans were also divided on Safehaven. Many intelligence officials, who were already overworked collecting German military data, said that they had neither the time nor the resources to pursue Safehaven duties. In a memo to his superiors in Washington in late December 1944, Bern OSS (Office of Strategic Services) chief Allen Dulles noted, "At present we do not have adequate personnel to do effective job in this field and meet other demands."[56] But according to a U.S. government report, Dulles spent much of his time in Bern constructing an "Old Boy" network of banking contacts. One of his closest personal friends was BIS president McKittrick, who was said to be an OSS source on Nazi gold looting.[57]

Still, neither Switzerland nor Germany showed any signs of breaking their convenient financial arrangements. For their part, Swiss banking officials said they did not "knowingly" purchase any looted gold from the Reichsbank, but the assertion is hard to believe, since the amount of Germany's gold reserves was well known to European bankers before the war. Following the war, officials of the Swiss National Bank said that they tried to ensure that the gold they received from Germany was not tainted. They insisted that each shipment be certified by a high-ranking official of the Reichsbank, such as Emil Puhl, and that gold bars be stamped with the Reichsbank symbol. But in order to disguise their war booty, the Nazis resmelted the gold at the Prussian mint, and ordered Reichsbank officials to redraft new documents attesting to the gold's German provenance. So, the Swiss would argue, there was no such thing as "identifiable" gold. In this way, U.S. intelligence officials estimate that the Swiss laundered $398 million worth of looted gold, which is equivalent to $4 billion at today's values.

Why were both minor and high-ranking banking officials in a neutral country with a reputation for fairness, pragmatism, and democracy, so eager to facilitate German financial transactions during the war? Greed alone cannot account for their cooperation. They were also influenced by the political and economic realities that faced their country.

Not only did the Swiss seem to crumble at the sight of German military might, but after the fall of France in June 1940, Switzerland was totally dependent on the surrounding Axis powers and occupied countries for survival. Switzerland, with few natural resources, depended for instance entirely on the Axis powers and their occupied countries for its fuel supplies. It also relied on the railway line from Genoa for the transport of raw materials and foodstuffs. On August 9, 1940, Germany and Switzerland signed a trade agreement that obliged Germany to supply Switzerland with raw materials, including coal and iron. In return, Switzerland agreed to supply Germany with transport facilities across its territory to bring up goods from Italy, a clearing agreement that allowed Germany a credit of 150 million Swiss francs and arms and ammunition for the German war effort—actions that violated international laws of neutrality.

In fact, Swiss neutrality was in some jeopardy: The Nazi high command planned for a possible full-scale invasion of Switzerland. The military plan was called "Operation Christmas Tree." Although it never got off the ground because the Nazis concentrated their expansionist efforts elsewhere, the plan called for the quick defeat of any Swiss resistance and the partition of the country with Italy: Germany would take the northern part of Switzerland and Mussolini's forces would occupy the remaining area south of a line running east from Lake Geneva.

In 1943, the Nazis put pressure on the Swiss, since Hitler continued to be troubled by Switzerland's persistent political independence and neutrality. He was afraid that once the Allies invaded Europe, the Swiss would allow them free passage through their territory. Heinrich Himmler, head of the Gestapo and the Waffen-SS, was keen to occupy the country, but Hitler's generals and economic advisers convinced him that it would not be a very strategic move. Switzerland's mountainous terrain, which had protected it over the centuries, made it a difficult region to conquer. And if the Swiss offered resistance, they could sabotage German military strategy simply by destroying the St. Gotthard and Simplon rail tunnels; the main transit route, for German supplies and arms to and from Italy would then disappear.

Still, the threat of a German invasion never quite went away, and from time to time, rumors swirled across the small country that Hitler, supported by a pan-German league operating out of one of the German-speaking cantons, would move into all of the German-speaking parts of the country. As the war in Europe continued to rage, tensions erupted among the different ethnic and linguistic groups of Swiss. Many French-speaking Swiss sided with the Allies, while some of their German- and Italian-speaking counterparts favored the Axis powers. Clearly, the Swiss acted out of fear as well as greed in their appeasement of the Axis. For most of the war, the Axis powers demanded that Switzerland impose a general blackout, contravening its privileges as a neutral area. The Swiss argued that belligerent aircraft could recognize neutral territory only if it was lit up at night; the Italians argued in favor of the blackout, suggesting that British bomber crews received an unfair advantage, since Swiss illumination assisted them in finding their northern Italian targets. After the fall of France, the Swiss government capitulated and enforced the blackout, which began in November 1940 and was lifted only four years later. Allied airmen, flying over Switzerland to reach northern Italian towns, missed their targets with alarming frequency, accidentally dropping bombs on Swiss territory.

The general Swiss policy of appeasement toward the Nazis was practiced by many of the country's leaders. During most of the war, the majority of the seven-man Swiss cabinet or Federal Council remained largely pro-German and anti-Communist. Press censorship blocked out news of flagging German military fortunes. However, General Henri Guisan, commander of the Swiss Army during the Second World War, exemplified the popular point of view when he declared after the fall of France that the Swiss should fight against the Nazis or even the Allies in order to preserve their independence. Guisan, however, was so keen on an Allied victory that he had even encouraged talks between his staff and the French. Similarly, the majority of the Swiss were anti-Nazi, say foreign diplomats and other observers who were stationed in the country during the war years. According to British diplomat John Lomax:

> The Swiss people would never have submitted to support the German war effort if the facts had been squarely placed before their public opinion. . . . The small ruling group were far from representing the pro-Allied sentiment of the Swiss people. One or two were pro-Axis; others were convinced that Britain would be beaten and were therefore disposed—as the French put it—to run to the help of the victors.[58]

Many Swiss who lived in the country during the Second World War also claim that the majority of them were hoping for an Allied victory. "The majority of the Swiss people did not support the Nazis," says Rolf Bloch, president of the Swiss Federation of Jewish Communities, although he does concede that some German-speaking Swiss were, like many of their leaders, pro-Nazi during the war. "Supporting the Nazis was against everything most Swiss believe in. It was against the old Swiss way of democracy. Nazism was anti-liberal, anti-parliamentarian, and anti-human."

Nevertheless, appeasing the Nazis became a strategy of survival, and for some Swiss it was a way of making huge profits. It is true that Swiss banks also did business with the Allies. For instance, the Bank Julius Baer greatly aided the Office of Strategic Services in Bern (the precursor to the CIA) by arranging for the foreign exchange the organization required to do business in Europe. Moreover, the Swiss National Bank held gold accounts for countries such as Canada and Britain. But overall the main beneficiaries of Swiss financial know-how were the Nazis—and the Swiss themselves.

Beyond rendering financial services to the Nazis, the Swiss also kept the Third Reich well stocked with munitions, machine tools, ball bearings, and electrical equipment during the war. In a 1943 letter to U.S. Secretary of State Cordell Hull, the chairman of the U.S. Joint Chiefs of Staff, Admiral William Leahy, worried that Swiss supplies of munitions to Germany were "materially decreasing the military effectiveness of our air attacks on the Axis."[59] In the letter, which has recently been declassified, Leahy, who was a fierce critic of Switzerland, worried that the Swiss were increasing munitions supplies "at the very time that the British and American combined bomber offensive is beginning to substantially affect German production of munitions."[60] Leahy argued that the most effective way of stopping the Swiss munitions supplies to Germany would be to impose an economic blockade around the country.

But the blockade was never imposed, although by the time the Allies liberated much of Europe in 1944 and early 1945, essential supplies from Germany and Italy to Switzerland had trickled virtually to a halt. Yet it was never a problem to move looted gold into the neutral country. Nazi gold continued to flow into Switzerland up until a month before Germany's unconditional surrender.

There was yet another stream of money and valuables entering Switzerland from Nazi-occupied territory, ironically and eerily mirroring the earlier influx of money from desperate Jews. And, in fact, though they didn't know it, some of this other money came from dispossessed Jews.

Just as the Jews had tried to take advantage of secrecy laws to safeguard their assets in Switzerland, so too did individual high-profile Nazis and other Germans, who broke their own laws to accumulate both large and small fortunes during the war. High-ranking Nazis traveled frequently to Switzerland, which was a center of European espionage as well as banking during the war. The Nazis or their couriers would also deposit artwork, jewelry, or other valuables seized from Jews and other victims, in Swiss bank vaults. Hermann Goering, Hitler's second in command and an avid art collector like his boss, managed to courier a self-portrait of Van Gogh (whose work was decreed "degenerate" by official Nazi censure), painted after the artist had cut off his ear, and Cézanne's *House in the Park* by diplomatic pouch to be placed in a Swiss bank vault.[61] Goering also had substantial holdings at banks in Lausanne and Davos, according to another U.S. intelligence report.[62]

One of Goering's techniques for confiscating valuable artwork was to work with well-known criminal underworld figures, who would do his bidding. Another U.S. intelligence document suggests that he used French detectives and criminals to track down valuable art belonging to French Jews. The document quotes from a November 21, 1940, letter that Goering sent to high-ranking Nazi Alfred Rosenberg: "I obtained them [the artworks] from hiding places that were very difficult to find . . . by means of bribery and the employment of French detectives and criminal agents." Although he did not offer any details in the letter about the people he employed, some historians believe that he may have been referring to organizations such as the "Bony-Laffont" gang, which turned over Resistance fighters and Jews to the Nazis in exchange for being left alone to continue their criminal activities without police interference. Inspector Bony was a Paris police detective who was reportedly involved in criminal activities. Henri Laffont was a Parisian mobster who, along with Bony, worked on behalf of the Gestapo, torturing their victims until they revealed where their valuables were hidden.[63]

Joachim von Ribbentrop, Hitler's minister of foreign affairs, transferred his assets to a Swiss bank in Geneva between 1941 and 1944. Franz von Papen, Hitler's deputy chancellor during the first two years of Nazi rule and later ambassador to Ankara, Turkey, deposited 500,000 Swiss francs at the Reifessenkasse, a Catholic savings bank in St. Gall. The German aristocrat reportedly put the money in trust for his children.[64]

Even Adolf Hitler's former chief tailor appears to have been involved in moving private Nazi funds into Switzerland:

> Scherrer, a Swiss, formerly chief tailor to Hitler, who retired to Morcote, near Lugano, between 1941 to '43 received 300,000 Swiss Francs through Scheidt, cashier of the NSDAP [National Socialist German Workers' Party] at Lugano. The two are now [1946] in disagreement about these transfers and are taking the matter to court. Scheidt, a German, was treasurer of the Nazi Party in Lugano. He appears to [have been] engaged in moving valuables and securities out of France into Switzerland. When he was apprehended recently by the Swiss police for interrogation, he had on his person 38,000 Swiss Francs.[65]

Over the years, unconfirmed reports have also circulated that Adolf Hilter himself had an account at the Union Bank of Switzerland, where he deposited his generous earnings from sales of *Mein Kampf* through Max Amann, his personal financial adviser and the Third Reich's most important publisher. In addition to managing his *Mein Kampf* royalties, Amann ensured that Hitler received huge fees from his contributions to the Nazi press.

Max Amann used coercion and his Nazi contacts to become the Third Reich's wealthiest and most influential publisher. Born in Munich in 1891, he started out as a business manager of the Nazi party in 1921, and a year later became director of the party's publishing house, Ether Verlag. Known as the "Hercules of the Nazi publishing business" and "a merciless man who sweated lesser Nazi workers for the least possible,"[66] Amann, diminutive and ruthless, was appointed in November 1933 president of the Reich Association of German Newspaper Publishers and president of the Reich Press Chamber. He used his influence to plunder the non-Nazi newspaper chains throughout Germany. Through enforced business deals and legal freeze-outs, Amann was also able to eliminate independent publishing in Germany. In 1942, Hitler praised Amann as "the greatest newspaper proprietor in the world . . . own[ing] from 70 to 80 percent of the German press."[67] Between 1934 and 1944, Amann's salary increased from 108,000 Reichsmarks ($43,200) to 3,800,000 Reichsmarks ($1,520,000). In addition to his salary from Ether Verlag, he owned a substantial interest in a printing company and was able to bank millions of dollars in Switzerland without paying income tax. After the fall of the Third Reich in 1945, Amann was tried as a "major offender" by the Central Denazification Court and sentenced to ten years' hard labor. He lost everything, including his pension rights, and died in poverty in 1957.

Other Nazis also used Swiss banks to maximize the earning potential of their deposits in wartime. A 1941 memorandum to the U.S. Treasury Department from the British legation in Bern notes that

The Bern Manager of one of the leading Swiss Banks told me yesterday in confidence that to his personal knowledge every leading member of the Governing groups in all Axis countries have funds deposited in Switzerland. Some of the leaders have fortunes here and even some of the smaller fry have considerable sums i.e. upwards of half a million Swiss francs. The Swiss banking system provides well for this since it is usual for accounts to be kept under numbers not names, the key to the accountholders names being kept with the Manager in his safe and never communicated to any third party.

My informant added that most of these accounts were originally opened and kept for months after the War began in dollars. Later the holders began to change over into Swiss francs. Later still another change occurred and on his advice in the case of his own clients, they began to transfer their accounts into "gold account." This process of change from dollars has had a considerable influence upon the movements of the Swiss franc/dollar cross rate of exchange.

During the past few weeks many of the holders have begun to close this "gold account" and to take the actual gold metal which is then deposited in a safety deposit box in the banks. This process according to his Axis clients gives the maximum of security that can be attained.[68]

Often, profits derived from the expropriation of Jewish businesses and properties in the Third Reich would find their way to Swiss banks. At Johann Wehrli & Company in Zürich, a bank popular with Nazis, American intelligence officers discovered the existence of the *Gustoloff Stiftung,* a "fund" named after the slain former director of the Nazi party in Switzerland, where "the assets and titles of property taken by the Nazis from Jewish businessmen in Germany and the occupied countries were placed."[69] Although Johann Wehrli, a private banker from a distinguished German family, did not oversee the day-to-day operations of his bank during the war, he left longtime employee Karl Kessler, a fervent Swiss Nazi, in charge. American intelligence officers suspected Kessler to be the person who administered Goering's private financial interests in Switzerland.[70]

U.S. intelligence officials also tracked the movements of Richard Holtkott, who reportedly profited "in a fabulous way during the Nazi regime" by acquiring properties in Germany "from Jewish persons dispossessed or threatened with dispossession by the Nazi regime" and stashing his profits in Swiss banks. The intelligence report on Holtkott listed some of the properties he acquired from Jews, including the Rheinische Linoleum Werke of Bedburg, near Cologne, where before 1933 Holtkott had been merely a member of the board of directors. "Holtkott himself made various promises to friends and families of Jews in Germany, offering to save them from the concentration camps for an appropriate fee. It appears that our informant was married to a Jewish girl and entrusted money to Holtkott to save the lives of her parents. Holtkott continuously asserted that in consequence of these payments the parents had been saved. Our informant has now learned that they were burned in a concentration camp, a circumstance which accounts for the present denunciation."[71]

THE SWISS RECORD in human traffic is as dark as its banking operations. Money and gold, Jewish and Nazi, were not the only commodities passing through Switzerland. As a neutral country in the midst of a war-torn continent, Switzerland was a magnet for anyone trying to escape Nazi persecution.

During the course of the war, Switzerland took in more than 295,000 refugees, most of them escaped prisoners of war, deserters, and hospital patients. Between 1939 and 1945, the Swiss government spent an estimated $82.8 million Swiss francs (about $172 million in 1997), compared with 178,000 Swiss francs (about $360,000 in 1997) before the war on maintaining refugees.[72] Its refugee policy, however, was extremely selective. Under orders from their superiors, the Swiss federal police helped the Nazi regime by turning back Jewish refugees, who had arrived in Switzerland to escape Nazi persecution. Recent reports suggest that although the Swiss allowed more than 25,000 Jewish refugees into the country, they turned away some 30,000 more during the course of the war. The Swiss police became so efficient in their treatment of Jewish refugees that nearly a year before the war started, Heinrich Rothmond, Bern's chief of police, invented a surefire way to identify Jews by suggesting that police officials stamp the passport of every Jewish refugee with a large red "J." This efficient practice, of course, was adopted throughout the Reich and in other countries occupied by the Nazis. Although they had been generally refusing entry to Jewish refugees as early as the summer of 1938, four years later the Swiss made it official. In 1942, they passed a regulation forbidding political asylum to persons who become "refugees only on racial grounds."

Swiss police who turned back Jewish refugees at the border would often advise Gestapo agents, who would round up the Jews on the other side of the border and escort them directly to concentration

camps or back to their countries of origin. The Swiss Evangelical
Relief Organization for Affiliated Churches in Germany published
the following letter in its 1942 annual report:

> According to information that I have received, my mother and my
> fourteen-year-old brother arrived in Geneva toward the end of Sep-
> tember and spent about a week in a camp. From there they were
> sent back again to France. . . .You can imagine in what a state of
> anxiety I have been since then. . . . My husband's parents and his
> brother, who had valid visas for Switzerland and France, were
> turned back by the Alien Police at the Swiss border post of St.
> Margrethe on August 28, 1939, and had to return to Germany.
> My father was sent to the concentration camp at Buchenwald and
> died there on November 14, 1939. My mother was deported to
> the east on November 13, 1941, and since then there has been
> no word of her.[73]

In his book *The Lifeboat Is Full,* Swiss writer Alfred Häsler describes the inhuman efficiency of Swiss border guards in their dealings with Jewish refugees. In late August 1942, after a week of
traveling through France on foot and without food, six Jewish refugees—a sixty-year-old woman, her daughter, her son-in-law, a fifteen-
year-old girl, her seventeen-year-old brother, and another man—
arrived on the French-Vaudois border, and entered Switzerland
illegally. A group of Swiss villagers took in the exhausted fugitives,
but the next day the local border guard ordered them expelled at
once. Under an armed escort of national police, the refugees were
forced to march on foot to the border, two hours away. A Swiss
journalist recounted the harrowing scene in a report published in *Das
Volksrecht* on September 2, 1942:

> The refugees wept, and everyone who was present wept with them.
> . . . The two children had to hold the old woman on her feet. So
> they trudged off, up the slope. The policemen stopped to buy cigars

for themselves and then followed peacefully behind them. When he was asked why at least a truck had not been called to transport them, one of the policemen retorted: "Because they're Jews! So they can walk—the old woman too." On the way the woman collapsed. "Shoot me," she begged in French. "Shoot: I can't any more." At this point the villagers went to their butcher, who had a car. He was a decent human being and he drove the absolutely worn-out woman to the hospital; the rest of the group was taken to prison. The farewell between mother and daughter was heart-rending: they were convinced that they would never see each other again. Weeping and protesting, the refugees were taken . . . to the border . . . and forced to cross back near the place where they had entered Swiss soil.[74]

Although Häsler noted that many Swiss protested the harsh treatment of Jewish refugees and sent angry letters to newspapers and to their local authorities calling for an unrestricted right to asylum, few officials did anything to try to reverse the policy. However, at least one Swiss bureaucrat decided to follow his conscience. Paul Gruninger, police chief in the St. Gallen canton on the Austrian border, falsified entry documents in order to save three thousand Jews fleeing Nazi persecution in Austria in 1938 and 1939. With the assistance of the local Jewish community, he wrote letters to families stranded at the border, issuing visas to some and falsifying entry dates on passports to mislead Swiss federal authorities into thinking that the Jews he saved had arrived before the August 19, 1938, border closing date for Jewish refugees set by the Swiss authorities. As a result of his humanitarian efforts, Gruninger was arrested by Swiss authorities in 1939, fined for disobeying orders, and convicted of fraud a year later. He was thrown out of the police force, stripped of his pension, and ostracized for the rest of his life. After his conviction he could not find a regular job in St. Gallen, and his daughter Ruth, who was eighteen at the time her father was fired from his job, had to abandon her studies to help support the family. In December 1995, twenty-three years after Gruninger died a broken man, the same St.

Gallen court where he had been convicted in 1940 granted him a full pardon.

Jews who were lucky enough to enter Switzerland suffered other official anti-Semitic indignities. When they were admitted into the country, they were immediately discriminated against by the authorities, who required that the Swiss Jewish community pay for the upkeep of the 25,000 refugees that the government allowed in. Rolf Bloch, current president of the Swiss Federation of Jewish Communities, recalls that the authorities regarded the refugees as people in transit to other countries, and would not grant them legal residence status. But by 1940, when Switzerland was surrounded on all sides by fascist states, there was nowhere for refugees to go. The Jewish community in Switzerland, which numbered no more than 15,000 people before the war, contributed, Bloch says, more than 10 million Swiss francs (about $23 million) to the upkeep of Jewish refugees, who were not allowed to work in the country because of their legal status.

Swiss authorities discriminated against Jewish refugees in yet other ways. In return for being granted a haven in Switzerland, they were forced to breach one of the country's most exalted principles: financial secrecy. Refugees had to fill out a form and agree to "give the authorities precise and truthful information about my financial situation and to give prompt and unsolicited notification of any change in my circumstances. I attest that I have given the authorities full information about my financial circumstances. I empower all persons who professionally or legally have or have had financial dealing with me, viz, banks, repositories, lawyers, etc. to disclose details of my personal finances."[75]

The Swiss may have forced Jews to yield their financial secrets, but in one case at least, they kept the darkest secret of the Germans—all in the name of what had already become a highly dubious neutrality. Recent evidence suggests that the International Committee of the Red Cross (ICRC) knew about the deportation and extermination of Jews in Reich-occupied countries in 1942, but chose to remain silent. In 1989, following a thorough examination of its World War II archives in Geneva, Swiss historian Jean-Claude Favez published a scathing account of the inaction of the humanitarian organization. He discovered a detailed report of a secret meeting of the International Committee members in Geneva on October 14, 1942. At the meeting several members demanded that information about the mass extermination of Jews be made public. Favez claimed that the Red Cross executive knew about what was happening to the Jews of Europe from their own delegates, who had heard about the gas chambers in Auschwitz and had seen smoke rising from the crematoria of other camps. Although ICRC delegates did not gain access to the camps until the Reich collapsed in May 1945, high-level ICRC officials knew of Hitler's plans to make Europe "Jew free." However, those committee members who demanded publication of Nazi atrocities against the Jews were effectively silenced at the October 1942 meeting and did not have the courage to publish the secret themselves for fear of losing their jobs. The humanitarian organization's then director, Karl Jakob Burckhardt, insisted on absolute secrecy. Philipp Etter, at the time Switzerland's head of government and a member of the International Committee, was also present at the meeting and also called for total secrecy. Burkhardt and Etter insisted that the Red Cross had no legal basis to intervene in the genocide of the Jews. Making these facts public would somehow jeopardize Swiss neutrality.[76]

While inaction and anti-Semitic policy dominated Switzerland's official refugee policy, individuals within the country did much to help Jews. In addition to committed professionals like Veit Wyler, Switzerland was home to some of the most progressive Jewish organizations, such as the World Jewish Congress (WJC), which had been founded in Geneva in 1936 to fight against Hitler's anti-Jewish policies and to defend Jewish communities in Eastern Europe, where anti-Semitism was particularly violent.

The World Jewish Congress, which today has representative offices around the world, was founded by a group of mostly young international lawyers committed to protecting European Jews. In 1936, one of them, a young man named Gerhart Riegner, put his legal career on hold for what he thought would be a few weeks in order to be secretary general of the WJC organization in Geneva. Riegner, who is now eighty-five and still associated with the WJC, says that in 1942 he received information from a very reliable source in Germany that the Nazis had launched a massive campaign to exterminate European Jews.

That summer, Riegner prepared a telegram in which he tried to warn the Allies about what later came to be known to the world as Hitler's "Final Solution." On August 8, 1942, Riegner wrote that all European Jews were to be deported to the east and "exterminated at one blow." He added that he was sending the information "with all necessary reservation as exactitude cannot be confirmed," but that his informant had very close connections within the upper echelons of the Nazi regime.[77] His telegram was sent via the American and British consulates in Geneva to Rabbi Stephen Wise, America's most prominent Jewish leader, and to MP Sidney Silverman in England. Silverman received the information, but Wise did not. Silverman transmitted the message to Wise, who sent the report to U.S. Undersecretary of State Sumner Welles. The undersecretary asked Riegner not to release the story until an attempt could be made to confirm the details. In the end, the Allies did nothing.

"It was the most tragic moment of my life," says the elderly Gerhart Riegner today, more than a half century later, as he watches the snow fall outside the window of his Geneva office. "It was terrible. So many Jews were dying, and nobody believed me."

THREE

DISPLACEMENTS

By January 1945, the Germans knew the war was lost. With the Allies advancing on every front, the Nazis evacuated several concentration camps and moved the prisoners in crowded cattle trucks and on foot farther and farther away from the front lines.

It was part of a desperate scorched-earth policy to destroy some of the most staggering evidence of genocide. On January 17, while 58,000 prisoners were moved out of Auschwitz-Birkenau, most of them on foot, in subzero temperatures, camp officials furiously set about destroying medical records and evidence of slave labor operations. A few days later, an SS detachment shot two hundred Jewish women who were too weak to walk, and blew up the buildings that had housed Crematoria I and II. When the Soviet Army reached the camp on January 27, 1945, they found that twenty-nine of the thirty-five storerooms had been burned down. In the six remaining storerooms, "they found part of the camp's legacy: 368,820 men's suits, 836,255 women's coats and dresses, 5,525 pairs of women's shoes,

13,964 carpets, large quantities of children's clothes, toothbrushes, false teeth, pots and pans. In abandoned railway cars hundreds of thousands of additional items of apparel were discovered, and in the tannery the Soviet investigation commission found seven tons of hair."[1]

Only seven thousand prisoners remained alive at Auschwitz when the Soviets arrived; the rest had been dispatched on the infamous "death marches," so called because weak and malnourished prisoners were often marched until they died. In general, the prisoners were moved to nearby, overcrowded concentration camps, but the marches also served a strategic purpose. The historian Martin Gilbert tells how some Nazi leaders desperately tried to fight, to hold out to the bitter end: "A new policy now drove the SS to prolong the agony of the death marches: the desire to preserve for as long as possible a mass of slave labor for all the needs which confronted the disintegrating German army: repairing roads and railway tracks, building up railway embankments, repairing bridges, excavating underground bunkers from which the battle could still be directed, preparing tank traps to check the Allied advance, and helping with the massive work involved in preparing mountain fortresses deep underground."[2]

Renée and Selma set out on one of the death marches from Auschwitz-Birkenau, and made it as far north as the Ravensbrück concentration camp. Thousands of prisoners, who were already malnourished and near death when they left Auschwitz, died of exposure and starvation on that weeklong winter march, which in many ways was far more grueling than the slave labor they had endured in the death camp.

"We wore only the striped prison uniform and wooden shoes," recalls Renée. "It was January. Our food was snow, our beds also snow."

Indeed, at one point Renée, exhausted and numb from the cold that pierced her flimsy prison rags, pleaded with her mother to leave her in the snow to die. This time it was her mother who saved her life. "I told my mother, let's just sit down and get it over with," she says, adding that prisoners who tried to rest during the march were immediately shot by the SS guards who were accompanying them. "I told her it would all be over in just a minute or two, but she refused, and so I had no choice but to keep going."

Following that momentary relapse, Renée was determined to survive at all costs. "My mother and I lived for each other," she says. "We fought to be at the head of the column, for those at the end were prodded on with guns. If any were tired and sat down, they were shot. Only about thirty percent lived through that march. Corpses were like flowers along the road."

On the way to find shelter in other concentration camps, the prisoners passed desperate German refugees, some on bicycles or battered motorcycles, others lugging overstuffed suitcases or pulling wagons piled with furniture and children. Everyone was fleeing the dreaded Soviet Army, but for the concentration camp inmates there seemed nowhere to go. At Bergen-Belsen, at Celle, near Hannover in the northwestern part of Germany, the camp administration broke down as thousands of new inmates were dumped into the compound. Raul Hilberg describes vividly how "the food supply was shut off, roll calls were stopped, and the starving inmates were left to their own devices. Typhus and diarrhea raged unchecked, corpses rotted in barracks and on dung heaps. Rats attacked living inmates, and bodies of the dead were eaten by starving prisoners."[3]

By the time Renée and her mother, along with columns of bedraggled and exhausted prisoners, reached the Ravensbrück concentration camp, they were covered with lice, their teeth had turned navy from malnutrition and lack of hygiene, and the exposed parts of their bodies were covered with sores. Ravensbrück, like most of the other German camps, was filled beyond capacity with dying Jews. "There were people on top of each other," remembers Renée. "There was a group of angry SS women who shot into the crowd of prisoners to keep them quiet. The SS women kept telling us that we'd better pray that Germany wins the war."

By early April 1945, the war was almost over. "I was behind a few SS men who took us out of the camp and then I saw another SS man on a motorcycle," recalls Renée. "The man on the motorcycle said, 'Ivan is closing in,' and that's when I knew that the Germans had lost the war."

But when they arrived at the concentration camps, the Soviet soldiers were overwhelmed by the thousands of survivors they saw before them. Because the soldiers did not have enough rations to feed the former inmates they encountered on the roads or in the camps they liberated, they encouraged the survivors to steal from the retreating Germans. Renée and her mother pilfered a loaf of bread and a tin of sardines from a demoralized German soldier, devouring everything in a matter of seconds.

In their desperation to avoid capture, prospective war criminals melted into the crowds in Germany or tried to get false papers to flee across borders. The men who had been instrumental to the Final Solution, the systematic murder of six million Jews, now scrambled to go into hiding. SS chief Heinrich Himmler wandered about Germany until he was arrested. He later swallowed poison. Rudolf Höss, the commander of Auschwitz between 1940 and 1943, managed to get false papers to cross the border into Denmark, but was quickly apprehended. Adolf Eichmann, who had been such an effective administrator of mass murder, called his men together to tell them the war was over. "While one of them was 'whimpering like a child,' Eichmann said that the feeling of having killed five million enemies [sic] of the state had given him so much satisfaction that he would jump laughingly into the grave."[4] Adolf Eichmann did, in fact, jump. After spending months in American custody, unrecognized, he disappeared. He was apprehended fifteen years later by Israeli intelligence agents in a run-down suburb of Buenos Aires.

Renée and her mother saw for themselves the cowardice of the defeated Germans. Just outside Ravensbrück, Renée watched with a mixture of horror and bleak amusement as a few SS officers changed into striped concentration camp uniforms, threw down their weapons, and tried to flee. "They tried to run away from the Russians," recalls Renée. "The Russians were very fair. They called once, twice, and three times before they shot them dead. I don't believe in killing, but at that time. . . ."

By the end of the first week of May 1945 the Germans had surrendered unconditionally, and an exhausted Renée was ecstatic. "I thought I owned the world. When we were liberated I thought this was the beginning and end of me, I felt on a high—I couldn't describe it—I thought I owned the world, to have lived and seen the Germans defeated."

But Renée's happiness was bittersweet, for when she finally managed to contact her aunt Paula and uncle George in New York, she found out that her family members who had fled to Riga had for all intents and purposes disappeared. Paula and George told her that uncle Adolf, uncle Harry, their families, and her grandparents had not communicated with anyone since the Germans marched into Latvia in 1941. Renée's father, Oskar Lang, had not been in touch since leaving for Poland before the outbreak of the war. Siegfried, Renée's brother, was still confined to a psychiatric hospital in London. His condition had not improved since the blitzkrieg of the city in 1940.

Meanwhile, as stateless Jews, Renée and her mother joined hundreds of thousands of displaced persons who wandered Europe in search of food, medical help, and a place to live. In the chaos that was postwar Europe, Renée and other uprooted Jews quickly discovered that not only did they not own the world, they owned nothing. Raul Hilberg noted,

Up to May 8, 1945, the Jewish masses could not be rescued from catastrophe; now the survivors had to be saved from its consequences. On the conquered territory of the former German Reich, some tens of thousands of Jews clustered around the liberated concentration camps: Bergen-Belsen in the British zone, the Dachau complex in the American zone, Mauthausen in Austria. Thousands of the worst cases among the camp survivors were taken to hospitals in Germany, Switzerland, and Sweden. Thousands more began to trek back to Hungary and Poland in search of lost families. To the south and east, the broken Jewish remnant communities formed a belt of restlessness, extending from the Balkans through Poland to the depths of Russia. The Hungarian-Romanian area still contained half a million Jews. Many were dispersed, most were destitute and all were insecure. In Poland the scattered survivors found possessions and homes in other hands. Not a few of these Polish Jews, emerging from labor camps and out of hiding, were greeted with the query: "Still alive?"[5]

The uprooted survivors had lived through a nightmare only to be thrust into a political quagmire. Many were treated with hostility and indifference when they made their way back to their own countries, and those who sought to emigrate to the United States or Palestine found huge bureaucratic and political obstacles in their way. Immediately following the war most countries still had immigration quotas. In the United States, the total quota allotted to both Jews and non-Jews born in Eastern Europe was 1,500 a month. Many Jews headed for Palestine, but were blocked by the British government, which only allowed immigration to Palestine at a very restricted rate. Many Jews grew frustrated and decided to make the journey on their own, even if they could go only halfway. By November 1945, thousands of Jews were spilling over the borders of a devastated Europe in search of a place to live.

In Germany, British authorities saw the influx of the Jewish refugees as a huge conspiracy to forcibly break the immigration barriers to Palestine. Lieutenant General Sir Frederick Morgan, who served as chief of displaced persons operations in Germany for the United Nations Relief and Rehabilitation Administration (UNRRA), told a reporter for *The New York Times* that a clandestine Jewish organization was orchestrating the influx of Jews into Germany from Eastern Europe. According to Morgan, these displaced Jews were "well-dressed, well fed, rosy cheeked, [had] plenty of money [and were] growing into a world force," who were planning to leave Europe. "They certainly do not look like persecuted people," said Morgan.[6] The British soon restricted Jewish admission to displaced persons camps in their zones of occupation in Europe, and even adopted a compulsory labor law for the Jewish residents of camps in their zone in Germany. No doubt the British themselves were aware of the cruel irony of requiring Holocaust survivors to pay for their upkeep in DP camps by donating their labor to rebuild the shattered German economy.

Because of British restrictions, displaced Jews headed to camps in the American zones, which were often already overcrowded and lacking in any basic facilities. Military authorities in all zones of occupation were so deluged with displaced persons and prisoners of war that they found it difficult to provide even essential food and other necessities for their charges. Between 1945 and 1948, American Jewish organizations scrambled to fill the gap left by the harried Allied victors to care for the urgent needs of a completely uprooted community of more than 250,000 people.

As these hundreds of thousands of souls wandered across a devastated Europe, the victorious Allied powers, dominated by the United States and the Soviet Union, began to deliberate postwar policy for the reconstruction of Europe, which would shape the history of most of the remainder of the twentieth century. At the Potsdam Conference, which took place from July 17 to August 2, 1945, on the outskirts of war-ravaged Berlin, the Allied powers formally divided up a defeated Germany into Allied zones of occupation, set up a new system of rule to abolish National Socialism, and drew up plans to reorganize the German economy and to collect reparations from the devastated country. All former German territory east of the Oder and Neisse rivers was transferred to Polish and Soviet administration.

But the fragile alliance that had linked the United States and the Soviet Union during the war had begun to fray even before Potsdam. Relations between the Soviets and the Americans had returned to the climate of tense mutual suspicion that had dominated their relations before the war. Incentives for mutual cooperation were not helped by the fact that on July 16, the day before the conference opened, the Americans' top-secret Manhattan Project concluded by successfully testing an atomic bomb, which the U.S. would use less than a month later with devastating force on Japan to end the war in the Pacific. Although the Americans and the Soviets managed to reach a workable compromise on the German question, both sides left the meeting even more deeply suspicious of each other. Joseph Stalin's foreign policy was transparent, and in the months leading up to Potsdam he began to assert his claim over much of Eastern Europe. The Soviets had already annexed Finnish territories adjacent to Leningrad, the Baltic states, western Ukraine, Bessarabia, and Moldavia during the war. The Americans, led by hard-liner Harry S Truman, were not amused and soon adopted a policy of "containing" Soviet expansionist threats, primarily by offering massive aid infusions to prop up shattered economies. In March 1946, former British Prime Minister Winston Churchill set the tone for more than four decades of Soviet-American relations in a postwar world when he warned of the implacable threat that lay behind a Communist "Iron Curtain." In Europe, the stage was set for the intense battle of nerves and wits that would characterize the Cold War.

Against this tense background, Switzerland got off easy. In fact, Switzerland's wartime and postwar negotiations with the victorious Allied powers were characterized by a pragmatic realpolitik that was part and parcel of the emerging Cold War. Although many Allied negotiators sought to punish Switzerland for its wartime financial services to the Nazis, they knew they needed Swiss banks to aid in the reconstruction of Europe, and later realized Switzerland's importance as a financial stabilizing force in a Europe that became sharply divided between those countries that rapidly fell behind the Iron Curtain and those that remained in the Western sphere of influence. The Western Allies were afraid of Switzerland's ability to do a thriving business with the new enemy. Switzerland, which had emerged unscathed from the war as the strongest capitalist country in the region, was already doing a great deal of business with the Soviets, buying large quantities of Siberian gold in exchange for hard currency.

The Allied–Swiss (Washington) Accord, signed among Switzerland and the U.S., the U.K. and France on May 25, 1946, after two months of tough negotiations, exemplifies this Cold War realpolitik. The accord, which flowed out of proposals made at the Paris Reparations

Conference in November and December 1945, was designed to forestall a Nazi resurgence by eliminating German assets in Switzerland.

Although proponents of Operation Safehaven in the U.S. Treasury Department felt that Switzerland should be severely reprimanded for laundering Nazi gold and fencing German assets during the war, State Department officials were more cautious. Led by Truman's special assistant, Randolph Paul, the American aim was to contain the Soviet threat at any cost, and they were reluctant to press Switzerland too hard. Moreover, the French and British negotiating teams wanted to rebuild their trade links in Europe, and needed loans on good terms from Swiss banks to prop up their shattered economies. The Swiss negotiators, led by the intractable Walter Stucki, the second in command at the Swiss foreign ministry, capitalized on the indecision and infighting within U.S. government agencies and among the Allies. Stucki and his team maintained rigid interpretations of international law, and refused to admit that Switzerland had done anything wrong by providing financial services to the Nazis. In his May 1997 groundbreaking two-hundred page report on Nazi gold, which involved eleven government agencies and thousands of documents, U.S. Undersecretary of Commerce Stuart Eizenstat characterized the Swiss as "obdurate" negotiators during the two tense months of talks in Washington:

> Throughout the discussions, the Swiss negotiators stood on their interpretation of international law and Swiss law. They showed little inclination to accept Allied arguments about the practical need or moral obligation to return to war-ravaged Europe some substantial portion of the profits they had earned in wartime commerce with Germany.[7]

The Americans should have known that they were in for a difficult time in Washington from their past experience with Swiss negotiators. Throughout the war, American and Allied diplomats issued stern warnings prohibiting the laundering of looted gold through neutral countries' banks. Nevertheless, Swiss banks continued to launder

Nazi gold, even as a German defeat appeared imminent. Three months before the end of the war in Europe, the Allies, led by the Americans, sent a mission to Bern to pressure the Swiss to halt their gold-laundering activities. They also wanted to find out the extent of German assets held in Swiss banks. In the last months of the war, the Allies drew up preliminary plans for dividing up a defeated Germany, and decided that German assets held outside Germany were to be impounded for the purposes of reparation, and to prevent Germany from rearming itself.

In February 1945, forty-two-year-old economist and diplomat Lauchlin Currie, special assistant to President Roosevelt and the intellectual leader of the New Deal economists in the United States, was dispatched to Switzerland to begin negotiating with the Swiss to turn over their German assets to the Allied powers and halt their financial services to the Nazis. The earnest, Canadian-born Currie, who was perhaps best known as the director of the lend-lease program to China during the war, arrived in Bern on the first train from a recently liberated Paris, and was welcomed at the train station by crowds of enthusiastic Swiss supporters. Since the Allied landings in Europe in June 1944, the German Army had been in retreat, and for the first time in four years Switzerland was no longer surrounded by Axis forces. Most Swiss looked forward to expanding their country's trade and ending their wartime isolation. More important, the recent liberation of France had cut off German supply lines to its western occupied countries, and as a result the Swiss were running out of essential items, such as coal. Many on the Swiss negotiating team desperately hoped that they could press their case for Allied aid with Currie and the other main Allied negotiator, Dingle Foot, British parliamentary secretary for the Ministry of Economic Warfare. During the three weeks of negotiations in Bern, Currie and his colleagues were wined and dined by their Swiss hosts, who were desperate for a favorable deal.

Currie carried with him a letter from President Roosevelt to Eduard von Steiger, president of the Swiss Confederation. The letter, which Currie himself had carefully drafted, promised to meet Switzerland's "most urgent needs and defend [its] liberties" if the country cooperated with the Allies and cut off all assistance to Germany. The letter appealed to Switzerland's historical tradition of democracy and fairness:

I know in these circumstances that you will be eager to deprive the Nazis of any further assistance. It would indeed be a trial to any freedom-loving Swiss to feel that he had in any way impeded the efforts of other freedom-loving countries to rid the world of a ruthless tyrant. . . . I hope also that you will lend every assistance in our efforts in the postwar period to track down and seize the property of our foe.[8]

The Swiss delegation was unmoved by such lofty sentiments, but committed to negotiating with the Allied team after Currie told them that the U.S. government was prepared to speed up requests for supplies through France if the Swiss curtailed cooperation with Germany and northern Italy. The Swiss were so desperate to restore their coal shipments that they appointed a mild-mannered academic named William Rappard to lead the negotiations. Hard-liner Walter Stucki, who was originally on the Swiss negotiating team, was pulled off because he was seen as too stubborn.

The negotiations were also threatened by divisions within the U.S. government on whether or not Switzerland should be punished. In the middle of the negotiations, General Walter Bedell Smith, chief of staff to General Dwight D. Eisenhower, suddenly canceled a previous offer to ship coal to Switzerland because he was furious at the idea of helping this neutral country that had collaborated with the Nazis. In the middle of the Swiss negotiations, Currie had to rush from Bern to the Allied military base at Versailles to placate General Bedell Smith and make sure that the offer to ship coal to Switzerland would be restored immediately. To make matters worse, stray Allied bombs fell on Swiss territory, resulting in damage to property and loss of Swiss lives. Currie had to send an urgent wire to Roosevelt, who was then at the Yalta Conference, to halt the bombing operations near the Swiss border.

On March 8, 1945, Currie breathed a sigh of relief. After many long hours of heated discussions, threats, and promises, the Swiss and the Allies had finally reached an agreement under which Switzerland would cut off trade with Germany and freeze German assets in Switzerland, including those held through Swiss nationals. The Swiss also agreed to limit their purchase of gold from Germany to the small quantities needed for the use of German diplomatic representatives in the country. Furthermore, they promised complete cooperation in helping the Allies return any "identifiable" gold to its rightful owners. (However, given that the Nazis had concealed looted gold by resmelting it and stamping pre-1939 dates on the new gold bars, Swiss bankers would stonewall and say that there was little in the way of "identifiable" gold in Swiss banks). In exchange, the Allies would allow a limited amount of fuel, food, and raw materials to be transported across a newly liberated Europe to Switzerland.

Although to many Swiss officials the Currie mission agreement smacked of complete capitulation, at least one observer noted that "the Swiss eventually reneged on almost every commitment they had been forced to make. They just stalled until the inauguration of the Cold War, when America's attention was diverted to much more pressing matters in Europe."[9]

Indeed, the ink was barely dry on the Currie mission agreement when the Swiss started to violate it. In addition to accepting a final shipment of looted gold from Germany in April, a month after the agreement was signed, Switzerland managed to pay only lip service to other key factors of the agreement. For instance, the attempt to conduct a proper census of German assets in Switzerland was pathetic at best. The Swiss Bankers Association and the Swiss Lawyers Association, both of which were dominated by Nazi sympathizers, criticized the Swiss government for lifting banking secrecy and giving in to American pressure by agreeing to freeze German assets and conduct the census. Although most of the other neutral countries eventually complied with the Allied policy, the Swiss balked, arguing that it was completely against international law. Bern contended that German assets inside Switzerland should be liquidated to pay off German debts owed to Swiss financial institutions. The banks even developed a press campaign to arouse public support for their position. Furthermore, the Swiss argued that the Allies had no right to make decrees affecting any assets held in Switzerland. Although Swiss government bureaucrats sent out standard questionnaires to lawyers and bankers, asking them to enumerate German assets, filling out the questionnaires was voluntary, and the Swiss government did not bother to check on the results. Based on these rather inconclusive reports, the Swiss Compensation Office, the government agency responsible for the census, produced a report stating that only $250 million worth (about $2.2 billion in 1997) of German assets was found in Swiss banks. The Swiss results were a fraction of the German assets that Safehaven investigators believed to be in the country.

In the United States, Switzerland's halfhearted attempts to fulfill its obligations under the Currie agreement did not go unnoticed. In June 1945, U.S. Democratic Senator Harley Kilgore chaired hearings of the Senate Subcommittee on War Mobilization to examine what he saw as a dangerous potential for German rearmament through Swiss financial institutions, and urged the United States government to take tougher action against Switzerland. The American media paid close attention to the testimony of Orvis A. Schmidt, director of foreign funds control for the U.S. Treasury Department and a member of the Currie mission. Schmidt noted that

[e]ven at this late date, the Swiss government is loath to take the necessary steps to force banks and other cloaking institutions to disclose the owners of assets held in or through Switzerland. This means that German assets held in or through Switzerland will not be identified. Thus, the true picture of German financial and industrial penetration throughout the world will be kept a secret. By the same token, Swiss banks will continue to profit by protecting, through their secrecy laws, Germany's war potential—the hidden assets of its financiers and industrialists.[10]

Despite the level of moral outrage that set the tone for the Senate committee hearings, the U.S. State Department would do little to punish Switzerland, even though U.S. intelligence agents had provided the government with copious reports about Swiss financial complicity with the Nazis during the war. As the negotiations got under way for the Allied–Swiss (Washington) Accord a year later, the U.S. chief negotiator, Randolph Paul, knew from Safehaven reports that more than $400 million worth (about $3.9 billion in 1977) of looted gold had passed through Swiss banks, and that an estimated $200 to $398 million in Nazi gold ($1.8 billion to $3.5 billion in 1977) still remained in the Swiss National Bank.[11] The U.S. negotiators also knew that German assets outside Germany totaled more than $750 million ($6.7 billion in 1997), and that the majority of these assets were being held in Swiss banks. According to one Safehaven report, "Switzerland cannot plead that she was ignorant of the despoilment and robbery which the Germans committed against the countries which were under her authority. . . . It is the view of the Allied Delegations that Switzerland is responsible for all gold shipped to her from Germany."[12]

But Randolph Paul was instructed by President Truman not to be too hard on Switzerland, since he felt that the country would be instrumental in helping the U.S. rebuild the shattered economies of Europe, thereby preventing them from falling behind the Iron Curtain. Against this backdrop of U.S. conciliation, the Swiss would get away with murder. Stucki, Swiss undersecretary of foreign affairs and a former ambassador to Vichy France, perceived as being too rigid by his own government in the negotiations for the Currie mission agreement just a year earlier, was under strict orders from his superiors in Bern to give as little as possible to the Allies in Washington. The American negotiators had their work cut out for them, as Stucki maintained from the outset that the Allies had grossly exaggerated the amount of gold looted by the Nazis. The Swiss argued that the Nazis had been hoarding gold for years as part of their secret prewar economy, and that the gold accepted by Swiss banks was indeed German gold, not looted gold. As for the amount of German assets in Switzerland, Stucki also maintained that the Safehaven estimates were grossly exaggerated.

According to British archival sources, "the Swiss maintained consistently that Switzerland could not be held liable to restore the entire amount of looted gold transferred from Germany to Switzerland, some of which was transferred to third countries. In the course of the negotiations they would admit that they had bought $88 million of gold traceable originally to Belgium, and about $415 million in total of German gold from 1939 to 1945, but they did not concede that they should restore this amount to the Allies."[13]

After several weeks of bickering, the Swiss put their final proposal on the table. They offered to give the Allies $58.1 million worth of gold (about $566 million in 1997), which comprised two thirds of the estimated $88 million worth ($857 million in 1997) of looted Belgian gold that they reluctantly conceded was in the Swiss National Bank. In addition, the Swiss agreed to divide the liquid German assets in Switzerland in half with the Allies, and make an immediate contribution to the International Refugee Organization (IRO) to assist in the resettlement of stateless victims of Nazism in Europe. Moreover, in side letters to the accord, the Swiss promised to look "sympathetically" at assisting victims of Nazism by recovering their heirless assets in Switzerland. In exchange, the Swiss would receive a blanket release from any further liability of its government and the Swiss National Bank in connection with looted gold, and the United States would unblock Swiss assets, transferred to American banks during the war for safekeeping.

Switzerland's opponents in the United States were furious with the Washington Accord. In a letter to President Truman, Senator Kilgore argued that "justice, decency and plain horse sense require that the allies hold Switzerland responsible for all of the . . . looted gold which they accepted from the Nazis and reject their proposition of settling for 20 cents on the dollar . . . fifty percent to reimburse certain Swiss nationals who, in their lucrative dealings with the Nazis, were finally stuck with some bad accounts because the Nazis lost the war . . . places the profit of those who dealt with the Nazis above the rights of those who were robbed and despoiled by the Germans."[14]

However, "justice" and "plain horse sense" seemed not to have prevailed during those two months (April–May 1946) of heated U.S.-Swiss talks in Washington. The attention of the Truman administration and the American public was focused on other, perhaps more pressing domestic and foreign issues. In the United States, coal miners and railroad workers were on strike, bringing the country to a virtual standstill. Outside the United States, the Soviet Union was trying to maintain its occupation of northern Iran, and American policy-makers worried about the military might of the Soviets as the world began to take sides in the emerging Cold War.

"The Allies knew that the Swiss wanted to keep the money," said Gian Trepp, a Swiss journalist who has written extensively about Swiss bankers' collusion with the Nazis. "In France and Italy you had a strong Communist party. The Allies did not want to alienate Switzerland."[15]

So on May 26, the Allies and the Swiss signed the Washington Accord keeping most of Switzerland's demands intact. Seymour Rubin, deputy negotiator on the U.S. team, recalls that the Americans were not displeased with the deal they had struck. "A lot of us, including myself, had some doubts," said Rubin, who is now eighty-three years old. "You know, you scratch your head [and ask]: 'Is that the best we could do?' We eventually came to conclude that it was the best figure."[16] In a recent interview with *The New York Times,* Rubin said he resented Eizenstat's conclusions that the U.S. negotiating team had been weak. For him, the primary motivating force for reaching an agreement with the Swiss was not so much the Cold War as American business interests in Europe.

"A lot of people in the United States were saying the same thing: The war is over and if we continue blacklisting Swiss companies, we can't do business with them but everybody else in the world will," said Rubin, adding that "nobody ever raised Cold War considerations—with the negotiating delegation, at any rate."[17]

In the same month that the accord was signed, the U.S. government began unblocking more than 4 billion Swiss francs (about $930 million then; $8.2 billion in 1997) worth of Swiss government and Swiss National Bank assets frozen in U.S. banks. By October, the United States unfroze the remaining private Swiss assets held in its banks. In his response to Senator Kilgore's letter, President Truman wrote "of the amount of looted gold purchased from Germany, almost two-thirds of the amounts fairly provable will be returned by the Swiss."[18] In reality, of course, far less would be returned, and Truman knew it.

In fact, soon after the signing of the accord, "State Department officials in Washington came to believe that the Swiss never intended to implement the agreement."[19] The accord was unworkable, and stood in the way of justice for at least one formerly Nazi-occupied country. The Washington Accord made it impossible for the Netherlands to bring legal action against Switzerland at the International Court of Justice when new evidence, which came to light only in 1947, suggested that an estimated 562 million Swiss francs worth of gold (about $131 million then; about $1.3 billion in 1997) had been looted by the Nazis from the Dutch National Bank and laundered in Switzerland between 1941 and 1944. When the Dutch government attempted to seek compensation, the Swiss responded that under the Washington Accord, no further claims could be made. The governments of the U.S., Great Britain, and France left the matter at that.

In the fall of 1950, U.S. negotiators even proposed to the Allies that the accord be publicly rejected because it was unworkable. But according to the Eizenstat report, France and Britain strongly resisted because they needed the hard Swiss currency that the accord promised, at least in theory, to provide. By unblocking Switzerland's assets so soon after the signing of the accord, the U.S. no longer had any leverage to pressure the Swiss to comply with the terms of the agreement. As one writer put it, the Washington Accord became a great example of Swiss perfidy—a "tribute to Swiss stamina, the national determination to stonewall in the face of overwhelming odds, and . . . the banks' consequent ability to protect their clients and their own interests."[20]

Abraham Hammersfeld, Vienna
Courtesy Herbert Stilman

Renée Lang, circa 1938. Renée Lang's photograph was displayed in the window of a popular photo studio alongside a picture of Adolf Hitler. A caption underneath her photograph described her as "the perfect Austrian woman." Courtesy Herbert Stilman

The dry-goods store owned jointly by Georg Stilman and Adolf Hammersfeld in Vienna in the 1930s. By the late 1930s, they had split their business, and each had his own dry-goods store in separate parts of the Austrian capital. Georg Stilman is pictured. Courtesy Herbert Stilman

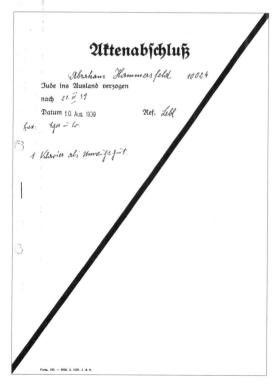

"File Closed." The last entry in Abraham Hammersfeld's Nazi file indicates that he left Austria on April 21, 1939. The file indicates that the only thing he took with him was a piano.

Courtesy Austrian State Archives, Vienna

Laufende Nr.	Gegenstand 10915	Ankaufspreis Reichsmark	Anmerkung
1	1 golgravierte Herrenuhr Springdeck Schaffhausen Letetie	100.--	W
2	1 Weissgoldarmbanduhr mit Brillanten	35.--	W
3	1 Schnur Barockperlen 8 Gramm mit Silberschliesse	8.--	W
4	1 Rosennadel mit Brillanten 6 Gramm Gold und Silber	120.--	W
5	2 Ohrgehänge mit Brillanten 4 Gramm Gold und Weissgold u. Platin	140.--	W
6	1 Ring mit 2 Brillanten 2 Gramm Weissgold Japanperle gebrochen	15.--	W
7	1 Ring mit Brillanten 1 Smaragd 2 ½ Gramm Gold und Silber Smaragd gebrochen	30.--	W
8	1 Damennadel mit Brillanten und Rose 2 ½ Gramm Gold u. Silber	20.--	W
9	1 Ohrring mit 1 Raute 1 Gramm Gold und Silber	7.--	W
10	1 Armkette 1 Durchsugskette 1 lange Kette 45 Gramm Gold	70.--	B I
11	3 Leuchter 1 Tasse 1 Tempelgerät 2 Körbe 1 Aufsatzteil 1 Salzfass 1 Becher 2 gr. 1 kl. Schöpfer 2 Vorleger 9 gr. 11 kl. Löffel 23 Gabeln 6 Fischmesser 8.000 Gramm Silber 1 Aufsatzteil mit Silber und Gips 14 Messer 4 Gabeln mit Silberhaften ca 100 Gramm Silber	178.--	W

	Summe	723.--	
	abzüglich 10 %	72.30	
		650.70	

Document from the Dorotheum auction house in Vienna, converted to the Public Purchasing Institute after the Anschluss, showing a list of the family heirlooms that Abraham Hammersfeld was forced to surrender in order to leave the country. The first item is Abraham's prized Schaffhausen pocket watch, which the Nazis severely under-valued at 100 Reichsmarks.
Courtesy Austrian State Archives, Vienna

DP Bride-To-Be Of Canuck Saw Fiends Told Of Doom

Witnessed Nazi War Criminals Receive Death Sentences, on Pass British Gave Her

Renee Lang, 24, described today with obvious delight shining in her vividly beautiful face how she felt when she heard Nazi war criminals receive the death sentence at the Nurnberg trials.

"I had watched the same prison guard hang my best friend so you can imagine how I felt when I heard the sentence passed 'shall be hanged by the neck until dead'," she said.

"One of my most valued possessions today is the pass granted me by the British Military Government to attend the trials. I saw the Beast of Belsen and Irma Grese receive their sentences and I shall never forget it."

FIRST WORD OF DAD

Renee Lang was born in Vienna, moved to Budapest to escape the Nazis in 1939 and three years later, along with her mother, was sent to the concentration camp at Auschwitz. Her father, a Polish citizen was sent to Poland and thence to Siberia where he worked as a lumberjack until three months ago when his family received their first word of him.

Transportation between the various camps "was on our feet," said Renee. "We wore only the striped prison uniform and wooden shoes. It was January. Our beds were snow. Our food was snow. My mother and I lived for each other. We fought to be at the head of column, for those at the end were prodded on with guns. If any were tired and sat down, they were shot. Several camps were full and did not have room for us. We prayed that Ravensbruk would, because we were so tired and cold. We were happy when they took us in. Only about 20 per cent. lived through that march. Corpses were like flowers along the road."

Renee and her mother were liberated in 1945. For a while they lived in a displaced persons camp in the Russian zone but a U.S. soldier in a jeep drove them to the U.S. zone, telling the Russian guards he was going to marry Renee.

"I had never seen him before, have never seen him since. I do not even know his name," laughed Renee.

WAS INTERPRETER

Renee was hired as interpreter and worked for the British Military Government until she obtained her exit permit for Sweden. While still in the displaced persons camp she met her future husband, Charl Appel, of 591 College st. He was then LAC Appel RCAF.

Renee joined her mother in Sweden about four months ago and arrangements were made through New York relatives to come to Canada to marry Mr. Appel. She will be married Sept. 7, Toronto.

RENEE LANG
Telegram Photo

One of the Canadian newspaper stories written about Renée Lang, among the first survivors of Auschwitz to arrive in Toronto
Courtesy Renée Appel

Villa Charlotte, the Hammersfeld summer house in Voslau, Austria Courtesy Herbert Stilman

PUBLIC   PASS valid only for date of issue

Admit (name) ......Fräulein Lang......

to War Crimes Court LUNEBURG on ....

Signature of issuing officer ....

Bürgermeister

STAMP

Signature of Holder

This pass will be shewn with military or other identity
card, and is only valid on the date of issue.   18236   ✳

*Renée Lang's cherished pass to the War Crimes Court at Lüneburg,
Germany* Courtesy Renée Appel

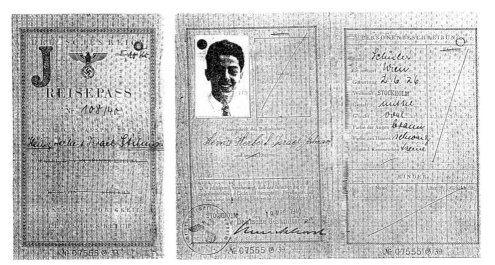

Passport issued to Herbert Stilman. The Nazis stamped a "J" on it and gave him the middle name "Israel" to identify him as a Jew. Courtesy Herbert Stilman

Senator Alfonse D'Amato sits with former Swiss bank guard Christoph Meili and his family—son David (two), daughter Miriam (four), and wife Giuseppina—before Meili testified before a Senate Judiciary Committee. Meili, who was fired for reporting the shredding of Holocaust-era documents at the Union Bank of Switzerland, told the lawmakers he was being threatened, harassed, and hounded at home, and feared for the safety of his wife and two children. He obtained refuge in the United States. Reuters/Mike Theiler/Archive Photos

World Jewish Congress President Edgar Bronfman (left) *waits to testify during House Banking Committee hearings on the disposition of assets deposited in Swiss banks by Nazi Holocaust victims. Bronfman questioned the role of the banks in the ongoing investigation, saying, "I am not totally convinced in my heart and soul that they are cooperating." Israel Singer, Secretary General of the World Jewish Congress, is pictured at right.*
Reuters/Mike Theiler/Archive Photos

Special Ambassador Thomas Borer, head of a Swiss Foreign Ministry task force handling the issues of Swiss purchase of Nazi gold during World War II and the dormant Holocaust accounts, testifies before the Senate Banking Committee hearings. In prepared testimony, Borer vigorously defended his country's response to the Nazi gold issue and said that Switzerland should not be treated as an international outcast.
Reuters/Mike Theiler/Archive Photos

As soon as its assets were unblocked in the United States, Switzerland threw up all sorts of problems over the accord's implementation, and took six years to comply with only some of its terms. With respect to the side-letter agreements on heirless assets, the Swiss would take another ten years to comply. As Stuart Eizenstat noted in his 1997 report,

American leadership at the time, while greater than that of our Allies, was limited. There was a demonstrable lack of senior-level support for a tough US negotiating position with the neutrals. Moreover, there was an even greater lack of attention to ensuring implementation of negotiated agreements. Because, for instance, the US government decided to unblock frozen Swiss assets in the US soon after the signing of the 1946 Accord, and, over the objection of the Treasury Department, decided not to pursue sanctions, most leverage was lost before Switzerland had met its obligations. Finally, neither the US nor the Allies pressed the neutral countries hard enough to fulfill their moral obligation to help Holocaust survivors by redistributing heirless assets for their benefit.[21]

Although the Swiss handed over $58 1 million worth of looted gold (about $566 million today) to the Allies after the signing of the accord in 1946, Swiss officials raised a fuss about some of the agreement's other key elements. For instance, they argued that they would not proceed with the liquidation of German assets until the Allies had established a fair Reichsmark–Swiss franc rate of exchange. The Swiss refused to make any payments to the IRO until a fair exchange rate could be reached. In 1948, the Swiss made a 20 million Swiss franc payment ($4.7 million then; about $41 million in 1997) to the IRO for the reconstruction of Europe.

The Swiss also raised concerns about the legal precedent of expropriating German assets in its own country, and insisted that the original owners' rights be protected through some form of compensation. But according to the Eizenstat report the U.S. State Department feared that paying compensation to German owners of liquidated assets in Switzerland would lead to pressure from many different German groups for compensation for other wartime losses and thus create a huge burden on West Germany's budget. After several failed attempts, the Allies finally agreed in the spring of 1951 to revise the Washington Accord, making West Germany an important negotiator. Switzerland and Germany entered into direct negotiations in order to determine Germany's wartime external debt to the Swiss. Meanwhile, an Allied-Swiss agreement was finally reached in August 1952, which called for a lump-sum payment of $121.5 million Swiss francs ($28 million then; $170 million in 1997) for liquidated German assets in Switzerland. Of course, this figure was far smaller than the one foreseen in the Washington Accord. This final lump-sum settlement was reduced by the amount of the 1948 payment that the Swiss had already made to the IRO, making the total 1952 payment, 101.5 million Swiss francs ($24 million then; about $214 million today). As part of the August 1952 German-Swiss accord, West Germany agreed to reimburse Switzerland for 121 million Swiss francs ($28 million then; $249 million in 1997), a figure that it had settled upon with the Allies for Germany's external debt to Switzerland. In order to pay back Switzerland, the Germans arranged financing through Swiss banks. The brutal irony did not escape Switzerland's critics. Nearly fifty years later, Eizenstat wrote that "thus over six years after the 1946 Washington Accord, this 1952 agreement was effectively paid for by Germany."[22]

Switzerland's total contribution to rebuild Europe amounted to a paltry $86 million, which comprised the $28 million payment and the $58.1 million worth of looted gold.

The latter payment was deposited by the Allies into a "gold pool," which had been established at the end of 1945 at the Paris Conference on Reparations, to be used for the restitution of German-occupied countries whose central banks had been looted by the Nazis. But like the Washington Accord, the issue of restitution in postwar Europe became so mired in geopolitical expediencies that in some cases it simply never took place.

The gold pool, which was created after rumors that American liberating troops were planning to keep the Nazi treasures they found as war booty, was to be supervised by a commission of the three Western occupying powers (Britain, the United States, and France) in Europe. Officials from these countries would evaluate claims from states that had had their federal treasuries expropriated by the Nazis. Claims were received from Belgium, the Netherlands, Luxembourg, Czechoslovakia, Poland, Austria, Yugoslavia, Italy, Albania, and Greece. The mandate of what became known as the Tripartite Commission for the Restitution of Monetary Gold, officially created on September 27, 1946, to implement Part III of the Final Act of the Paris Reparations, was to redistribute gold to claimant countries "in proportion of their losses." In June 1947, the commission issued a questionnaire to all members of the Inter-Allied Reparations Agency (IARA), Poland, and Italy, calling for a statement of wrongful removal of gold from their national treasuries during the war.

In addition to the $58.1 million worth of gold handed over by the Swiss as per the terms of the Washington Accord, the gold pool also included the gold and other valuables from the Reichsbank vaults that the Nazis had dumped at Merkers. According to one historian, the total amount of gold found at the salt mines near Merkers was worth $241,113,302 ($2.3 billion in 1997).[23] Finally, the Tripartite Commission's pool also included gold seized by the Allies at various Reichsbank branches in Germany. The total amount that the Tripartite Commission had at its disposal was worth close to $330 million (about $3.2 billion in 1997).

By the time the Tripartite Commission began to redistribute the looted gold in 1948, a good part of Europe was already behind the Iron Curtain. While the commission sought to reward countries such as Austria and Italy, which were important to the Western balance of power in Europe, they were quick to punish countries under the Soviet sphere of influence. Although Austria received all of its looted gold from the commission's gold pool, shipments to Poland, Czechoslovakia, and Albania, for example, were tied up in legal red tape for decades. Poland which quickly fell under Soviet influence after the war, did not receive its share of the gold pool until 1976, and the Czechoslovakian claim was postponed following the 1948 Communist coup in Prague. The Czech claim was not settled until 1981. Although distribution of Albania's share of the Tripartite Commission gold was supposed to occur in 1946, it was held up after Albania laid mines in the Corfu Channel, killing British seamen and destroying British ships. The United Kingdom, one of the controlling parties of the Tripartite Commission, refused to distribute the gold until Albania paid compensation to the British government. Albania did not receive its portion of the gold until October 1996, after the fall of communism in the country.

Switzerland wasn't the only neutral country that had done its business with the Nazis during the war and got off easy as a result of geopolitical realities. Portugal, which had accepted between 93 and 122 tons of gold from Nazi Germany during the war, about half of which is believed to have been looted from occupied countries, was eventually let off the hook by the Western Allies. After the war, American officials tried to pressure Portugal to surrender forty-four tons of gold to the gold pool by freezing its assets in the United States. But the fascist regime of Antonio Salazar did not give in to U.S. demands, declaring that Portugal was not aware that the gold that the Nazis traded for Portuguese textiles and wolfram had been looted. In 1953, the Allies gave up the pressure, largely because the Cold War was in full force and the Americans wanted to keep a strategic base in the Azores, off the coast of Portugal. After the war, Portugal began to secretly sell off the Nazi bullion to the Far East through its colonial enclave in Macao. A recent New York Times report suggests that "according to a government official who was himself involved in supervising numerous shipments, the China-bound gold was flown from Portugal to Macao, and from there moved across the Chinese border. The former official said some ingots sent to Macao were still embossed with the seal of the Dutch Treasury, which had been plundered by the Nazis; others were marked with swastikas. A number of bars were carried from Macao to the Philippines and Indonesia, strapped on people's bodies, the official said."[24]

In another postwar compromise that let the Swiss off easy, the Allies decided against dissolving the Bank for International Settlements (BIS) in Basel, even though it was well known in financial and diplomatic circles that the financial institution was responsible for helping the Nazis launder a significant amount of gold. Delegates to the 1944 Bretton Woods Monetary Conference had passed a resolution to dissolve the BIS, which had been dominated by Nazis on its board throughout the war. However, a postwar investigation of gold-washing activities through the bank was inconclusive because neither the BIS nor the Swiss National Bank would open their files for Allied perusal. Bank directors used stalling tactics to defer the publication of the banks' financial statements. To this day, many questions remain unanswered about the BIS's gold-laundering activities.

Although they had strong suspicions about the BIS's wartime activities, the victorious Allies decided to leave the bank intact, realizing that the institution, which had initially been set up to sort through complex reparations payments from the First World War, would be valuable to them as they tried to put war-torn Europe back on its feet. As one historian noted,

> the BIS was far too valuable an institution to dissolve amidst the great devastation of postwar Europe. It was soon evident that the prevailing opinion among Western Europe bankers—including the central banks—was that the BIS definitely served a purpose and should be continued as an institution. It represented a financial source that could complement the efforts of the International Monetary Fund and the International Bank for Reconstruction and Development; it had flexibility and experience, and its geographic location made it an ideal meeting place for Europe's banking community to exchange views and do business.[25]

By 1946, the BIS began to resume many of the transactions that had been suspended during the war, and its board of directors agreed to open negotiations on a settlement for the looted Nazi gold that had passed through the bank. However, because the evidence available at the time suggested that relatively little of the looted gold could actually be traced to the BIS, the bank was compelled to hand over only 3,740 kilograms of gold to the Allies.[26] By 1950, the United States had formally acknowledged that the Bretton Woods resolution calling for the dissolution of the bank was no longer valid.

Neither Thomas Harrington McKittrick, the American president of the BIS from 1940 to 1946, nor BIS Director and Reichsbank Vice President Emil Puhl were properly taken to task by Allied officials even though the two had colluded on Nazi gold laundering. McKittrick became a vice president of the Chase National Bank in New York. In 1950, he invited Emil Puhl to the United States as an honored guest. Puhl, who had cooperated with Allied officials at Nuremberg to give evidence against his old boss, Walther Funk, had been handed a rather light sentence of five years.

The headline of McKittrick's obituary, published on January 22, 1970, in *The New York Times,* refers to him respectfully as T. H. MCKITTRICK, WORLD FINANCIER. In addition to his educational and professional backgrounds, and his memberships in the American Ornithologists' Union, the American Club in London, and the American Geographical Society, the obituary mentions his six-year tenure at the BIS.[27] Of course, there is no reference to his dealings with high-level Nazi party financial officials or the BIS's role in laundering Nazi loot.

Similarly, other Nazis who played important roles in the shady financial transactions of the Third Reich were either acquitted by military courts or handed relatively short sentences. The Third Reich's financial wizard, Hjalmar Schacht, who was instrumental in setting up Hitler's secret war economy, was acquitted at Nuremberg in 1946. Although he was later sentenced to eight years in a labor camp by a court in Stuttgart, Schacht was eventually released. In 1950, he was acquitted of all charges connected with his involvement in the Third Reich, and even courted by the government of Juan

Domingo Perón to take up a financial advisory post in Argentina.[28] Schacht decided against the Argentine offer, but in the 1950s he launched a highly successful career as a financial adviser to developing countries, founding his own foreign trade bank in Dusseldorf in 1953.

Walther Funk, president of the Reichsbank and Hitler's minister of economic affairs, who had come to a secret agreement with the SS to launder valuables confiscated from Jews at concentration camps, was found guilty of war crimes, crimes against peace, and crimes against humanity, and sentenced to life in prison by the Nuremberg Tribunal on October 1, 1946. However, after serving a fraction of his sentence at Spandau prison, Funk was released in 1957 for health reasons. He died three years later at the age of sixty-nine.

Many other Nazis, including men who were directly responsible for the murder of millions of Jews, escaped prosecution right after the war. Aided by sympathetic officials of the Swiss International Committee of the Red Cross and by the Vatican, who provided them with passports and travel documents, several thousand Nazis found refuge in South America, particularly in Argentina. Hundreds of high-ranking Nazis, such as Josef Mengele, Adolf Eichmann, and SS officer Erich Priebke, all made their way to Argentina in the years immediately following the Second World War with the aid of either the Vatican or Swiss Red Cross officials.

Europe immediately following the war was racked by instability and chaos, where individual concerns for justice were often trampled under the intense power struggle between the Americans and the Soviets. For many survivors of the war, Europe was a cutthroat world dominated by black marketers who sought to make a profit on human misery. Many of the once grand European capitals had been decimated by bombs and reduced to piles of rubble, where refugees foraged for food and unscrupulous carpetbaggers and some soldiers carved out small black-market fortunes. In the postwar period, many European cities were reminiscent of Harry Lime's Vienna in the film *The Third Man*. In the film, written by Graham Greene and directed by Carol Reed, Harry Lime, an American hood who is running a profitable black-market business in diluted penicillin, captures the climate of Social Darwinism that pervaded postwar Europe when he says: "The world doesn't make any heroes. . . . Nobody thinks in terms of human beings. Governments don't, why should we? They talk about the people and the proletariat. I talk about the suckers and the mugs. It's the same thing. They have their five-year plans and so have I."

Given none of the recognition or preferential treatment granted to some former Nazis, collaborators, and governments, and scrambling for survival in DP camps and cities reduced to rubble, it's little wonder that many Holocaust survivors like Renée Lang wanted to leave Europe as quickly as possible. In their haste to escape the horrors of the war-ravaged Continent and rebuild their lives in the New World, it's not surprising that many of those who suspected or knew that their relatives had deposited money in Swiss banks did not rush to Switzerland to claim their legacy.

"I couldn't wait to get rid of Europe," says Renée. "I thought of nothing else. I wanted to get out of there as soon as possible."

Although she thought about making the trip to Switzerland to seek out her grandfather's account immediately following the war, she quickly abandoned the idea. She had other things on her mind, the most important of which was a twenty-four-year-old Canadian airman, Charles Appel.

Charlie, as he was known to his fellow recruits, was a handsome, good-natured Jew from Toronto who took it upon himself to help Holocaust survivors scattered in displaced persons camps throughout Germany. In the late spring of 1945, Charlie wandered the British occupied zone of Germany searching for concentration camp survivors. Charlie, whose parents were born in Poland but moved to Canada well before the Second World War, had become a one-man aid agency during the two years he was posted in Europe. In Eindhoven, Holland, where he was stationed in December 1944, Charlie even organized a Hanukkah party for the town's Jewish community. Later, he took it upon himself to help Jewish refugees communicate with relatives abroad by using his Allied armed-forces mail privileges, collecting letters from Jewish refugees and sending them off to their worried relatives. For many Jews, the communiqués sent through Charlie's good offices were the first bits of news that they had received about their loved ones since the beginning of the war.

When Charlie marched into the Bergen-Belsen concentration camp with his unit in the spring of 1945, what he saw changed his life. The mass open-pit graves, full of dirt- and blood-smeared emaciated cadavers, and the stick-figure people depicted in the black-and-white snapshots he took home to his family in Toronto, could never convey the horror of what the young Canadian soldier saw as he stood motionless in the middle of the camp on a cold day in 1945. "You wouldn't believe that human beings could have done that," he would later tell his family in Toronto. "You just wouldn't believe it."

As a result of his experience in Bergen-Belsen, Charlie intensified his search for Jewish victims, offering to do what he could to help them. That was when he met twenty-two-year-old Renée Lang at a displaced persons camp in Lüneburg, Germany. Despite her gaunt features, Renée, who had found a job as a translator for the British while she and her mother waited for an exit visa to Sweden, was the most beautiful woman he had ever seen.

Renée and her mother had been luckier than the vast majority of uprooted Jewish survivors. The biggest constraint for the Langs at the camp was having to share their room with four other women in the crowded barracks. At first, Renée wanted nothing to do with the fresh-faced, tousle-haired Canadian soldier. She seemed more interested in following the progress of the military tribunal set up at Lüneberg to try the Nazi war criminals responsible for the hanging of the brave Polish girl Roza Robota and the three other valiant women who had participated in the uprising at Auschwitz. Renée's pass to attend the trials remains one of her most treasured possessions, preserved in a photo album that contains a few keepsakes of the years immediately after the war. She also looked forward to seeing the trial of Reichsführer Heinrich Himmler, who was brought to Lüneburg after being captured by British troops. But the head of the Gestapo and

Waffen-SS, who was also one of the architects behind the mass murder of the Jews, swallowed a vial of poison concealed in his mouth before he could be brought to trial.

Somehow, when she wasn't attending the Nazi trials, Charlie managed to get Renée's attention long enough to ask her to marry him. On his daily visits to the camp, he eventually won her over. In lieu of flowers or chocolates, he presented her with more utilitarian gifts to woo her. He gave her an old uniform and a white silk parachute when they first started "walking out." Renée, who was longing for clothes after her ordeal at Auschwitz, found a seamstress at Lüneburg who converted the parachute and the uniform into two smart outfits.

"After that you could say I fell in love," she says.

In the spring of 1946, Renée and her mother had obtained their Swedish visas and left for Stockholm while Charlie made his way to Toronto, where he established a fur business with his brother Israel. Although Renée and Charlie planned to marry, Renée, who was still considered a stateless person, needed a Canadian immigration visa to travel to Toronto. The plan was that she would wait in Stockholm until Charlie could arrange for her visa. An old family contact named Marcus Kaplan, who had helped the Stilmans settle in Stockholm before their departure for the United States, helped Renée and her mother obtain jobs doing piecework at his men's suit factory.

While in Stockholm, Selma wrote the Viennese Jewish community center inquiring about her husband, Oskar. She heard nothing for almost a year until the spring of 1947 when a telegram arrived at her flat. Selma waited until her daughter returned from work at the factory before the two opened the telegram, which they both feared would only impart bad news. As she read the brief message that her husband had survived the war in a Siberian labor camp, tears of joy rolled down Selma's face. Two months later, a rake-thin Oskar Lang, who had registered with the Viennese Jewish community center upon his release from a Soviet prison camp, arrived in Stockholm.

"It was a very emotional meeting when my father arrived in Sweden," recalls Renée. "We cried and cried, and I think my father even cried to see us all alive. He started to tell us of the horrors he experienced at the labor camp, but when he heard what had happened to us at Auschwitz, he was flabbergasted. It was no picnic what he went through, but he told us it was like a resort compared to what we had experienced."

Oskar, who had joined the Polish Army in 1938 when he arrived in his native country, was lucky enough to have been in the Russian sphere of influence when the Germans marched into the country in September 1939. As a result, he spent the war years working as a lumberjack in a Siberian labor camp. Although rations were meager at best and he endured torturous cold and harsh working conditions, the labor camp was far better than what would have awaited him if he had been captured by the invading Nazis.

The Langs began putting their lives back together, ecstatic that they had all survived the war. The only permanent casualty was Renée's brother Siegfried, who had spent the entire war in a London psychiatric hospital following his nervous breakdown; he never fully recovered and would remain hospitalized for the rest of his life.

"We were free," says Renée. "We could do what we wanted. We appreciated little things so much. In Sweden, I enjoyed watching the lake and walking the streets, going to museums. I cannot describe to you what it meant to be free."

Although Renée and her mother were happily reunited with her father in Stockholm, there was still no word of her grandparents and uncles in Riga. The Langs made frantic requests to obtain information about their family from authorities in Riga immediately after the war, but their efforts were in vain.

HANS HAMMERSFELD LAY slumped on his hard wooden bunk in a Russian labor camp, struggling with a particularly difficult mathematical equation. Now a gangly, awkward teenager, he had immersed himself in math and physics problems to pass the long winter months. A fellow inmate had loaned him the textbooks, which he had found lying around the camp. Perhaps they had been salvaged from the belongings of a group of students who had perished of disease or malnutrition. Hans didn't wish to give their provenance much thought; he was simply content to sit quietly in the drafty barracks for hours at a time going over complicated equations.

As refugees from the German Reich, Hans and his family had been interned in a series of Russian labor camps, where the mattresses were made of straw and icicles hung from the showerheads. Since their daring escape from Mitau across the Russian border in 1941, they had had no communication with the outside world and didn't even know the war in Europe had come to an end.

For several months before they were interned, Hans, his uncle Harry, and Aunt Bronia had lived what seemed to the teenager an exciting adventure as they hitchhiked their way through the Russian countryside, sleeping in haylofts, hopping freight trains and even a barge on the Volga River. But the adventure came to an end when they were picked up by Soviet authorities and shut away in a series of internment camps for the duration of the war.

By sheer coincidence, Hans managed to be reunited with his parents at one of the labor camps. Hans's mother, Edith, who had been stuck in Riga with Adolf when war broke out between the Germans and the Soviets, was so overwhelmed to see her young son alive that she fainted on the spot. Ever since that happy meeting across a barbed-wire fence in a dust-blown internment camp, the family was inseparable except for Aunt Bronia, who died of starvation during the family's first incarceration. In her selfless concern for her husband, who was suffering from typhoid fever at the time, Bronia gave most of her food rations to Harry to ensure that he survived.

In the spring of 1947, two years after the end of the war, the remaining Hammersfelds were released by the Soviets and made their way back to Vienna, a journey that took them fifty-six days by ramshackle train. When Renée received the news of their survival a few weeks before she left Sweden, she sent a telegram to her aunt Paula and uncle George Stilman in New York. Paula opened the RCA radiogram, which arrived at her dry-goods store on Second Avenue in April 1947, with trembling fingers. After years of aching worry about her family in Europe, Paula dreaded the arrival of the telegram that she was sure would bring her only bad news. Bracing herself for the worst, she carefully opened it. Tears of joy and relief rolled down her face as she read and reread the brief message: JUST RECEIVED CABLE FROM VIENNA . . . HARRY DOLFI EDITH HANSI BACK FROM RUSSIA HAPPY RENEE LANG.

On the way back to Vienna, Harry Hammersfeld feared the worst about his parents in Mitau. Nobody could tell him anything conclusive. One person said a neighbor had seen the two elderly Hammersfelds dragged from their flat by an angry mob, who led them at gunpoint to a forest on the edge of town. According to the neighbor, they were forced to dig their own graves before they were shot dead. Another neighbor said the elderly Hammersfelds were herded into a truck and driven to a concentration camp, where they died of starvation and exposure. At the National Archives of Latvia in Riga, the last entry in the Hammersfeld file reads: "We can provide no information regarding the Hammersfeld family . . . or their demise in . . . 1941 since none exists in the fragmentary documentation that survives from the German occupation."[29]

Harry was devastated. Of all the Hammersfeld children, he was probably the closest to his parents. He strained to recall the last painful memories of his mother and father, alone and helpless in the Mitau flat. How had they looked during that last embrace? What had they said to him?

That was when he remembered something about a bank account in Switzerland. But what bank? Who was it that he had to contact? Hadn't his father given him a number? A code? After the trauma of losing his wife and his six years in an internment camp, Harry was at a loss to remember such business-related details.

There was nothing left to do for his parents except to say *Kaddish*, the Hebrew prayer for the dead, at his father's tiny old synagogue in Vienna's Second District. Harry then made his way to the Palace of Justice. A businessman well versed in legal procedures, he knew that if he was to recover the last vestige of his father's legacy, which might be locked away in a Swiss bank vault, he would first have to declare his parents officially dead, and name himself and his surviving brothers and sisters as the legal heirs. In a small office in a corner of the imposing Justizpalast, Harry Hammersfeld took a deep breath and dictated the few painful facts he knew to a bored Austrian bureaucrat who laboriously typed everything onto a sheet of paper, backed by a carbon:

> I, Harry Hammersfeld, fled with my parents from Austria to Riga in 1939 and lived there myself. In 1941 my parents moved to Mitau, 27 kilometers from the border, where I left them. . . . At the outbreak of the German/Russian war I fled to Russia but couldn't take my parents with me. They fell like many other emigrants into German hands, and very probably were sent into a concentration camp. Reports mention 50,000 persons were liquidated in September 1941 from this area, and my parents were surely among them. I returned in 1947, and if my parents were alive, they would have given some sign. I ask to have Abraham Hammersfeld declared legally dead.[30]

Abraham Hammersfeld, patriarch, businessman, scholar, and Jew, was declared officially dead. In a few short years the Nazis had managed to expropriate his home, his possessions, his business, his very life. As if to make matters worse, the Austrian bureaucrat, wearily typing the death certificate, even managed to expropriate Abraham Hammersfeld's identity. He spelled his name wrong. And from that day forward, the Hammersfeld family name officially lost an "m."

BY THE SUMMER of 1947, a few months after her father had arrived in Sweden, Renée had obtained her Canadian visa and crossed the Atlantic on the maiden voyage of the *Queen Mary*. As the boat docked in New York Harbor on August 5, 1947, a nervous Renée stood on deck, straining to catch a glimpse of her handsome fiancé, who had made the trip from Toronto to meet her. Renée stayed in New York with her aunt Paula and uncle George, who were so glad to see her that they threw the young couple a big party.

"Everybody wanted to talk to Renée," recalls her cousin Herbie, a kindly, white-haired patriarch. "Everybody crowded around her at the party, and wanted to know how she had made it out of the concentration camp alive."

When Charlie and his bride-to-be flew into Toronto a few days later, they were met at the airport by a local reporter, eager to write about one of the first Holocaust survivors to arrive in Canada. Renée became something of a media celebrity. The *Toronto Telegram* printed two stories about the arrival of the beautiful young concentration camp survivor under the sensationalist headlines DP BRIDE-TO-BE OF CANUCK SAW FIENDS, TOLD OF DOOM and TORTURE CAMP HOPE SOON TRUE FOR GIRL.

Renée told the newspapers that she was happy to be alive, and throughout the rest of her life she would remind herself every now and again that it was "plain luck" that had allowed her to survive her ordeal at Auschwitz. "You know there were better ones than me who did not survive," she said. "Our survival was based on pure luck. Maybe Mengele had a good breakfast and a good night's sleep the day he decided about my mother and me. Do I know why we should have been allowed to survive while others died? It was luck, nothing else."

On September 7, 1947, Renée and Charlie were married at the Ostrovtzer Synagogue on Cecil Street in Toronto After a honeymoon in Niagara Falls, Renée began to settle down to a quiet life in Toronto. The newlyweds moved in with Charlie's parents on College Street in the heart of Toronto's old Jewish enclave. Renée apprenticed as a dental hygienist and arranged for her parents to move to Toronto. She vowed never to return to Austria or revisit the horrors of the past.

"I promised myself that I would never forgive them [the Germans] for what they did to my youth. . . . I had my life ahead of me and I wanted no more of the terrible past."

Although her past was always with her, and she had only to glance at the number tattooed on her left forearm to remember the horrors that had robbed her of her privileged youth and her grandparents, Renée preferred to remember the happy times in Vienna, the long Sunday afternoons at the Café Sweden, and the family vacations in Voslau. In her dark moments, however, she couldn't help but wonder, just how did her grandparents die? Were they dragged out of a tiny flat by an angry mob in faraway Mitau? Were they forced to strip and stand shivering, waiting for death? Were they forced to dig their own graves? What did they think about before they died?

In New York, when Renée returned, Aunt Paula had pulled out the last letter she had received from her father, and she cried as she silently read again of his helplessness in his last days in Mitau. Although Paula and George were overjoyed by the news that Harry, Adolf, Edith, and Hans had survived the war, they would now have to sit *shiva* (the traditional Jewish mourning period) for Abraham, Lotte, and Harry's wife, Bronia. On the day they received the news of the Hammersfelds' return to Vienna, the Stilmans closed their dry-goods store early and headed home to prepare a package to send to them. Paula gathered up all of her son Herbie's old clothes and packed them in a cardboard box along with canned goods and other essentials. George removed a crisp $50 bill from his wallet, carefully flattened it out on the kitchen table, and wrapped it in cellophane. He then emptied a can of cocoa into a bowl, put the cellophane-wrapped money in the tin, and replaced the chocolate powder and the lid.

"It was a lot of money back then," says Herbie, who by then had returned from his tour of duty in Italy and Egypt, and had fallen head over heels in love with Brigitte Schenkein, a German-Jewish girl he recently met in New York on a blind date. In Italy, Herbie had worked as a hospital-tent repairman; in North Africa, he acted as a translator for German prisoners of war. "But we knew that conditions in Vienna were terrible, and that they had no money. They arrived in Vienna on a cattle train from Russia, so you can imagine what kind of state they were in."

As it was for so many other Jews who returned to Vienna after the war, life was a struggle for the Hammersfelds. Destitute following their internment, they relied on the soup kitchen of the *Kultusgemeinde* (Jewish community center), at Schottenring, 25. According to newspaper reports, Austria's food shortages were the worst in postwar Europe. "Vienna is the worst spot in Austria and the kernel of the problem," said John Wraight, an official with the United Nations Relief and Rehabilitation Administration on a relief mission to Vienna in June 1946. "Austria is at least as badly off as or worse than Germany."[31] The situation was exacerbated in the year after the war when the country's population swelled with some 300,000 foreigners living inside or outside displaced persons' camps.

Everywhere they went in the city, Jews were confronted with the bitter memories of the Anschluss, the expropriations, the loss of family members. "Wherever I go, I feel the shrouds of the dead beating the air around me," observed writer Friedrich Torberg.[32] Many survivors who had been relatively healthy during their incarceration began to develop physical problems when they returned to Vienna. Only five thousand Jews returned to Vienna after the war. Many of them died, or left the city almost as soon as they had arrived.

"We seemed to live in a state of limbo and what I remember best about these days is waiting," recalled one survivor. "Everyone hoped this one or that one would come back. Arthur Hochermann, who had fled to France and had survived Auschwitz, came back and was overjoyed when told his wife was on the way. Then, when it became clear that she had died at just about the time when he had entered Vienna, he broke down. He died a short time afterward."[33]

There was little anyone could do to seek compensation or restitution. Vienna, which had been divided into Allied and Soviet spheres of influence after the Potsdam Conference in 1945, was emerging as a Cold War battleground. Frequent skirmishes broke out among Russian, French, and British soldiers. Returning Jews often got caught in the crossfire. Oscar Wilheim was one such Jew. The administrator of Jewish-owned properties awaiting restitution, Wilheim informed the Austrian government and foreign press that he had been ordered by Soviet authorities to liquidate the so-called Austrian Settlement Company, of which he was the government-appointed administrator. But he announced that he was refusing to do so, and began to denounce the wholesale Soviet seizures of Jewish land holdings in the Soviet occupation zone.

The Austrian Settlement Company had taken over the holdings of the German Settlement Company, created by the Germans as a holding company for properties seized from Jews. According to a report in *The New York Times*, "The Russians proceeded to take a great part of these holdings on the basis that they had been German properties and were now Russian. The settlement company's records showed that the Russians had seized about twenty-five of the larger Jewish land holdings, totaling around 17,000 hectares."[34] Despite protests from Austrian Chancellor Leopold Figl, Wilheim, sixty, was arrested and sentenced to two years of hard labor in Siberia for disobeying the Soviet command's order.

Fellow Austrians also made it difficult for returning Austrian Jews to seek restitution. "It was devastating to go back," says historian Gertrude Schneider, who returned to Vienna in June 1945 with her mother and sister after their liberation from a concentration camp. "We found the city in rubble, and as Jews we were treated like dirt. When we went back to our old neighborhood, people seemed angry with us. They just looked at us and said, 'Ah, yes, we knew you'd come back. You people always come back.' "

The department store that Gertrude Schneider's father, Pinkas Hirschhorn, had owned in the Fourteenth District had been reduced to rubble by an Allied bomb, and the family flat had been taken over by neighbors. The family eventually forced its way into another flat, which had belonged to a cousin, only to find that it had been taken over by their cousin's maid, who had denounced her former employer as a Jew to the Nazis. As a result, the cousin was sent to a concentration camp and was never heard from again. In order to secure her right to the flat, the maid employed the help of her son, a former Nazi official who was working for the American Zone command. The Americans, who were using former Nazis against the Soviets in Vienna, were quick to side with the maid and ordered Schneider's

family out of the flat. However, in a daring feat of Cold War diplomacy. Schneider's mother managed to get a Russian-Jewish official
onside. The Americans, who did not want to provoke a problem with
the Russian Zone commanders, eventually allowed Gertrude Schneider's family to stay in the flat.

"Those who robbed the Jews and harmed them in a variety of ways
during 1938, and later, pretended to have been the most righteous
all along and were absolutely unwilling to part with their ill-gotten
assets," wrote Gertrude Schneider.[35]

In the postwar period, Austrians seemed to suffer from a collective
amnesia about their willing role in the Anschluss and in the humiliation and deportation of Jews to Nazi death camps. Many of them
seemed to forget how tens of thousands of their non-Jewish compatriots had crowded outside the Hofburg on Tuesday, March 15,
1938, to welcome Hitler after his triumphant march into Vienna.
They also apparently forgot how many ordinary Austrians had willingly participated in the robbery and denunciation of Jews after the
Anschluss and during Kristallnacht. Indeed, according to Simon Wiesenthal, Austrians comprised one third of all personnel who carried
out the Final Solution.

For years, however, Austrian politicians denied all responsibility
for their involvement in Nazi crimes. "Austrians considered themselves the first victims of Nazism and as such they felt they shouldn't
have to pay any restitution or offer any kind of help to the Jewish
victims," says Austrian historian Brigitte Bailer, noting that the victimization theme was further emphasized at the Potsdam Conference
in 1945. For geopolitical expediency and to keep Austria onside in
the emerging Cold War, victorious Allied leaders absolved Austria of
any responsibility to pay reparations, and chose to consider Austria
as Nazism's first victim.

The result was that anti-Semitism permeated official policy regarding restitution to returning Austrian Jews. For instance, former
political prisoners who had spent the war years in Nazi concentration
camps could register at City Hall, where they were able to obtain
apartments, clothing, and food directly from the city of Vienna. Jews,

on the other hand, registered at the Kultusgemeinde, which received most of its funding from Jews abroad and had no power to help local Jews retrieve apartments or other possessions that had been confiscated by the Nazis or by their own neighbors. Similarly, when the Jews wanted to join the newly created *K. Z. Verband* (concentration camp organization), which was linked to the government, the political prisoners refused to accept them, wrote Schneider, adding that "it is perhaps because of these occurrences, that many Jews, born and bred in Austria, realized that there was no future for them in that country and emigrated, leaving the field to the political concentration camp survivors, who may have been anti-Nazi, but were also anti-Semites."[36]

To make matters worse, many Austrian politicians were extremely duplicitous in their public efforts to offer restitution and compensation to Jews. According to Gertrude Schneider:

While members of the government were ostensibly friendly to Jewish concentration camp survivors, with some of them having spent time in camps themselves, the reality was quite different. The British historian Robert Knight unearthed records at the Vienna State Archives dated 1945 to 1952 that show a very ugly picture. Perusing those records, it becomes frighteningly clear how differently the members of Parliament expressed themselves when they were among themselves compared with what they said in public. State Chancellor Karl Renner, the later president of Austria, for instance, found it impossible for the country "to be responsible for whatever was owned by those Jews who had been no more than small tradesmen and peddlers," and Austrian Chancellor Leopold Figl, in a discussion about restitution, said, "All those Jews would like to get rich quickly," and then energetically denied, when confronted by Austrian Jews living in the United States and England, that anyone in his government was anti-Semitic. In this obvious untruth, Figl was seconded by the Viennese Mayor Theodor Koerner, who called the Austrians "too cosmopolitan to be prejudiced against Jews."[37]

Austrian Jews did finally receive some token restitution and compensation for their suffering when the government recently paid out $7,000 to any former Austrian persecuted by the Nazis, but for many this was too little, too late. As for reclaiming their expropriated property, the process was equally agonizing. Gertrude Schneider says it took her mother twenty years to get restitution for the family business and for their apartment.

The Hammersfelds, who made their way back to Vienna following their internment in Siberia, were luckier than most Jews in their position. Despite their years of hard labor in a Siberian work camp, Harry, Adolf, Edith, and Hans were in relatively good health and eager to rebuild their lives in the city. For the first few years after their return, it seemed that things were going well. Hans, who in 1947 would be celebrating his seventeenth birthday, was looking forward to going back to school, and despite his spotty education over the years, was soon able to enroll at university to study engineering. Harry, whose round black-framed spectacles and earnest good looks made him look a lot like a middle-aged Harold Lloyd, soon remarried and tried to reactivate his old textile connections in Europe.

Adolf even managed to get back his dry-goods store. Hans Allnoch, the well-connected Nazi merchant who had expropriated the store in 1938, had disappeared after the war, abandoning all of his ill-gotten holdings. Adolf reopened the store and even rehired his trusted employee Aloisia Celnar, now Greisinger, to work for him. Following the Allnoch expropriation in 1938, her husband, Johann, had found a job as a tram operator.

Although the Hammersfelds seemed to have luck on their side in Austria, they had none in Switzerland. Armed with Abraham's official death certificate and proof of their status as his legitimate heirs, the Hammersfeld brothers got nowhere when they approached Swiss diplomats in Vienna with their claim in the years immediately following the war. Swiss bureaucracy was simply too daunting, and they had other, more pressing matters to attend to.

. . .

MANY OF THE problems that stood in the way of Jewish restitution in Austria were repeated in Switzerland in the years after the war.

On April 20, 1947, Frances Greenfield, an American citizen, wrote the following letter to the U.S. Department of State from her home on University Avenue in the Bronx:

> I am looking for information concerning the location of bank accounts of my deceased sister. I know that she had her money in the National Bank in Zuerich [sic], Switzerland, and she changed banks at the outbreak of hostilities in Europe. I do not know to which bank she transferred. My sister's name was Gisella Tuttmann, born in Vienna, February 14, 1898. My brother-in-law's name was Salo (Zalo) Tuttmann, born in Czernowitz, birth date unknown. My niece's name was Hertha Tuttmann, born in Vienna, August 29, 1928. The account may be deposited under any of these names. The last known address was in Vienna II, Untere Augartenstrasse, 4, previous to their removal to a final concentration camp.[38]

On June 25, a State Department official forwarded Greenfield's letter to the officer in charge of the American legation in the Swiss capital, Bern. By mid-July, the legation's commercial attaché had sent off a formal inquiry about Greenfield's assets to Switzerland's Federal Political Department. On August 6, a bureaucrat working for the Swiss department's Division of Foreign Affairs, responded in a letter, written in French, that his department could not find an account of Greenfield's description in a Swiss bank. But the response appears not to have been good enough for the Americans, who called the Swiss ministry and politely yet firmly requested them to do another search.

The phone call seems to have paid off because five days later a ministry official wrote to the American legation, noting "that there is evidence of certain assets in Switzerland but if Mrs. Greenfield desires to obtain detailed information she will be obliged to supply proof of the decease of the person or persons in whose names the account or accounts are recorded, as well as documentation that Mrs. Greenfield is either the sole heir or represents the heirs of the deceased."[39]

In a memorandum from the American legation in Bern to the secretary of state in Washington, an official named Harrison expressed some surprise at the Swiss response when he noted that "Swiss banking secrecy laws prohibit supplying information concerning bank deposits in Switzerland unless the inquirer can prove his or her right to such information."[40]

In other words, the same secrecy laws that had made it so attractive for European Jews escaping Nazi persecution to deposit their assets in Swiss banks were now making it difficult for legitimate heirs, like Greenfield, even to inquire about dormant accounts. This was further complicated by the fact that many Jews who had perished in the Holocaust had entrusted their assets to reliable third parties— lawyers like Veit Wyler—whose identities were not necessarily known to their heirs.

The situation was tainted with a cruel irony for the Holocaust survivors and their families who wrote letters to Swiss banks, or in some cases even made their way to Switzerland after the war to search for their deceased families' assets. For in every instance they were confronted with a coldly efficient Swiss bureaucrat or banker who was under a strict legal obligation not to reveal any kind of account information as stipulated by the 1934 banking secrecy law. In order even to begin the search for a dormant account, the potential heir would have to supply, among other things, a legal death certificate that clearly showed that an account holder had died. In the chaos that was postwar Europe, where the victorious Allied powers tried to rebuild shattered countries and repatriate millions of displaced persons, a death certificate for a family member who perished in a concentration camp was not an easy document to obtain. For, as many Holocaust survivors were quick to point out, officials at camps like Auschwitz and Treblinka did not issue death certificates; nor did the members of the deadly Einsatzgruppen after one of their killing sprees.

Frances Greenfield's predicament was typical of individual heirs whose claims in the years immediately following the war were first mired in Swiss bureaucracy and then lost in the geopolitical compromises characteristic of a deeply divided and bipolar world. It is not known whether Greenfield continued to press her claim with the Swiss, or whether, like many other heirs, she just gave up when confronted with the country's crushing bureaucracy.

Although international Jewish organizations clamored for restitution of confiscated Jewish property, indemnification for survivors who had suffered damage or injury, and reparations for the rehabilitation of the displaced, they initially focused their efforts on Germany. They seemed to have their work cut out for them because, initially at least, restitution legislation benefited only a small number of Jews. According to Raul Hilberg,

> the restitution laws had been designed for the upper middle class; they covered the kind of property that was substantial enough to be preserved in identifiable form. For those who had never possessed such assets, there was as yet no remedy. The masses of the poorer Jews who had lost their relatives, their health, their liberty, and their economic prospects could not make use of restitution laws. These Jews could be served only by a money grant, and such payment had to be obtained out of the public funds of the country that was responsible for the misery: Germany. This was a much tougher proposition.[41]

In addition to lobbying for broader compensation and restitution legislation from Germany, Jewish organizations were paying attention to other issues, such as the trials of high-ranking Nazi war criminals at Nuremberg in 1945 and 1946, and the establishment of the State of Israel in 1948. In the chaotic postwar era, few people lobbied for the opening of dormant Swiss accounts belonging to Jews who had perished in the Holocaust.

"Our first priority was to deal with the hundreds of thousands of displaced persons in the concentration camps, and then to fight for the State of Israel," says Gerhart Riegner, honorary vice president of the World Jewish Congress, who served as the organization's secretary general during and after the war. "Then we fought for reparations from Germany and then we looked to restitution in the Eastern countries. There were always other priorities that took a long time to overcome."

Moreover, the Cold War became the biggest barrier to seeking justice, especially in the case of Swiss banks. As one historian pointed out, "The postwar situation confronting the Jews was far from ordinary. They were in the midst of a cold war, and neither side was dependent on their support."[42]

By 1952, Swiss bankers and the Swiss government thought they had long since dealt with the issue of restitution once and for all when they fulfilled their obligations under the Washington Accord. In a 1946 letter to Walter Stucki, head of the Swiss negotiating team on the Washington Accord, Randolph Paul, special assistant to President Truman, emphasized that "the property within Switzerland of victims of Nazi action who have since died and left no heirs are put at the sole disposal of the Allied Governments for purposes of relief."[43] Through the Swiss Clearing Agency, set up after the war to distribute German assets, some 6.5 million Swiss francs ($1.5 million in the postwar period; about $13 million today) were identified as belonging to people persecuted by the Nazi regime, and were returned to the appropriate beneficiaries. However, this amount did not include the 4 billion Swiss francs ($930 million in the postwar period; about $8.2 billion in 1997) worth of Swiss assets frozen in the United States during the war. Members of the Swiss Bankers Association claim it was impossible, in the postwar period, to identify how much of that money had actually belonged to Holocaust victims.

In 1954, the Israeli government intensified pressure on the Swiss government to deal with the dormant accounts of Jewish depositors who had perished in Nazi concentration camps. Israeli government officials presented a diplomatic note, based on Article 8 of the Paris Reparations Conference of December 1945, which stated that neutral governments had "to make available whatever assets they had of Nazi victims who had died and left no heirs." It was only in the early 1960s, following lengthy negotiations with Jewish organizations and banks, that Swiss legislators passed a law that allowed bankers to lift the sacred veil of bank secrecy. The new law allowed banking secrecy to be broken in order to identify unclaimed funds held by Swiss banks for foreigners "persecuted for racial, religious or political reasons." The law also imposed criminal penalties for noncompliance with its provisions.

When the legislation was finally passed in 1962, the Swiss government issued an international appeal for Holocaust victims and their families to make claims if they believed they had money in Swiss banks before the war. The law set up a registration office inside the justice ministry and ordered all banks, insurance companies, lawyers, trustees, and others to report and hand over all heirless and dormant accounts within six months. Claimants had until 1973 to make claims. The government received more than seven thousand responses. However, by the end of the six-month period, only 961 dormant accounts were identified as belonging to victims of Nazi persecution. Under Swiss banking practice, there are no time limits on dormant accounts. Unlike in the United States, where assets in dormant accounts revert to the banks after a period of time, dormant accounts in Switzerland are allowed to remain virtually untouched. Furthermore, when an account is finally closed by the account holder, banking officials are required to hold on to account records for a period of ten years.

The accounts identified under the 1962 law totaled approximately 9.5 million Swiss francs, or $8.3 million. Three quarters of the amount was returned to its rightful owners, and the rest was split between the Organization of Swiss Jewish Communities and the Swiss Refugee Aid Society.

Critics say that the 1962 legislation was flawed. Not only was there no outside accountability for the banks, but it was not always possible for a banker to ascertain from an account holder's name whether or not the person was a Jew. And no additional searches were undertaken to look behind the numbered accounts, or to seek the help of third parties who might have been able to assist in identifying the account holders. Safe deposit boxes, where Nazi victims might have deposited wills, deeds to property, jewelry or patents, were not included in the search. In essence, critics say that the search entailed little more than the checking of surnames. The registration office set up to deal with the heirless accounts never produced a final report.

"The searches were not done well," says Beat Brenner, financial editor of the *Neue Zürcher Zeitung,* Switzerland's leading business newspaper. "It was an impossible search because it was done by types of refugees. Banks had to look for foreigners who were victims of religious or political persecution. So if you are a Swiss victim or a homosexual victim of Nazism, a banker couldn't look for your account."

Swiss historian Jacques Picard agrees, adding that in 1962 a respected international law professor named Paul Guggenheim, who was a legal consultant to a variety of Jewish groups, suggested that legislators should appoint a mixed commission of experts and Swiss officials to oversee the process of searching for dormant accounts. "If they had followed Guggenheim's proposal, we wouldn't be dealing with this issue now," says Picard.

Paul Guggenheim's son Daniel, himself an international banking lawyer, believes that the 1962 law was probably doomed from its inception. "The thing is that in these days [the 1960s] banking secrecy was like a religion practiced not only by bankers but also by the legal profession, which even more vehemently opposed this legislation. The weakness of the 1962 law was probably that the banks themselves had to make a declaration without any possibility for an impartial body to check them. [The law] it is true, foresaw criminal sanctions but it had, I suspect, little practical effect."

In fact, recent evidence suggests that only twenty-six out of a total of five hundred banks responded to the search for dormant accounts in 1962. "This raises questions of how assiduous everybody was in responding and how much follow-up there was," says Paul Volcker, former chairman of the U.S. Federal Reserve Board and coordinator of an audit on how Swiss banks are conducting current searches for dormant accounts. He notes as well that the lack of response by many banks in 1962 also raised the issue of how questionnaires were formulated.[44]

For its part, the Swiss Bankers Association (SBA) has noted that the banks had followed the legislation "diligently" and with "due care" in 1962, and that one of Switzerland's largest banks had even employed two rabbis to go over the accounts and deposits. Although the SBA admitted that the amount of the assets found seemed "paltry" by today's standards, it pointed out that the amount was "in line with the then estimates of the Swiss Jewish Society, which, in 1947, had spoken of unclaimed assets 'worth only a few million francs.' "[45] Although it was within the purview of the law to search for Eastern European claims, many bankers did not want to risk the money passing to Communist regimes rather than to the legitimate heirs.

After the ten-year search that began in 1962, Swiss bankers considered the issue of Jewish dormant accounts dead and buried, even though many Holocaust survivors and their heirs continued to search for their assets. At the height of the Cold War, business was brisk for Swiss bankers, and they were busy with a host of new foreign account holders, which included everyone from industrialists to corrupt Third World dictators, spies, tax evaders, drug traffickers, and money launderers. In fact, business was so good that few in the banking community paid much attention to the gathering storm of Jewish anger over the dormant Holocaust accounts. So when the storm finally hit in 1995, the Swiss were caught completely off guard.

FOUR

REOPENING
THE FILE

I n the 1960s, thoroughly settled into her new life in Canada, Renée spent no time dwelling on the past and had little desire to make the trek from bank to bank in Switzerland to search for her grandfather's account.

But she could never leave the past too far behind her. In 1950, she gave birth to a baby girl whom she named Charlotte in memory of her grandmother. Six years later she had a son, whom she named Aubrey after her beloved grandfather, Abraham. In the same year, 1956, Renée and Charlie moved into the comfortable suburban bungalow—with its two-car garage, immaculately trimmed hedges, and lush backyard—that they still inhabit. Just before the birth of her first child, Renée quit her job as a dental hygienist and devoted herself entirely to caring for her family.

In the early 1950s, she sponsored Uncle Adolf, Aunt Edith, and Hans, who had had enough of Vienna and were eager to begin new lives in Canada. Renée's parents also came to Canada from Stockholm. Oskar and Selma Lang soon began managing a neighborhood convenience store in downtown Toronto, a job they shared until Oskar's death in 1973 at the age of eighty-two. Selma, who was several years younger than her husband, died eighteen years later.

"They worked every day from seven in the morning until midnight," recalls Renée. "They were so happy to be in Canada, happy to be alive and happy to be able to work hard."

Uncle Harry, his new wife, Paula, and his two young daughters, Lotte (also named in honor of the elder Mrs. Hammersfeld) and Anita, also tried to make a go of life in Canada in the 1950s, but they missed their native Vienna, where Harry had managed to start up a successful textile firm after the war, and so they returned to Austria. Still, they visited Toronto frequently, and the occasions were always used as excuses to throw big family reunions. On a visit to the city in the summer of 1963, the happy-go-lucky Harry, who was then fifty-eight, surprised his favorite niece, Renée, with an expensive gold bracelet.

"Uncle Harry just showed up one day with this beautiful bracelet and gave it to me," she recalls, adding that he also bought her daughter Charlotte, a young teenager at the time, her first pair of high-heeled shoes. "He was always so good-hearted and so spontaneous. I remember when I was a teenager I once said I admired a diamond ring he wore on his little finger, and you know, he took off that ring and gave it to me on the spot."

But on that trip to Canada in 1963, Harry Hamersfeld suffered a fatal heart attack in his hotel room. "It was one of the saddest days of my life," says his tall, soft-spoken nephew Hans, who, like Renée, thought of Harry as more of a second father than an uncle. "I was very close to Uncle Harry. He had been like a father to me when we were in Siberia."

Indeed, it was as if their last link to Europe had been permanently severed. After Uncle Harry's death, few of the Hammersfelds, now mostly living in Toronto and New York, had any desire to go back to Vienna. Although Renée traveled every year to England to visit her brother Siegfried, who was still institutionalized, she could not face going back to Austria. For the first time in her life, Renée was a full-fledged citizen, and could travel anywhere in the world on a passport. This was a new and exciting concept to a formerly stateless Jew who could not escape Austria after 1938 because she did not have the proper documentation.

"Charlie and I traveled a lot," says Renée, who goes to Israel at least once every two years to visit the women she and her mother shared their DP camp barracks with after their liberation from Auschwitz. The Appels also visit Siegfried every year in England. "It felt so good to have a passport, to be able to go from place to place as a citizen."

In addition to her excitement over her new Canadian citizenship, Renée rediscovered a spiritual dimension in her life. The girl who never really thought much about her Jewish heritage when she was growing up in Vienna before the Second World War became a committed religious Jew and a Zionist. When the new State of Israel was established in May 1948, Renée and Charlie were ecstatic, and attended local celebrations at Toronto's Maple Leaf Gardens. In the 1960s she met David Ben-Gurion, who headed the struggle for Jewish independence in Palestine and was Israel's first prime minister, at an official dinner to raise money for the young Israeli state in Toronto. "Charlie and I were sitting far away from Ben-Gurion's head table, but when he walked by our table on his way out, I stood up, pushed through his bodyguards, and grabbed his hand," says Renée. "I said 'Shalom, Ben-Gurion,' and he looked me in the eye and shook my hand. I walked back to the table and told Charlie I had just met the builder of Israel, and I would not wash my hand for a week."

In between her domestic duties, Renée campaigned passionately on behalf of Jewish charities. After the establishment of the State of Israel, Renée went door to door in her neighborhood selling Israel bonds. By selling individual bonds valued at $100, she soon sold over $100,000—no small feat in the space of a few years for a full-time mother and housewife.

"I called people on the phone, I walked through pouring rain, and bothered everyone I knew when I was selling Israel bonds," says Renée, who likes to show off the elegant Woman of Valor pin—one of Israel's highest awards—that she always wears on her lapel. "My strong Jewish identity came after the war, after what they did to me. It was the proudest moment of my life when they presented me with that pin, and that's why I wear it all of the time."

EDGAR BRONFMAN ALSO likes to show things off—like the lavish collection of artwork in his office. On the wall next to his desk hangs a tapestry by Joan Miró, behind his chair an oil by Jean-Paul Riopelle. There are sculptures, religious artifacts, and antique furniture tastefully arranged in the opulent fifth-floor Park Avenue office that used to belong to his father, the legendary liquor baron from Montreal, affectionately known as Mr. Sam.

His most prized possession—the one he delights in showing visitors—is a replica of the Torah that King David carried into battle. Edgar Bronfman's Torah is an exquisite illuminated scroll that sits under a Plexiglas case on a museum-style pedestal across from his desk. The Torah, a gift from Bronfman's friend, rabbi, and Jewish activist Israel Singer, is there for a purpose: to remind him of the wisdom of the ancient Jewish kings, who would march into battle carrying the sacred scroll containing the first books of the Bible and the law of the Jewish people that was handed down from God to Moses on Mount Sinai. According to tradition, before launching into battle the kings would hold up the Torah as a symbolic gesture to their enemies that they would allow them one last chance to appeal to reason and to that most sacred tenet of Judaism, the law.

"They always appealed to the rule of law first," says Bronfman, sixty-eight, a broad-shouldered, rather imposing Jewish leader in his own right. "And if their enemies chose to ignore it, well, then they fought like hell."

This is the philosophy that has guided Edgar Bronfman, who in his capacity as president of the World Jewish Congress has become a kind of modern-day monarch of world Jewry. And since taking over the leadership of the organization in 1981, some of the battles he has fought have been of biblical proportions—and none more so than his recent campaign against the Swiss banks. In the 1980s, Bronfman took on a superpower to fight for the rights of Jews to practice their religion in the atheistic Soviet Union or be free to leave the country, and he won, succeeding in getting many Jews to freedom. In 1986, he helped to expose former UN Secretary General Kurt Waldheim as a suspected Nazi war criminal whose German army intelligence unit had reportedly ordered the deportation of Greek Jews to Auschwitz during the war. The accusations were hurled against Waldheim during his successful run at the Austrian presidency in the spring of 1986. A year later, Waldheim became the first Austrian head of state to appear on the U.S. "Watch List" of suspected war criminals, and was barred from entering the United States after a lengthy Justice Department investigation, which cited evidence that "Kurt Waldheim assisted or otherwise participated in the persecution of persons because of race, religion, national origin, or political opinion."[1]

The incendiary accusations against Waldheim did not come without controversy. Waldheim threatened to sue Bronfman for defamation, and many European Jews, including prominent Nazi hunter Simon Wiesenthal, who lives in Austria, feared that Bronfman's actions would fuel anti-Semitism. But as Bronfman is quick to point out, "Jews don't create anti-Semitism, anti-Semites do." The Waldheim issue heightened the divisions between American and European Jews. On the whole, European Jews, who have suffered the worst anti-Semitism in the modern era, prefer a low-key, diplomatic approach to Jewish issues, rather than the aggressive, cowboy-style, in-your-face tactics often favored by their American counterparts.

"Many Jewish leaders believed this 'attack' [on Waldheim] would create bad will, and worse," wrote Bronfman in his 1996 memoir, *The Making of a Jew*. "I believed it was a moral imperative, and everywhere I went, the audiences I spoke to were 100 per cent behind me."[2]

In the campaigns to help Soviet Jews and to expose Waldheim, Bronfman, who has an estimated personal fortune of $3 billion and ready access to everyone from Bill Clinton to Fidel Castro and the Pope, says he first appealed to reason and the law. When that didn't work he didn't hesitate to fight "like hell" in his desire to obtain dignity and justice for the Jewish people.

Edgar Bronfman inherited his gruff, forthright manner, and philanthropic drive, from his father, a Russian-born Canadian distiller and a self-made man who built his fortune on liquor during Prohibition. Samuel Bronfman, a stocky, diminutive man who had a habit of using language that would "make a sailor blush,"[3] was a committed Zionist, president of the Canadian Jewish Congress, and a vice president of the World Jewish Congress. He was also a formidable businessman. Edgar Bronfman is chairman of the board of the Seagram Company Ltd., the business built by Sam Bronfman, which is today a $22 billion concern that has 80 percent control of Universal Studios Inc., in addition to Tropicana Dole Beverages, G. H. Mumm & Cie, Martell and Co., and 5.3 percent of Time-Warner. In true Bronfman dynastic tradition, Seagram is today controlled by Bronfman's son, forty-two-year-old Edgar junior.

Bronfman developed his philanthropic drive in middle age. As a teenager, he had rebelled against Judaism, and it wasn't until after his father's death in 1971 that he rediscovered his faith, and along with it a burning desire to help his fellow Jews around the world. The year of his father's death, Nahum Goldmann, one of the founders of the World Jewish Congress and himself a legendary figure, approached Bronfman to join the organization. Goldmann was best known as the postwar chair of the Conference on Jewish Material Claims Against Germany, which negotiated hundreds of millions of dollars in compensation and restitution for Jewish victims of Nazi aggression after the war. Goldmann, a committed Zionist, was born in Lithuania, but benefited from a high German education when his parents moved to Germany in 1897. As a European Jew, Goldmann was not always in agreement with the brash tactics of his American counterparts, but nevertheless he took Bronfman under his wing.

"[W]e differed in our approaches and in our backgrounds," wrote Bronfman in his memoirs. "He was a European Jew, born in the Pale of Settlement, and a little chary of brash American Jews. I am a transplanted Canadian, an American citizen, perceived to be a successful businessman, with all that implies. I live in New York City, where Jews are unbelievably secure, and am too young to have any real memories of the horrors of the Holocaust. "[4]

Bronfman flourished under the rather domineering tutelage of Goldmann. Today he is a respected philanthropist, holding several international distinctions. In 1986, he was named a Chevalier de la Légion d'Honneur in France, and holds several honorary degrees. In Argentina, an entire university arts faculty has been named in his honor.

At the beginning of his tenure at the World Jewish Congress (WJC), Bronfman joined forces with Israel Singer, an ordained rabbi and former political science professor from New York City, and the two set out to change the world—for Jews. Bronfman credits Singer, currently secretary general of the WJC and "one of the brightest . . . most hardworking, driven, and at the same time, nicest"[5] people he has met, with bringing him back to his Jewish roots by instructing him in the Torah and the Talmud. Today, Bronfman says he reads a portion of the Talmud daily and frequently calls up Singer when he has questions related to Jewish scripture.

"I've had a marvelous life because my grandparents came to North America from that part of the world [Russia], and so I had this great desire to pay back a little of what they gave me," says Bronfman, who estimates that he currently devotes 40 percent of his time to World Jewish Congress matters, regularly flying around the world on his private jet to do the organization's work. During his time as WJC president, Bronfman says he has already spent "in the seven figures" to bankroll the organization. In a recent mailing campaign to raise money for the organization, Bronfman personally pledged to match all contributions of up to $25,000.

Under his dynamic leadership, the World Jewish Congress has been transformed from a rather plodding, largely unknown Jewish lobby run by a group of earnest international lawyers, to a major world player—an umbrella body made up of 80 Jewish organizations from around the world, with a 285-member governing board and a $6 million annual budget.

Today, the headquarters of the World Jewish Congress are no longer on the outskirts of Geneva, overlooking a bucolic stretch of parkland on one side and a block of United Nations buildings on the other, but deep in the heart of Manhattan, just a few blocks away from the Seagram Building on Park Avenue. Although the organization maintains its Geneva office, its main work is coordinated by eighteen members of an executive cabinet that oversees the day-to-day operations of the group, out of the New York headquarters. In addition to its lobbying efforts for Jewish causes around the world, the other main priority of the organization is fund-raising. The bulk of the WJC's budget comes from more than 200,000 individual donors in the United States.

Elan Steinberg is the forty-three-year-old plain-talking executive director of the World Jewish Congress in New York. Since 1995, he has juggled the coordination of WJC research into declassified Operation Safehaven intelligence files at the National Archives in Washington and an almost daily barrage of camera crews, photographers, and print journalists who seem permanently camped out in the organization's suite of offices. These days, Steinberg can spare only five minutes for interviews, which are usually conducted with the persistent, nerve-shattering ring of telephones in the background.

"We know that a lot of people don't agree with our tactics, but so what?" says Steinberg in between interviews with CNN and National Public Radio. "It's not our responsibility to be nice to the Swiss and get them off the hook. We represent the Jewish people, and we are trying to achieve truth and justice for those who have been victimized for more than fifty years."

Later, in an interview with *The New York Times,* Steinberg outlines the strategy that will carry the World Jewish Congress into the next millennium. "For a long time the World Jewish Congress was meant to be the greatest secret of Jewish life, because the nature of diplomacy after the war was that it was quiet diplomacy. This is a newer, American-style leadership—less timid, more forceful, unashamedly Jewish."[6]

Indeed, Bronfman's strategy remains unashamedly aggressive in his latest campaign against the Swiss government and Swiss banks. Bronfman admits that when fellow members of the WJC executive first discussed strategy, he instantly took up the old Torah approach, and planned to appeal to the Swiss love of diplomacy and the law. When that didn't work, they didn't hesitate to fight like hell to be heard.

Ever since Nahum Goldmann lobbied Germany for wartime reparations for Holocaust victims, the issues of compensation and restitution have been on the organization's agenda, even if they have sometimes taken a back seat to more pressing issues, such as fighting for the rights of Jews persecuted behind the Iron Curtain. So it wasn't until the early 1990s, after the fall of the Berlin Wall, that Bronfman and Singer began giving serious thought to restitution. In 1992, the World Jewish Restitution Organization, of which Bronfman is the president, was created by a coalition of Jewish groups around the world, which sought the return to their Jewish owners of properties and other assets expropriated by Communist governments after the Second World War.

As a result of the collapse of communism, Holocaust survivors who had lived behind the Iron Curtain for more than fifty years after the end of the war began to clamor for the return of family assets, some of which they believed had been deposited in Swiss banks. Switzerland, the seemingly benign neutral country, best known for fine watches and chocolate, became the focus of a new struggle for restitution and justice, and many Holocaust survivors from around the world enlisted the aid of Jewish organizations, like the WJC, to gain access to family assets that might still be languishing in Swiss bank vaults.

A myriad of fiftieth-anniversary commemorations of the end of the war throughout Europe also contributed to the renewal of the restitution issue in 1995, sparking a collective reexamination of, among other things, the behavior of neutral countries during the conflict. In Switzerland, historian Jacques Picard published *Switzerland and the Jews, 1933–1945 (Die Schweiz und die Juden, 1933–1945)*, a condemnation of Switzerland's treatment of Jewish refugees who had tried to escape into the country during the war. Although his book did not focus on the financial assets that persecuted Jews had deposited in Swiss banks, it provoked collective introspection about Switzerland's wartime role, and debunked the myth of the compassionate, alpine neutral that had survived Nazi aggression thanks to solid resolve on the part of its wartime leaders, and a formidable army.

"I was concerned with the myth that Switzerland made of itself," says Jacques Picard, whose family on his father's side was Jewish, and who took part in the French resistance movement during the war. His interest in researching Jews in wartime Switzerland stemmed from the fact that his parents, who were traumatized by Nazi persecution, could never bring themselves to talk about the Holocaust. "For years, the Swiss believed that Switzerland was a lonely rock in Nazi-occupied Europe and that it was not invaded because of military deterrence factors. These myths were sustained during the Cold War, as was the myth that Switzerland took in all Jewish refugees."

The renewed search for Jewish assets in Swiss banks, which began when Edgar Bronfman and his entourage arrived in Switzerland fifty years after the end of the Second World War, came to epitomize the debunking of the Cold War myth.

"It's true that Switzerland bought its neutrality," says Bronfman. "But looking back, you can't condemn people for what they did. Lots of people did a lot of not-nice things to survive during this period of time. People do it all the time. But if you want to have a good future, you have to acknowledge your past."

Indeed, once Bronfman and his aides began to ask publicly about the long-forgotten Jewish assets, other wartime issues, such as the Nazi laundering of looted gold through Swiss banks and the Swiss treatment of Jewish refugees, came to the surface. "This is not just about money, it's about justice," says Bronfman, who plunged energetically into the case. "This is the last chapter of the Holocaust."

Trusting that his Torah approach would work on the Swiss, Edgar Bronfman set off in his private jet. On September 12, 1995, he arrived in Bern with a letter from then Israeli Prime Minister Yitzhak Rabin, authorizing him and the World Jewish Congress to act on behalf of the Jewish people to seek restitution for Holocaust victims who had deposited assets in Swiss banks to safeguard them from the Nazis. In addition to meeting with then Swiss President Kasper Villiger, Bronfman and his aides were scheduled to meet with the Swiss Bankers Association (SBA). Arriving early for their meeting, Bronfman and his entourage were shown into a bare room where there was no furniture.

"Nobody even offered us a chair," recalls Bronfman, who stood uncomfortably in the middle of the bare room, waiting for the Swiss bankers. At the appointed time, members of the Swiss Bankers Association, sporting conservative navy and gray suits, made their entrance, and one of them promptly read from a prepared statement. In a stiff monotone, Georg Krayer, chairman of the SBA, said that the association had agreed to conduct its own preliminary search for dormant accounts and would create a set of guidelines by which Holocaust victims and their families could make claims to conduct searches. (When they conducted their internal search, SBA members discovered $32 million worth of assets in dormant World War II accounts that might belong to victims of the Holocaust.) After reading their statement, the bankers asked Bronfman if he had any questions.

"This kind of reception was beyond cold and rude," he says, his bushy eyebrows furrowing in anger as he recalls the meeting. "So I told them that I didn't come to Switzerland to discuss money. I came to discuss process. If they expected me to tell the world that that's all there was, then I had to know that for a fact. I wasn't going to take their word for it."

Bronfman describes the Swiss bankers' gesture as a bribe. At the time, he and the World Jewish Congress suspected that there might be up to $7 billion worth of Jewish assets hidden in Swiss banks. "They [the SBA] had bought off groups before, and this was just a bigger bribe," he said. "I realized what they really wanted us to do was to take the money and run."[7]

The meeting was a harbinger of things to come in the WJC's deal-ings with the Swiss. Nevertheless, Bronfman and his aides left that first meeting with a small sense of hope. At least the Swiss bankers had agreed in principle to the WJC's suggestion of an independent audit of their procedures. The two organizations promised to work together and set up a commission to investigate the unclaimed World War II assets in Swiss banks.

THE DAY AFTER Bronfman's awkward meeting with the Swiss Bankers Association, a young Jewish immigration lawyer from To-ronto named Sergio Karas emerged fresh from an early-morning shower in his room at the quaint Helmhaus hotel in the heart of Zürich Old Town. Wrapped in a plush, white bathrobe, he caught the tail end of a BBC World Service television broadcast that im-mediately piqued his interest. Something about Nazis, the Holocaust, and Swiss banks.

Sergio Karas, who was in Zürich on unrelated business, shaved and dressed in a hurry, and made his way downstairs for a quick breakfast in the hotel dining room before setting out for a day of meetings. As he sat down to drink his coffee, his eye caught the large, bold headline plastered on the front page of the *Tages Anzeiger,* a leading Swiss newspaper, which another hotel guest had left at the table next to his. Karas, whose German is fairly good, skimmed the article, which detailed the Swiss Bankers Association's decision to create new guidelines under which Holocaust survivors and their heirs would be able to apply for new searches for family assets. Leav-ing his breakfast half eaten, Karas made his way back to his room, where he promptly called a Swiss lawyer, Caterina Nägeli, whom he had arranged to meet on other business.

"Why did I get so interested?" asks Karas, recalling his initial ex-citement when he heard about the dormant Holocaust accounts. "I saw the issue as an opportunity to work for justice. Fifty years of holding on to people's money is not right. How would people's lives have been different if they had had access to that money? How many kids would have gone to university? I felt I was on the side of seeking justice for people. I like that because too often lawyers are seen to be on the side of scumbags."

Karas, who has a crusading streak, has built his career representing the desperate and the downtrodden. The waiting room of his immigration-law practice in downtown Toronto is often crowded with veiled Muslim women from Asia and Africa, cradling crying babies, and Central American political refugees, dressed in ill-fitting suits and nervously clutching official-looking documents. All are fleeing persecution from their native countries, and all have put their faith in the good-looking lawyer who grew up in Argentina and knows what it's like to live under a repressive regime.

By the time he arrived at Caterina Nägeli's office on Grossmünsterplatz around the corner from his hotel, he had already made up his mind to help Holocaust survivors seek restitution from Swiss banks. He pitched the idea to Nägeli and found her enthusiastic. In a conference room overlooking the city of Zürich, the two young lawyers plotted their strategy. They would jointly represent Holocaust survivors or their heirs who wanted to make claims against Swiss banks. Because lawyers in Switzerland are prohibited from actively seeking clients, Karas would make the rounds of Canadian synagogues and advertise their services in North American Jewish newspapers.

"Sergio thought we could do something good together to help people," says Caterina Nägeli. An earnest thirty-nine-year-old lawyer, Nägeli was immediately intrigued by the story. Raised on the myths of Switzerland's role in World War II, she was shocked to learn that five decades later Swiss banks might still be holding on to the assets of Jews persecuted by the Nazis. "There is a certain fairy tale that you grow up with here that the Swiss have always been neutral, good people and good fighters."

A partner in a small firm that specializes in a wide variety of legal work, Nägeli, a tall, striking blonde, retains the youthful idealism that propelled her through law school—a keenly developed sense of altruism that was born when she left Switzerland in her early twenties to live and work with Indians in the Peruvian jungle. Like many intellectual idealists, she decided to study the law to help people seek justice. And now, like Sergio Karas, it seems she has found the perfect mission.

Although Karas admits thinking that the Swiss issue might revive a diminishing client base in the wake of Canadian government cuts to legal-aid programs, his primary motivation was personal. "I wanted to do it for my father," says Karas, who is the son of a Holocaust survivor from Poland.

Sergio Karas was born in Buenos Aires on May 22, 1959, the only son of Aria Karas and Ana Smoisman. Sergio's mother came from a family of Jewish gauchos, rugged, Yiddish-speaking homesteaders and cowboys who came from Russia to carve out a life in the hard-scrabble expanse of the Argentine pampas in the nineteenth century. Sergio's great-grandparents on his mother's side arrived in the province of Entre Rios in the 1880s as part of a massive exodus of Jews from Russia. The exodus was financed by Baron Maurice de Hirsch, a prominent German financier and philanthropist, whose worries about fierce anti-Semitism in Russia gave birth to the Jewish Colonization Association, an ambitious organization that would finance large-scale resettlements of persecuted Jews in North and South America. Baron de Hirsch's organization negotiated with the Argentine government to purchase huge tracts of land in order to establish Jewish colonies in the remote South American country. By 1881, boatloads of Russian Jews were making their way to Argentina under de Hirsch's plan. On the windswept pampas, the Jewish settlers established agricultural cooperatives, synagogues, and yeshivas. Although the men soon adopted the distinctive wide-brimmed hat and loose-fitting trousers of their gaucho neighbors, most of the settlers retained their Jewish traditions. They did not milk their cows on Saturday, and many, like Sergio's great-grandmother, spoke only Yiddish and refused to learn Spanish.

Sergio's father, Aria, grew up in Lodz, where his father, a middle-class Polish Jew, owned a bakery. When Aria was fourteen years old, the Nazis marched into Poland, and overnight the family's stable existence fell apart. The Karas business was taken over by Nazis, and the family was forced, along with the other Jews, into a ghetto in the poorest part of the city. Aria's older brother, Mario, who was tall and blond and could easily pass for an Aryan, escaped to Krakow, where he obtained false identity papers and escaped to France and then to Argentina, where the Karas family had relations. Following the liquidation of the Lodz ghetto in 1944, Aria, his parents, and younger brother were shipped to Auschwitz. Aria never saw his parents again, and found out only after the war that his eleven year-old brother had died after having much of his blood drained by a concentration camp doctor for the German war effort in the last desperate months of fighting. Following the war, Aria wandered around Europe for three years before tracking down Mario in Buenos Aires, who arranged for him to be smuggled into Argentina, which had ironically also become the premier destination for escaping Nazis after the war.

'We came together with the Nazis on the same boats, but the difference even there was that the Nazis were given special treatment and the Jews were not welcome," recalls Aria.

The favorable treatment of Nazis by Argentina's dictator Juan Domingo Perón, who took office in 1946, was as much a result of the leader's own fascination with fascism as the fact that Nazi loot was being exchanged for blank Argentine passports and residency permits. Pedro Bianchi, a junior diplomat in the foreign ministry from 1946 to 1948, estimates that Argentina's federal police issued at least two thousand Argentine passports and eight thousand identification cards, which were sent to Vienna via diplomatic pouch, where they were distributed to Nazis in the years immediately following the war.[8] The historian Ronald Newton has described how Perón was interested in attracting German scientists, technicians, and other professionals to his developing country, and didn't care if they were wanted war criminals. Perón did not bother "to distinguish among technicians, political irreconcilables, and war criminals and spoke of [admitting] 'several thousand.' La Prensa once wrote of 'seven thousand *cedulas en blanco'* [blank identity cards] that Perón had placed at the disposal of refugees, both technicians and non-technicians; Simon Wiesenthal estimated there were 7,500."[9]

In addition to allowing free entry to Nazi war criminals, Argentina also provided a haven for their wealth. While the war was still going on in Europe, many high-ranking Nazis with Swiss bank accounts began transferring their assets to Argentina, which had a sizable German-speaking and Swiss population. According to one American intelligence report, a manager at a well-known Nazi-dominated bank "withdrew cash sums from their personal accounts in the Wehrli Bank and transferred part of them to Argentina to form the three 'S' companies—Securitas, San Juan and Stella." These financial management groups maintained secret numbered accounts that were reportedly owned by Germans. "Evidence shows that accounts ostensibly held for various neutrals are actually cloaking German interests . . . another account, held in the name of Moriz Carl Bunge of Zürich and containing assets in excess of 3 million pesos, actually proved to belong to the Henkell family of Wiesbaden, Germany, of which the wife of Joachim von Ribbentrop is a member. In establishing these accounts in Argentina, Wehrli and Company transferred assets held in their name from throughout the world."[10]

Indeed, the transfer of Nazi assets from Switzerland to Argentina became so widespread in the last months of the war that U.S. Secretary of the Treasury Henry Morgenthau directed his office to send a U.S. Treasury Department representative to Argentina to investigate Nazi holdings. In a recently declassified memorandum to a colleague, written in February 1945, Morgenthau notes that "there is no place where field planning and action is more urgently needed than in Argentina. It is unnecessary for either of us to cull the extensive series of dispatches sent by the mission concerning Nazi activity and penetration in the economy of Argentina in order to appreciate the importance of the problem. More recent reports indicate clearly that Argentina is not only a likely refuge for Nazi criminals but also has been and still is the focal point of Nazi financial and economic activity in this hemisphere. In the light of these facts,

I feel certain you will agree that we should have someone in the field who is well-versed in the financial aspects of this problem."[11]

After conducting a preliminary study, an official at the American embassy in Buenos Aires reported on sizable German holdings in the South American country: "The best estimates in millions [of] Argentine pesos are: insurance companies 40; farms and ranches 500; banks 105; commercial firms 500. Patents, securities, money and miscellaneous not included in foregoing, though undoubtedly run into many million pesos . . ."[12]

A U.S. State Department memorandum from 1945 lists some of the Argentine assets of high-ranking Nazis: "[Hermann] Goering previously sent more than $20,000,000 of his personal fortune . . . via the Schweizer Bank of Geneva. . . . Goering is also reported to have transferred some funds to Argentina by a Nazi submarine in the spring of 1945. . . . Nazi Propaganda Minister Joseph Goebbels has $1,350,000 in a safe deposit box in a German controlled bank in Buenos Aires under the name of a friend of German origin. . . . Foreign Minister Joachim von Ribbentrop has a large sum deposited in the name of his cousin, a German named Martin, who recently received $500,000 from a Swiss bank from the account of a Nazi diplomat."[13]

According to Argentine journalist Jorge Camarasa, who has written extensively on Argentina's links with the Nazi regime, between 1942 and 1944, just as the war began to turn against Germany, more than two hundred German companies set up offices in Argentina, transferring huge amounts of money through local branches of German banks, such as the Deutsche Bank, the Banco Alemán Transatlántico, and the Banco Germánico del Río de la Plata.[14]

Camarasa also notes that a great deal of artwork, including several works by sixteenth-century Italian painter Antonio Canaletto, confiscated in France from Jewish families, ended up at the now defunct Wildenstein Gallery in Buenos Aires. In the 1960s, Argentine investigators found a painting in Buenos Aires by the Venetian master Francesco Guardi, which had been confiscated by the Nazis in Europe and shipped to Argentina. Camarasa believes that some Nazi gold and other valuables may have been transferred to the country via German submarines in the closing year of the war.[15]

Ironically, much of the Nazi loot that made its way to Argentina at the end of the war may have eventually made its way back to Swiss banks. In the summer of 1947, Eva Perón, the high-profile wife of the Argentine leader, embarked on an official visit to Europe, where she not only met with notable fascists, such as Croatian leader Ante Pavelic, but also opened up at least one bank account on a visit to Bern. It was not until after her death in 1952 that Perón investigated the accounts. Perón sent a group of Argentine envoys to Switzerland, where they found a safe-deposit box at a Credit Suisse branch in Bern, registered under the name Juan Duarte, Eva's brother and coordinator of her European tour, which had taken place between June and August 1947. A CIA file dated March 23, 1972, suggests that Eva Perón may have deposited "millions of dollars" in a Swiss bank during her European tour.[16] Argentine historians say that much of the Peróns' wealth may have been derived from the sale of Argentine residency documents for Nazi war criminals fleeing Europe.

In a country ruled by a Nazi-loving regime, Aria Karas was not surprised to be greeted with intense anti-Semitism, nor was he startled to find that Josef Mengele, the notorious extermination camp doctor whom he recognized from Auschwitz, was living a few blocks from his brother Mario's agricultural implements factory on the city outskirts. Like Adolf Eichmann, Mengele had fled to Argentina after the war with the aid of some pro-Nazi members of the Catholic Church and the Italian Red Cross. In their desire to rid Europe of what they saw as a godless Soviet menace that would threaten the existence of the Church, high officials at the Vatican helped hundreds of Nazi war criminals evade justice immediately following the war.[17] In 1949, Mengele, who had escaped detection in chaotic postwar Europe, was able to secure a Red Cross passport from the Swiss consulate in Genoa, Italy, through his connections to an underground SS organization with ties to the Vatican. In Buenos Aires, Mengele lived quite happily in the large German community first under the alias Helmut Gregor, and then under his own name. He actually had his real name listed in the Buenos Aires telephone book, and even applied for a divorce from his wife in Germany by registering at the West German consulate in 1954. Two years later, he was able to travel to Switzerland under his real name to visit with his twelve-year-old son Rolf. However, by 1960, Mengele had become frightened by the specter of Israeli secret agents, who had tracked down Eichmann and secretly abducted him to Israel, where he was tried and sentenced to death for crimes against the Jewish people and crimes against humanity. Mengele left for Paraguay and then Brazil, where he died in a swimming accident outside São Paulo in 1979.

Another Nazi who made Argentina his residence after the war was Erich Priebke, the SS captain who had ordered the murder of 335 Italian Jews at the Ardeatine Caves outside Rome. He admitted in an interview on the Italian state-run RAI TV that the Roman Catholic Church had helped him escape to Argentina in 1948, with a passport provided by an official at the Geneva-based International Committee of the Red Cross. Priebke lived a quiet life in the resort town of Bariloche until an American TV crew tracked him down in 1994. In an interview with an ABC TV reporter, he admitted his part in the Ardeatine Caves massacre, and in 1995 he was extradited to Italy to stand trial.

Although the Perón regime eagerly welcomed thousands of Nazis, including high-ranking members of the SS and wanted war criminals, Jews were a different matter. Jewish refugees trying to escape the horrors of Nazi Europe were met with a cold reception in Argentina. "Legal Jewish immigration . . . was strongly discouraged, despite the vociferous lobbying of Jewish groups in Buenos Aires. Until July 1947 the most obvious obstacle was the presence of an energetic anti-Semite, Santiago Peralta, as director of the Dirección de Inmigración; but after his departure, matters did not noticeably improve. The US government, with an important involvement in Argentine immigration policy after 1947, omitted to urge greater tolerance toward the Jews."[18]

In fact, when Aria Karas arrived in Argentina in 1948, one of the most popular sayings was *Haga Patria, Mata un Judío* ("Serve Your Country, Kill a Jew"). Despite intense anti-Semitism, Aria managed to live rather well. He married Ana, who was studying pharmacy in Buenos Aires, and built a prosperous textile business. Still, life under a succession of military regimes proved too much for the Karas family. In the late 1970s, the military dictatorship opened the markets to cheap textile imports, which practically destroyed the local industry. The Karas business suffered a huge blow. In addition, the anti-Semitic regime had been launching an internal "Dirty War" against political opponents, mostly idealistic university students like Sergio Karas, who was studying law at the University of Belgrano. If they didn't pick him up off the street one day, they would surely call upon him for his compulsory military service. Jewish men in the Prussian-influenced Argentine military were objects of scorn and discrimination. For all these reasons, the Karas family decided to pack up and move to Canada in 1980.

FIFTEEN YEARS AFTER fleeing Argentina, Sergio Karas, a bachelor who is known in local legal circles as a workaholic, sat in his small Toronto law office, its walls crowded with framed newspaper articles detailing his legal successes with refugee claimants over the years. On his filing cabinet a framed photograph of his dog, Prince, a bright-eyed sheltie who died in 1990, was proudly displayed.

"Prince was a great dog," Sergio said gently.

It was more than a month since he had returned from Zürich, and the day after he had placed an ad about Swiss banks in a local Jewish newspaper. The phone was ringing off the hook. The callers were all Holocaust survivors who suspected that their families had indeed stashed their assets in Swiss banks more than fifty years ago. They all seemed to share the same sense of urgency, and almost always related the same vague stories about parents or grandparents who had somehow managed to smuggle their assets to Switzerland before being deported to a concentration camp, where they were never heard from again. No, nobody had an account number, a code word, or even the name of a bank. Karas promised to send them an information package, which included an explanation of the new guidelines for filing claims to Swiss banks along with articles about his own work. For those who were hooked up to the Internet, he told about his new Web site, which also listed any information he could find about Swiss banking claims. Few of the elderly claimants who came to see him knew anything about the Information Highway. For the most part, they arrived with yellowed documents and personal letters stashed in old shoeboxes.

One of the most insistent callers was a spirited elderly woman who said she was born in Vienna, where her grandfather had been a prosperous textile exporter. Her grandfather had told her about money he had deposited in a Swiss bank account just before he escaped to Latvia in 1939. But the grandfather had been killed in Latvia, and she had been split up from the rest of her family during the war, ending up at Auschwitz with her mother. No, she had no banking information, but could she please make an appointment to see him in person? She was uncomfortable talking about such things on the telephone.

Renée Appel, whose respect for punctuality was instilled in her as a child in Vienna, arrived early for her two o'clock appointment with Sergio Karas on October 30, 1995. She was accompanied by her cousin, a lanky and balding but still handsome Hans Hamersfeld. Renée, now seventy-two and a grandmother of two toddlers, retained the majestic beauty and stature of her youth. Elegantly coifed and dressed, her hands adorned with gold rings and bracelets, she stood out from the nervous and bedraggled refugee claimants who also sat waiting for Sergio Karas. Hans, now sixty-five, the proud father of three grown children and a successful businessman who runs a company that leases coin-operated laundry machines, sat rigid in a straight-backed office chair and looked uncomfortably around the waiting room.

As soon as Renée had read Sergio Karas's ad in the *Canadian*

Jewish News, she had called Hans, who called the other Hamersfeld cousins, Herbie in New York, and Charlotte and Anita, Harry's two daughters, in Vienna. Everyone agreed to pitch in for the legal fees necessary to make a claim against the Swiss banks. Although Hans's father, Adolf, and his uncle Harry had already tried unsuccessfully to inquire about Abraham Hammersfeld's Swiss account before they died, the grandchildren were determined to find it now, more than five decades after the war.

It wasn't that anyone in the family was desperately in need of the money. They had all done well over the years, building prosperous middle-class lives in Toronto, New York, and Vienna. No, the money wasn't driving their claim, they told Karas. During the meeting, Renée and Hans interrupted each other to tell Karas about their family's story during the war—a story that they found surprisingly easier to tell a total stranger than their own children. Renée painfully recalled the events of the day in April 1939 (she could no longer recall the day of the week) at the Negerlegasse flat in Vienna, which was the last time she had seen her grandfather. She told Karas how Abraham, his face lined with worry, had taken her aside in his library and told her about the bank account in Switzerland.

"I only want what belongs to my family," she said. "I want justice. I resent the fact that Switzerland should hold on to that money and get rich off the Jewish tragedy."

Sergio Karas sat transfixed. He had quickly realized there was something more behind Renée and Hans's desire to find Abraham's bank account. Renée and Hans told him that their parents had approached the Swiss consulate in Toronto in the 1950s to try to find the money, but had hit a brick wall. "I felt they were still haunted by their past, and really wanted to find the money to put it all behind them once and for all," recalled Karas after his first meeting with Hans Hamersfeld and Renée Appel. "What stood out for me was the incredible journey they'd taken. It was not your typical story about people who went through the Holocaust. They were very well spoken and had a very vivid memory of these events. They were convinced that there was an account belonging to their grandfather, somewhere in a Swiss bank."

Somewhere in a Swiss bank. It certainly seemed that Karas and Nägeli had their work cut out for them. Although they could provide him with no banking information, Karas immediately trusted Hans and Renée. There was something impressive about their forthright manner and intensity. Furthermore, everything about their story rang true and was repeated by every other Hamersfeld family member old enough to remember the stories from the war. Karas knew from his father that most Jews living in Europe just before the Second World War did not have the kind of assets that would warrant opening up a Swiss bank account. The Jews most likely to have put money in Swiss banks were upper-middle-class professionals and business people from urban centers like Vienna. People very much like Abraham Hammersfeld.

Karas took extensive notes during his meeting with Hans and Renée, and then sent off a fax to his colleague, Caterina Nägeli, in Zürich. Nägeli prepared to send the claim to the Swiss banking ombudsman's office, set up by the Swiss Bankers Association in 1992 to settle disputes between Switzerland's 450 banks and their clients. In the fall of 1995, the ombudsman's office was charged with handling claims from Holocaust survivors and their heirs around the world. The Contact Office for the Search of Dormant Accounts Administered by Swiss Banks, the newly created department in the ombudsman's office, would function like a clearinghouse, sending the claims to Swiss banks. Upon receipt of the claims, the banks would conduct searches based on the information available in the claims, and send replies back to the ombudsman.

As Nägeli drafted the claim on behalf of the Hamersfeld grandchildren, she worried about the effectiveness of the procedure. "The banks can say what they want to say," she notes, in reference to the thirty claims that she and Karas have now prepared on behalf of clients. "Where is the scrutiny? How can the ombudsman make sure that the banks are actually searching through their dormant accounts?"

These are the same questions that troubled Edgar Bronfman during his first meeting with the Swiss Bankers Association. To make matters worse, Switzerland's largest bank contemptuously announced that in its own private search for Holocaust assets its officials had found far less than their critics were accusing them of holding in their vaults. In February 1996, a spokesman for the Union Bank of Switzerland said that an internal investigation had yielded the equivalent of $8.9 million in dormant accounts that may have been opened by Jews fleeing Nazi persecution during the Nazi era. "That is today's value, with interest and compound interest," said Robert Studer, chief executive of the Union Bank at a press conference in Zürich. "I think I can say in this case that the original amounts were peanuts." Studer estimated that the original assets may have totaled somewhere between 100,000 and 500,000 Swiss francs ($84,000 and $357,000 in 1997).[19]

The "peanuts" comment sent shock waves around the world, angering Jewish leaders and Holocaust survivors, who used it as evidence that the Swiss were not taking their concerns very seriously. Robert Studer and the Swiss Bankers Association, a self-regulating body accountable only to its own members, further antagonized Jewish organizations by refusing to reveal how they had conducted the searches for dormant accounts.

How to make the Swiss listen had preoccupied Bronfman ever since that ill-fated meeting in Bern in the fall of 1995. He had long since left his Torah behind, and now favored a loud, aggressive approach to shake up the Swiss people. However, he knew that, on its own, the World Jewish Congress could not muster enough popular support or political credibility to take the Swiss to task on an international scale. So in a move that was remarkable for its political savvy, Bronfman enlisted the aid of U.S. Senator Alfonse D'Amato, a high-level influence broker and one of the most powerful politicians in the state of New York.

When Bronfman contacted him for lunch in early 1996, D'Amato, the Republican senator from Long Island, had just taken a beating in the polls. His Senate committee hearings on Bill and Hilary Clinton's involvement in the Whitewater influence-peddling and fraud scandal were going nowhere; he was picking on Clinton when the president's approval in the polls was almost 60 percent. The American journalist Leonard Lurie, who has written a book about D'Amato's career, saw that the senator's attacks against the Clintons over Whitewater were quickly backfiring at a time when "the president was delivering on his campaign promises. The deficit was declining, employment was rising, NAFTA had passed, and a push for universal health insurance was progressing for the first time since Harry Truman proposed it. Taking on a popular president seemed like a thankless task. . . ."[20]

With only two years of his third term in the Senate left, Alfonse D'Amato was looking for a popular cause to propel him into a fourth term. Bronfman gave him a sure-fire winner—one almost certain to appeal to D'Amato's large constituency of Jewish voters. In his run for the Senate in 1992, D'Amato had managed to get only 40 percent of the Jewish vote. Jewish voters make up about 10 percent of the New York state electorate. What could be an easier target for this brash, pit-bull senator than the gnomes of Zürich, who had not only helped the Nazis launder gold, but now were holding on to the assets of Holocaust survivors?

"D'Amato was desperate to find something to lift his standing in the polls," says Lurie. "The Swiss issue was the perfect campaign platform."

Indeed, D'Amato offered Bronfman nothing less than putting Switzerland and its banks on trial in the United States. A few months after D'Amato met with Bronfman, the U.S. Senate Banking Committee, which D'Amato chairs, abandoned hearings on Whitewater and started to concentrate on Swiss banks. The growing battle against Swiss banks became such a popular issue in the United States that Bronfman even managed to get Bill Clinton to support the cause that was now being spearheaded by one of his biggest political enemies. Alfonse D'Amato, who had been known in New York as "Senator Pothole" and was once the Senate's least popular member with constituents, was now being called the "Scourge of Switzerland." Thanks to the Swiss scandal, D'Amato saw his approval rating jump by 12 points in a year to 37 percent[21]—not stellar, but according to political observers in the United States, he was making a comeback riding on the Swiss banks issue.

"He has shown leadership, courage, and stamina on the issue," said David Harris, executive director of the American Jewish Congress.[22] U.S. State Department spokesman Nicholas Burns went one step further when he claimed approvingly that the senator was "doing the Lord's work" by taking on the Swiss banks.[23]

"There are two heroes in Washington on this whole question—President Clinton and Senator D'Amato," said Elan Steinberg of the World Jewish Congress. "It might be the odd couple of politics, but a more powerful combination you can't dream of."[24] For his part, President Clinton appointed U.S. Undersecretary of Commerce Stuart Eizenstat, who as special envoy for property claims spearheaded an important probe into the role the U.S. government played in the disposition of Nazi assets immediately following the Second World War.

For the Swiss, who had already endured the moral indignation of another U.S. senator, albeit a Democratic one, D'Amato's hearings seemed a throwback to 1946, when Senator Harley Kilgore of West Virginia had criticized the United States' wishy-washy attitude toward both Germany and Switzerland. Kilgore criticized plans to leave large German cartels like I. G. Farben intact after the war, arguing fiercely that penalties against high-ranking Nazis had not gone far enough. However, in Switzerland he is best remembered as one of the harshest critics of the Washington Accord.

Almost fifty years to the day after the signing of that agreement, D'Amato seemed to be taking up where Kilgore left off. By the time the hearings got under way, the senator would not only be demanding the return of the dormant assets, he would demand that the U.S. government reconvene the Washington Accord, investigate the laundering of Nazi loot through Swiss banks, and put out a call for a generalized boycott of Swiss banks.

On the morning of April 23, 1996, D'Amato assembled representatives from Jewish groups, a Holocaust survivor from Long Island who claimed to have funds in Swiss banks, U.S. Undersecretary of Commerce for International Trade Stuart Eizenstat, and Hans Baer, chairman of the Bank Julius Baer and Baer Holding Ltd., and a member of the executive board of the Swiss Bankers Association. From the beginning it became apparent that the purpose of the committee hearings was not so much to arrive at a course of action as to capitalize on increasing media interest in the issue and to embarrass Swiss bankers into a full capitulation.

"This morning the committee meets to take up an important matter that has implications that go back to World War II, the Holocaust, and it involves more than money, more than millions and tens of millions and maybe hundreds of millions and maybe more than that," said D'Amato by way of opening the committee hearings. "But it involves the systematic victimization of people."[25]

Although D'Amato made a plea to "get the facts" and for an "honest accounting" of the situation, his own comments were laced with innuendo and ill-conceived remarks. At one point, he referred to the irony of "secrecy laws originally enacted to shield assets of the Holocaust victims from the Nazis [and] now being used as a sword against those victims and their families."[26] It didn't matter that this remark was patently untrue and that banking secrecy laws had a completely different genesis—the speech was effective, and D'Amato's version of the origins of banking secrecy was soon cited as fact by careless journalists around the world.

Despite D'Amato's errors and exaggerations, few would deny Edgar Bronfman's remarks that the banking committee hearings were "of great historical significance," if only as a method of forcing Switzerland and its bankers to rectify the injustices of the past.[27]

'Our collective mission here is nothing short of bringing about justice," said Bronfman in his address at the April 1996 hearings. "We are here to help write the last chapter of the bitter legacy of the Second World War and the Holocaust."[28] Once again Bronfman repeated the request he had made to the Swiss Bankers Association (SBA) in Bern a few months earlier for "a transparent mechanism to conduct a verifiable audit of all Nazi-era assets, those deposited by

Jews and those assets stolen from the Jews by the Nazis and also deposited in Switzerland."[29]

A few weeks before the Washington-based banking hearings, the SBA had sent a letter to Israel Singer at the World Jewish Congress reconfirming its willingness to participate in such an audit. A few weeks later, on May 2, the Memorandum of Understanding Between the World Jewish Restitution Organization, the World Jewish Congress, and the SBA was signed in New York. The agreement called for independent auditors and impartial investigators to "examine the methodology of the individual banks, the Swiss Bankers Association and the Office of the Ombudsman as regards the search for accounts and assets in question." Moreover, the auditors would have "unfettered access to all relevant files in banking institutions regarding dormant accounts and other assets and financial instruments deposited before, during and immediately after the Second World War." The memorandum provided for a Committee of Eminent Persons, representatives appointed by Jewish organizations and the SBA, to oversee an investigation into the *methodology* by which Swiss banks search for dormant accounts. Contrary to rather confused reports in the world press, the committee's mandate was never to match individual claimants with accounts, as this would contravene banking secrecy regulations. Bronfman's original concern had stemmed from the fact that the Swiss Bankers Association is a largely self-governing body that patrols its own members. There is virtually no outside scrutiny of its activities or those of the office of the ombudsman, which is itself funded by the association.

In the summer of 1996, Paul Volcker, former head of the U.S. Federal Reserve Board, was appointed as a "neutral" chairperson by the committee, whose members are evenly divided between Swiss and Jewish organizations. Paul Volcker prepared to assemble a group of auditors licensed to audit Swiss banks to begin evaluating the identification of dormant or heirless accounts deposited by Jews fearing Nazi persecution. Volcker's audit procedure would be completed in two phases. The first phase would involve gathering background information on banking practices from the 1930s and 1940s. Mem-

bers of Volcker's team would conduct interviews with present or retired bank employees and presumed depositors or their heirs who
might be able to cast light on the treatment of dormant accounts.
Auditors would then conduct "pilot" audits of four or five banks chosen as representative of those that might have been recipients of
funds from persecuted Jews. Volcker estimated that these preliminary
audits would probably be conducted on a private bank, a cantonal
bank, a regional bank, and two offices of the big three Swiss commercial banks (Credit Suisse, Union Bank of Switzerland, Swiss Bank
Corporation).

The second phase would involve an audit of all the relevant offices
of Switzerland's 450 banks. In order to avoid even the hint of a
conflict of interest, the audit would "be arranged in a manner that
avoids any of the accounting firms' investigating institutions with
which they have a continuing commercial auditing relationship.
Moreover, in all cases, the oversight of the effort will be by a senior
partner drawn from the international firm rather than from the Swiss
affiliate" of the auditing company.[30] The committee would need at
least two years to finish its report, but Volcker believed that "if the
job is to be done in a careful and comprehensive manner that once
and for all may command confidence and represent a true 'closing
of the books'—and there is no point in doing it otherwise—the
schedule adopted is ambitious rather than laggard."[31]

Although Bronfman would have preferred a quicker study, noting
that most Holocaust survivors are old and feeble and may not have
the luxury of waiting another few years for restitution, his strategy of
getting D'Amato, arguably the most ferocious bully in American politics, to take on the Swiss banks was working like a charm.

As Bronfman himself so aptly put it, "I got their attention."

EDGAR BRONFMAN NOT only managed to get the attention
of the Swiss when he began asking hard questions about the dormant
accounts, he opened a Pandora's box of unresolved Jewish postwar
issues, the most pressing of which became restitution and the activ-

ities of that little-known agency, the Tripartite Commission for the Restitution of Monetary Gold. More than fifty years after the end of the Second World War, questions were being asked by yet another abrasive pit-bull politician of the D'Amato school of diplomacy. Greville Janner, British Labour MP, chairman of Britain's Holocaust Educational Trust, and a vice president of the World Jewish Congress, was leading a charge to reopen negotiations involving the Tripartite Commission's final gold distribution.

After the war the Tripartite Gold Commission (TGC), administered by representatives from Britain, France, and the United States, had been charged with redistributing some $330 million worth of looted Nazi gold to the ten claimant countries whose national treasuries had been plundered. The TGC was charged with redistributing only "monetary gold"—defined by the Allied governments as "all gold which, at the time of its looting or wrongful removal, was carried as a part of the claimant country's monetary reserve, either in the accounts of the claimant Government itself or in the accounts of the claimant country's central bank or other monetary authority at home or abroad." The TGC did not accept claims from individual victims of Nazism.

"Nonmonetary" or "body gold" wrenched from the bodies of concentration camp victims, in addition "to the assets of victims of Nazi action who had since died and left no heirs," was to go to the Intergovernmental Committee for Refugees to help fund the rehabilitation and resettlement of displaced victims of Nazism. The organization would receive $25 million in German monetary gold as its first installment.

Although the victorious Allied powers did their best to separate monetary and nonmonetary gold when they came across hidden Nazi treasure troves throughout Germany, evidence unearthed in Operation Safehaven reports suggests that some of this gold could have been mixed, either by the Nazis themselves or by Allied troops. Did the Nazis melt down the gold fillings and wedding rings of concentration camp victims and send the gold bars to Swiss banks? Did the gold distributed by the Tripartite Commission, which still has a "residue" of 5.5 tons stored in New York and London and waiting to be distributed, contain nonmonetary gold? Following the distribution of Albania's share of the gold in October 1996, the TGC, which is run out of the British embassy in Brussels, was preparing to redistribute the leftover "residue" gold among the ten original claimant countries.

The redistribution was put on hold. "Some 5.5 tons of gold will remain," said Greville Janner in a debate in the British House of Commons in November 1996. The Labour MP for Leicester West says his interest in helping victims of the Holocaust stemmed from his experience as a junior war-crimes investigator for the British government at the end of the war. "I ask the Government to say that they will not agree to the distribution of that residue unless and until the origins of that gold have been researched and investigated. I am sure that the Government will agree with Honorable Members on both sides of the House that insofar as it is individuals' gold, that proportion should be returned—if not to the individuals who lost it, at least to their families and successors, who are still living in need and poverty as a result of the Nazi looting and the Nazi holocaust."[32] In pursuit of his claim, Janner wrote copious letters to then British Foreign Secretary Malcolm Rifkind, then U.S. Secretary of State Warren Christopher, and then French Foreign Minister Hervé de Charette. Janner was so convinced of the righteousness of his cause that he began short-lived legal proceedings earlier in the year in Britain to try to stop the last disbursement of gold to Albania.

Janner, known for his gruff and pushy manner, was treated a bit like a ranting revisionist for questioning the provenance of the remaining Tripartite Commission "gold pool," but his claims appear to have some validity. Evidence of the mixing of monetary and nonmonetary gold first came to light at the Nuremberg Trials with the cross-examination of Albert Thoms, head of the Precious Metals Division of the Reichsbank during the war. During the last frenzied year of the Nazi war effort, as gold expropriated from the national treasuries of Nazi-occupied countries was running out, the Nazis resorted to melting down gold jewelry and gold fillings of concentration camp victims. While on the witness stand at Nuremberg, Albert

Thoms was asked what happened to the gold teeth that were wrenched from the mouths of concentration camp victims. Thoms answered that "they were melted down by the Prussian State Mint. The gold was then refined and the fine gold was returned to the Reichsbank."[33] Although it is clear that the Nazis melted down some of the nonmonetary gold, it is impossible to know how much of the Nazi ingots captured by American troops after the war were made up of this gold.

Also still unverified is how much of the nonmonetary gold ended up at the Swiss National Bank when the Nazis exchanged gold for foreign currency during the war. Perhaps the $58 million worth of gold that the Swiss transferred to the United States under the terms of the 1946 Washington Accord contained the tainted gold, argued both Greville Janner and Edgar Bronfman.

Further mixing of the two types of gold may have occurred after the war when American troops discovered the huge caches of German loot in mines and bunkers. The largest of these troves, which contained more than $241 million (about $2.4 billion today) worth of gold, stolen artwork, and part of the SS concentration camp booty from the Reichsbank, was found in the huge mine in Merkers, near Weimar. As the war came to a close in April 1945, Hitler ordered, on the advice of Walther Funk, president of the Reichsbank, that gold, stolen artwork, and a great deal of the SS booty from the Reichsbank vaults be moved to the Kaiseroda salt mine in Merkers for safekeeping and to avoid damage by Allied bombing, which had destroyed part of the Reichsbank in Berlin.

American soldiers who found the cache of gold and other valuables in the fifteen miles of underground tunnels at the Kaiseroda mine shipped it for sorting to the newly named Frankfurt Exchange Depository (FED), which had functioned as a Reichsbank building during the war. The gold was sent to Frankfurt by heavily armed and guarded convoy on April 15, 1945. From there it was to be distributed to claimant countries by the Tripartite Gold Commission, which began its work a year later. Evidence suggests, however, that some mixing of an unspecified amount of gold may have occurred in the

FED. According to American historian Arthur Smith, Jr., "The FED also had some minted gold looted by the Germans from individuals, which had not been held by any government's central bank or any other recognized monetary authority, and thus did not strictly count as part of a nation's monetary reserve. . . . [C]ontrary to announced policy, gold coin that had come from concentration camps and had less numismatic than monetary value was earmarked for the gold pot."[34]

In May 1997, the U.S. State Department's report on Nazi gold noted that mixing of monetary and nonmonetary gold certainly occurred at the FED, where American troops failed to follow orders from Washington to analyze chemically the assembled gold to determine its provenance:

> The smelted SS gold was indistinguishable in appearance from gold
> bullion stolen from central banks across Nazi-occupied Europe. . . .
> In deciding to include gold coins and bars without mint markings,
> there is no doubt that the U.S. Government consciously contrib-
> uted gold and coins at Merkers belonging to concentration camp
> victims and other civilians to the Tripartite Gold Commission gold
> pool.[35]

Similarly, a huge nonmonetary treasure trove, called Shipment 16, found by U.S. troops at the Buchenwald concentration camp in the last month of the war, may have been mixed with monetary gold when it was sent to the FED for sorting and safekeeping before being shipped to the Intergovernmental Committee for Refugees.

A few weeks after the Fourth and Sixth Armored Divisions of the U.S. Army reached the Buchenwald concentration camp on April 11, 1945, German inmates told them about a cache of loot in a nearby quarry. Buried in a bunker in the quarry just outside the SS barracks, U.S. military officials found hundreds of bags, suitcases, and barrels containing U.S. currency, gold coins, gold bars, diamonds, precious stones, seven thousand pounds of silver tableware, more than six hundred bags of fountain pens, and boxes containing hundreds of weddings rings and gold fillings.[36] The convoy that transported Shipment 16 to the FED consisted of "six two and a half ton trucks, two armored cars, one MP motorcycle, and one Chevrolet."[37]

Furthermore, British and American troops launched "Operation Sparkler" to round up gold, silver, and jewels that had been overlooked in Germany after the initial occupation began. According to Smith, the operation was planned on the basis of lists of gold rings, dental fillings, watches, and other jewelry noted in the files of the Reichsstelle für Edelmetalle. The sweep reportedly netted $150 million (about $1.5 billion in 1997) worth of nonmonetary valuables,[38] of which $40 million (about $390 million today) ended up in the monetary gold pool.

As a result of the uncertainty of the provenance of the gold in the Tripartite Commission's pool, on both sides of the Atlantic, Greville Janner and Edgar Bronfman lobbied the governments of Britain, France, and the United States—the original trustee governments of the commission—to distribute the 5.5 tons of "residue" gold (currently sitting in vaults at the Bank of England in London and at the Federal Reserve Bank in New York) to Holocaust victims and their heirs through the World Jewish Restitution Organization. However, as then UK Foreign Secretary Malcolm Rifkind noted in a letter to Greville Janner, there are "formidable legal and administrative obstacles in the way of . . . using the gold held by the TGC to benefit individual claimants, as you and Mr Bronfman have proposed"[39]— one of the obstacles, of course, being that the commission's mandate, as set out at the Paris Reparations Conference, was not to deal with individual claims. Some legal experts say that in order to use the "residue" gold for individual claims, all of the nations that signed the Paris Reparations Conference would have to reconvene and renegotiate the terms of the Tripartite Commission's agreement.

"The legal implications of what Bronfman and Janner are proposing are quite severe," says a British legal expert who does not want to be identified. "Even if they manage to reopen negotiations, the chances of the gold going to Jewish victims are slim. What about the other victims of the Nazis? A number of non-Jewish victims, such as merchant seamen and captured POWs, never get anything in the way of compensation or restitution."

However, Edgar Bronfman and Greville Janner have made progress. On February 3, 1997, the United States Britain, and France agreed at least to freeze the distribution of the 5.5 tons of "residue" gold, worth approximately $68 million, until the three trustee governments can ascertain whether the TGC pool did in fact contain nonmonetary gold.

"We've taken the first step, freezing the money in place," said Stuart Eizenstat, who is also responsible for sorting out the diplomatic problems related to the looting of Nazi gold. "But we don't have any agreement yet on what to do next."[40]

When asked if he considers the Tripartite Commission's decision a victory, Bronfman replies with some surprise, "A victory? It's justice more than a victory. Obviously some of this gold belonged to people who died in the Holocaust, but now it's the right thing for these governments to realize that this gold should go to the benefit of Holocaust survivors to make their lives a little more dignified. They are getting very old and they need walkers, glasses, and medical help to live out their last years."

Not content with his progress on the Tripartite Commission, back in London Greville Janner sought to reopen yet another contentious postwar agreement. In a letter to Malcolm Rifkind, he noted that he wanted the Swiss government to accept a "review and renegotiation of the Washington Accord of 1946 to return non-monetary gold held from plundered nations."[41] His call for the reopening of the Washington Accord was given a further boost by the publication of a report by Britain's Foreign Office suggesting that the Swiss might still be holding nine tenths of the gold looted from Nazi-occupied countries.

As one international legal expert notes pressuring the Swiss to return the gold, even if it was taken by the Nazis, may be impossible under international law, since Swiss banks exchanged it for Swiss currency. "The Swiss weren't just taking in gold," he says. "They were giving the Germans back value for that gold."

Reopening the Washington Accord will be a difficult undertaking, since Switzerland will have to acquiesce to renegotiating what it still considers to be a binding agreement. The Swiss government has not ruled out reopening the agreement, but has said that it will take no decisions until it has the chance to do a proper reckoning of its own. Such an inquiry, Swiss officials estimate, could take five years.

But Greville Janner, for one, is not prepared to wait. Like Bronfman, he says he is worried that victims of the Holocaust, many of whom have been waiting for restitution and compensation for fifty years, do not have the luxury of waiting much longer. Besides, it's not in Switzerland's best interests politically to have international Jewish organizations on its back.

"The longer they wait, the longer Switzerland will remain an international pariah," says Janner in an interview in the sitting room of his opulent London townhouse in residential Golders Green. With his collection of silver menorahs and kiddush cups arranged on the mantel, Janner considers himself a good Jew and a crusader for the Jewish people. In his capacity as chairman of Britain's Holocaust Educational Trust, Janner works with a small staff of young researchers to lobby the British government to take action on issues related to the Holocaust. He says he devotes much of his time to the trust, which may explain why he's so impatient—some might even say rude—when having to answer reporters' questions.

"Look," he says, by way of cutting off the conversation, "we've been incredibly successful so far. We've managed to get the Holocaust on the front page of *Time* and *Newsweek*."

The next step, he says, is to get some sort of monetary settlement from Switzerland for its role in laundering Nazi gold and holding on to dormant Holocaust accounts. When asked what form this settlement would take, Janner does not mince words: "I don't care it it's compensation or restitution, just as long as it's money."

GIZELLA WEISSHAUS WOULD probably agree with Greville Janner's sentiments. The sixty-six-year-old Romanian-born Holocaust survivor says that she has been waiting more than fifty years to recover her father's assets from Swiss banks. On October 1, 1996, Gizella Weisshaus, acting "on behalf of herself and all other persons of all national origins, ethnic groups, races, creeds and colors, similarly situated as victims and survivors of the Nazi Holocaust," launched a $20 billion class-action suit against Switzerland's largest and most important banks. She is the first Holocaust survivor in the United States to sue Swiss banks for unclaimed accounts opened by Jews escaping Nazi persecution. According to her lawyer, she has been joined in the class-action suit by more than ten thousand plaintiffs.[42]

"Our people are not getting younger," said Gizella Weisshaus, a mother of six and grandmother of twenty-seven, who currently lives in a Hasidic community in the Williamsburg section of Brooklyn. "I'm considered one of the youngest survivors, so there's going to be nobody left to claim this money. That's why I felt this was the only way to force them to disclose these so-called dormant accounts. We are the survivors, and we are entitled to the money and information."[43]

Her story is typical of many Holocaust survivors whose family assets may still be languishing in Swiss banks. In 1944, just before her father, a prosperous currency dealer named Eugene Stern, was arrested in her hometown of Sighet, Romania, he assembled his family and told them that he had hidden money and other valuables in the walls of the family home and had transferred the rest to Swiss banks. She was deported to Auschwitz, where all fifty-five of her family members perished—she was the only one to survive. After the liberation of the camp, the fifteen-year-old girl returned to her family home, where she found some of the assets hidden in hollowed-out places in the walls and ceiling. However, she had no luck with Swiss banks. She tried three times to reclaim her father's assets in Switzerland, to no avail.

In 1950, Gizella Weisshaus emigrated with her husband, Joseph, to the United States. Weisshaus, who now carries an electronic pager so that her lawyer can reach her at any time, said she decided to sue because she was angered by the Swiss authorities' estimate that an investigation of the dormant accounts could take up to five years. For her, filing a lawsuit on behalf of those who survived the Holocaust is nothing short of a *mitzvah*—a good deed.

"Why did they choose me?" asked Weisshaus, referring to the Nazi guards who chose her to work while they sent the rest of her family to the gas chambers at Auschwitz. "I was the chosen one to keep up the family, and I am doing the right things. There were some people who said they didn't believe in God anymore. But I couldn't think that way. So . . . filing this lawsuit I had to do. Because of their memory. And because I was chosen to do this."[44]

Ed Fagan, the New York City attorney who has taken on the Weisshaus suit, found his firm overwhelmed with thousands of inquiries from Holocaust survivors from around the world who want to join what is already a huge class-action suit.

"The lawsuit seeks three things," Fagan said. "One is . . . for an accounting to compel them [Swiss banks] to disclose all the information about the accounts that were opened from 1933 to 1945. The second count is a count for what's called 'conversion.' They took property, and they've kept it for fifty-one years, and the third count is for unjust enrichment. They became unjustly enriched from the backs and the life blood of these people. . . ."[45]

The Weisshaus suit has spawned other bold legal attempts to wrest funds from various Swiss banks. There are at least three other large class-action suits under way. One, filed in Brooklyn federal court, has been brought on behalf of five plaintiffs living in New York, California, Britain, and Canada. In January 1997, the World Council of Orthodox Jewish Communities filed a class-action lawsuit against Credit Suisse, Union Bank of Switzerland, and Swiss Bank Corporation. Their council's lawyer, David Berger, did not list what damages the suit would seek. "We are not putting a number in this except that they're huge," he said.[46] The latest suit is against insurance companies throughout Europe that allegedly handed over to Nazi authorities the proceeds of life-insurance policies taken out by Jews during the war.

Although the class-action suits have attracted a great number of Holocaust survivors and their families, many believe they will only exacerbate problems with Swiss banks and get in the way of others who are seeking to find their families' assets rather than receiving monetary damages.

"These big U.S. claims are doing tremendous damage," says Sergio Karas in his small office in Toronto. "I get very nervous when people talk about these huge global settlements. The class-action suits have done nothing but provoke mass hysteria and Swiss-bashing. They're just perpetuating the myth about Jewish lawyers who just want money."

Since the class-action suits were launched in New York, Karas has had several calls from people he suspects of being charlatans and opportunists, who want him to represent them in a billion-dollar class-action suit because they see it as a chance at easy money.

"I wish I had one hundred dollars for everyone who calls me to say that they will divide half the booty with me if I find their money for free," says Karas, who charges a retainer in order to attract serious clients, and adds that he has so far lost money on the thirty claimants he is representing from across the United States and Canada. "The true measure of the quality of the claim is whether or not somebody is willing to risk a few bucks to do the search. I had a lady calling me recently who said she is a Holocaust survivor. She said she didn't have any money in Swiss banks but wanted to make a claim anyway because she said the Swiss have too much money. I told her I couldn't help her with that. She seemed very insulted that I wouldn't take on her case and that I wouldn't do it for free."

Caterina Nägeli agrees. Like Karas, she favors the quiet but determined legalistic approach to recover their clients' dormant assets. In early December 1996, as she sat hidden behind her desk, stacked with legal texts and client files, Nägeli looked out over the Gothic spires of the fifteenth-century Wasserkirche, just off the Helmhaus square, to the sparkling blue waters of the Limmat Canal, which divides the Old Town from the city's financial district, where the world's most important banks have their offices. Nägeli squinted at the afternoon sun, which formed dancing spots of light on the stack of neatly typed documents that comprised the Hammersfeld claim.

Well, everything certainly seemed to be in order. She signed one of the documents before inserting the Hammersfeld claim into a white envelope, neatly addressed to the attention of Switzerland's banking ombudsman, whose office, like those of the banks, is on the other side of the canal.

FIVE

THE LETTER
OF THE LAW

The Contact Office for the Search of Dormant Accounts Administered by Swiss Banks, where Caterina Nägeli forwarded the Hammersfeld claim, is a modest suite in a converted flat in a nondescript residential building on Zürich's Seestrasse. It is next door to the Judaica Bookshop and above a hairdressing salon called the Coiffure Simmer and a photo shop, where a big sign in the window guarantees that you can get a strip of passport photos taken in a few minutes.

Set up in 1995 by the Swiss Bankers Association, the Contact Office acts as a clearinghouse for Holocaust survivors and others seeking to make claims against Swiss banks for the retrieval of assets in dormant accounts. When an inquiry is sent to the office, it is reviewed by Hanspeter Häni, the ombudsman for Swiss banks, who then sends out a questionnaire to the potential claimant. The questionnaire asks for details about the applicant, the assumed bank customer, and the relationship between the two. Under the guidelines of the Swiss Bankers Association, several conditions must be met before a search can be initiated. First, the claimant must be able to substantiate that such an account might exist, the claimant must supply the name of the person whose account is sought, explain that the bank customer has been dead or presumed dead for at least ten years, prove their claim to the existing account, and pinpoint in which region of Switzerland to conduct the search.

However, most people who send in claims to the ombudsman have little information, and the banks have to conduct most searches on the basis of very flimsy evidence. Unlike the bureaucrats in the post-war period who demanded that Holocaust survivors produce death certificates and other formal documentation, the Contact Office is much more lenient, and does not insist that official documents be submitted if these documents do not exist.

"We accept photocopies of proofs," says Hanspeter Häni. "We accept no proof."

In fact, the ombudsman sometimes has little more than a name to go on. Typical claims include statements such as "My uncle told me he had received money from my father and had given it to a courier in Budapest, who was to deposit it in Switzerland"; or "I recall that my father set up bank accounts; I don't know where, but probably in Switzerland"; or "I heard as a young child that my father was sending funds abroad just in case we would go to the U.S.A." From this point of view, the Hammersfeld claim, which is based on Renée's memory of her grandfather telling her a few months before the outbreak of war in 1939 that he had money in a Swiss bank, is typical. The difficulty in undertaking a search based on this kind of limited information is that it is not even clear if Jews escaping Nazi persecution opened accounts in their own names. After the Nazis made it illegal for Reich citizens to have assets abroad in 1935, contravening the law was punishable by death. Sometimes, in order to guard themselves against Gestapo agents who had infiltrated many banks to ferret out undeclared German and Jewish assets, Jews deposited their assets through a third party. What if Abraham had hooked up with a trustee or lawyer such as Veit Wyler and decided not to inform his children and his grandchildren, for their own safety? As one Swiss lawyer put it, "Only the *bon Dieu* knows what happened to those accounts."

Many of the country's bankers agree, adding that most wealthy account holders transferred their assets to the United States before and during the war. "The possibilities of what could have happened to these assets are infinite," says Hans Baer, chairman of the Bank Julius Baer, the only Jewish bank in Zürich just before the war. "What you have to remember is that there is an extremely close relationship between the Swiss banker and his client. Often, it's closer than the relationship he has with his own children. So during the war maybe there were Jewish refugees who said, 'First I want to save my life, and if anything happens to me, you keep the money because you have been a nice guy and a good banker.' That Jewish refugee isn't necessarily thinking of his third cousin in Australia, who may one day have a claim on his assets. He's thinking of survival."

Hans Baer's view is repeated by Paul Volcker, former Federal Reserve chief, who by the spring of 1997 was already well into the first phase of his investigation. "We are dealing with a period when strong and comprehensive exchange controls were in place and there were specific prohibitions in Germany on travel and the transfer of Jewish wealth abroad, with harsh penalties to any found in violation," he told a U.S. House of Representatives committee on banking chaired by Republican James Leach in December 1996.

Those familiar with the conditions before and during World War II emphasize that many of the deposits of fearful and persecuted persons—perhaps the bulk—were made clandestinely through third parties acting as agents. The names of the beneficial owners might have been deliberately withheld even from the banks receiving the deposits. The agents could have been Swiss or non-Swiss—lawyers or accountants, or simply friends or others. In some cases, frightened people, with invasion imminent or under way, may have dealt with unscrupulous alleged agents, with the funds never reaching Swiss banks or other safe havens as promised.

Legitimate agents may themselves have retired or died without adequate records, or even have succumbed to the temptation to divert funds illegally, in the conviction that true beneficiaries were, in any event, untraceable or dead. As is well known, potential beneficiaries of dormant accounts are often able to provide only sketchy indications of either the bank in which the funds are deposited or the name of the deposit holder. It is those difficulties that have been one factor in the relative lack of success so far of the Swiss Ombudsman. In practice, he has had to request searches through a large number of records from outside the banking system and with a weak description of accounts.[1]

Volcker noted that the search for assets is also complicated by the fact that many of the small banks that existed in the 1930s have since merged with larger financial institutions or, in some cases, have gone out of existence. Searching through dormant accounts is also a very slow process, and banking officials must literally sort through crates of old documents because accounts dating back to the 1930s are not available on computer databases.

Despite these difficulties, the Contact Office never turns anyone away. Once the questionnaires are returned, Hanspeter Häni and his skeletal staff of four assistants send off the information to the 450 Swiss banks across the country. The banks are then obliged to check their records and conduct an internal search of their dormant accounts, which in Switzerland are defined as assets in banks (accounts, custody accounts, or safe deposit boxes) about which the banks have had no contact with the beneficial owners or their trustees for at least ten years. Unlike just about every country in the Western world, where funds revert to the bank or to the state if there is no activity on an account for a specified period of time, in Switzerland there are no time limits and no provisions for the absorption of dormant assets by the bank or the state. An account is considered closed only when an account holder or proxy withdraws the balance. Documentation on a terminated customer relationship is then held by the banks for ten years after the closing of the account, when it is usually destroyed.

If a bank finds one of the names on an application in its records, it then takes over the responsibility for dealing directly with the claimant and may request more information. If nothing happens after two months from the date of sending the information to the banks, Häni's office informs the claimant that their search has been unsuccessful. With Häni acting as a mediator between the claimants and the banks, searches are done without breaking banking secrecy laws, which maintain that information on bank accounts may be released only to authorized proxies and successors of former customers.

Of the 2,229 people who applied to the Contact Office in 1996, 1,055 returned the ombudsman's questionnaires. Of those returned, 892 questionnaires were admitted to the search proceedings. (Häni sent the others back, requesting more information.) The majority of the claims were from the United States and Israel, with 70 percent coming from relatives of victims of the Nazi regime. The rest related to the search for assets that had become dormant before or after the war for other reasons. In the first year after the establishment of the Contact Office, Swiss bankers found the equivalent of $1.28 million belonging to eleven depositors. Only five of those depositors were victims of the Holocaust, who had combined deposits of 11,000 Swiss francs, or $8,800. In three of those cases, the bank customers were murdered by the Nazis; two others were Jewish customers who lived in Romania. Confidentiality regulations prevented Häni from elaborating on the other six depositors or any of the banks involved.

The World Jewish Congress called the findings "pathetic." One congress official called Häni a "photocopying service for Swiss banks." Kalman Sultanik, a vice president of the World Jewish Congress in New York, blasted Häni, but in his anger confused the role of the Swiss banking ombudsman with that of the Swiss banks.

"After 2,000 inquiries and 1,000 formal claims, the Swiss ombudsman has returned not a cent," said Sultanik, who was mistaken in his assertion that Häni is charged with returning money. "He has rejected every claimant for a year. This is a cruel farce perpetrated on Holocaust survivors by the Swiss banking industry."[2]

The outrage wasn't limited to Jewish groups. In Switzerland, the liberal press also condemned the findings. An editorial in the *Basler Zeitung* newspaper noted that

the amount found in Swiss banks by the Banking Ombudsman . . . after nearly a year of work is small. Questions should be asked about the procedure. If the banks limit themselves to reacting to requests from descendants of Holocaust victims, this won't be enough to restore lost trust. They should do everything in their power to identify and find the rightful owners of unclaimed assets. . . . The miserable results so far show how justified the reproach is that the banks waited until the problem of Jewish assets went away by itself.[3]

A day after Häni called a press conference to announce the banks' findings, the daily *Tages Anzeiger* featured a front-page cartoon showing a Swiss banker tossing a few coins from a fortress to a group of people below carrying a sign reading DORMANT WEALTH. The banker is shouting down at them: "You should be satisfied now."

Only the conservative *Neue Zürcher Zeitung* said that Häni's findings were in line with realistic expectations, and indicated that few heirs would be found for the $32 million that the banks say remain in dormant accounts of all kinds, not just those opened by Jewish victims of Nazi persecution.

Following the announcement at the press conference, Hanspeter Häni became an object of international scorn and ridicule. The World Jewish Congress began to raise questions about the independence of the ombudsman, whose office is funded by the Swiss Bankers Association. "It's just another example of the Swiss dragging their heels," says Edgar Bronfman. "The concept of an ombudsman to deal with this issue is unbelievably ridiculous."

On the other hand, bankers like Hans Baer believe that the work of the Contact Office in helping claimants find their assets is of vital importance, but that Häni is not a miracle worker: "It is crucially important to treat all potential claims seriously and sensitively and to work with claimants to substantiate their claims, as the Ombudsman is doing," say Baer. "However, a responsible institution cannot simply pay someone an indeterminate amount based on little more than a hope that there is an account somewhere in Switzerland belonging to some relative."

Although his office was indeed set up and is currently funded by the members of the Swiss Bankers Association, Häni, an economist and former banker, bristles at the charge that he may be somehow beholden to the banks. "If I accepted the orders of the banks, I could close my offices today," he says. "I don't give out money. I am simply a mediator. The banks ask us for documentation, and it's up to them to find out if a claim is legitimate."

Häni, whose traditional responsibility as ombudsman involved fielding complaints from customers of Swiss banks, has tried to clarify his new role as the first point of contact for those searching for dormant assets. "I have one single principle in my position as Contact Office in the search for dormant accounts: Everything that can be returned to the legal owners must be returned. And I would never have taken on this task if I had not been convinced that all the institutions involved were totally unanimous on this point."[4]

Häni, a forty-seven-year-old father of two teenagers, who describes himself as "very average," is also the epitome of Swiss professionalism. At first glance, the rake-thin, middle-aged Häni, with his impeccably groomed, wide brown mustache, thinning hair, and immaculately pressed dark suit, has the air of an ascetic. He is sparing with his time—"I can only spare a half hour," he notes at the beginning of an interview—and periodically consults a large German-English dictionary to make sure that he has hit upon the precise English word that best conveys his thoughts, which he can formulate in Switzerland's official languages. Although precision, integrity, and rigid self-discipline seem to be his guiding principles, Häni is not a caricature of the bloodless Swiss bureaucrat. For one thing, he seems to feel deeply for the plight of the claimants, many of whom have sent him hand-scrawled letters recounting their families' painful experiences during the war. "I can't imagine that a survivor of the Holocaust would make a claim just for fun. It can't be very fine to review again and again the details of those who perished so horribly," says Häni, who sometimes receives as many as twenty claims per day. Due to the sheer volume, he has recently doubled his staff and moved to a larger office.

Despite his efforts to clarify the work of the Contact Office, whose colorful brochures cheerfully promise that "the Swiss Banking Ombudsman can help you," Häni says his office has been the subject of a great deal of misinformation in the media. For instance, many in the world's press have made him out to be a nasty Swiss bureaucrat in cahoots with the Swiss banks, and have criticized the Contact Office for charging claimants 300 Swiss francs (about $214) to conduct a search. He does not usually respond to press reports, but in an effort to appear more open, his office has reduced the processing fee to 100 Swiss francs (about $71) and even waived it in almost one hundred cases where the applicants said they could not pay. Häni, however, believes the fee structure should be in place to ward off potential opportunists who may want to abuse the system. Still, his office now often absorbs the expense of sending each claim to hundreds of bank branches across the country.

Häni is extremely wary about meeting with journalists. He says he has yet to read a magazine or newspaper article that gets the dormant-accounts issue right. "The reports—unrealistic to any unprejudiced eye—of billions being held by the banks have led to additional expectations and further pushed up the ideas held by inquiring parties about the sums that could be found," said Häni at his November 1996 press conference in Zürich.

Almost all the searching parties assume that money will be found for them. . . . The search for dormant assets is encountering major, almost fathomless interest in the media and thus among the public at large. This interest is often in crass contrast to the knowledge of the actual proceedings. The complexity of the subject matter

and the several layers involved leads to grotesque misunderstand-
ings in some cases and erroneous information if dealt with super-
ficially.[5]

However, few reporters seemed to be paying attention, since
most of them concentrated on the rather anticlimactic results of
that first search. One of the problems lies in the complexity of the
Swiss issues—the dormant accounts and the Nazi gold—which are
usually lumped together by the press. Perhaps those who had expected the banks to find the billions of dollars that the World Jewish Congress promised confused the value of the dormant assets
with that of the Nazi gold. Although today it is well known that
Hitler did indeed launder more than $5 billion (at today's values)
through Swiss banks, nobody can say conclusively how much the
dormant assets of Holocaust victims are worth or that they will
ever be found. As Häni himself noted, "In terms of figures, the results of our activities may seem disappointing at first glance. I myself consider the results encouraging just because *something* has
been found."[6]

For Hanspeter Häni and other banking professionals who had been
saying all along that there is probably not a lot of money left in Swiss
banks belonging to persecuted Jewish depositors, the results were
expected, partly because few depositors on the eve of the Second
World War had liquid assets. Many deposits were made in securities
or bonds, which lost their value over time. For instance, many banks
reported to Häni's office that they had found worthless bonds from
the kingdom of Romania from the 1930s, and securities from now
defunct German companies such as *Deutsche Reichsbahn* (German
Imperial Railways) or the Gelsenkirchen Mines. Many German depositors may have also deposited their assets in Reichsmarks, which
were worth approximately one tenth of their original value after the
German defeat.

"It is unthinkable that large sums are going to be found," says Hans
Baer. "Securities deposited before the war became worthless in currency. You also have to be careful about the issue of interest. You

have to look at currency and the fluctuation of currency to determine interest."

Beat Brenner agrees. Flicking ashes from a smoldering cigarette into an ashtray overflowing with yellowed butts, Switzerland's foremost financial journalist punches numbers into a calculator. The earnest, bespectacled Brenner, who works for *Neue Zürcher Zeitung,* is trying to calculate the original worth of the five deposits found by the banks in 1996. "Let's see, assuming a steady interest rate of three percent per year over a fifty-year period, I don't think those deposits were originally more than $2,500, combined."

No matter how much or how little money is found, for those on the side of justice, restitution—not money—is what's important. Almost two months before Häni announced the banks' rather paltry findings, a prescient editorial in *The New York Times* noted that "the search will not be easy and the amount of gold and other assets may prove smaller than imagined. But in a matter of historical accountability like this, monetary value is less important than honesty and openness. This is a reckoning long overdue."[7]

But for Edgar Bronfman and his supporters, the ombudsman's performance was just another example of Swiss stonewalling. A week after Häni's announcement of the results of the 1996 search, British MP Greville Janner, who was on a visit to Switzerland to pressure Swiss bankers and politicians into conducting a speedier search for the dormant accounts, demanded that the Swiss set up a multimillion-dollar fund to compensate those who could not get their assets out of Swiss banks. A spokesman for the World Jewish Congress suggested that the fund, which Janner called a goodwill "gesture" on the part of Swiss banks, should be valued at between $100 million and $200 million.

Although a few Swiss bankers seemed receptive to Janner's idea, their critics were skeptical. "Switzerland will fight like hell not to give up money and not to give up banking secrecy," said Jean Ziegler, an outspoken Socialist parliamentarian, between voting sessions at the Swiss Parliament in Bern. "You can be sure there are billions of dollars' worth of Holocaust money in Swiss bank vaults."

Ziegler's assertion is based on a career of railing against Swiss banks. A professor of sociology at the University of Geneva, he has spent much of his time in the Swiss Parliament criticizing what he believes to be questionable banking practices, and Switzerland's international reputation as a haven for money-laundering activities. As a result of his books *La Suisse Lave Plus Blanc* (*Switzerland Washes Whiter*), an ironic exposé of money laundering in Swiss banks, and *Le Bonheur d'Etre Suisse* (*The Happiness of Being Swiss*), which attacks Swiss hypocrisy and complacency, Swiss banks have slapped seven libel and commercial defamation suits against him, claiming damages of over $6 million. But the legal actions haven't dulled Ziegler's attacks, which have become so virulent that he recently saw his parliamentary immunity lifted to allow court actions to proceed against him. He has recently published another controversial book, *Die Schweiz, das Gold und die Toten* (*Switzerland, the Gold and the Dead*), in which he argues that the Swiss helped to prolong the Second World War by laundering gold for the Nazis.

"We must now open our vaults and just admit that we were accomplices to Hitler," said Ziegler, rushing back to the Swiss parliamentary chamber for an important vote "This is morally indefensible. Let's ask for pardon. If we cling to the problem of the law these survivors will all die."

A few seconds later, the heavyset Ziegler dashed back into the main hallway outside the chamber, where a group of journalists were comparing notes. "Beware the Swiss banks," he said in a breathless whisper, and then he disappeared.

CLINGING TO THE law has had dubious results for Swiss bankers in the past. The reason Swiss banks became such popular havens after the Second World War for the ill-gotten gains of Third World dictators and drug traffickers was because the bankers followed their own laws on banking secrecy to the letter, and only reluctantly put provisions into place to help third-party investigations, and then only when Switzerland's own reputation was on the line.

After the banking law of 1934 permanently enshrined the principle of banking secrecy, Swiss banks attracted not only the assets of Jews fleeing Nazi persecution, but also a whole host of money launderers, deposed dictators, drug lords, and crooked businesspeople in search of a place to hide their assets from either tax authorities or criminal prosecutors in their native countries. No matter where they lived in the world, their money was almost always entrusted to the Swiss. So it's no surprise that Swiss banks became the depositories of choice for such well-known dictators as Argentina's Juan Perón, Cuba's Fulgencio Batista, and Haiti's Jean-Claude "Baby Doc" Duvalier, who is said to have deposited over $7 billion, allegedly stolen from the treasury of the Caribbean country, the poorest in the Western hemisphere, that he once ruled. Another dictator, Zaire's ex-president Mobutu Sese Seko, is said to have $4 billion in Swiss banks, although Swiss authorities have been able to find only $3.4 million so far. Switzerland came under fierce international criticism for allowing Mobutu to stay in the country to recuperate from a cancer operation while fighting engulfed Zaire in 1977. The international pressure was so intense that Switzerland eventually refused him a visa to return, despite his reputed wealth in these banks. The Swiss foreign ministry publicly accused Mobutu of condoning human-rights abuses and canceling elections. By May 1997 when rebel leader Laurent Desiré Kabila took over control of the country, which he renamed Democratic Republic of the Congo, the Swiss Federal Council ordered a one-year block on Mobutu's assets in Switzerland.

Bank secrecy has even stymied governments—including Switzerland's own. Throughout the 1950s and 1960s, Swiss bankers resolutely held on to principles of banking secrecy, making it impossible for anyone other than the beneficial owners of accounts to access banking information. For instance, the secrecy was so stringent that Juan Perón was never able to collect the money allegedly deposited by his wife, Eva, in 1947, because she did not open a joint account with her husband. In 1959, the French government accused Swiss banks of using Arab money to finance major arms deals for Algerian

rebels. But the banking secrecy rules prevented even the Swiss government from conducting an investigation.

Swiss banks also helped Philippine dictator Ferdinand Marcos or-
chestrate one of the largest thefts in history, although in this case he
was eventually thwarted by the Swiss government. which bowed to
international pressure and blocked his assets. Documents found in
Marcos's bedroom safe in the abandoned Malacanang Palace, in Ma-
nila, and in his luggage, which U.S. authorities confiscated upon his
arrival in Hawaii after being defeated by Corazón Aquino in the elections of February 1986, clearly show how the Marcos family smuggled huge amounts of money and other assets to Swiss banks.

For several months after taking power in 1965 until his ouster
from the Philippines in 1986, Ferdinand Marcos stashed anywhere
from $5 billion to $10 billion in gold and other assets, pilfered from
the Philippine national treasury, in Swiss banks in Zürich, Geneva,
Fribourg, Lucerne, and Lausanne. He and his aides also set up several Lichtenstein foundations, which helped hide the real ownership
of his accounts. Investigators say there were even gold shipments
sent by the Marcos family directly to Switzerland from the Philippines. Some gold shipments continued after the Marcos family down-
fall, causing the Swiss Bankers Association to be on alert for "unusual
transactions" conducted by Philippine nationals.[8]

In fact, the Swiss were so worried that an international scandal
involving the deposed dictator would develop that they blocked his
assets before any request came from the Philippine government to
conduct an investigation. On March 24, 1986, a Filipino businessman attempted to withdraw $213 million in cash from the Credit
Suisse in Zürich by presenting a power of attorney signed by Ferdinand and his wife, Imelda. The bank was prepared to provide the
funds the next morning, but alerted agents in the Swiss finance ministry. Members of the *Bundesrat,* the Swiss Council of Ministers,
were also informed of the situation. Operating under Article 102.8
of the Swiss Constitution, which states that the Federal Council
'shall watch over the external interests of the Confederation, partic-

ularly its international relations, and it shall be in charge of external affairs generally," the Federal Council ordered an emergency freeze on all assets held in Switzerland by Ferdinand Marcos and his family. On March 26, the Federal Banking Commission notified all six banks where Marcos or his associates held accounts that they would be violating banking secrecy by allowing the withdrawal of the Marcos family assets. The unprecedented decision, which was clearly motivated by political considerations to avoid international criticism of Switzerland, stunned bankers, "who said they feared it could compromise Switzerland's reputation as a haven of banking secrecy."[9]

It was precisely this intractable concern for banking secrecy that had damaged Switzerland's reputation abroad in the first place. In the 1970s, Swiss banks came under fire, especially from U.S. investigators, for their stubborn refusal to lift the veil of banking secrecy for the purpose of assisting in exposing and prosecuting illicit activities. The Swiss government could demand that banking records be made available to foreign governments that had mutual-assistance agreements with Switzerland concerning criminal investigations. However, there were a series of bureaucratic hurdles that had to be crossed before the Swiss would cooperate. The most troublesome was the issue of "double criminality," which required that the crime being investigated be classified as a crime in both Switzerland and the other jurisdiction.

For instance, until 1987, insider trading—the act of buying or selling publicly held securities using information that is not available publicly—was not illegal in Switzerland, but rather considered an "administrative" problem. For this reason, the U.S. Securities and Exchange Commission could not access the Swiss banking records of anyone suspected of conducting insider trading through Swiss financial intermediaries. Judges in the United States were so frustrated by Swiss intransigence that they resorted to fining some Swiss banks up to $50,000 per day for their refusal to cooperate on a certain case. Furthermore, U.S. prosecutors threatened to ban some Swiss banks from trading in the United States until they cooperated. The Swiss eventually capitulated to U.S. pressure. In 1982, the Swiss and the

United States signed a Memorandum of Understanding that stated that until insider trading was made a criminal offense under Swiss law, it would be "considered" a crime for the purposes of the mutual-assistance treaty signed by the two countries in 1973.

To this day, the issue of "double criminality" continues to be a frustrating obstacle in investigating tax evasion. In Switzerland, tax evasion is not a crime, and the government does not require banks to break secrecy regulations in order to assist foreign prosecutors seeking evidence of tax evasion in Switzerland by their nationals.

While to the outside world this sort of behavior is seen as intransigence and arrogance on the part of the Swiss, to Swiss bankers it represents nothing short of survival in the increasingly competitive world of international banking. "What you have to realize is that this kind of banking is all about image," says Daniel Guggenheim, an international banking lawyer based in Geneva. "Switzerland is the only country in the Western world where the bank data belongs to the bank and to the client. This secrecy can only be maintained if Switzerland and its banks appear powerful and do not cave in to international pressure."

Still, in an effort to appear at least cooperative and deflect criticism abroad, Swiss bankers have periodically decided to clean up their image. In 1977, the Swiss Bankers Association, the Swiss National Bank, and Swiss commercial banks adopted a "good conduct" code. The so-called "Know your client" agreement was designed to prevent illegally acquired funds from being used by Swiss banks by requiring the verification of depositors' integrity. Although depositors could still be represented by Swiss agents, the intermediaries now had to provide a declaration to the banks that they personally knew the "economic beneficiary" of the account, and that the funds being deposited had not been obtained illegally. However, it was a halfhearted measure, because one large loophole still existed. The so-called *Strohmänner,* or dummy clause, allowed lawyers and notaries to take responsibility for a customer's good standing by using a newly created "Form B" account. Form B allowed Swiss lawyers and notaries to open, as intermediaries, accounts on behalf of their clients by declaring that *to the best of their knowledge* the beneficial owner was not corrupt. Since legal professionals are shielded by their duty of secrecy to their clients, the beneficial owner of the account could still remain unknown. This inadequacy was finally corrected in 1991 when the Swiss government, through the Federal Banking Commission, abolished so-called Form B or anonymous accounts. As of June 30, 1991, all Swiss banks must know and record the identity of the beneficial owners of all bank accounts.

Despite these measures, Switzerland was still a haven for assets derived from organized crime, where criminals or their intermediaries could show up with suitcases full of cash and deposit them in Swiss banks. So in 1990, Switzerland enacted new legislation to curb its growing money-laundering problem. (Article 305 *bis* of the Swiss criminal code prohibits the concealment of criminal proceeds. According to this provision, money-laundering crimes are punishable with imprisonment of up to five years and by fines of up to 1 million Swiss francs [about $714,000]. In 1994, Swiss legislators drafted a law requiring bankers and all other money managers to report suspicious transactions to the police, and the bill was passed by Parliament in November 1996. This obligation to report is also extended to nonbank-asset managers, such as investment funds, life insurance companies, and financial trustees. The bill also provides for police powers to freeze suspicious assets pending an investigation.)

However, both foreign and Swiss prosecutors believe that the laws do not go far enough, and Edgar Bronfman's and Alfonse D'Amato's recent accusations about Swiss bankers have come in the wake of several international scandals, when the country's own investigators are demanding changes. While Bronfman began to level his attacks against the banks for holding on to the assets of Holocaust victims, Swiss investigators found about $130 million in Swiss accounts that were tied to the brother of Mexico's disgraced former president, Carlos Salinas de Gortari. Swiss authorities believe that some of the money belonging to Raúl Salinas came from drug trafficking. A few years earlier, when high-level Italian politicians and businesspeople were accused of widespread corruption, the flow of bribes was traced back to Swiss banks. Similarly, organized-crime rackets in Eastern Europe and Russia are increasingly using Swiss banks to launder their profits.

Carla del Ponte, Switzerland's crusading chief federal prosecutor, wants to cleanse the Swiss banking system of dirty money, and hopes that international criticism over the dormant accounts will spur Swiss bankers into cleaning up their image. She says that banks should be required by law to report dirty money. She also wants to see Switzerland classify tax evasion as a crime, since some of the larger deposits in Swiss banks are made by foreigners evading tax collection in their home countries. And she wants strict legislation to cover financial services other than banks, such as fiduciaries and asset managers, who are often hired to open accounts and act as shields through which money is laundered.

"Swiss bankers are retarding our progress," says Carla del Ponte, who earned her reputation as a muckraking prosecutor in Ticino, Switzerland's Italian-speaking canton. In 1985, the plain-spoken del Ponte helped Italian and American investigators crack the so-called Pizza Connection, a Mafia drug-and-arms ring that used Swiss banks to launder money. Heroin from the Middle East was shipped through Sicily to the United States, and the profits were laundered through Swiss-bank branches in the Bahamas. As a result of her crusade against some of the world's most notorious criminals, del Ponte lives under twenty-four-hour security and is driven to work in a bulletproof car. In addition to hiring a group of highly trained bodyguards, the Swiss Federal Justice building where she works, near downtown Bern, has been transformed into a veritable bunker, with metal detectors, security cameras, and heavy steel doors leading to her offices. She says that she rarely sees her teenage son, who lives with his father, del Ponte's ex-husband, for his own security. In 1992, while she was still a prosecutor in Ticino, del Ponte embarked on a trip to Sicily to pool her information with her friend and colleague, Sicilian magistrate Giovanni Falcone. While del Ponte went to visit the Palermo cathedral, Falcone was assassinated by the Italian Mafia. A year later, del Ponte was not the least bit surprised to find herself the next target on the Mafia's hit list.

Despite numerous death threats, Carla del Ponte continues her war against organized crime, and now Swiss banks. "It's very important for us to block the criminal's ability to launder money, and to get bankers to cooperate with us," she says. "The dormant accounts don't really affect our work here, but maybe they will be enough to force them to clean up their image."

The scandal over the dormant accounts, arguably the biggest in Swiss banking history, couldn't have come at a worse time for the country's bankers. While many of them say that so far the scandal has not affected their business, the threats of international boycotts from Jewish groups must give them pause, especially when a few of the larger banks are undergoing massive restructuring to deal with an increasingly competitive global banking marketplace and the dismal state of the Swiss economy, in which banks have traditionally contributed nearly 10 percent to the Gross Domestic Product. The financial journalist Beat Brenner describes Switzerland as going through its worst recession since the Second World War, with the national debt double its 1990 level. Economic growth has remained stagnant since 1991, and the decrease in the real value of real estate has been staggering. Residential holdings are down by 35 percent, commercial holdings by 45 percent.

In 1996, the Union Bank of Switzerland, Swiss Bank Corporation, and Credit Suisse announced major restructuring plans. The most dramatic change came in November when the Union Bank, the country's largest, announced that it would cut eight hundred jobs, or nearly 4 percent of its entire staff in Switzerland, and take a write-off of 3 billion Swiss francs ($2.3 billion). The bank's loss for the 1996 financial year was estimated to be more than half a billion francs, or $776 million.[10] The 3-billion-franc charge was intended to cover projected loan risks for the next few years. Moreover, Credit Suisse announced a net loss for 1996 of $1.7 billion, the first deficit in the banking group's 140-year history.[11]

These announcements are indicative of the malaise gripping the entire Swiss banking industry, where for too long banks have concentrated their efforts on off-balance sheet items, such as their brokerage and insurance businesses, at the expense of their core banking activities. Restructuring, coupled with the allegations that Swiss banks plundered the assets of Holocaust victims, led to a small but nevertheless persistent degree of uncertainty in the country's financial markets. When Jewish groups threatened to call for an international boycott of Swiss banks, the stocks of the big three Swiss banks took a beating. If a boycott were imposed, it could cause significant damage, as it could involve the withdrawal of funds managed by the banks under private banking activities. "The big Swiss banks derive roughly 50 per cent of their profits from their private banking activities," said Madeleine Hofmann, a banking analyst at Credit Suisse. "If this area were affected, then that would certainly be negative because that is an important business."[12]

In an industry where image and reputation are key considerations, the protection of banking secrecy used to be seen as fundamental to continued growth. Another analyst pointed out that "even a mere perceived reduction of this protection in the eyes of private clients could lead to a substantial reduction in banking activity in this country."[13]

However, according to the Swiss historian Jacques Picard, Swiss banks risk much more today by obsessively protecting secrecy at the cost of "doing the right thing." Picard says, "The difference between the 1950s and today is that there has been a huge internationalization of capital. Big banks realize there are consequences for the damage to their reputation."

And, indeed, Edgar Bronfman himself astutely noted that the scandal over dormant accounts struck at the very heart of the Swiss banking industry. "As a businessman, I often deal with bankers, and I know that the most important asset any banker can have is his reputation, the trust of his customers," he told the Senate banking committee in Washington in 1996. "If we cannot have faith in the integrity and trustworthiness and the honor of the banker to protect our deposits, to give a faithful and accurate accounting, then we must go elsewhere."[14]

Some described the consequences for Swiss banks in rather apocalyptic terms: "The credibility, the veracity, the very integrity of the entire Swiss banking industry is at stake in this matter, and the burden of proof lies entirely with the Swiss banking industry," said Republican Congressman Spencer Bachus before the U.S. House of Representatives banking committee hearings. "This may be terribly unfair. I'm inclined to think that it does sound harsh. But . . . that is the case and if you ignore that fact, you do it at the peril of your entire industry."[15]

In this kind of self-righteous moral climate, Swiss bankers were at a loss to fight back. They could hardly invoke the complex realities of banking secrecy to a world that increasingly viewed this scandal in terms of moral absolutes. Most of the world's press pitted the "evil" Swiss bankers against the defenseless, feeble Holocaust survivors who had been trying vainly to pry their family assets from Swiss bank vaults for more than fifty years. But at least one of the profiles of Holocaust survivors who claimed they were heirs to small fortunes in Swiss banks was somewhat inaccurate.

In June 1995, The Wall Street Journal's Peter Gumbel recounted the fruitless efforts undertaken by the three daughters of a man named Moses Blum, who before being interned at the Dachau concentration camp in 1938 had reportedly deposited his assets at the Bank Julius Baer in Zürich. Mr. Blum's daughters, who live in England and Israel, began to search for the account in 1987 after the death of their mother, Frieda Blum, who in her will had asked her heirs to contact the Baer bank. After their first inquiry, the daughters received a letter from the bank saying that it couldn't search farther back than the previous decade.

After the publication of The Wall Street Journal article, which appeared on the first page of the highly respected financial newspaper, the Bank Julius Baer issued a terse clarification. According to the bank, Frieda and Moses Blum had indeed held a joint account at the bank, but it was opened nine years after the end of the war and closed in 1972.

> In 1987 and 1988 the daughters of a foreign couple inquired about a presumed bank account of their parents who had died in 1957 and 1987 in a western European country. No inquiry was made about possible assets of a relative who was missing or who had not survived the end of World War II. The result of the internal research by Bank Julius Baer was that the couple in question had opened an account with the bank a decade after the end of World War II, and that the surviving widow had subsequently closed this account, and disposed of the relatively small balance, in the early seventies. Besides the mere fact of the opening and the cancellation of the account, the bank had no further information left in 1987, as all the relevant documents and records had been destroyed after the statutory period of ten years had elapsed. Accordingly, the bank was not in a position to give the daughters any detailed information about the account relationship that their mother had terminated over one and a half decades before her death.[16]

The Wall Street Journal did not provide a response and clarification about the Blum claim until October 7, 1995, nearly four months after its initial story on dormant accounts. By that time it didn't matter if the newspaper's original story had been accurate or not: It quickly spawned similar pieces in newspapers around the world. Before they knew what had hit them, Swiss bankers were under attack from all sides. By the time Edgar Bronfman got to Switzerland in September 1995, the case of dormant accounts of Holocaust victims in Swiss banks had spiraled into an international moral issue. "We had morality and the whole world on our side," said Edgar Bronfman, "because Swiss banks are just not very popular, so it was hard for them to fight back."

Swiss legislators quickly realized that not only was one of the country's most important industries at stake, the country itself was in danger of turning into what the British MP Greville Janner called an "international pariah." No Swiss institutions were spared the intense international scrutiny that followed in the wake of the media avalanche in 1996. In addition to the demand for the renegotiation of the Washington Accord, and a full accounting of Switzerland's wartime financial dealings with the Nazis, the age-old concept of Swiss neutrality and the World War II activities of respected Swiss organizations such as the International Committee of the Red Cross were suddenly called into question.

"We realized early on that what we had was a very serious *political* problem on our hands. This was not just a methodological problem of banks, but a huge problem for Switzerland," says Verena Grendelmeier, a Zürich-based television journalist and Swiss parliamentarian, who in March 1995, several months before Edgar Bronfman made his first trip to Switzerland, launched an initiative in the Swiss Parliament to lift banking secrecy and return assets in dormant accounts. "I felt that we should do something for the fiftieth-anniversary commemorations of the Second World War, and the issue of dormant accounts was something that was still outstanding," says the soft-spoken fifty-eight-year-old former actress and theater director.

It was the international outcry, however, that propelled Verena Grendelmeier's initiative through the Swiss Parliament at record speed. In December 1996, the parliament unanimously passed a federal decree to lift banking secrecy so as to facilitate an investigation into all assets that had reached Switzerland before and during the war as a result of Nazi rule. Usually it takes more than two years to pass Swiss legislation.

The federal decree, which lifts banking secrecy for a period of three to five years, calls for a sweeping investigation of all financial transactions between Switzerland and the Third Reich from 1933 to 1945. It will cover the extent and fate of assets of all kinds that were transferred to banks, insurance companies, attorneys, notaries, fiduciaries, asset managers, and any other third-party depositors. In addition to examining the dormant accounts of Nazi victims, the investigation will also scrutinize accounts held by members of the Nazi party and the laundering of looted gold through Swiss banks. To be conducted by a team of both Swiss and non-Swiss "experts from various fields," the investigation will also review the wartime role of the Swiss National Bank and any postwar measures covering unclaimed assets taken by the Swiss government. The decree prohibits the destruction of legal records from the period being investigated. Those who do not cooperate are liable to criminal prosecution, and may be punished with imprisonment or fined up to 50,000 Swiss francs (about $36,000). According to Grendelmeier, the Swiss Parliament has reportedly created a 5 million Swiss-franc (about $3.6 million) budget for the investigation.

"I was the one who threw the first stone, but I could not know that a whole wall would come crashing down around me," says Grendelmeier. Her salt-and-pepper hair is stylishly close-cropped. Her long, graceful fingers seem to be constantly balancing a smoldering cigarette. "I'm not interested in mountains of gold to be found. I'm interested in justice. For us Swiss the most important thing is that we can install a commission of experts and historians. Then we have to let them work."

During an interview with Grendelmeier in December 1996, a swath of bright winter sunshine streamed in through the windows of the salon where the bespectacled parliamentarian sat smoking and contemplating the events of the past year.

"Up to now we have had a version of history which was not wrong, but we only had one part of it," she said, referring to some of the myths that the Swiss have embellished to explain the country's ability to fend off a Nazi invasion during the Second World War. "Hitler was more interested in a free Switzerland than in an occupied country. He needed money in convertible value and the whole world knew it. If he would have occupied Switzerland, he would have had only Reichsmarks, which were not convertible, and therefore not strategic. Then of course the blackmailing and the pressure started, but until the end of the war we couldn't know: Does he destroy us or does he invade us?"

Bathed in sunshine, Grendelmeier rose frequently in midthought whenever the persistent beeper she carried in her purse went off, signaling that her presence was required in the chamber for a parliamentary vote. The vote would soon be taken on Grendelmeier's historic legislation to investigate the country's financial dealings with the Third Reich.

The Swiss Parliament meets four times a year for three weeks at a time in Bern, a quaint capital city of broad medieval streets and cobblestoned squares where local farmers regularly set up stalls to sell their produce. The markets, where everything from cheese to fresh-baked rye bread and vats of sauerkraut is available, seem to be just about everywhere in Bern, including outside the magnificent, domed nineteenth-century federal parliament—the Bundeshaus— where the collection of stalls sometimes restricts the entrance to the building.

There is a strange Alice-in-Wonderland, fairy-tale quality to this city, where lunchtime residents stand mulling over their next moves in open-air chess matches, rolling four-foot wooden statues of brightly painted laughing kings, queens, and pawns across chessboard squares neatly painted on the pavement. At Christmastime, stocky men dressed as gnomes, wearing brightly colored leotards and absurdly pointed shoes, stand in the covered shopping arcades that line the downtown streets, soliciting donations for local charities. The official mascot of this alpine city is a rather ferocious-looking bear.

Like Verena Grendelmeier, who is from Zürich, most members of Parliament who hail from other parts of Switzerland hole up at one of the city's hotels when the parliament is in session. This is why most deal-making actually takes place in the city's hotels or at the Wandehalle, the high-ceilinged hall just outside the chamber, where parliamentarians gather to discuss legislation. Members of Parliament do not have offices here, just small, elegant lockers and a cluster of desks, each with its own brass lamp and computer, in alcoves just off the Wandehalle, which is also known as the *Salle des Pas Perdus* (Room of the Forgotten Steps).

"It's much more practical this way," says Alessandro Delprete, the Swiss Parliament's extremely efficient press attaché. "I guess you could say it's very egalitarian and Swiss." Indeed, this is a country where the president takes a tram to work or drives his own car. In fact, when Edgar Bronfman showed up for a meeting here recently, many observers may have been shocked to see the president of the World Jewish Congress arrive with an entourage of aides and body-guards in several chauffeur-driven cars. The president of Switzerland made a less dramatic entrance, driving his own Mercedes.

Among the Swiss, Bronfman's forthrightness and lavish gestures are often taken for arrogance. "I've never seen these guys not travel in style or stay in first-class hotels," said one banker. "It doesn't look right. You can't fight for social justice from the balcony of the Hilton."

According to Grendelmeier, the brash, aggressive lobbying meth-ods used by Bronfman and D'Amato are quite foreign to the Swiss. She herself has been a victim of D'Amato's signature attacks, which are becoming increasingly similar to those of Joseph McCarthy, the Republican senator famous for holding up mysterious lists of sup-posed Communist agents in his crusade to purge the United States of Communists in the 1950s. A few months after Grendelmeier made her speech to Parliament, her last name appeared on one of D'Amato's lists. It was in a State Department memorandum entitled "List of Swiss Lawyers in Zürich Said to Be Hiding German Assets," dated May 22, 1946. On the list were the names of her father, Alois, who died in 1983, and his law partner. Verena Grendelmeier, who had been informed of the list by a German journalist, was ap-palled.

"Certainly it was a huge shock when I saw it," she says. "But my family was condemned without being accused. My father is dead. I cannot ask him if he took in German money. And maybe he did take in money. And if he did, I am certain that it could not be Nazi money, but Jewish money. And if he did take in any money, he surely returned it after the war. I'm not sure what happened, but how do I defend my father?"

Indeed, to those who knew him, it seems rather unlikely that Alois Grendelmeier would have acted as a trustee for Nazi assets. He started his career in the Zürich law offices of Vladimir Rosenbaum, a left-wing Jewish lawyer. Verena Grendelmeier remembers that her father was a vigorous opponent of the Nazi movement and a founder of the center-left Independence Party, of which she herself is today a member. In fact, after the war she found out that her mother's hairdresser was a spy for the Nazis. Had the Nazis invaded Switzerland, her parents would have been among the first on the Nazi hit list in Zürich.

"I am ready to face my own family story, to see my family in a different light, but first I have to have facts and figures," she says. "This stupid phrase, 'said to be,' means nothing to me. It's up to Mr. D'Amato and the World Jewish Congress to find out what the hell they are reproaching me for."

D'Amato's list of lawyers also shook up the placid community of Lugano, a sleepy mountain resort town of wide boulevards, lined with expensive boutiques and banks. Known as the "Rio de Janeiro of the Old World," Lugano hugs a magnificent, sparkling bay, bordered by the rolling foothills of the Alps. The city, the largest in the Italian-speaking canton of Ticino, is a premier holiday destination as well as a tax haven for wealthy Italian nationals.

Waldo Riva, patriarch of one of the most prominent legal families in Lugano, was "said to be" hiding German assets during the war by American intelligence officials. The allegation shocked his son, Pierfranco Riva, himself a prominent Luganese lawyer who has taken over his father's old office on the Via Pretorio. Waldo Riva was cited by U.S. intelligence officials along with several other prominent Lugano-based lawyers. As with Grendelmeier's father, the charge seemed ludicrous to anyone who knew Waldo Riva, who died in 1987. According to his son Pierfranco, Waldo's mother was a German Jew, much of whose family perished in concentration camps or in Allied combat. In fact, says Pierfranco, Waldo Riva's clients included many Jews who were persecuted by the Nazis and sought him out to act as their trustee to set up Swiss bank accounts. After the war, Waldo Riva served as Lugano's honorary consul to West Germany.

"It looks to me like this American intelligence service is not very intelligent," said Pierfranco Riva in an interview in his elegant office where Renaissance frescoes cover the ceilings and espresso in delicate porcelain cups is served by slim, smartly dressed young women. "This 'said to be' means nothing, but it can be very damaging. One can accuse my father of being an accomplice of the Allies but not of the Nazis. My father was an honest man, and nobody has come since the end of the war to claim any money."

Riva noted that the infamous list first surfaced in 1990 when it was published by Zürich's weekly SonntagsZeitung and by a Swiss law journal. Although at least one of the lawyers on the 1946 list, Wilhelm Frick, was a known Nazi collaborator, most of the others did not have definitive connections with the Nazi party.

Toward the end of 1996, Senator D'Amato's office was producing one of these formerly classified "discoveries" to an eager international press corps on an almost daily basis. According to D'Amato's documents, taken piecemeal out of the National Archives in Washington, Switzerland had laundered between $400 and $800 million worth (about $4 billion and $8 billion today) of Nazi gold during the war, plus it had knowingly taken in Dutch and Belgian gold, and the gold that had been melted down from the dental fillings of victims of the Holocaust. Switzerland concluded secret deals with the government of Poland to use the money of Polish Holocaust victims to compensate Swiss industrialists in the postwar period. It's not that this information, much of it contained in U.S. intelligence files that had been declassified for years, was wrong, but that these were not the sensational revelations D'Amato made them out to be. For instance, much of the so-called classified information on the Nazi laundering of looted gold had been available to the public for several years, and had actually been the subject of several academic works, including an extremely thorough and comprehensive study by American historian Arthur Smith, Jr., who in 1989 published a book titled *Hitler's Gold*.

"I've listened all morning and this afternoon to things that, to a large extent, in outline were known for a number of years," Arthur Smith told the banking committee hearings of the U.S. House of Representatives in December 1996. "I'm surprised about the fact that much of it is presented as new and sensational. I began research on this subject in 1980; and, by 1989, I published the book you referred to. It received absolutely no attention."[17]

Smith said that American government officials had known about Swiss financial collaboration with the Nazis since the spring of 1946, after the signing of the Washington Accord. So what D'Amato was telling the world was old news repackaged to create sensational stories.

At least one Swiss diplomat publicly berated D'Amato for his cowboy-style tactics: "Publishing single documents out of context and without regard to the historical realities constitutes sensationalism and throws doubts upon the seriousness of purpose."[18]

For American journalist Leonard Lurie, it's just another example of the senator's "bullying" style: "Here is a man in the U.S. Senate who is theoretically a patriot, yet his whole endeavor has been to destroy the president of the United States through the Whitewater scandal. Do you think," he asks, "that such a man would hesitate to destroy Swiss banks?"

In a speech before the House banking committee hearings in December 1996, D'Amato defended his actions:

I think it's a bit cavalier for those—maybe because they find what we are unearthing to be embarrassing—to take the Senate Banking Committee to task for releasing these documents and/or releasing them, as they say, piecemeal. We're only finding them piecemeal. Indeed, some of these documents they had had—the Swiss government and the Swiss Bankers Association—in their possession for 50 years. And I say how dare they then accuse us of some kind of misdeed because we, for the first time, unearthed these documents. Some of them did not come into our possession until two or three weeks ago. That they should be offended because we are shocked by what we find? That's absolutely unconscionable.[19]

In addition to exploiting sensational bits of information, such as attacks on deceased Swiss lawyers, from the National Archives— quite a few of them taken out of context—D'Amato also relied on the emotional testimony of Holocaust survivors, many of whom had been nowhere near Switzerland during the war, as ammunition against the Swiss.

"D'Amato had a whole stable of widows waiting to testify," said one prominent Swiss banker.

Other witnesses chosen by D'Amato's staff to testify before the Senate banking committee gave testimony about family bank accounts in Switzerland that, upon close examination by banking officials, revealed more about their own complicated family politics than Swiss banking practices. In April 1996, Greta Beer gave a moving, albeit confused account of going with her elderly mother from bank to bank in Switzerland in the 1960s to find her father's bank account. She said the bankers treated her and her mother with contempt. At one point, a Swiss banker asked Beer's elderly mother if she had been "hit over the head by a German soldier with the butt of a gun."[20] Beer, a New York City tour guide who lived in Queens, was born to a wealthy family in Romania, and believed that her father had assets in Swiss banks. After he died of natural causes in 1940, the family left Romania to escape the Nazis and the Communists.

"My father had the greatest trust in the Swiss banks. And they broke that trust," she said.[21]

Swiss banker Hans Baer, who testified at the same hearing, was so moved by Greta Beer's story that he invited her to spend a week in Switzerland at his expense to search for her family's assets She traveled to Zürich a few months later. Upon researching her claim, banking officials did indeed find her father's account, but also discovered that other members of her family had withdrawn the funds long ago.

"I told her that she had to be happy that we had found what had happened to the account," says Baer, a stocky, good-natured banker, who has set himself up as a kind of intermediary between Edgar Bronfman and the Swiss Bankers Association. "But it shows you that you have to be careful when you make accusations. Without proof it's hard to accuse anyone."

Carlo Jagmetti, Switzerland's ambassador to Washington, called the Beer claim a tricky case. "They [Swiss bankers] found her account but they discovered her uncles had taken everything from her account in the past. . . . Had she had money, . . . she would have gotten it right away. Accusations should not be made before records have been carefully analyzed, and sinister motives should not be attributed to measures taken out of genuine concern."[22]

D'Amato wasn't the only person who saw conspiracies. It's not difficult to see why many normally sober and intelligent Swiss politicians and businesspeople believed the attacks were part of a wider conspiracy among the world's banks to discredit Switzerland. At the end of January 1997, New York state and municipal governments warned that they would consider blacklisting Swiss banks, and one reporter noted how politicians jumped at the chance to attach themselves to the popular Swiss-bashing. "[N]ow other politicians are scurrying to follow D'Amato's lead on the Swiss bank issue. New York City is debating a proposal to bar any city investments in Swiss banks, and New York Governor George Pataki soon will order audits to determine if any looted assets were transferred to Swiss bank branches in the state."[23]

Peter Vallone, the president of the New York City Council, introduced a bill to bar city funds from being deposited in Swiss banks until a compensation fund was set up for Holocaust victims. A spokesman for the council also said that the government body would consider whether to require the city's pension funds to divest themselves of the $50 million the city of New York holds in the stock of

Credit Suisse, the Swiss Bank Corporation, and the Union Bank of Switzerland.

"Internationally this has done a lot of damage to Switzerland," said a Zürich-based banker who did not want to be named. "We can only see it as a conspiracy of banks in New York."

More and more, the Swiss saw the international outrage against them as a plot by their competitors in London and New York. *Finanz und Wirtschaft,* an influential Swiss business paper, noted in an editorial, "Certain circles are using the tragic fate of Holocaust victims to discredit the still extant advantage Switzerland as a financial center and its banks have in global competition."[24]

Marc Suter, a deputy from the Radical Democratic Party, agreed. "It is no coincidence that especially harsh tones are coming from the City of London or the New York senatorial campaign," he said. "One reason this storm of indignation is roaring through the Anglo-Saxon newspapers may be to weaken Switzerland as a financial center, to undermine Swiss banking secrecy or to deflect attention from their own shortcomings."[25]

However, as angry as D'Amato has made them, some Swiss politicians do not criticize the senator for trying to get ahead in American politics. "The first duty of any parliamentarian in any country is to be elected," says Grendelmeier. "I don't fault D'Amato for raising an issue to help him get elected; I'm just upset at the way he's doing it."

Others say that Switzerland owes a great deal to D'Amato and the World Jewish Congress for opening up an important debate on the country's wartime role. "They imposed a national discussion in Switzerland," says Ueli Haldimann, the earnest young editor in chief of the *SonntagsZeitung.* "If pressure did not exist from outside, we wouldn't be going through this process."

Still, politicians like Lili Nabholz, a fifty-one-year-old Swiss parliamentarian, lawyer, and chair of the legal-affairs committee, shake their heads when they're reminded of Switzerland's rude brushes with D'Amato. "Look, we're trying to be as objective as possible here," says

Nabholz, who, along with Grendelmeier, spearheaded the creation of the parliamentary commission that is examining Switzerland's financial relationship with the Third Reich. "We are not interested to hold up a piece of paper as an accusation, which seems to be very popular in the United States. We are interested in doing serious work. Once the report of the commission is on the table, then the discussions can start. This is not an issue to play political games on. We hope it will be recognized in the international community that we are doing everything to clarify this issue. We are trying to do our best."

While Switzerland's critics have applauded the creation of the parliamentary commission, the major complaint is that the proposed timetable of three to five years is much too long. The British MP Greville Janner wants everything done in two months. D'Amato seems to want it to be done even sooner, and claims that the five-year timetable is just another example of Swiss stonewalling:

> While we understand that the people today who head the Swiss Bankers Association and the Swiss government are not responsible for the acts that took place 50 years ago plus, they are responsible for their own actions or in-actions today—make no mistake about that. You will hear testimony from the heirs of those victims. Some of them are well into their 80s. Imagine, saying we'll report in three to five years. What kind of confidence does that give us? It would suggest that the stonewalling continues.[26]

Today there are about eighteen thousand Jews scattered throughout Switzerland. While most of them welcome the long overdue debate on Switzerland's wartime role, they would prefer that it was conducted a little more quietly.

"It is true that the Swiss banks did not have the right attitude during and after the war," says Daniel Guggenheim, the international lawyer based in Geneva. "But I don't like this scapegoat idea, perpetuated by the World Jewish Congress and Mr. D'Amato. The World Jewish Congress lives in a dream world. Nobody is as black-and-white as they make them out to be. It's amazing. They fight against stereotypes, but use them all the time to fight against the Swiss."

Daniel Guggenheim, who is third cousin to the American art collector Peggy Guggenheim, was born in 1938 and grew up in a country where not until the nineteenth century were Jews permitted to feel like citizens. Jews were particularly unwelcome in Geneva, the city of the French Reformer Jean Calvin. In the sixteenth century, Geneva attracted wealthy Protestant refugee families from all over Europe, who settled in the region during the Protestant diaspora of the sixteenth century. Until 1866, Swiss Jews could not vote, be elected to public office, or live in their area of choice. Things were so bad that Guggenheim's great-grandfather paid for his cousins to move to America. In the 1930s, while most Swiss were indeed anti-Nazi, they were not necessarily pro-Jewish, says Daniel, whose father, Paul, a respected international banking lawyer, was president of the legal commission of the Swiss Federation of Jewish Communities after the war.

"As he often told me, he considered it his duty, despite the fact he was a nonpractising Jew, to show full solidarity with other Jews," says Daniel Guggenheim, sitting behind a large mahogany table piled with legal textbooks in his elegant offices on the Rue des Granges, a tiny cobblestoned street nestled in Geneva's Old Town—a neighborhood of narrow, winding alleyways and immaculately preserved seventeenth-century row houses that Guggenheim jokingly refers to as the "Calvinist ghetto." Next door to Guggenheim's office stands the house where Swiss-French philosopher Jean-Jacques Rousseau was born. A few doors down, Argentine writer Jorge Luis Borges lived out his last days.

"In the days before the Second World War, my father had to fight even the Swiss Jewish community over letting in Jewish refugees," says Guggenheim, completing his thought. Despite his commitment to Jewish issues, Paul Guggenheim was sometimes shocked by the divisions that racked even the relatively small Swiss Jewish community. "You have to remember that there was also a great deal of racism within the Jewish community here. You could let in certain kinds of Jews, but nobody wanted the Polish Jews, for instance."

Despite this, Paul Guggenheim devoted much of his career to campaigning on behalf of important Jewish causes. According to his son Daniel, Paul, along with Gerhart Riegner of the World Jewish Congress, was one of the first to notify U.S. President Franklin Delano Roosevelt of the mass extermination of Jews in Europe. Paul Guggenheim filed an affidavit that warned of the Holocaust with the U.S. consulate in Geneva, which sent it off to Roosevelt, who promptly ignored it. Following the war, Paul Guggenheim lobbied to have Swiss banks release the funds belonging to victims of the Holocaust, which resulted in the 1962 law temporarily lifting banking secrecy.

If his father were alive today, says Daniel, he would not approve of the lobbying tactics of "these Jewish American cowboys" of the World Jewish Congress. "They have turned themselves into figures of the arrogant Jews demanding money, and this is very dangerous."

Rolf Bloch, the jolly, rotund president of the Swiss Federation of Jewish Communities, shares Daniel Guggenheim's concern over the abrasive tactics used by fellow Jews in North America. But he also knows from past experience that "silence doesn't work" and that "Jews must speak up." Still, Bloch is Swiss, and works tirelessly on behalf of Swiss Jews with quiet, diplomatic resolve, knowing instinctively when to press an issue, and when to be quiet. For instance, for years he has been assembling evidence about how the Swiss Jewish community during the war was forced to pay for the upkeep of the 25,000 Jewish refugees who were allowed into the country. Bloch figures the Swiss government owes the Jewish community more than 15 million Swiss francs (about $10.7 million). He wants the money to return to the community, but says he is waiting for the right time to present his case. "Now is not the time to push. There are other issues to be resolved first." An attentive, kindly gentleman of sixty-seven who regularly wakes up at five o'clock in the morning to juggle the affairs of Camille Bloch Chocolates, the company his father founded, and the work of the Swiss Federation of Jewish Communities, Bloch says, "I have always felt a strong moral obligation as a survivor of World War Two in Switzerland. I owe it to my fellow Jews to give part of my work to Jewish organizations."

As part of his obligation to Switzerland, Bloch accompanied the Swiss governmental and banking delegation that appeared before the U.S. House of Representatives banking committee hearings, and eloquently conveyed the dilemma of Swiss Jews, torn between their desire to achieve justice for victims of the Holocaust and fairness for Switzerland.

"What I told them in Washington was that I was bleeding for justice for victims of the Holocaust but also for fairness for the Swiss," he said, noting that his family has lived in Switzerland for 150 years. "Fairness means that one does not present documents out of context. One does not generalize and construe a collective guilt."

IN HIS SUBURBAN office in an industrial park on the outskirts of Toronto, Hans Hamersfeld was thinking about Switzerland, his grandfather, and the elusive Swiss bank account. It was a Friday morning, and Hans was looking forward to a weekend of skiing with his family in northern Ontario. As he made his hotel reservations, his secretary walked in with the morning mail. Among the bills and junk mail, a white envelope with a Swiss postmark caught his eye. It was a letter from Caterina Nägeli, his lawyer in Zürich, informing him that the family's first claim to the Swiss banks had met with failure.

It was the end of November 1996, and as the first blizzard of the season raged outside his office window, Hans calmly read over the stiff, legalistic form letter from Ombudsman Hanspeter Häni several times as if to comprehend its meaning.

We have studied your completed questionnaire and carefully processed the documentation submitted therewith together with the information which you provided on the presumed depositors (names and any additional designations) as illustrated by the enclosed data sheet. This material was passed on to every bank in Switzerland. We must unfortunately now inform you that no positive reports were received from any of the banks applied to. This indicates that no dormant accounts (accounts, custody accounts or safe deposit boxes) are held in any Swiss Bank under any of the names or designations cited by you. It only remains for us to assure you that inquiry was treated with the utmost diligence. We regret that we are unable to give you a more satisfactory reply.[27]

"I'm not sure what it means," said Hans, who immediately phoned his cousins Renée and Herbie to inform them of the results of the first search.

That night, when he returned to the elegant suburban home he shares with his Spanish-born wife, Carmen, Hans made himself a cup of herbal tea and did something he hadn't done in years. He searched through old family letters in a worn cardboard box, looking for some clue that might unlock his grandfather's Swiss account. As he flipped through the pile of yellowing letters, he lingered here and there over old postcards from his uncle Harry on business trips in Czechoslovakia, and the 1945 telegram from Renée to the Stilmans informing the family that she and Selma had survived the war. As he dug through the box, he was overwhelmed by a flood of memories that had been so painful he had never really been able to bring himself to discuss them with his own children. They came to him all at once, in no particular order, and he recalled things he hadn't thought of in years. He remembered the winter that he had gathered scraps of wood to build a sled in a Siberian labor camp. He remembered the seders at the Negerlegasse flat and his grandmother's collection of Chinese porcelain cups so fine you could see right through them if you held them up to the light.

"It's amazing the things you remember, the things you've hidden for so long," he said, recalling the anti-Semitism he had endured at school in Vienna after the Anschluss, his first encounter with the SS officer who bought him an ice-cream cone and took him to the park when he was eight years old, and the rushed journey to Stockholm—his first time on an airplane—and then the boat trip across the Baltic Sea to Riga, where he lived with his grandfather, who took him to synagogue and taught him his first words of Hebrew.

"Why didn't Grandfather repeat the banking information to me when I was in Riga?" wondered Hans, instinctively looking up at his parents' photographs, which occupy a place of honor on the piano in his living room. "Why didn't Grandfather say something to me?"

As he sipped his tea, Hans contemplated what to do next. He would think about it on the weekend, on the ski slopes, where he always did his best thinking. On Monday he would ask his lawyer, Sergio Karas, to try filing another claim. He was determined to find the account through every legal means possible. Like his grandfather, he would put his trust in the law. More than fifty years after the death of Abraham Hammersfeld, his grandson was determined to uphold his principles.

Hans Hamersfeld's trust in the law to salvage what remained of his grandfather's legacy may seem like a brutal irony to an outside observer. But Hans didn't give it a second thought.

"Everything is destiny," he said with a long sigh. "Sometimes we are just so helpless to control our own lives." For Hans, it seemed that there had always been an outside force determining how and where he would live his life. As a Jew, he had been forced to leave Austria and then Latvia to escape the Nazis. In Russia, he and his family were interned by the Soviets precisely because they were Austrians, citizens of the enemy Third Reich. Even his settlement in Canada had not really been by choice, but through a series of happy events that began when his cousin Renée fell in love with a good-hearted Canadian soldier at a displaced persons camp in Germany. And now destiny in the form of Swiss bankers and the Swiss government would determine whether or not he and his family would be able to find a bank account that represented much more to him than money. It was a final vestige of a grandfather, whom destiny had also taken away.

Hans drained the last of his tea, and carefully placed the old letters and postcards back into the cardboard box. He stood for a few minutes watching the snow fall outside his living-room window, thinking about his grandfather. And then he went to bed, so that he could get an early start on his ski trip.

BUYING
RESPECT

The man with the most difficult job in Switzerland was also dreaming of the ski slopes.

Thomas Borer, a thirty-nine-year-old career diplomat, was in charge of saving Switzerland's international reputation in the wake of the scandal over the dormant Holocaust accounts and the Nazi gold issue. It was a week before Christmas, and Borer, barely two months into his new job, was already overworked.

"I need a vacation," he said, glancing around his cluttered office, where paintings were propped up against walls, waiting to be hung, and cardboard boxes full of official documents took up almost every square inch of floor and desk space. Borer's visitors were obliged to move stacks of legal texts and government documents to free up a place to sit on his couch.

For a country known around the world for its unwillingness to take sides in any sort of international debate or to expose its own internal matters to global scrutiny, this very public probe into Switzerland's wartime dealings with the Nazis was decidedly un-Swiss. But after more than a year of being pilloried by their opponents, even the Swiss recognized that they needed to do something to end their public row with Jewish groups and Alfonse D'Amato, which was turning into what UN Secretary General Kofi Annan called "a public relations disaster"[1] for Switzerland.

Borer, who in addition to his new job was also deputy secretary general of the Swiss Federal Department of Foreign Affairs, had not yet had a chance to make the final move into his new office. He had just returned to Bern from his first trip to Washington as head of the Swiss government Task Force on the Assets of Nazi Victims. While in Washington to testify at the House banking committee hearings, Special Ambassador Borer, as he was known in Switzerland, had had meetings with his country's most vocal critics. He had tried to re-assure people like Alfonse D'Amato and Edgar Bronfman that this time Switzerland was indeed serious about conducting an independent investigation into the country's financial dealings with the Third Reich. In fact, hours before he testified in Washington, the Swiss Parliament had unanimously approved the legislation to lift banking secrecy for five years and to create the commission of experts to conduct the "sweeping study" of Swiss financial dealings with Nazi Germany.

"Ja, ja, everything went well," said Borer, who was speaking in German-accented English to one of the New York legal consultants he had hired to help him coordinate his political strategy in the United States. "D'Amato said that he doesn't trust the Swiss, and he doesn't trust the banks, but he trusts me."

It was probably because Borer is eminently likable and nonthrea-tening. He is the very antithesis of his predecessor, of sorts, Walter Stucki, the aggressive and rigid envoy who was sent on the now infamous 1946 mission to the United States to hammer out the terms of the Washington Accord. Whereas Stucki, a bald, middle-aged dip-lomat, was known for his hard-line negotiating style, Borer is friendly, conciliatory, even charming. But unlike Stucki, who went to Wash-ington with precise instructions from the Swiss Federal Council to give the Allies very few concessions in the Washington Accord, the young, handsome diplomat with thinning light brown hair seems to have a much more difficult and certainly very public responsibility. For he has the herculean task of repairing Switzerland's tarnished reputation abroad. His mandate is to coordinate "swift" action on the part of the Swiss federal authorities in all questions pertaining to the issue of assets transferred to Switzerland between 1933 and 1945. He is in charge of making sure that the Foreign Ministry cooperates with officials of the Swiss Federal Archives, the Finance and Justice Ministries, the Swiss National Bank, and the Swiss Bankers Association. He also travels around Switzerland, speaking at town hall meetings and community centers to make sure that the Swiss people understand their government's response to the international scandal. Internationally, he is Switzerland's goodwill ambassador—the man whose increasingly important task is to pacify and reassure Switzerland's most virulent opponents.

"We decided we needed to do something to save Switzerland's image," says a Swiss foreign ministry official who does not want to be identified. "At first we were so surprised by the magnitude of the criticisms from the outside world. We had been reactive in the past, and now we felt it was time to become proactive. We wanted someone who was young and dynamic and understood Americans."

So they hired Thomas Borer, an international lawyer born in Basel whose credentials for "understanding Americans" include a year spent as legal counselor at the Swiss embassy in Washington in 1993, and an American-born fiancée who works in telecommunications.

In addition to Borer, Swiss officials also hired other young bureaucrats and academics, placing ads in newspapers throughout Switzerland calling for "young" English speakers to act as Borer's assistants.

It was the end of the workday in Bern, but the beginning of the workday in New York and Washington, and Borer's telephone was ringing off the hook with overseas callers. He was balancing his telephone headset on his left shoulder, talking to his New York–based legal consultant, while typing an E-mail message on his computer.

His other line was ringing now, so he put the New York lawyer on hold and, switching into French, spoke to the Swiss foreign minister's secretary. But while he was on the phone with her, his sleek, black cellular telephone rang, and he realized he had run out of hands. He abandoned the E-mail in midsentence and put the foreign minister's secretary on hold to answer the cellular caller, who turned out to be his girlfriend.

"I promise I will make it happen this time. I will," said Borer, who was promising to take his fiancée on a two-week ski vacation in the Swiss Alps. Since he took over his post, they had had little time together—what with Borer traveling all over Switzerland and flying to Washington and New York for high-level meetings with U.S. politicians.

Borer had good reason to be stressed out. As the Swiss government's envoy on his country's financial relationships with the Third Reich, he had been under almost constant scrutiny from critics in the United States, who said he wasn't moving fast enough to resolve the issue. In Switzerland he had recently come under fire from parliamentarians who were upset that he had convinced the government to spend more than $20,000 on American public relations consultants to help him with his presentation before the House banking committee hearings in Washington. "This is not like the United States," said Borer. "Switzerland is not the kind of place where you hire image consultants. It's very conservative on these things." For his part, he insisted that he had hired not image consultants, but legal experts, who nevertheless give him advice on how to present his country's case before U.S. politicians, like D'Amato.

In New York and Washington, politicians and lobbyists found Borer to be well-intentioned but rather pompous, and sometimes a little bit awkward. "He's a Swiss cowboy from the Alps, who's engaged to a former Miss Texas and thinks he knows everything about America," said Elan Steinberg, executive director of the World Jewish Congress in New York. "I once dated a girl from Texas and that didn't get me any closer to understanding America."

Even some Swiss observers agreed. "This man is a disaster for

Switzerland, and has absolutely no feeling for the American public," said Daniel Guggenheim.

Despite the opposition, Borer soldiered on, offering to speak with just about any politician in the United States to save Switzerland's reputation: "I'd meet the devil if it helped." His main task, as he explained it, was to interpret American reaction to the Swiss and translate the Swiss way of thinking to the Americans. For Borer, the job was a challenge—even more difficult than his first overseas posting as an economic attaché at the Swiss embassy in Lagos, Nigeria, in 1937.

"I'm thirty-nine years old and getting older by the day with this job," he said, adding that his biggest challenge was convincing American politicians that Switzerland was truly committed to conducting a proper investigation of the dormant accounts and Nazi gold. "To the Americans, we are the really bad, bad guy in Europe now, but the truth is that we are honest, no-nonsense people who also want to get to the bottom of this issue."

Before Thomas Borer arrived on the scene, Switzerland had no discernible strategy for dealing with its critics. Depending on the accusations hurled against the country by Jewish groups and American politicos, Swiss government officials either reacted with shocking aloofness or dug in their heels and became overly defensive. Indeed, in the first few months of the scandal it seemed that the Swiss government was content to stay out of the fray altogether and let the Swiss financial institutions fend for themselves. At the end of September 1996, as D'Amato, Bronfman, and Britain's Greville Janner stepped up their campaign against Swiss banks, Winterthur, the country's second biggest insurance company, made a rather bold step to save Switzerland's reputation, by taking out a full-page advertisement in the *Financial Times* of London, quoting a 1944 speech by then British Prime Minister Winston Churchill on Switzerland's noble wartime role:

Of all the neutrals **Switzerland** has the greatest right to distinction. She has been the sole international force linking the hideously sundered nations and ourselves. What does it matter whether she has been able to give us the commercial advantages we desire or has given too many to the Germans to keep herself alive? She has been a **democratic State,** standing for freedom in self-defence among her mountains, and in thought, in spite of race, largely **on our side.**[2]

The 50,000 Swiss-franc (about $35,700) ad was a dramatic gesture to remind the newspaper's global readership of Churchill's defense of the Swiss. The idea for it came from Winterthur President Peter Spaelti, who is also a former member of Parliament. Reprinted in leading dailies in Switzerland, the ad sought to restore confidence in the country.

"It is certainly a reaction to the attacks that have arisen, not in the sense that we have anything to hide . . . but one cannot see this in such a one-sided way," said Winterthur spokesperson Anna-Marie Kappeler. "This is also a mouthpiece for many Swiss who say: 'Not everything was wrong. We were in an extreme situation, under pressure, a small country.' . . . This was the message and many people were waiting for it."[3]

But not even Winston Churchill could dignify Switzerland's tarnished wartime record. Less than a month after the ad appeared, Switzerland was hit by another public relations nightmare: Senator D'Amato brought forth evidence that Switzerland had struck secret deals with Communist countries to use the unclaimed dormant accounts of Holocaust victims and others to compensate Swiss nationals for property nationalized by Communist regimes in Eastern Europe. D'Amato's allegations were backed up by Swiss historian Peter Hug, who had discovered evidence in Switzerland's National Archives in Bern that the country had indeed struck these secret postwar deals with several Eastern Bloc countries.

The Swiss government handled this revelation as it had dealt with most of the others. At first, officials vehemently denied it, then they stonewalled, and finally they gave in only days later when they were presented with the indisputable evidence, much of it found by their own Foreign Office researchers in the National Archives.

The revelations about Switzerland's postwar secret deals with Communists in Eastern Europe began in mid-October 1996 when D'Amato announced that his researchers had found evidence that Switzerland had signed a compensation treaty with Poland, with a secret annex attached. The New York senator's office released a March 22, 1950, statement from Switzerland's then foreign minister saying that the heirless property of Polish citizens in Switzerland would be deposited in a Swiss bank account for the Polish National Bank. The statement, which was found in the archives of the American Jewish Distribution Committee, further noted that the Polish government would use the money from dormant accounts belonging to Poles in Switzerland to compensate Swiss citizens, banks, and life insurance companies that had had their assets confiscated or "nationalized" in Poland.[4]

Two days after D'Amato's allegations were made public, the Swiss Foreign Office announced that it had found, in the National Archives, secret letters between Poland and Switzerland dating from 1949, detailing the agreement. These unpublished letters, which were part of the public treaty between the two countries, noted that Polish citizens' Swiss bank accounts and life insurance policies that went unclaimed for five years would be turned over to Poland. Under the public part of the treaty, Poland was to pay Switzerland 52.1 million Swiss francs (about $41.6 million then; about $275 million in 1997) in compensation for confiscated Swiss property. The deal was struck after mounting pressure from Swiss businesses and individuals who were actively seeking compensation from Eastern European countries whose new Communist regimes had confiscated foreign-owned property.

Switzerland's critics pounced on the revelations.

"The Swiss immorally transferred Jewish assets to Poland," said Kalman Sultanik, a vice president of the World Jewish Congress in New York.[5] Sultanik and others demanded that the Swiss pay millions of dollars in compensation to Jewish restitution groups. Senator

D'Amato called the actions "unconscionable" and went on to blast the "immorality" of the Swiss government and financial community. "Never in banking history could you deem something to take place like this," he said. "This was long after the war. This was in 1949. This is not a situation [that] I've heard some say 'oh, well they [the Swiss] felt threatened. They were surrounded. They had to, in some cases, kind of look the other way.' "[6]

Even the diplomatically reserved Rolf Bloch, president of the Swiss Federation of Jewish Communities, could not control his anger. "We do not agree that Switzerland should use funds stemming from Holocaust victims to make it easier for the Poles or other states to compensate Swiss for nationalized property," he said. "We demand a quick determination of the facts and of the amount of the money involved and that these be given to the heirs or to the fund set up by federal decree in 1962 to distribute dormant assets to charitable organizations."[7]

When news of the secret deal first surfaced, Swiss Foreign Minister Flavio Cotti vehemently denied any wrongdoing. He noted that the claim was "totally without foundation,"[8] despite the secret letters unearthed at the archives. In addition to the covert deal with Poland, government researchers found evidence that Switzerland had concluded similar pacts with Hungary, Romania, Bulgaria, and the former Yugoslavia.[9] However, money related to secret compensation agreements was disbursed only to Hungary and Poland, according to Swiss historians.

To make matters worse, historian Peter Hug of the University of Bern wrote a damning article in the *Neue Zürcher Zeitung,* detailing his findings on the secret deals. Swiss government officials, who could no longer deny the evidence before them, were quick to point out, however, that funds from the dormant accounts of Holocaust victims had not been used to compensate Swiss industrialists. Moreover, they pointed out that although the deals might look immoral and unfortunate today, they were completely correct under private international law. Nonetheless, while the Swiss may indeed have had the law on their side when they signed those deals, they did not have the morality, argued Hug.

Following an intensive examination of more than 6,500 boxes of documents at the Swiss National Archives in Bern over several months, Peter Hug said the Swiss used dormant account money to compensate Swiss business on at least three occasions between 1960 and 1975. He told a reporter for *The New York Times* that on one of these occasions, money from dormant accounts of presumed Holocaust victims was "distributed directly among Swiss businessmen" to meet their claims for compensation for assets seized in Hungary after that country's Communist takeover.[10] Moreover, according to Hug, Switzerland agreed in 1950 to help Hungary—which, like Poland, was eager to acquire hard currency—search for the dormant Swiss accounts of Hungarians who had perished in the war. However, when in 1973 the Swiss government sought parliamentary approval for a bilateral compensation treaty with Hungary, it did not mention a confidential protocol that credited Hungary with 325,000 Swiss francs (about $229,600 in 1997) from unclaimed accounts whose beneficial owners were Hungarian nationals.[11] In addition, Hug contended that money from dormant Holocaust accounts left unclaimed after the 1962 law—set up to return the unclaimed assets of victims of Nazi persecution—also went to make secret payments to Hungary and Poland. Under the provision of the 1962 law, that money should have gone to support Jewish charitable organizations. However, in 1973 when the Swiss struck the compensation agreement with Hungary, the 325,000 Swiss-franc payment was withdrawn from the special government account, said Hug. "The money stayed in Switzerland."[12]

For compensations in Poland, Swiss officials paid more than 460,500 Swiss francs (about $390,000 today) into a separate Polish government account at the Swiss National Bank in 1975. "Account N" was a clearing account into which were deposited Polish receipts from the sale of coal to Switzerland, along with funds from dormant accounts held by Polish citizens before 1939, and the Swiss compensation claims were all to be offset against each other.

"At the start of each month, beginning January 1, 1951, the balance of 'Account N' will be credited to the Swiss government, which will use it as a partial payment toward the global compensation fixed in the first and third articles of the [public part of the] treaty," said the secret protocol. A separate protocol estimated that the value of the Polish dormant accounts in Switzerland was close to $1.6 million (about $9.6 million today).[13]

According to Hug, at the insistence of Swiss banks, the secret agreement between Poland and Switzerland provided for Poland, not Switzerland, to act as a guarantor that legitimate heirs would inherit the dormant accounts. However, when Switzerland deposited the money, it did not provide a list of the beneficial owners of the accounts. "For me what is morally very, very questionable is that for 50 years Switzerland did nothing to try to find the people this money actually belonged to," said Hug.[14] During one payment in 1975, Switzerland again refused to include the names of the beneficial owners of the accounts despite repeated requests from Poland. The Swiss also refused to give out a list of possible heirs to Hungarian authorities, citing a Cold War policy of hiding the identities of the account holders from Communist regimes for fear of endangering the lives of the account holders or their heirs.

Recently declassified documents in Washington suggest that the United States knew about parts of the agreement between Poland and Switzerland, and sent a diplomatic note of protest to the Swiss on December 23, 1949. The note referred to information which had come to the State Department's attention "in relation to the commercial and financial agreement between Switzerland and Poland of June 25, 1949, which is now before the National Assembly for ratification." The note complained that the Swiss-Polish agreement "is said to contain a provision whereby the assets in Switzerland of Polish nationals who had died without heirs would be turned over to the Government of Poland."[15] However, geopolitical expedients during the Cold War prevented the United States from getting further involved in the situation in Poland.

It wasn't until Senator D'Amato raised the issue in the fall of 1996 that the international spotlight focused cn Switzerland, some forty-seven years after the postwar agreements were signed. While Switzerland remained defensive and continued to offer flimsy excuses for its participation in these unethical deals, other countries were quick to denounce them as immoral. Even some of the Eastern European signatories to the compensation deals with Switzerland expressed disapproval.

Poland, now a democracy, declared that its former Communist rulers had acted unethically in the 1949 compensation agreement with Switzerland. After conducting a two-month probe into the deal, Polish Foreign Minister Dariusz Rosati noted that it "contained many legal flaws . . . it was not ratified by the Polish parliament, . . . the way in which the money was accepted was unlawful as inheritance procedures were not carried out." Rosati added that his government would now try to identify any surviving heirs by asking Swiss authorities to provide details of the beneficial owners of the dormant accounts. Ten days later, Switzerland gave Poland the names of fifty-three Polish citizens, including several Holocaust victims, whose Swiss bank accounts were declared ownerless after the Second World War. A few days later, Switzerland handed Hungary a similar list of thirty-three people, most of them victims of the Holocaust, whose bank accounts were declared heirless after World War II and were credited to Hungary.

It was in the midst of the international outrage over the revelations of Switzerland's postwar agreements with Eastern Bloc countries that Swiss officials appointed the very able and congenial special ambassador, Thomas Borer, to prop up Switzerland's international image.

"We had to do something fast to save our international reputation," said a Swiss foreign ministry official who did not want to be identified. "The [revelations of] the Polish deal were a huge blow to us."

Borer made all the right moves, and tried to put his Swiss sensibilities—for accuracy, precision, and the law—on hold. He did not bother to explain away complicated agreements, such as the secret Eastern European protocols, that were morally indefensible and too complex to explain away in a sound bite. If he had contempt for his

American opponents, for their grandstanding style and irreverence for the facts, he didn't show it. For Thomas Borer knew that the battle to save Switzerland's reputation would not be won with academic or legalistic explanations of the past. It would be won with sensitivity, compassion, and remorse.

At his first official appearance in Washington to testify before the House banking committee, Borer represented himself as a sensitive diplomat, personally committed to seeking the truth about Switzerland's wartime dealings with the Third Reich. He explained the various efforts under way in Switzerland to probe the issue, including the historic parliamentary commission, made up of nine historians from all over the world, who would have complete freedom to comb through official archives and thoroughly review Switzerland's wartime role.

In what appeared to be an effort to bolster his commitment to Jewish concerns, Borer noted that he grew up in Basel, the same place that Theodor Herzl had convened the First Zionist Congress in August 1897. And, perhaps on the advice of his American legal advisers, he made a point of mentioning that he had been to the Holocaust Museum in Washington. Twice.

"On a personal note, I want everyone to know the seriousness with which I personally view my current assignment," he said. "Yesterday afternoon, after preparing for today's hearing, I visited the Holocaust Museum. I had been there once before when it opened in 1994. This time, I wanted to reflect in the surroundings of such an important memorial about whether Switzerland is, about whether I am doing enough. . . . I believe my country is doing everything it can and the initiatives I described today will resolve all questions in a sensitive, moral and just manner. We are doing the right thing . . . Swiss political will and civic morality converge in their response to all those who were persecuted or perished during the war. We recognize that accounting for one's past is the key to the future."[16]

For all of his eloquence, Thomas Borer made one big mistake: He did not stay to hear the testimony of the Holocaust survivors who spoke after him. In her testimony before the banking committee,

Auschwitz survivor Alice Burger Fisher made a point of noting Special Ambassador Borer's quick exit. "I am insulted to see that Ambassador Borer, on behalf of the Swiss government, didn't see fit to stay to hear the statements of the victims and the depositors," she said, before launching into her story about her inability to obtain her father's holdings in Swiss banks.[17]

Edgar Bronfman was also unimpressed, and immediately after Borer addressed the members of the House banking committee, Bronfman blasted the Swiss government and financial institutions for taking so long to distribute dormant assets to their rightful heirs. "Until now the pace has been slower than that of a snail," said an indignant Bronfman. "For all the discussions in the past year, not one franc has passed hands. And Holocaust survivors now in their twilight years are dying. . . . This is why the imperative to uncover historical truth must be also weighed against the flesh and blood needs of the aging victims."[18]

Borer seemed to anticipate the criticism and the World Jewish Congress's predilection for quick answers. "We are fully aware that nothing less than our reputation as an honorable country and reliable friend is at stake," he said, perhaps addressing his comments in Bronfman's direction. "As you may know, the Swiss have a reputation for being no-nonsense people, attached to values of hard work and exacting precision. There lies in our national character a strong preference for realism over fantasy, or compromise rather than ideology."[19]

In a private December meeting with Borer in New York, Bronfman repeated World Jewish Congress demands for an initial financial "gesture" from the Swiss government of $250 million to help needy Holocaust survivors waiting to find out about their families' dormant accounts. At that meeting, his first with representatives of the World Jewish Congress, Borer fixed Bronfman with a sympathetic gaze, nodded at all the right points, and told him he was personally committed to helping Holocaust survivors. He would try to persuade his government to agree to the fund. Bronfman, who was still smarting from his brush with Swiss officialdom a year before, still wasn't willing to put his complete confidence in Special Ambassador Borer, but he did admit that Borer was "actually a nice guy."

After the House banking committee hearings, Borer returned to Switzerland, confident that he had made a good impression. One U.S. congressman had called his speech a "powerful statement of commitment"[20] to seek the truth. Surely, Switzerland was now on the road to repairing its damaged international reputation. The $20,000 plus the Swiss government had spent on Borer's legal strategy had certainly been well spent. Or at least that's what Borer claimed to have told his boss, Foreign Minister Flavio Cotti.

Things were going so well that Borer now felt that he could put a few things on hold. The paintings in his office could wait another few weeks to be hung; the stacks of legal files could also wait. "I was told not to go to the United States because I would be butchered," he confessed. "But I think things worked out well." So well that Borer and his fiancée could now in good conscience embark on that long-awaited ski vacation in the Alps.

However, just as Borer was making reservations at a popular resort, Flavio Cotti's French-speaking secretary was back on the line. A slightly more relaxed special ambassador picked up the phone, mumbled a few words in French, hung up the phone, and rushed out of his office.

"I'm sorry, but I have to go," he said, straightening his tie. "Flavio Cotti wants to meet with me, and he doesn't like it when I'm late."

LESS THAN A month after Thomas Borer's Washington debut, all of his diplomacy and international goodwill in repairing Switzerland's tarnished image would come crashing down like a house of cards. Not even Special Ambassador Borer could save Switzerland from an unfortunate series of blunders by senior members of its own government and financial organizations.

The spectacular series of faux pas began on the last day of 1996, arguably Switzerland's most traumatic year in the international spotlight. On December 31, outgoing President Jean-Pascal Delamuraz gave the traditional year-end interview to the Swiss press. (Switzerland has a one-year rotating presidency whereby cabinet members take turns serving as president.) In a long interview with the French-language *Tribune de Genève*, Delamuraz, who was also economics minister, offered what he thought was an accurate reflection of the mood of the Swiss people and his fellow cabinet members.

"This is nothing less than extortion and blackmail," said Delamuraz, referring to the World Jewish Congress's repeated demands for "an interim fund" for Holocaust victims waiting to find out about their families' assets in Swiss banks. "This fund would make it much more difficult to establish the truth. Such a fund would be considered an admission of guilt. No one . . . appears to see that apart from dogged research into historical truth there is also a strong political desire to destabilize and compromise Switzerland. . . . Economic competition is fierce [for Swiss banks] and this affair proves it. This has one link in Washington and another in London, where it is a matter of nothing else than trying to demolish Switzerland's status as a financial centre."[21]

Although Delamuraz might have thought he was accurately conveying the frustration and paranoia of many of his compatriots, in the international arena he had put his foot squarely in his mouth. Thomas Borer cut his ski vacation short and rushed back to Bern to try to remedy the situation. But there was very little he could do. Journalists from around the world reprinted parts of the *Tribune de Genève*'s interview, with headlines like SWISS PRESIDENT CALLS HOLOCAUST CLAIMS "BLACKMAIL."[22] The words "blackmail" and "extortion" were the only ones that Switzerland's legion of keen critics remembered from the unfortunate interview. And they pounced on them with remarkable ferocity. It did not help that incoming Swiss President Arnold Koller supported his colleague's comments, noting that he did not like getting pushed around by Switzerland's critics, whom he accused of "arrogance and unfair methods."[23]

Avraham Burg, head of the Jewish Agency, a quasi-governmental body in Israel, called Delamuraz's comments "a conspiracy by the Swiss president to destroy negotiations between us in order for the

Swiss to avoid taking responsibility for their actions . . . during the war."[24]

In the United States, Jewish groups reacted predictably. "It is the height of 'chutzpah' for the head of a state which made billions of dollars as a result of its financial dealings with the Nazi Third Reich to label, 55 years later, the demands for justice and restitution for its victims as 'blackmail,'" said Rabbis Marvin Hier and Abraham Cooper, leaders of the Los Angeles branch of the Simon Wiesenthal Center, in a joint press statement.[25]

Jewish groups in Switzerland reported an onslaught of anti-Semitic activity in the wake of Delamuraz's comments. Martin Rosenfeld, executive director of the Swiss Federation of Jewish Communities in Bern, said the organization had received a rash of anti-Semitic letters, some of them calling for a return of Hitler's gas chambers for the Jews. He said that most of the letters he received were from older people objecting to Jewish demands for compensation fifty years after the war.

"The whole thing arose after the comments from Delamuraz and the subsequent uproar," said Rosenfeld. "It had been quiet before. Many feel justified by Delamuraz, and also have the feeling that if a cabinet member is allowed to express himself this way, then the threshold of anti-Semitism has been lowered. . . . It is not the case that the Swiss are especially anti-Semitic. There was always a latent anti-Semitism but until now people did not dare to express it openly."[26]

Indeed, Delamuraz's comments opened the floodgates for a lot of pent-up Swiss hostility against Jews—especially American Jews and Israelis. In one letter, published by the *Neue Zürcher Zeitung*, the writer noted that "the Jews want to see money from Switzerland. . . . Nothing other than money, money, money. . . . If peace with the Palestinians made money, then the Jews would have forced it by now."[27]

The liberal newspaper *SonntagsZeitung*, which appeals to a younger generation of Swiss, noted in an editorial that Delamuraz had broken a taboo in Switzerland. "He [Delamuraz] accused Jewish organizations of indecent behavior," wrote the newspaper's young

editor-in-chief, Ueli Haldimann. "That was a signal and now old prej-
udices about Jews are breaking out again openly. Not just among
neo-Nazis. Latent anti-Jewish feeling is still present, especially
among the older population."[28]

A journalist writing in the *Tages Anzeiger* went one step further:
"When I hear Minister Delamuraz and his many friends, it sounds
as if this were from the Middle Ages: The Jew who claims his basic
rights is tiresome and 'extortionist.' The Jew should not be so brazen,
but rather remain nice even if Switzerland still hesitates after half a
century to own up to its long-established failures and compensate via
a fund what still can be compensated."[29]

Switzerland's biggest coalition party, the Social Democrats, demanded that the Swiss cabinet distance itself from the remarks of
Minister Delamuraz. The World Jewish Congress demanded the
same thing and threatened to boycott Swiss banks if Delamuraz did
not offer an apology. But the Swiss cabinet stood firmly behind Delamuraz, as did the majority of the Swiss people, in opinion poll after
opinion poll. For his part, Delamuraz refused to apologize at first,
although he did concede that he "regretted" that his remarks had
been misunderstood and could have offended the feelings of Holocaust survivors and their families.[30]

Delamuraz finally did give in to international criticism. A fortnight
after his explosive interview with the *Tribune de Genève*, Delamuraz
wrote World Jewish Congress President Edgar Bronfman to say he
was "very sorry that I offended your feelings as well as those of . . .
the Jewish community at large. I assure you this was not my inten-
tion. The information on which I had based my statement regarding
the fund was inaccurate. I look forward to [the] return of constructive
work together with the Swiss authorities and the Swiss banks, to
resolve outstanding questions which will further our goals of truth
and justice."[31]

The groveling apology had its desired effect. The World Jewish
Congress called off its plan to boycott Swiss banks, and continued
negotiations with the Swiss authorities over the WJC's "interim fund."

However, no sooner had Thomas Borer and his colleagues in the

Swiss government breathed a collective sigh of relief than the country was plunged into another spectacular scandal.

On Thursday, January 9, after business hours, Christoph Meili, an earnest, bespectacled twenty-nine-year-old security guard, was making his usual rounds at the Union Bank of Switzerland's head office on the elegant Banhofstrasse, Zürich's financial center, when he noticed two large bins on wheels filled with old ledgers and documents in the bank's shredding room. Meili gave a quick glance behind him before walking briskly into the shredding room. Picking his way through a pile of documents stacked in the two bins, he was startled by what he saw before him: German contracts from the 1930s and 1940s, and ledgers with handwritten entries in fountain pen, which looked as if they might be from the nineteenth century.

Christoph Meili doesn't quite know why he stopped to read the documents, or why, fifteen minutes later, he found himself stuffing a sheaf of those same documents and one large ledger under his shirt. Something just didn't seem right about those bins of documents waiting to be destroyed, recalled Meili.

"I thought to myself: 'Wait a minute. This is historical material,' " Meili told a reporter from The New York Times. "There were more than 40 pages about real estate and they were from 1933, 1934, 1937. I saw the dates of payments and credits. I saw street names and numbers, and I saw that some of them were from Berlin."[32] Meili noted that some of the data he spirited out of the bank included information on "forced auctions," or expropriations of properties in Berlin between the years 1930 and 1940, records of loans granted to both Swiss and German firms between 1920 and 1926, and handwritten minutes of Central Bank meetings dating back to 1875.

The next day Meili called the Israeli embassy in Bern and asked what he should do with the large ledger and fifty-nine loose-leaf documents he had taken from the bank. An embassy official replied rather brusquely that he should either drive the documents to the embassy in Bern, which is about an hour from Zürich, or drop them in a mailbox. Meili decided instead to bundle the documents in a shopping bag and take them to the Israeli Cultural Center, a Jewish community center in Zürich that is devoted primarily to child care. Werner Rom, director of the center, was shocked when he saw the documents and, at first, suspicious of Meili. Rom decided to find out as much as he could about the young security guard and paid him a visit at his modest home in a working-class neighborhood in Baden, just outside Zürich, where Meili lived with his wife, Giuseppina, and his two young children. Meili is a typical Swiss, although he did admit to a reporter from *The New Yorker* to having lived "a chaotic life" until he nearly overdosed on a meal cooked with marijuana, and rediscovered God.[33]

"I wanted to see what kind of a person he was," said Rom, who spoke to both Meili and his wife. "They are simple people, but they are good people—they have a lot of dignity."[34] Rom warned Meili that he would most definitely lose his job if he made the documents public. After consulting his father, a small businessman, and his wife, both of whom counseled him against going public, Meili nonetheless made up his mind to tell the world about what he'd found.

"When God put these documents into my hands, I had to act on them," he said, adding that he did not give much thought to the continuing debate about Swiss banks' ties to the Third Reich when he took the documents.[35]

So, a few days later, on January 14, Meili did indeed go public. As Rom had predicted, Meili immediately lost his job at the private security firm that serves the Union Bank of Switzerland. He also became the subject of a criminal investigation into whether he had violated bank secrecy laws by turning over the documents to the Israeli Cultural Center. He said he was grilled for hours by law-enforcement officials, who wanted to know what his motives were for going public with the documents. Did he belong to a political party? A terrorist organization? Did he receive money to go public? No, said Meili repeatedly. He just *sensed* there was something wrong when he saw all of those weighty historical documents waiting to be destroyed. It was his duty as a Swiss citizen to save them. Meili, a minor functionary who said he acted with his conscience, brought to mind another man, Paul Gruninger, the Swiss police chief from St.

Gallen, who had also followed his conscience in 1938 and 1939 by falsifying entry documents to save three thousand Jews escaping Nazi persecution in Austria and Germany.

Meili's naive and impulsive act plunged the Union Bank of Switzerland, and the whole country, for that matter, deeper into scandal. The shredding incident stunned both Switzerland's critics and its supporters, especially since it occurred less than a month after the Swiss Parliament passed the law that created the commission to investigate the country's financial relationship with the Nazis. The law made it a criminal offense to destroy any historical records that could shed light on the period.

The Union Bank of Switzerland (UBS) snapped into action immediately, calling the shredding a "deplorable mistake," but noted that its in-house historian said that the documents had nothing to do with the present discussions about the Holocaust. The bank's explanations, however, seemed somewhat suspect, especially when Gertrud Erismann-Peyer, its senior spokesperson, noted that Erwin Haggenmueller, the bank's archivist, was acting entirely on his own in seeking to destroy the documents. She also noted that Haggenmueller, a longtime UBS vice president who had been put in charge of the bank's archives in 1993, had kept no inventory of what was destroyed. For this reason, Swiss authorities were not able to say whether the bank had violated the 1996 law to protect historical materials from the Nazi period when Haggenmueller shredded a large quantity of documents, which filled three large packing crates, each measuring three feet square and three feet deep, and two plastic garbage bags, four to five feet high.

"The historian made his judgment that these documents had nothing to do with the present discussion about the Holocaust—nothing, and that is the point," said Erismann-Peyer,[36] adding that Haggenmueller had "coincidentally" begun a three-week process of determining what should be destroyed just as the law prohibiting the destruction of documents went into effect. Haggenmueller did not get a chance to tell his part of the story. He was suspended from his job a few days after the shredding incident. The UBS dispatched a security detail to his home, on the outskirts of Lucerne, to make sure he did not speak to the press.

Further doubt was cast on the UBS when investigators discovered that some of the material waiting to be shredded came from a UBS subsidiary called the Eigenoessische Bank. It had been one of Switzerland's largest banks during the Second World War, and its fortunes were intimately tied to the rise and fall of the Third Reich. When the Nazi regime collapsed, so too did the bank, which was taken over by the UBS in 1945.

According to Swiss journalist Gian Trepp, who has written four books on Swiss banks, "There were several Swiss banks that cultivated close connections with Germany in the 1930s and Eigenoessische was one of them. They attached their fate to the fate of Nazi Germany. What that means is that anything about Eigenoessische has a possible relevance to the Holocaust."[37]

Switzerland's critics reacted to the document shredding with disbelief. "When you think about all of the publicity this issue has had in Switzerland," said Alfonse D'Amato, "it seems pretty remarkable that they let this stuff sit around for 50 years and then start shredding this month."[38]

The tall, soft-spoken Meili, became the "Document Hero" to Jewish groups around the world. He received fan mail from Israel and the United States. A tree was planted in his name in Israel. In February, the Israeli Parliament invited Meili to the country as a guest of honor. "You are not only a hero to us, the Jewish people, but to history," said Abraham Foxman, national director of the New York–based Anti-Defamation League. Foxman presented Meili with a golden menorah and a donation of 50,000 Swiss francs ($36,100) toward his legal defense. At least two Swiss banks refused to take the money when Meili tried to deposit it.

"Maybe he did break the law to prevent a crime," said Foxman, referring to the criminal investigation into whether Meili had broken banking secrecy by stealing the documents. "What crime? The crime of hiding the past. There are thousands of people, simple people, who during the years of the war were clerks, were secretaries, were messengers, were recorders. They know some of the truth that has been shredded in the past and has disappeared."[39]

Perhaps emboldened by the media attention and the plaudits from Israel, Meili appealed to other Swiss citizens to do the same thing he did if given the chance. "I would like to make an appeal that if there are people in Switzerland who know of these things, they have the courage to do something so that light is shed on the subject."

However, people in Switzerland were as divided in opinion on Meili's actions as they were about their country's relationship with the Third Reich. Swiss left-wingers wanted to use Meili in a campaign to get rid of banking secrecy laws. The Swiss government cited Meili as an example of a good citizen who could show the world that the Swiss were really upstanding, conscientious people, not Nazi-loving anti-Semites. But many others did not see Meili in a positive light. Robert Studer, chairman of the Union Bank of Switzerland, questioned Meili's motives on national television.

"What I currently know allows me to assume that the motives Meili has stated for his actions aren't the only ones," said Studer, who refused to elaborate. Studer is not known for his media savvy. It was Studer who, in early 1996, announced at a news conference that his bank had found less than $10 million in dormant accounts that might belong to Holocaust survivors, and had cavalierly called the findings "peanuts." With regard to Christoph Meili, Studer went on to suggest that the security guard could have tried to prevent the shredding by bringing it to the attention of his superiors.[40]

A few days after Studer questioned Meili's motives on television, the unemployed security guard hired a lawyer and sued Studer for slander. The suit, which did not name any damages, alleged that Robert Studer had maligned Meili by questioning his motives for taking the documents.

In protest, Meili closed his own account at the Union Bank of Switzerland. He later said that he had received so many death threats from angry compatriots that he had to pack up his family and move to New York. In May 1997, the U.S. Senate approved a bill to grant asylum to Meili and his family in the United States.

Zürich's *Blick* newspaper best summed up the whole incident when it ran a bold front-page headline: DEAR UBS. IT STINKS!

For Special Ambassador Thomas Borer, the headline might just as well have read DEAR SWITZERLAND: IT STINKS! The shredding scandal coming on the heels of the "blackmail" comment from an outgoing head of state was nothing short of a public relations nightmare. For most of January and early February 1997, Borer rarely saw his fiancée. He spent much of his time locked up in meetings with the country's highest officials or on the telephone to his New York legal advisers, trying to come up with some way of cleaning up the mess. Members of the Federal Council, who had been divided over the creation of Bronfman's "interim fund," were now locked up in debates for hours over how they could make such a fund palatable to the Swiss without stirring up anti-Semitism or right-wing political opponents.

While Borer met in closed-door sessions with political leaders to hammer out the logistics for a Swiss government fund, the actions of a respected Swiss diplomat put Switzerland back under the harsh glare of the international spotlight.

On January 24, 1997, editors of the *SonntagsZeitung* received a leaked confidential document outlining Switzerland's new strategy to deal with the demands of Jewish organizations. The internal foreign office memo, written by Carlo Jagmetti, Switzerland's ambassador to Washington, referred to the allegations being made by Jewish organizations as a "war" that Switzerland "has to fight and win on two fronts: external and internal." Jagmetti also noted that Switzerland's opponents in this war "cannot be trusted," and that Jewish claims must be settled in one general payment so that "peace would return on all levels." When Jagmetti's remarks were published in the *SonntagsZeitung* two days later, Jewish organizations in Switzerland and abroad called his comments insensitive, even anti-Semitic, and demanded his resignation.

The outspoken Avraham Burg, chair of the Jewish Agency in Jerusalem, condemned the Swiss ambassador's choice of words. "We will not leave a single such remark on the public agenda," said Burg, adding that he had received a death threat from Switzerland following Delamuraz's "blackmail" comments. "Verbal violence leads to incitement, racism and murder. We will excise it from its roots."[41]

Even the U.S. government registered a formal complaint. "If it's true the Swiss ambassador made these remarks it betrays a fundamental lack of understanding of the commitment the United States government has to its own citizens and of the search for justice for people who had their human rights fundamentally violated during the Second World War," said State Department spokesman Nicholas Burns. "It is very troubling."[42]

The Swiss ambassador had raised hackles a few months earlier when he disparaged Greta Beer's claim to Swiss banks and publicly condemned the "misrepresentations and distortions"[43] of the accusations against Switzerland, particularly with regard to the $20 billion class-action lawsuit against the country's biggest banks. He had also publicly disputed allegations that Switzerland had signed secret deals with Communist countries after the war to compensate Swiss citizens with the dormant assets of Holocaust victims.

In all of these cases, Jagmetti said he was just trying to get closer to the truth, and arguing for a more accurate and informed look at Switzerland's wartime role. But as Thomas Borer had found out early on, there was little room for accuracy and the facts in such an emotionally charged issue. Although Jagmetti was probably right in what he said about "war," the thirty-five-year veteran of the Swiss diplomatic corps was vilified by Switzerland's opponents and the international press. He must have realized he couldn't win the international public relations game, so a day after the *SonntagsZeitung* article appeared, he announced his resignation, offering to take his retirement, which was scheduled for July 1997, several months earlier.

Reading from a prepared statement at a Washington press conference, Jagmetti, sixty-four, said that his remarks were taken out of context, and explained why he was taking early retirement. "I no longer find it appropriate to continue my activity as ambassador in this country until the retirement date . . . originally envisioned," said the once respected diplomat, whose solid career had seen him posted to some of the world's most important international capitals, including Brussels, Paris, Rome, and London. "The leak, the resulting stories in the media and the reaction that followed from persons affected and from the public have created an intolerable situation for me."[44]

He noted that he was particularly offended by the statement that the remarks he made in the classified memo were somehow anti-Semitic. "The allegation of anti-Semitism is a particularly despicable one that gratuitously offends my longstanding upholding of human values at large," he said.

CARLO JAGMETTI'S FINAL statements spoke to the very crux of the problem between Switzerland and its critics in the United States—a serious lack of cultural awareness, which he himself had been unable to rectify:

> Sensitivities in America or in Switzerland are not identical; the art of communications or the use of language diverge in many respects . . . misunderstandings can and unfortunately will arise on occasion. Whatever harsh words I used in the text of this internal, not for public consumption, confidential document, were meant to energize our decision makers to advance this issue as quickly as possible. My words were and are a call for the Swiss to get our act together. . . . Nothing is more important to the people and government of Switzerland than establishing the complete truth in this matter as swiftly and humanely as possible. . . . If it is determined that assets that belonged to victims of the Holocaust are still being held in Switzerland, my government will not rest until they are returned to their rightful owners or a relevant charity.[45]

For his part, Foreign Minister Flavio Cotti did little to pacify international public opinion over Jagmetti's remarks. While he condemned the leaking of the confidential report and said he would ask the Swiss cabinet to authorize a criminal investigation, he did not apologize for his ambassador's actions or give any public indication that such harsh comments, even made in a confidential memo, were at all inappropriate. Cotti stood by his ambassador, and regretted that such a conscientious and successful diplomat should end his career in such a way.

As a result of all the embarrassing high-level gaffes, many Swiss joined Jewish groups to lobby for Edgar Bronfman's "interim fund." Many ordinary citizens tried to repair their country's image and distance themselves from their seemingly uncaring rulers. They signed petitions urging the government to set up a substantial fund as a good-faith gesture. Church groups held silent demonstrations in solidarity with victims of the Holocaust and against anti-Semitism. Schoolchildren collected donations for impoverished Holocaust survivors in Eastern Europe. Swiss academics, writers, and politicians started a private aid fund, hoping to raise more than 1 million Swiss francs ($686,000) in their first campaign for Jews in the Belarus capital of Minsk and for Warsaw's Jewish Historical Institute. The group took out a full-page advertisement in Swiss papers, noting that "we the undersigned nationals and residents of Switzerland feel discredited by the behavior of our country's banks and government. . . . The standing and credibility of Switzerland as a democratic nation are compromised and imperiled."[46]

Even Swiss banks, their reputation hanging in the balance and under threat of U.S. boycotts, offered to donate the $32 million in dormant accounts that had been identified almost a year earlier to a fund for impoverished Holocaust survivors. Then, at the urging of Rainer Gut, chair of Credit Suisse, the banks offered to double their donation.

Such gestures did not go unnoticed by Borer and Swiss cabinet officials, who worked furiously behind the scenes to salvage their country's reputation. On February 26, 1997, the Swiss Federal Council approved a decree creating a special fund for needy victims of the Holocaust, which would be administered by an executive body made up of four Swiss representatives and three others, chosen by the

World Jewish Restitution Organization. According to the decree, the fund would be used to "support persons in need who were persecuted for reasons of their race, religion, or political views or for other reasons, or otherwise were victims of the Holocaust." Although the fund would also support Gypsies, homosexuals, and disabled people who had suffered Nazi persecution, Swiss officials said the bulk of the monies would be distributed among Holocaust survivors who were now living in Eastern Europe, where they had been cut off from compensation because of the Cold War. All that remained for the Swiss government was to commit a specific amount of money.

A week later, Swiss President Arnold Koller stunned the world when, in a speech to Switzerland's Federal Council, he committed his government to donating 7 billion Swiss francs ($4.7 billion) to the new fund, which would be known as the Swiss Foundation for Solidarity.

"Today we do not have to feel ashamed that we escaped the war," said President Koller in a special morning session of Parliament. "Every country defended primarily its own interests. And we, too, were entitled to this right. We had the right to survive. But nevertheless the question arises as to whether and to what extent all Swiss citizens managed to satisfy the high moral demands during the war period. That means that we have to publicly admit self-criticism and admit the dark sides of that difficult period."[47]

If the staggering amount of money was meant to be the kind of ostentatious gesture that would appeal to Switzerland's mostly American critics and deflate criticism abroad, it worked. Bronfman called the fund "a victory for the Jewish and Swiss peoples" and pledged to cooperate with the Swiss authorities in disbursing the money for long-term relief efforts. Even Greville Janner, the British MP, offered grudging praise. "They don't want to be the pariahs of Europe, therefore they have proposed to do what is right and set up this fund."[48]

The foundation was indeed a great public relations victory for Switzerland, restoring its humanitarian image as the land of compassion and the Red Cross. Immediately after the announcement of the fund, private Swiss banks jumped on the bandwagon and established their own multimillion-dollar fund for needy Holocaust survivors. Just to make sure that the world would not overlook the significance of this gesture, Koller announced that the historic foundation would be officially set up with great fanfare in 1998 to coincide with the one hundred and fiftieth anniversary of the modern Swiss constitution.

For about a split second, Koller and some of his fellow cabinet members basked in the international praise that followed the spectacular announcement. But only for a split second, because now they would have to explain this magnanimous financial gesture to a country where economic growth had remained stagnant for the last several years, the bottom was falling out of the real-estate market, and unemployment was uncharacteristically high. Koller's plan did not draw universal support, even from his own colleagues. The plan, which was worked out with Special Ambassador Borer in unusually tight secrecy, drew only limited support from the cabinet, with three of seven cabinet members arguing that the idea was simply too hastily thought out.

In order to appease his critics, Koller was quick to note that the foundation would not be funded through higher taxation or any cost-cutting government measures. Rather, he and his aides had figured out a somewhat convoluted way in which the fund wouldn't really represent a financial burden. In order to raise the principal for the foundation, Switzerland would revalue its undervalued gold reserves and use a substantial portion of the difference to set up the fund. The Swiss National Bank's gold reserves are based on a legally fixed price that is equivalent to $117 per ounce, compared to the current market price of $350 per ounce. While these reserves are currently valued overall at 12 billion Swiss francs (about $8.6 billion), their market value is much higher. According to Hans Meyer, the chairman of the Swiss National Bank, the foundation would sell the gold transferred to it in the market for a period of approximately ten years "and invest the proceeds in interest-bearing assets."[49] With sound investments the fund could generate up to $400 million a year for its long-term relief activities, financial analysts noted.

In a further effort to stifle opposition at home, Koller gave the new foundation a broad mandate. He took the emphasis away from Jewish issues and the Holocaust by making sure the fund would also benefit "victims of poverty and catastrophes, of genocide and other severe breaches of human rights." In order to fend off internal criticism that Switzerland would be spending too much money, the government decree establishing the fund noted that at least half of the fund would be spent in Switzerland.

Despite all the planning, Koller still met with opposition in Switzerland. His biggest hurdle was to convince the Swiss people that the foundation was the best thing for the country, especially since in the end it would be the Swiss people who would probably have to go to the polls to approve the extraordinary measures. For in order to permit a revaluation of Switzerland's gold reserves, the constitution would have to be changed, probably by popular referendum. The only other time in history that the government had tried to change the constitution was in 1992, when the Swiss voted whether or not to join the European Union (EU): They voted no. So, how likely would the majority of Swiss voters be to agree to part with 7 billion Swiss francs of what were, after all, public assets? Many Swiss seemed eager to rectify their country's international image by signing petitions and collecting pocket money, but would they be willing to part with such a sizable chunk of public money?

Christoph Blocher, a fifty-seven-year-old millionaire and a leading figure in the ultraconservative Swiss People's Party, had some objections to the foundation. "The Federal Council has lost its head," said Blocher, whose party is the smallest of the four that make up the governing coalition, and the most vocal opponent of compensating Holocaust victims at Swiss public expense. Blocher, whose party successfully blocked Switzerland's membership in the EU in 1992, said that after Koller's announcement of the foundation his party's offices were swamped with phone calls from supporters. "These are public assets, not just money. What is this really about? Looked at soberly, it is about demands for money from Switzerland. What is not so clear is what Switzerland should be paying this money for."[50]

HERBIE STILMAN WONDERED the same thing. On a bright winter morning, he sat in the kitchen of his high-rise apartment in Queens, reading the newspaper and shaking his head. "He's right in a way," said Herbie, referring to Christoph Blocher's opposition to the Swiss foundation. "Why is Switzerland paying out this huge amount of money? I don't think it's about justice, or a concern for what they did in the past. They're just buying themselves respect, that's all."

When Arnold Koller announced the multibillion-dollar fund, Herbie and his cousins Renée and Hans did not quite know how to respond. They worried about what would become of their claim to collect their grandfather's assets. Would the banks continue to search now that the Swiss government had offered a solution to the problem? And just who would be entitled to that compensation fund? Would it be given out to claimants, or to other Holocaust survivors who never had assets in Swiss banks?

"This whole thing has really gotten out of hand," said an angry Sergio Karas, who was still representing the Hammersfeld family claim. Karas worried that individual claims would get lost in the shuffle now that world attention was turning to the Swiss foundation. "The Swiss seem content to throw money at the problem and leave it at that. And who will get the money? My clients feel that they will be left out. They feel that they will be sacrificed in favor of the Eastern European Jewish communities and in favor of whoever the World Jewish Congress considers to be 'needy.' "

Herbie buried his head in the morning newspaper. "All we want is what belonged to Grandfather," he said. "Whether it's twenty dollars or two thousand dollars or two hundred thousand dollars, it doesn't matter. We just want it back."

SEVEN

A MORAL ACCOUNTING

In the fall of 1937, a thin and gawky Herbie Stilman, eleven and a half years old, walked behind the towering figure of his grandfather as he made his way to his pew for High Holiday services at the Levias Chaim synagogue in Vienna's Second District.

Abraham Hammersfeld was smartly dressed in his customary dark three-piece suit. A large white *tallis,* or prayer shawl, its collar gleaming with silver brocade, was draped around his shoulders, its fringes reaching down below his waist. Herbie felt rather uncomfortable in a starched white shirt and his best suit—a dark woolen blazer and trousers that made him itch. As the oldest male grandchild, Herbie took the seat of honor beside his grandfather, and reached for a prayer book to practice reading Hebrew. Abraham was devoting much of his spare time to helping Herbie prepare for his bar mitzvah, which was a year and a half away. The tall, mustachioed patriarch beamed as he looked down on his grandchild, whose tall, bony frame was bent in silent contemplation of ancient scripture.

During the holiest part of this Rosh Hashanah service, when the rabbi lifted the Torah out of the Ark, Abraham Hammersfeld did what many Orthodox Jews traditionally do. He cast his eyes downward, covered his forehead with his prayer book, and gently embraced his eldest grandson, covering him with the protective folds of his prayer shawl so that he could not look upon the Torah. The gesture was symbolic of showing humility before the unveiling of the sacred text—the laws of the Jewish people that God delivered to Moses on Mount Sinai.

The new Jewish year 5698 would be filled with uncertainty and dread for the Hammersfelds and all other Austrian Jews. But those assembled in that tiny synagogue in Vienna's Second District, happily exchanging Hebrew blessings for a joyous new year, could hardly imagine what Hitler had in store for European Jewry. In his grandfather's warm embrace, eleven-year-old Herbie Stilman was blissfully ignorant of the horrors that awaited him and his family in the next several months. Nothing could hurt him under the warm, secure canopy of his grandfather's prayer shawl, he thought.

Less than a year later, Herbie, his sister Sylvia, and their parents, Paula and Georg, along with Adolf, his wife, Edith, and their son Hans fled to Sweden to escape Nazi persecution. A haggard Abraham Hammersfeld, who looked as if he had aged ten years in just a few months after the Nazi Anschluss, took a taxi to his son-in-law Georg's flat to see his family off. When he said goodbye to Herbie he made him promise to continue his Hebrew studies so that he would be prepared for his bar mitzvah, which would now have to take place in Sweden. How Abraham regretted not being able to accompany his family!—if only to share in the joy of watching his eldest grandson pass through the most important rite of Jewish manhood.

A few months after arriving in Stockholm, Herbie received a gift from his grandfather in preparation for the bar mitzvah, which would take place in Stockholm's main synagogue on June 10, 1939. Abraham had sent him his *tefillin,* a ceremonial leather prayer apparatus worn by Jewish men on the forehead and arms. The tefillin, traditionally passed down from a grandfather to his eldest grandson on his bar mitzvah, contain tiny Torah scrolls encased in black leather boxes. When Herbie opened his grandfather's packet, he found that one of the tefillin was severely damaged. The Torah scroll had been unraveled by Nazi mail inspectors, and the sacred text containing the laws of Judaism—the laws that Abraham Hammersfeld had followed so diligently throughout his life—was indiscriminately stamped with swastikas and ominous Nazi eagles. As he glanced upon the vandalized tefillin and the desecrated Jewish laws, Herbie knew he would never see his grandfather again.

MANY YEARS LATER, as he walked down Vienna's Negerlegasse, the narrow cobblestoned street where his grandfather used to live, Herbie's eyes welled up with tears as he remembered the tefillin and his grandfather's embrace. The grandchild, now close to the grandfather's age the last time he saw him alive, cast his mind back to the last Rosh Hashanah of his Viennese childhood in 1937. He could remember everything so vividly: the pungent residue of the sulfur cream that Grandfather used to shave, the ticking of Grandfather's Schaffhausen pocket watch, and the warmth and security that suffused his entire body when Grandfather pulled him under his prayer shawl.

"I only knew Grandfather for twelve and a half years of my life, and my most profound memory is of being a little boy hiding under his tallis and feeling so safe," said Herbie, who returned to the Austrian capital in spring 1972 to revisit his childhood home.

Everything was smaller than he remembered it. The street where his grandparents used to live seemed tiny and cramped with its nineteenth-century tenement buildings pressed so close together. Herbie stood outside Negerlegasse, 1, a drab and rather nondescript corner block of flats, the dusty vestibule crowded with rusted bicycles, no doubt belonging to the university students who shared some of the larger apartments. Herbie stood in silence for several minutes before he summoned the courage to go inside. Walking slowly up the three flights of stairs, the middle-aged man from Queens became the twelve-year-old Viennese boy again, on his way to share a festive meal with his grandparents or to sit in the book-lined library poring over the encyclopedia as Grandfather read about exotic places and exciting scientific discoveries.

Herbie felt as if his heart would burst out of his chest as he approached flat 18. His sharp knocks shattered the silence of the peaceful summer afternoon, and seemed to echo throughout the drafty building. Herbie waited for what seemed like an eternity until an old, stocky woman, wearing a scarf around her head like a babushka, hesitantly opened the door.

"What do you want?" asked the woman in German.

Herbie explained that he was the grandson of Abraham Hammersfeld who used to live in her flat before the war, and—well—he was in Vienna and thought he would come by and see the old neighborhood.

"Hammersfeld?" asked the old woman.

"Yes, Abraham Hammersfeld," said Herbie excitedly, hoping she would be able to tell him something—anything—about his grandfather.

"Hammersfeld? Hammersfeld? No, I've never heard of Hammersfeld," said the old woman, opening the door another few inches. "Do you want to come in?"

As Herbie walked into the old flat, a chill swept his entire body. "I just stood still for a moment and looked around," he said. Walking through the small, drab rooms, he was shocked to find some of his grandparents' furniture intact. The mahogany table where he had sat at so many seders was still in the same place in the dining room. Passing through the louvered French doors into the main bedroom, he recognized his grandparents' antique brass bed. Although it was tarnished and the old mattress seemed to sag with the weight of so many years, it was the same bed under which he and his cousins Renée and Hans used to hide their treats on Purim.

He wanted to ask the old woman how long she had lived in the flat and how she had acquired his grandparents' furniture, but his eyes welled up again, and the most he could muster was a hoarse *"Danke, Frau"* before walking out the door.

Confronting the past has been heart-wrenching for the rest of the Hamersfeld grandchildren. Until a few years ago, Hans Hamersfeld found it difficult to talk about the war years with his own family. He returned to Vienna on a bus tour of Europe with his eldest son in the 1980s, but he could only bring himself to spend a night there. He said he felt uprooted, like a stranger.

"All the sites that I knew as a kid appeared so different to me when I went back," said Hans. "I remembered everything was much bigger when I was a kid, and when I went back everything was all of a sudden so tiny."

Renée, who spent the longest of all of the Hamersfeld grandchildren in Vienna before escaping with her mother to Hungary in 1943, has never returned to her birthplace.

Now in their early seventies, Renée and her husband, Charlie, travel to Europe at least once a year, mainly to visit Renée's brother Siegfried, who never recovered from his nervous breakdown during the Blitz, and is now in a Jewish nursing home in London. Renée refuses to return to Vienna or even to speak German. Indeed, when she flies over Germany and Austria, and the pilot announces that they are flying over "German airspace," Renée gets sick to her stomach and has trouble breathing. Even Oskar and Selma, Renée's parents, refused to go back to Austria after the war. Neither had any regrets about not seeing the land of their youth before their deaths, and both are now buried in a Jewish cemetery on the outskirts of Toronto.

Renée's hatred of Germany is so intense that she studiously researches everything she buys to make sure it isn't made there. A few years ago she bought an expensive grandfather clock, insisting on repeated assurances from the merchant who sold it to her that the clock was not made in Germany. When she took it home and proudly displayed it on a shelf in her living room, her son Aubrey discovered that part of the clock was indeed German-made. An infuriated Renée promptly returned it and demanded her money back.

"I have to face myself in the mirror every day," she says. "I hate the Germans for what they put me and my family through. It only happened once in a lifetime and I hope nobody else has to go through what I went through because it is really unbelievable."

For Renée, who still retains some happy memories of growing up in Vienna, going back to Austria might simply be too traumatic. How would she react if she saw her grandfather's old office building on Wipplingerstrasse, its elegant nineteenth-century façade destroyed and crudely replaced in the early 1950s by a concrete mural of Soviet dockworkers? Wipplingerstrasse, 35, where Abraham managed his wholesale textile firm, is today the headquarters of the *Oster-reichischer Gewerkschaftsbund,* or the Austrian Union Movement. Despite the changes to the building, the old Hammersfeld firm seems to be intact, albeit under a different name. The back entrance to the building lists a textile firm that makes linens for hotels, pensions, and restaurants. Perhaps it's just a coincidence that the same kind of firm, once owned and operated by Abraham Hammersfeld, is still open for business in the same building. If it is indeed a coincidence, then it's the kind that seems so commonplace in modern-day Austria and other formerly Nazi-occupied countries in Eastern Europe, where many of the Jewish businesses expropriated by the Nazis were never reclaimed by their original owners, who either perished in concentration camps or just never bothered to return to reclaim their assets.

"Most of the Jewish families didn't want to come back to reclaim their property, and the Austrian state had no real mechanism in place to deal with this after the war," says Austrian political scientist Irene Etzersdorfer, who has completed one of only a handful of studies of Nazi expropriations in Austria.

Nazi hunter Simon Wiesenthal, himself an Austrian Jew, agrees: "Many of the survivors of the concentration camps just never came back. The past is simply too painful."

What would Abraham Hammersfeld's reaction be if he could see his old flat occupied by strangers? The truth is that if he returned to Vienna today, he would hardly recognize it. There are few Jews left in the Second District, where he used to live. Before the war, Vienna's vibrant Jewish population hovered at around 200,000. The streets in the Second District were lined with kosher butcher shops and Jewish bookstores. Today, the few small, family-run Jewish businesses that are left intact are little more than curiosities in a city where the Jewish population currently numbers between 8,000 and 12,000, depending upon whom you talk to. At Vienna's Jewish Museum, which is just down the street from the headquarters of the Dorotheum Auction House, where Renée dutifully delivered the Hammersfeld family heirlooms in 1939, there are dusty shelves full of hundreds of silver and brass menorahs and other relics of Jewish religious life. There are no neatly printed museum labels explaining their origins. The objects are simply lumped together in a storage area on the museum's top floor, like sentimental keepsakes someone doesn't have any use for anymore but cannot bear to throw away.

Around the corner from Negerlegasse, nobody has bothered to repair the old synagogue, which was partially destroyed during Kristallnacht. In fact, you wouldn't even know that the decaying building, a stone's throw from Abraham's old flat, had once been a synagogue except for a nicely appointed plaque affixed to the entranceway of the building, commemorating the site as one of Vienna's notable nineteenth-century synagogues. Since the war, the building has been converted into a tenement, where extended Islamic families from Turkey and Iran are crowded into tiny apartments.

The only vestige of Jewish life is a small, makeshift yeshiva, which has been set up in a grimy room on the second floor of the building. The yeshiva, little more than a sad collection of hand-me-down chairs, a few wooden pews stacked with coats, and two large work tables covered in cheap, floral-print vinyl tablecloths, is run by a stern, dark-suited ultra-Orthodox rabbi who delivers his lectures in a high-pitched wail, and carries a sleek cellular telephone in one of the pockets of his black overcoat. His tiny yeshiva, which is on the Grosse Schiffgasse, is often crowded with Jewish refugees from Iran and the former Soviet Union. Men sit in the front, according to Orthodox custom, and the women, their heads covered with colorful scarves, cradle sleeping toddlers in ragged, mismatched clothing behind a Plexiglas barrier in the back.

At the Israelitschen Kultusgemeinde, the Jewish Community Center, where Eichmann cut his teeth as a young bureaucrat, efficiently dispatching thousands of Jews on forced-emigration schemes before the Second World War, two Israeli security guards sporting buzz cuts and automatic weapons stand at attention. Security has been tight following a rash of anti-Semitic incidents by local neo-Nazi skinheads, who, like their predecessors fifty years ago, don't like Jews or new immigrants. Around the corner from the community center, swastikas and slogans, such as *Auslander Raus* (Foreigner Out) spray-painted on a wall, are small but vivid reminders that the xenophobia that inspired the murder of millions is still alive and well in this otherwise highly civilized society. It is little wonder that unexpected visitors to the Israelitschen Kultusgemeinde must submit to an intensive twenty-minute interrogation by the Israeli security detail before being allowed to pass through a series of metal detectors and automatic, bulletproof, sliding doors.

In Austria, many people still practice what Austrian historian Gertrude Schneider called a "selective amnesia" about their compatriots' role in Nazi atrocities. A generation of Austrians prefer not to recall that the overwhelming majority of the population welcomed their fellow Austrian Adolf Hitler when he marched into the country in 1938. Or that many ordinary Austrians and Nazi party members alike willingly participated in the harassment of Jews. Or that one third of the Nazis who implemented the Final Solution were Austrian.

While many Austrians would prefer to leave the past behind them, many Jews fear they will be doomed to repeat it. In 1991, a Gallup poll found that 50 percent of Austrians fully or partly agreed with the statement that the Jews bear the blame for their own persecution throughout history. Nineteen percent said that it would be better for Austria not to have Jews in the country. In a recent study, completed in 1996, researchers at the University of Vienna found that 53 percent of respondents in Austria said that Jews have too much influence on an international level. There is a rather sadistic joke making the rounds in the more liberal Viennese intellectual circles that the only safe time for a Jew to walk the streets of Vienna is between two and four in the morning. At 2 A.M. the young anti-Semite neo-Nazis go to sleep, and the old ones don't get up until 4 A.M.

"If you live in a place like this you are always reminded of the past, you are always at the crossroads of history," says Robert Liska, vice president of Austria's Federation of Jewish Communities. Liska's family is originally from Czechoslovakia. His father, who is now Austria's preeminent furrier, jumped off a cattle train en route to Auschwitz during the war. His mother survived on false Christian papers in Budapest. Today, Liska, a soft-spoken talmudic scholar, helps run the family business in Vienna in addition to his work for the Austrian Jewish community.

"No one has any illusions that Jews are liked by people here," says Liska. "We have a sense of reality."

Nor does Austria's Jewish community have any illusions about the new direction in which their country seems to be going. Populist Austrian politician Jorg Haider and his ultranationalist Freedom Party are building on the familiar resentments and anti-immigrant sentiments of the past. Many political scientists say that the historical conditions that led to the birth of fascism in Germany in 1933 are now ripe in Austria, and many are predicting that Jorg Haider could easily emerge as Austria's new chancellor after the next elections in 1998.

"It is a very frightening time in Austria," says historian Brigitte Bailer, who has done a great deal of research on the rise of Haider's Freedom Party in Austria. "Haider is copying the strategy and tactics of the National Socialists. He even quotes directly from *Mein Kampf*. And right now he has all of the right socio-economic conditions to get himself elected."

Indeed, the fall of the Berlin Wall in 1989 unleashed a wave of xenophobia in Austria as a flood of economic refugees from Eastern Europe poured into the country. Moreover, economic instability is on the rise. Unemployment is increasing in the country, where public services and welfare have recently been decimated by savage budget cuts designed to meet one of the criteria for Austria's full economic integration into the European Union. As a result, there is a strong backlash in the country, mostly from an older generation of Austrians, over its 1995 entry into the European Union.

On the other hand, as Austria moves boldly into a new Europe and into the future, many Austrian baby boomers have been wrestling with the past, and, more specifically, their country's treatment of the Jews. The Mauerbach auction in the fall of 1996 reminded Austrians of the rich prewar Jewish heritage of the country and how much of it was snuffed out by Nazi tyranny. At the official opening of the auction, then Austrian Chancellor Franz Vranitsky repeated an apology he had made a few years earlier, exploding the postwar myth that Austrians were merely victims of Nazism.

In this new climate of collective World War II guilt, some ordinary Austrians are doing extraordinary things. In 1984, working with Austrian government support, a group of mainly non-Jewish historians founded the country's most important research center on Nazi crimes against Jews and Austrian resistance during the war. The Austrian Resistance Archive occupies a few drafty rooms on the second floor of Vienna's old Rathaus, or city hall, and is staffed mostly by earnest volunteers, born after the war. Others are accounting for the past in more modest ways. A young professional Viennese couple, both of them non-Jews, recently decided to name their firstborn son Solomon "for all of the Solomons that we helped to murder during the Second World War."

In the midst of this collective *mea culpa* among Austria's younger generations, Jews themselves are wrestling with memory, or more specifically with how they want to be remembered by future generations of Austrians. Do they want to celebrate longstanding Jewish contributions to the country, or do they want to be remembered as victims of modern civilization's greatest pogrom? The debate is currently raging in the Jewish community, and is epitomized in the controversy over the city's first Holocaust memorial.

The city of Vienna made a rather halfhearted attempt to commission an anti-Nazi memorial in 1988. But "The Monument Against

War and Fascism," designed by Viennese artist Alfred Hrdlicka and built in Vienna's Albertinaplatz, was not popular with local Jewish leaders, partly because the monument features a sculpture of an old Jew scrubbing the sidewalk, too reminiscent of those whom the Nazis forced to clean the city's streets with toothbrushes and boiling water right after the Anschluss. Many Jews found the sculpture degrading, especially when passersby started to use the monument as a bench. Furthermore, Hrdlicka's monument does not specifically refer to the evils of Nazism.

So three years ago, Vienna's mayor, acting on a suggestion from Simon Wiesenthal, designated the Judenplatz, a small, medieval Jewish square in the heart of old Vienna, as the site for a new memorial specifically devoted to the Holocaust. Many Jews were immediately opposed to the idea, especially after archaeologists discovered the remains of a medieval synagogue on the site. There are conflicting accounts of what had actually happened to the old synagogue. Some historians say that the building, along with a group of Jews who were praying inside, was burned to the ground in a pogrom in 1421. Others say that a group of defiant Jews who would rather die than be converted to Christianity set fire to the synagogue and died in the ensuing blaze. In any event, a five-hundred-year-old plaque in Latin still hangs in the square, commemorating the slaughter of "Hebrew dogs."

"The excavations are extremely important for the Jewish community and its identity," says Avshalom Hodik, a medieval historian and executive director of the Vienna Jewish community center. "It shows the greatness of the medieval Jewish community in Vienna, that Jewish history is an integral part of the history of this country, with its own significance. It shows that Jews were not victims of just the Holocaust."

In addition to their opposition to the construction of a Holocaust memorial on a site where Jews may have committed mass suicide, Hodik and other critics also have difficulty with the monument's proposed form. The winning design, chosen from among several submissions by artists from around the world, is a large concrete abstraction of an inside-out library, where the books have their spines facing outward. Measuring about twelve feet high, twenty-four feet wide, and thirty-three feet long, the design by English artist Rachel White-read will have inscribed on its base the names of Austrian sites where Jews were killed during the war. Many critics say Whiteread's design reinforces the stereotype that Jews are valued only for their contributions to intellectual culture. Shouldn't Jewish farmers, workers, or doctors also be mourned? Others use the monument to voice their displeasure with Simon Wiesenthal, whom many Jews still believe did not do enough to condemn former Nazi Kurt Waldheim, who successfully ran for president of Austria in 1986.

"Why is Wiesenthal privileged to speak in my name?" asked Leon Zelman, head of the Jewish Welcome Service in Vienna, who opposes the monument. "I went to the Mayor and he told me that the Jews want it. I said: 'Who are the Jews? Wiesenthal?' I'm not against a monument. But make the excavation the monument so children can understand the background of the Holocaust and put the Whiteread someplace else."[1]

The controversy has delayed the construction of the memorial, and there is now a new proposal before the city council to create a public exhibition area for the old synagogue below ground, with an entrance through a building on the Judenplatz, which would become a museum. Meanwhile, Viennese archaeologists have cordoned off the Judenplatz excavation site as they continue to dig up the past.

ACROSS THE BORDER in Switzerland, they are also digging up the past. It's been a rather messy undertaking, because for the last few years the Swiss have had to dig through decaying layers of self-created myth before they could hit the bedrock of truth.

But the truth is proving to be painful and controversial because it undermines Switzerland's collective identity as a modern, democratic nation, devoted to international humanitarian principles, and law and order.

"The truth is always hard for everyone," says Frédéric Koller, a

young reporter with Geneva's French-language *Journal de Genève.*
"Everyone always has something to hide."

The Swiss are no exception. For more than fifty years they chose
not to acknowledge their wartime financial dealings with the Nazis.
Swiss schoolchildren learned that their country was a bastion of compassion and democracy during the war. Like the Austrians, who cultivated the myth that Austria was the first victim of Nazism, the Swiss
believed that their gallant little country could withstand a Nazi invasion on the strength of its army and impregnable mountain terrain.
But the truth, which has only recently emerged in a very public way,
thanks to unrelenting pressure from Edgar Bronfman and Alfonse
D'Amato, is that Swiss business and political leaders struck a Faust-
ian bargain with their fascist neighbors. Switzerland was allowed to
survive as an independent, democratic state in the midst of the Second World War in exchange for acting as the Third Reich's banker.

"This scandal has been a pretext for us to reopen certain discussions," says Antoine Maurice, editor-in-chief of the *Journal de Genève,* which has set up discussion groups on the Internet,
encouraging the Swiss to debate what their country did in the past
and where it is going in the future. "It has a deeper psychological
aspect. We are revisiting our past and seeing Switzerland in a bad
light. Prior to this we had a vision of Switzerland that was not only
neutral but heroic. This is the first time we are having a debate, as
Germans had in their country, about our role in World War Two."

Today, many Swiss are so guilt-ridden about their country's role in
the Second World War that something as seemingly benign as an
advertising campaign for a local watch company can spark a national
debate about ethics and morality. Swatch, the official timekeeper
during the World Ski Championships in Sestriere, Italy, in early
1997, decided to salute the accomplishments of Swiss athletes who
won two gold medals at the competition with an ad that noted, "As
always whenever there is gold, a good part of it ends up in Switzerland." Many Swiss business executives said that the ad, designed to
sell the popular plastic watches made by Ste. Suisse Microélectro-
nique et d'Horlogerie SA, was insensitive at a time when the country

was emotionally confronting its role in the laundering of looted Nazi gold.

"This is over the top," said one irate ad agency executive. "It's too much. This is a very touchy subject for Swiss people. You can't joke about it. We would never have run this ad."[2]

In another attempt to appease their country's critics, authorities at Swissair stopped serving Swiss chocolates, wrapped up like gold bars, on both domestic and international flights.

Not everyone in Switzerland is so guilt-ridden or so eager to participate in what has become a very spirited national debate. Today, as in Austria, it's mainly a younger generation, born after the war, who are boldly trying to come to grips with their future by taking responsibility for their past. It is largely their parents who prefer not to deal with that past, and rail against Switzerland's critics, whom they accuse of deliberately trying to destroy their country's financial institutions and undermine its hallowed international reputation. The internal debate not only pits generation against generation, but ethnic group against ethnic group. The Italian and French Swiss are on the whole much more committed to participating in a broad debate on the past, just as they are willing to embrace a modern, progressive future, which means opening Switzerland up to the world and becoming a part of the European Union. However, most of the older German-speaking Swiss would prefer to bury the past. These are the same people who also seek a return to Switzerland's intractable isolationism. In 1992, they overwhelmingly blocked the country's entry into the European Union when a referendum was held on the question.

Switzerland's reckoning with its past started even before Edgar Bronfman arrived in Bern for his ill-fated meeting with the Swiss Bankers Association in the fall of 1995. Earlier that year, then Swiss President Kaspar Villiger officially apologized for his country's wartime treatment of Jews. He said that his government particularly regretted the decision to turn away 30,000 Jewish refugees from Swiss borders and send them back into the hands of the Gestapo.

He also apologized for the Swiss urging the Nazis to stamp a "J" on passports to identify their holders as Jewish.

The long, painful process of self-examination that led to Villiger's apology actually began six years earlier, with the end of the Cold War. When the Berlin Wall crumbled in 1989, so, too, did Switzerland's *raison d'être* as the only neutral haven in the middle of a divided Europe.

In the climate of moral absolutism that pervaded the Cold War, the concept of neutrality in Europe seemed clearly delineated as did Switzerland's international role. Switzerland was the go-between, the important neutral middle ground in a bipolar world divided between the West and the "Evil Empire" of communism behind the Iron Curtain. International organizations such as the United Nations set up their offices in Geneva, and the city played host to superpower summits that allowed Communist leaders to meet their Western counterparts on uncompromising ground. In order to preserve that neutrality, Switzerland itself avoided taking any compromising moral stands. It refused to join the United Nations or NATO or to take sides in any international conflicts.

"During the Cold War, we Swiss thought that we were the best in the world, that our democracy functioned with the precision of a fine watch," says Antoine Maurice. "But the truth is that Switzerland got a moral free ride during the Cold War."

Even before the Cold War began, the concept of Swiss wartime neutrality itself may have been little more than an illusion, as demonstrated by Swiss financial dealings with the Nazis. In reality, Switzerland was only neutral when it was convenient to be neutral. During the Second World War, many Swiss institutions hid behind neutrality when they were forced to make difficult decisions. The International Committee of the Red Cross (ICRC), the world's most respected humanitarian organization, is a case in point. Although ICRC officials knew as early as 1941 that Jews were being herded into concentration camps and exterminated en masse by the Nazis, the organization chose not to get involved, rationalizing that it was not within the ICRC's mandate to interfere with the laws of Germany, a sovereign country. It didn't seem to matter that German leaders had completely disenfranchised a significant part of their population, practically overnight, and were systematically putting them to death both in Germany and in Nazi-occupied countries. As the ICRC self-servingly noted in one of its own publications, "relief for Jews rested on no juridical basis."

> No convention provided for it, nor gave the International Committee even the shadow of a pretext for intervention. On the contrary, conditions were all against such an undertaking. Chances of success depended entirely on the consent of the Powers concerned. And there were all the other tasks, which the Conventions or time-honored tradition permitted the International Committee to undertake, or which, with so great difficulty, it had succeeded in adding thereto. To engage in controversy about the Jewish question would have imperiled all this work, without saving a single Jew.[3]

Such fastidious and self-righteous respect for the rule of international law at a time when the worst crimes against humanity were being committed just outside Switzerland's borders is a truly "moral failure," to borrow the phrase used by the president of the Red Cross to describe his organization's reluctance to act to prevent modern civilization's greatest genocide.

"We have taken another look at our share of the responsibility for the almost complete failure by a culture, indeed a civilization to prevent the systematic genocide of an entire people and of certain minority groups," said ICRC President Cornelio Sommaruga on the fiftieth anniversary of the end of the Second World War in 1995. "But believe me, every moment spent today on our humanitarian responsibilities to assist the victims of war and political violence reminds me of our institution's moral failure with regard to the Holocaust, since it did not succeed in moving beyond the limited legal framework established by the states. Today's ICRC can only regret the possible omissions and errors of the past."[4]

Not only has the ICRC lost face in the international community for its refusal to speak out against the Holocaust, but its continued single-minded adherence to neutrality is rapidly turning it into an anachronism in a multipolar world, where conflicts are no longer characterized by two easily identifiable, opposing sides. Today's conflicts are not measured in black-and-white absolutes but are multisided brutal civil wars and ethnic rivalries in places like Chechnya, Bosnia, Rwanda, and Liberia, where the warring parties don't necessarily adhere to the rules of states as set out in international treaties such as the Geneva Convention, which is the guiding principle of the ICRC.

Like the ICRC, Swiss neutrality is an anachronism in the so-called new world order. The nation that identified itself as the neutral bulwark in the uneasy peace that characterized the Cold War is now suffering a massive identity crisis. As the Swiss journalist Beat Brenner puts it, "We could define ourselves by monolithic institutions. [But] after the end of the Cold War it was no longer clear what we were or what we wanted to be in the new world order."

In fact, Switzerland is an unexpected victim of the Cold War, and many Swiss are only now realizing it. For the world no longer needs Switzerland, which is why the Swiss themselves are grudgingly determined to become part of the world. Although it still refuses to join the United Nations or peacekeeping operations in troubled countries, Switzerland is slowly shedding its isolationist past. In 1992, it joined the World Bank and International Monetary Fund. In 1995, in a huge break with Swiss tradition, the country allowed NATO troops to pass through its territory on their way to Bosnia, and in 1996 Switzerland's defense minister asked to join NATO's Partnership for Peace. Perhaps as a way to make up for its discriminatory refugee policy during the Second World War, Switzerland has now agreed to give sanctuary to 400,000 refugees from the former Yugoslavia, which is equivalent to more than 5 percent of the total Swiss population.

If Switzerland did indeed have a "moral free ride" throughout much of modern history, it's now being forced to pay for it, retroactively and with interest. There are the emotional costs of the debate over Swiss national identity. In addition to the work of the Volcker commission that is currently auditing dormant accounts in Swiss banks, another commission of Swiss and foreign historians is painstakingly combing through government and bank archives to get closer to the truth about the country's financial relationships with Nazi Germany.

And then there are also the monetary costs of atonement. The country's leaders hope that appeasing its critics will save its international reputation. So, on the advice of Special Ambassador Thomas Borer, Switzerland's leaders are keeping their mouths shut and engaging in high-priced repentance. Switzerland's big three banks have reluctantly acknowledged that their treatment of the heirs of Holocaust survivors after the war was not as sensitive as it could have been. While they still refuse to break banking secrecy and indiscriminately open their dormant accounts, they are nevertheless trying to make amends, setting aside, along with Swiss industry, the $200 million to help the needy survivors of the Holocaust. The Swiss government, which finally recognized that its own institutions were morally bankrupt during the war, will also seek to make amends with its proposed $4.7 billion fund for victims of the Holocaust and other human-rights abuses around the world.

At the beginning of his campaign to seek justice for Holocaust survivors with assets in Swiss banks, Edgar Bronfman noted that "each dollar recovered represents a little piece of dignity, not just for the survivors who will benefit but for all mankind, who will have demonstrated that it remains morally unacceptable for anyone to profit from the ashes of man's greatest inhumanity to man."[5]

But can you put a price on justice, especially after profiting from the ashes of man's greatest inhumanity to man?

Yes. It is a necessary corollary as other significant restitutions have shown—such as the American government's restitution to the American Japanese interned as enemy aliens during World War II. "It's not about money, it's about justice," said Bronfman. "But you cannot have moral restitution without some sort of financial restitution."[6]

The question whether there can ever be restitution for the destruction of an entire civilization has divided Jews since the end of the Second World War. In the early 1950s there were large demonstrations in Israel over whether to accept reparations from Germany for the mass extermination of six million Jews. Government opposition leader Menachem Begin led thousands of angry demonstrators, who protested outside the Knesset building in Jerusalem that accepting German reparations implied recognizing and even forgiving Germany less than a decade after the Holocaust.

Today, the World Jewish Restitution Organization (WRJO), is fighting to reclaim Jewish assets. But the WJRO's aggressive tactics are not only alienating government officials throughout Eastern Europe, they are infuriating local Jewish populations in the region, upsetting the delicate balance that these communities have had to forge with local governments to survive under godless and often hostile Communist regimes.

In addition to heading up the World Jewish Congress, Edgar Bronfman is also head of the WJRO, and has brought the same righteous urgency that characterized his assault on Swiss banks to recovering Jewish properties in Eastern Europe. It seems to be the WJRO's *modus operandi* to blunder into situations where it has little knowledge of local conditions, and create a scandal so loud that local officials are cowed into giving them their way. Many Jews fear that the World Jewish Congress and the World Jewish Restitution Organization's grandstanding could result in an angry backlash, making conditions worse for Jews, especially in countries with proven track records in anti-Semitism. Others are afraid that such aggressive lobbying by Jewish groups could result in Palestinian demands on Israel for the return of confiscated properties.

Bronfman has been asked so often whether his tactics will rekindle anti-Semitic behavior that he now anticipates it in his speeches and interviews: "Anti-Semites create anti-Semitism, not Jews. If someone wants to use our pleas for justice [as the pretext] for anti-Semitism, that's going to be their problem not my problem."[7] He ducks such responsibility for his actions.

In Switzerland, Bronfman and his aides did not bother to consult local Jewish leaders before they launched their campaign against the country. The joint World Jewish Congress–D'Amato campaign against Switzerland was sometimes based on distortions and simplifications of extremely complex historical events and international legal agreements. "We were not consulted, and this led to all types of distortions," says Rolf Bloch, president of the Swiss Federation of Jewish Communities, who has recently been appointed by the government to help oversee the distribution of funds for Holocaust survivors and others under the government's proposed foundation. "Switzerland may have profited from the war, but it did not knowingly or deliberately profit from the Holocaust. Switzerland was not Auschwitz, yet those accusations make it seem as if the Swiss supported the extermination of Jews."

D'Amato has at times turned a morally just cause for restitution into a media circus, based on questionable pieces of paper taken piecemeal out of the National Archives in Washington, and often presented as historical fact in a sensational fashion to a gullible international press, eager to capitalize on the world's rather prurient fascination with Nazi atrocities. The worst part is that this righteous American-led campaign against Switzerland relied on the tragic stories of human suffering, painfully recounted—in the media and before government committees in Washington—by a parade of old and feeble Holocaust survivors, who relived the most traumatic parts of their lives for a global audience, but are no closer to achieving justice than they were at the end of the war in 1945.

But as the Swiss scandal has shown, people have some peculiar ideas about the meaning of justice, and many fear that class-action lawsuits seeking billions in damages will do little to help the cause of Holocaust survivors, and will just perpetuate the two-thousand-year-old stereotype of the Jew who is only interested in money, primarily because the majority of lawyers pressing these suits are doing so on a contingency basis. As Swiss parliamentarian Verena Grendelmeier commented about the class-action suits against Swiss banks, "Law and justice under this aspect quickly degenerates into big business."

Jewish critics agree. "No people can present the world with an unlimited number of moral demands," said Efraim Zuroff of the Simon Wiesenthal Center's Israel office in an interview with *The Jerusalem Report*. "Our efforts would be far better invested in issues related in bringing war criminals to justice. Putting all our efforts into reclaiming material assets will only reinforce anti-Semitic stereotypes, especially in poor countries in Eastern Europe."[8] In the interview, Zuroff adds that the WJRO's aggressive restitution attempts have hurt his own campaign to bring Nazi war criminals to justice in places like Lithuania, where high-ranking government officials recently tried on local television to discredit his work by implying that his motives had nothing to do with justice, and everything to do with money. As a result, Jewish communities in Hungary, Czechoslovakia, and Poland have tried to maintain a respectful distance from the WJRO, preferring not to jeopardize their own moral standing by making claims to their respective governments.

Today, the noble battle for restitution for the victims of Nazi atrocities has degenerated into a bitter row that is threatening to divide the very people it is supposed to dignify and unite. For now that Bronfman and the World Jewish Congress are being congratulated for having won a big part of the battle for Jewish dignity and restitution in Switzerland, how are they going to divide up the spoils? So far, there are no firm plans. Bronfman has repeatedly said that the money will go to needy Holocaust survivors. But what is the definition of "needy," and who will decide who is deserving? As with the Eastern European situation, just about everybody agrees that the first payments should go to meet the special needs of aging Holocaust survivors, but beyond that there is no consensus about what to do with the rest of the money. Should it go to American Jewish educational organizations, to Israel? There is even one proposal on the table that part of the money be earmarked for "successor communities," such as ultra-Orthodox Hasidic sects.

"The Holocaust has been used for every purpose, including fund-raising by U.S. Jews for Israel," said Efraim Zuroff. "It's outrageous that we would take restitution funds out of Eastern Europe for educating American Jews. Funding its own education is the job of American Jewry. Restitution money should be used for social and educational purposes in Eastern Europe, period."[9]

Similarly, when the organizers of Vienna's Mauerbach sale announced that they had raised more than $14.5 million after the auction in late October 1996, many Jews in Austria wanted to know who had a legitimate right to the money. Albert Sternfeld, a seventy-year-old Viennese Jew whose family has lived in Austria for generations, says that Jewish organizations risked adding insult to injury by donating the proceeds from an auction of art expropriated by the Nazis to recently arrived Jewish immigrants from Russia and Iran who had no right to receive it. Nearly a year following the auction, there are indeed plans to give the money to the Austrian Jewish community, but nobody is saying just how the funds will be distributed. "We're still in the process of working out a formula and procedure for the distribution of funds," says Saul Kagan, one of the auction organizers, and the executive vice president of the Committee for Jewish Claims on Austria, an international body of twenty-two Jewish communities, based in New York.

Many Austrian Jews who watched the Mauerbach auction are furious about what they see as the steering committee's rather vague plans for what to do with the proceeds. "It sounds very plausible and fair to give the proceeds to the Austrian Jewish community, but it is not," says an angry Albert Sternfeld, whose family escaped Nazi tyranny, although most of their property was confiscated by enterprising Austrian neighbors and Nazi thugs. More than fifty years after the war, Sternfeld said he and others are still waiting for restitution.

"They're just perpetuating the expropriation process," he says, in reference to the Mauerbach auction's organizers. "Jews who were not here before 1938, who came after the war, have no business receiving the proceeds of what was stolen from Jews who had been here before 1938. This is not the way to make good after more than fifty years."

How do you make good after fifty years? Do you turn the memory of the Holocaust into an excuse for a global fund-raiser? How do you bring about justice for the expropriation and murder of a civilization?

The truth is that no amount of money will ever compensate for the humiliation, torture, and murder of six million people. According to historian Raul Hilberg, "If we were to survey the hurt inflicted by the Germans upon the Jews, we would have to consider the suffering and dying of the victims; we would have to measure the impact of these deaths on those who were closest to the victims; we would have to think about the long-range effects of the entire destruction process upon Jewry as a whole. All this adds up to a vast, almost nonassessable loss. What, then, is to happen after such damage has been done? When ordinary justice prevails, there is an expectation of compensation for every wrong, and the bigger the injury, the greater will be the claim for payment."[10]

If we were to survey the hurt inflicted by Swiss indifference on thousands of Jews who sought refuge within Switzerland's borders and sought to protect their assets in its banks, we would find moral debts long overdue. The first debt is owed to the heirs of Jewish depositors, who have been waiting for years to reclaim what is rightfully theirs. At the end of the war, when they arrived to collect their families' assets, the Swiss treated them with icy indifference. In 1962, responding to years of pressure from Jewish organizations, Swiss bankers made only a halfhearted attempt to return the money in dormant accounts to their rightful heirs. Now, if there is to be any justice at all, every effort must be made by the Swiss Bankers Association and the Swiss government to find these heirs.

The second debt is owed to the Swiss people themselves, whose leaders have traded on time-worn myths of Swiss neutrality, bravery, and compassion for their own political expediency. Today, the evidence suggests that Switzerland acted less than honorably during the war. Although the country was technically neutral in law, it clearly sided with the Axis forces, and hid behind its neutrality when it was convenient to do so. When members of the International Committee of the Red Cross had the chance to act to prevent genocide, they remained silent and invoked neutrality. After the war, when Swiss officials were called upon to account for their transactions with the Nazis, they invoked neutrality. As a neutral during the Second World War, the Swiss argued, they should not be expected to pay any type of compensation or reparations. And they got away with it, even though they did have to pay a token amount as their "contribution" to the reconstruction of Europe under the terms of the Washington Accord of 1946. Additionally, they were never called to a proper accounting because there were "more pressing" issues after the end of the Second World War—such as thousands of displaced persons wandering around a devastated Europe, and the urgent aggression of the Cold War, which was to dominate the agenda of the world community for nearly fifty years.

Today there is no Cold War, no more excuses. In the new world order, the Swiss can no longer trade on the moral credit that came with being the aloof intermediary between enemy superpowers. They can no longer hide behind their neutrality or their official history. As many of its people now understand, in order to proceed boldly into the future, Switzerland first needs to reclaim the truth about its past.

But Switzerland is not the only country that needs to reexamine its past. Other neutral and nonbelligerent countries, such as Portugal, Spain, Sweden, Turkey, and Argentina, helped the Nazis launder looted gold and other assets, in addition to helping the German war effort by selling the Nazis critically important goods and raw materials. These activities continued despite several warnings by the Allies to cease trade with the Nazi regime, as it became evident in 1943 that Germany would probably lose the war. Like the European neutrals, Argentina's military governments turned a blind eye to the flow of Nazi assets into their country during and after the war. Furthermore, Argentine officials eagerly helped thousands of Nazi war criminals escape from justice by selling them Argentine citizenship.

As in the case of Switzerland, these countries looked upon neutrality as a convenient excuse not to take a moral stand during the war or to conduct a proper moral accounting after it. As Stuart Eizenstat, U.S. undersecretary of commerce for international trade, noted,

> In the unique circumstances of World War II, neutrality collided with morality; too often being neutral provided a pretext for avoiding moral considerations. Historically a well-established principle in international law, neutrality served through centuries of European wars as a legitimate means by which smaller nations preserved their political sovereignty and economic viability. But it is painfully clear that Argentina, Portugal, Spain, Sweden, Switzerland, Turkey and other neutral countries were slow to recognize and acknowledge that this was not just another war. Most never did. Nazi Germany was a mortal threat to Western civilization itself, and had it been victorious, to the survival of even the neutral countries themselves.[11]

In the wake of the Swiss scandal and under pressure from Alfonse D'Amato and Edgar Bronfman in the United States, who are only now beginning to address the role of these so-called neutrals, Sweden, Portugal, Spain, and Turkey are opening up their World War II archives to public scrutiny, and engaging in public debates about their silent complicity with the Nazis. Argentina has been a bit slower off the mark, although President Carlos Menem recently promised to open up the central bank archives to determine if the Nazis laundered looted gold through the South American country.

Even Israel is accounting for its past. In a bizarre footnote to the story of heirless World War II assets, an Israeli academic recently found nearly $70 million (today's value) worth of unclaimed funds, reportedly belonging to German Jews who had deposited their assets in British-controlled Palestine before the Second World War. Many of the depositors had died in the Holocaust, and only those heirs who knew of the deposits and had the proper proof were able to recover them after the war. Unlike Swiss banks, funds that remained dormant in prestate Israel banks for fifteen years or more were taken over by the state. The Israeli government is now accepting claims from heirs, who have the proper documentation, to recover their families' legacies.[12]

Despite the collective soul-searching triggered in the wake of the Swiss-Nazi scandal, at least one country, the United States, has failed to account publicly for its behavior during and after the war. In fact, Alfonse D'Amato and Edgar Bronfman have been so wrapped up in their fury against Hitler's silent financial partners abroad that they have completely overlooked historical events in their own backyard. For just as Switzerland and other countries hid behind the veil of neutrality, the Allies, and particularly the United States, hid behind a cloak of moral superiority. American officials cavalierly overlooked the suffering of millions of Jews. Although they knew about the Final Solution, they chose not to bomb railway lines leading to the death camps. Despite reports of Nazi atrocities against Jews in the Third Reich, the United States, like Switzerland, set up strict quotas on allowing Jewish refugees into the country.

And when it had a chance to work for justice after the war, the United States simply chose not to act. Although the Allies had received numerous reports about the laundering of looted gold through Swiss banks during the war, they chose not to punish Switzerland too harshly under the terms of the Washington Accord. In the immediate postwar period, Britain and France needed favorable terms on Swiss bank loans to rebuild their shattered economies, while the United States was arming itself for a different conflict. Emerging Cold War imperatives prevented President Harry S Truman from taking Switzerland and the other neutrals to task; his government let Switzerland get away with murder in the Washington Accord, and conveniently overlooked the rights of Holocaust survivors as they began to clamor for restitution.

Today, instead of pressing for the redrafting of postwar agreements that seemingly let neutral countries off the hook, perhaps Alfonse D'Amato and Edgar Bronfman should turn their righteous moral spotlight on their own country. The cathartic reexamination of history that they so rudely forced on Switzerland in recent months is now long overdue in the United States. Perhaps it's for this reason that U.S. Undersecretary of Commerce for International Trade Stuart Eizenstat so vigorously criticizes his country's postwar leaders for failing to bring about justice in his groundbreaking report on the Allied response to the Nazi gold looting. His undertaking is perhaps the first step to a collective soul-searching desperately needed in the United States.

HOW TO ACCOUNT properly for the past had been on Sergio Karas's mind ever since that brisk September day in 1995 when he chanced upon the fateful article in Zürich's *Tages Anzeiger* that launched him on his crusade to retrieve the assets of Holocaust survivors in Swiss banks.

Eighteen months later, in March 1997, just after the Swiss government announced its $4.7 billion plan to compensate Holocaust victims, Karas was very worried. Shouldn't the Swiss wait until they had the results from the Volcker commission before dispensing funds to Holocaust survivors? How would they determine who gets the money from the Swiss government fund? And, most important, how would individual claimants achieve justice? How would his own clients achieve justice?

Karas mulled over these questions as he straightened his tie and pulled out the gold-plated case that he uses to dispense his business cards—smart white rectangles of fine linen card-stock with a discreet red Canadian maple leaf, strategically but tastefully placed next to "Karas & Associates, Immigration Lawyers," as if to remind would-be clients of his proven track record in immigration matters. Karas stood in a long lineup of journalists, Jewish dignitaries, and Canadian businesspeople waiting to meet Edgar Bronfman, who had just finished giving a speech to a gathering of Canada's business elite in the faded splendor of the grand ballroom of Toronto's Royal York Hotel. Karas had been writing to Bronfman for the last year about his concern that the World Jewish Congress had forgotten about those ordinary claimants who had been pressing to find their families' assets in Swiss banks since the end of the Second World War—people like his clients, who had so far met with nothing but failure.

Despite Bronfman's multibillion-dollar resolution to the Swiss scandal, negotiated with the hard-line bravado of a Seagram business deal, there had been no resolution for Karas's clients. While many other Holocaust survivors had been calling local Jewish organizations to find out how they could benefit from the proposed Swiss fund for victims of the Holocaust, Karas's clients were still waiting to access their families' assets in Swiss banks. Although the Swiss banking ombudsman, Hanspeter Häni, announced that he had found only some $8,000 worth of dormant Holocaust accounts, Karas's client list kept growing. In addition to the Hammersfeld family claim, he now had claims from Holocaust survivors from all over Europe and the United States, and had dutifully sent them off to his partner in Zürich, where Caterina Nägeli passed them on to the ombudsman.

Karas was angry. He feared that Bronfman's loud lobbying had drowned out the small voices of those who were seriously pressing their individual claims. Now, with billions of dollars from Swiss banks and the Swiss government earmarked for Holocaust compensation funds, he worried that Swiss bankers would no longer see any purpose to searching for hard-to-find individual claims, which might contain no more than a few hundred dollars, but were nevertheless important to the families of survivors seeking to reclaim something that had belonged to their families, a last piece of the past.

Two years of fighting the Swiss banks had made Karas cynical, and he was resolute in his conviction that restitution had not yet been made. Instead, there had only been more expropriation. Jewish organizations may only be adding insult to injury and unwittingly preventing restitution to the rightful owners of the accounts, he says. First, his clients had been victims of World War II; then of the Cold War; now they were being victimized by a new kind of war, a war of image and power waged in the media. Memory, which in many cases is the only thing that a Holocaust survivor has managed to hold on to, was being exploited to advance the political career of an opportunistic U.S. senator and to wrench financial compensation from the Swiss. Karas is not interested in billions of dollars, he is interested in justice. "I just want my clients to get what used to belong to their families. That's all."

So now, Karas says he also finds himself at odds with the World Jewish Congress, who, he says, did not answer his letters or return his telephone calls. Which was why he was standing in line on his lunch hour, wearing his best black three-piece suit and a smart red tie, determined to meet the billion-dollar diplomat who seemed to have so much power. (The World Jewish Congress says it diligently answers all letters and has no recollection of receiving any from Karas.)

Karas took a deep breath as he approached the lectern, where Bronfman was basking in the praise of well-wishers. One aging Holocaust survivor even bowed to kiss Bronfman's hand in gratitude. Clutching a business card that he was ready to slip into Bronfman's hand, Karas prepared to launch into the few phrases he had been going over in his mind: "There is no justice, Mr. Bronfman" and "My clients don't want compensation. They want restitution."

Karas approached the smiling Edgar Bronfman and extended his right hand in greeting. "Mr. Bronfman, I . . ." But at that moment a group of television reporters overwhelmed Bronfman and elbowed Karas out of the way.

"At least I gave him my business card," said Karas, trying to cheer himself up as he prepared to head back to his office. "Maybe one day he'll give me a call."

But as he watched Bronfman, who was straining to hear a reporter's question under the glow of a television camera, Karas knew he was on his own: "Doesn't he understand that all of the money he's raised from Swiss banks and the Swiss government hasn't brought us any closer to justice?"

.   .   .

''IF ALL THE money in all the Swiss banks were turned over," said writer and Holocaust survivor Elie Wiesel, "it would not bring back the life of one Jewish child."[13]

Or of one mother, or of one sister, or of one uncle, or of one grandfather.

In the fall of 1996, an elegantly dressed Viennese opera singer sat in the swish restaurant of the Vienna Hilton sipping coffee and contemplating a stack of documents from the Austrian State Archives. They were photocopies of the original expropriation documents that her grandfather had carefully filled out fifty-eight years earlier, listing all of his worldly possessions. She winced whenever she saw the Nazi reminders—a stamp of a defiant eagle perched upon a swastika, or the salutation "Heil Hitler!" typed at the end of an official letter. She eagerly scanned the documents for clues to a life she had only heard about in family lore. She knew by heart the stories of her strong-willed cousin Renée, determined to survive the horrors of Auschwitz, and the stories of her cousin Hans, who had taught himself mathematics in a Siberian labor camp. And then there was cousin Herbie, and his family's long, roundabout route to America, only months before the Japanese bombing of Pearl Harbor forced the United States into the war. And then, of course, there was her own father, Harry, the gambling *bon vivant* who was nevertheless responsible for saving most of the Hammersfeld clan by arranging for visas to get them out of Austria.

She knew little about her grandfather except that he was deeply religious and liked to read Goethe and Schiller. Yes, she said, scanning the official government documents, this was her grandfather, Abraham Hammersfeld, the textile merchant and Jew who lived at Negerlegasse, 1, flat 18, Second District, married to Lotte Hammersfeld (née Faust), and whose firm was on Wipplingerstrasse, 35, First District. And then she stopped in midsentence, overwhelmed with emotion, and momentarily closed her eyes as if to regain her composure.

"You know I never knew when Grandfather Hammersfeld was born," said Anita Ammersfeld, who was born after the Second World

War to Harry and his second wife, Paula. "I never knew." And she slowly repeated the date out loud—"24, 12, 1874"—as if the sounds of the numbers were satisfying some deep inner longing.

It was no more than a date, a series of numbers, but to a granddaughter who dreamed of a ghost of a grandfather she'd never met, those numbers somehow brought him closer to reality, and perhaps allowed her to recover a part of herself.

Thousands of miles away in a suburban living room in Toronto, another granddaughter pondered the importance of numbers. There are the numbers on her left forearm—81006—that remind her daily of the horrors of the past. But the ones that nag at Renée, now seventy-four, are the elusive numbers to a bank account somewhere in Switzerland. "He may have told me all of the details of the bank account. I'm sure he did, but I can't remember the account numbers."

If only she could remember what her grandfather had said at that tearful meeting in his library in April 1939, maybe, just maybe, she could recover her family's final inheritance—the one thing from that horrible past that should have remained inviolate, untouchable, even by the Nazis.

If only she could remember the numbers.

EPILOGUE

As this book was going to press, the Swiss Bankers Association made its most strenuous attempt to date to establish the ownership of assets belonging to Holocaust victims. The organization published a list of 1,756 names of dormant account holders in major newspapers around the world on July 23, 1997. Aging Holocaust survivors and their heirs eagerly scanned the list of names—printed in small type and spread out over two broadsheet pages—for those of family members who might have opened accounts with Swiss banks before the war.

Those who recognized a name on the list were invited by the Swiss Bankers Association to make a claim against the banks. The organization also promised to publish, in October 1997, a complete list of World War II–era dormant accounts of Swiss citizens, many of whom may have held powers of attorney for Jewish depositors.

The publication of this first list came as researchers at the World Jewish Congress unearthed more explosive documentation in the National Archives in Washington, which this time suggested that financial institutions in the United States and Canada had helped the Swiss launder Nazi gold during the war. In Canada, an inquiry is now under way to find out how tainted Reichsbank gold was laundered through the Bank of Canada.

On that humid July morning, Renée Appel sat in her housecoat in the kitchen of her neatly appointed home in suburban Toronto, poring over the names on the Swiss Bankers Association's list, which included at least six Nazi officials as well as Holocaust victims and other account holders from around the world. Renée squinted as she scanned her local newspaper for the name of her grandfather, Abraham Hammersfeld. It took her awhile to get to the H's and she read slowly so as not to miss any names—Halfin, Haller, Hanau . . . no Hammersfeld.

Renée folded the newspaper and sat at her kitchen table in silence.

GLOSSARY

Wherever possible, I have converted currency values into 1997 United States dollars.

Currency Values, 1939: $1.00 = RM = 2.50 (Reichsmarks); $1.00 = SF4.30 (Swiss francs). All other currency values are based on conversion rates established by the May 1997 "Report on U.S. and Allied Efforts to Recover and Restore Gold and Other Assets Stolen or Hidden by Germany During World War II," coordinated by Stuart E. Eizenstat, undersecretary of commerce for International Trade and special envoy of the U.S. Department of State on property restitution in Central and Eastern Europe.

To ascertain the value of nongold assets in 1997 United States dollars, multiply the figure by the following:

1945—8.9; 1946—8.2; 1947—7.2; 1948—6.6; 1952—6.0;
1962—5.3

In 1946, the value of gold was $35 an ounce; in 1997, it is nearly ten times that amount (multiply by 9.74).

Deutsche Arbeiterpartei (DAP): German Workers' Party, founded in 1919 by Anton Drexler

Einsatzgruppen: special mobile killing units that carried out the massacres of Jews, Communists, and others on the Eastern Front during the Second World War

Generalgouvernement: German-occupied Poland, administered by Hans Frank, the Nazi party's leading jurist, from his headquarters in Krakow

Gestapo (*Geheime Staatspolizei*): Secret State Police

ICRC (International Committee of the Red Cross): a Swiss humanitarian aid agency, founded in 1863 by Jean-Henri Dunant

NSDAP (*Nationalsozialistische Deutsche Arbeiterpartei*): the National Socialist German Workers' Party

OKW (*Oberkommando der Wehrmacht*): the High Command of the entire German armed forces

OSS (Office of Strategic Services): U.S. intelligence-gathering agency under Allen Dulles, which was based in Europe and had contacts with the German Resistance

Ostministerium: Reich Ministry for the Occupied Eastern Territories, created in 1941 under Alfred Rosenberg

POW: prisoner of war

Reichsicherheitshauptamt (RSHA): Reich main security office, formed in 1939. It comprised, among others, the intelligence division, the Gestapo, the criminal police, and the SD.

SA (*Sturmabteilungen*): the storm troopers, or "Brown Shirts," founded in 1921 as a private army of the Nazi party under Ernst Röhm

SD (*Sicherheitsdienst*): Security service of the SS founded in 1932 and directed by Reinhard Heydrich. It became the only intelligence service of the Nazi party.

SS (*Schutzstaffel*): protection squads, which were formed in 1925 and at first acted as the black-shirted personal bodyguard of Hitler. Under the leadership of Heinrich Himmler, the organization grew into the most powerful organization within the Nazi party and the Nazi state.

SBA (Swiss Bankers Association): the self-regulating organization that represents Switzerland's more than four hundred fifty banks

SHAEF (Supreme Headquarters, Allied Expeditionary Forces): General Dwight D. Eisenhower's headquarters in Europe

Waffen-SS: Armed SS elite. These were the combat formations of the SS, which also included non-German SS units after 1940.

Wehrmacht: Germany's armed forces

Wehrwirtschaft: War economy

Wehrwirtschaftsführer: War economy leader

WJC (World Jewish Congress):   A nongovernmental Jewish organization, founded in Geneva in 1936 to represent world Jewry and raise awareness of the Nazis' anti-Semitic policies, particularly in Eastern Europe. Today, the organization is based in New York, and works to advance restitution efforts and the status of Jews in the former Eastern bloc.

WJRO (World Jewish Restitution Organization):   Founded in 1992, it is a coalition of international Jewish organizations seeking to reclaim the communal properties of Europe's Jewish victims of Nazism and communism. Chaired by Edgar Bronfman and Avraham Burg, who is also the head of the Jewish Agency in Israel

WVHA (*Wirtschafts und Verwaltungshauptamt*):   Economic and administrative main office of the SS, formed in 1942 and headed by Oswald Pohl. The WVHA administered the concentration camps and managed the economic enterprises of the SS.

NOTES

ONE: ''FILE CLOSED''

1. Steven Beller, *Vienna and the Jews, 1867–1938: A Cultural History* (Cambridge, England: Cambridge University Press, 1989), 164.
2. William L. Shirer, *The Rise and Fall of the Third Reich: A History of Nazi Germany* (New York: Ballantine Books, 1992), 464–465.
3. Shirer, 450.
4. Shirer, 477.
5. Martin Gilbert, *The Holocaust* (London: William Collins Sons & Co., Ltd., 1986), 59–60.
6. Gertrude Schneider, *Exile and Destruction: The Fate of Austrian Jews, 1938–1945* (Westport, Conn.: Praeger Publishers, 1995), 15.
7. Letter from Abraham Hammersfeld to Harry, Vienna, July 27, 1938.
8. A Record of the Assets of Jews as of April 27, 1938, Abraham Hammersfeld, State Archives, Vienna, filled out on July 13, 1938.
9. Memorandum of the American Consulate General to the State De-

partment, dated June 13, 1938, Vienna, by John C. Wiley, American Consul General, Subject: Jewish Situation.

10. Hannah Arendt, *Eichmann in Jerusalem* (New York: Penguin Books, 1994), 44.

11. Arendt, 46.

12. Nora Levin, *The Holocaust: The Destruction of European Jewry, 1933–1945* (New York: Thomas Y. Crowell Company, 1968), 102.

13. Permit to Purchase Application, signed by Johann Greisinger, August 30, 1938, State Archives, Vienna.

14. Ibid.

15. Letter from Abraham Hammersfeld to Harry Hammersfeld, Vienna, July 27, 1938.

16. Letter from Renée Lang to Harry Hammersfeld, Vienna, July 11, 1938.

17. Letter from Abraham Hammersfeld to Georg and Paula, Vienna, December 24, 1938.

18. As quoted in Levin, 101.

19. Schneider, 26.

20. Georg Stilman, letter undated.

21. Letter from Renée Lang to Sylvia, Vienna, December 3, 1938.

22. Letter from Adolf Hammersfeld to Georg Stilman, October 27, 1938.

23. Letter from Franz Celnar to Josef Burckel, Nazi governor of Austria, January 4, 1939, State Archives, Vienna.

24 Ibid.

25. Letter from Josef König to the Vermogensverkehrstelle, Vienna, January 18, 1939, State Archives, Vienna.

26. Nicholas Faith, *Safety in Numbers: The Mysterious World of Swiss Banking* (London: Hamish Hamilton, 1982), 83–84.

27. *Bundesgesetz über die Banken und Sparkassen* (Federal Law Relating to Banks and Savings Banks of November 8, 1934, as amended by federal law of March 11, 1971—Office Collection of Federal Laws and Regulations of the Swiss Confederation, 1971).

28. Constance Howard, "Switzerland," in *Survey of International Affairs, 1939–1946: The War and the Neutrals,* edited by Arnold Toynbee and Veronica M. Toynbee (London: Oxford University Press, for the Royal Institute of International Affairs, 1956), 147.

29. T. R. Fehrenbach, *The Swiss Banks* (New York: McGraw-Hill Book Company, 1966), 58.

30. Fehrenbach, 59.
31. Larry McShane, "Document Shows Nazi Extortion," Associated Press, November 16, 1996.
32. Faith, 85–86.

TWO: TRANSFERS

1. Letter from Selma Lang to Paula Stilman, Vienna, June 28, 1940.
2. Letter from Selma Lang to Paula Stilman, Vienna, August 6, 1940.
3. Letter from Selma Lang to Paula Stilman, Vienna, January 1, 1941.
4. Gertrude Schneider, *Exile and Destruction: The Fate of Austrian Jews, 1938–1945* (Westport, Conn.: Praeger Publishers, 1995), 64.
5. Herbert Rosenkranz, "The Anschluss and the Tragedy of Austrian Jewry, 1938–1945," in *The Jews of Austria*, edited by Josef Fraenkel (London: Vallentine, Mitchell & Co., Ltd., 1967), 516.
6. Letter from Abraham Hammersfeld to Georg Stilman, Riga, March 1, 1940.
7. Letter from Abraham Hammersfeld to Paula Stilman, Riga, undated.
8. Letter from Abraham Hammersfeld to Paula Stilman, Riga, March 25, 1940.
9. Letter from Abraham Hammersfeld to Paula Stilman, Riga, May 31, 1940.
10. William Shirer, *The Rise and Fall of the Third Reich: A History of Nazi Germany* (New York: Ballantine Books, 1992), 1110.
11. Martin Gilbert, *The Holocaust* (London: William Collins Sons & Co., Ltd., 1986), 182.
12. Captain Paul Salitter, Shutzpolizei, Düsseldorf, December 26, 1941; TR-3/138, Yad Vashem Archives.
13. Letter from Abraham Hammersfeld to Paula Stilman, Riga, undated.
14. Letter from Abraham Hammersfeld to Paula Stilman, Riga, undated.
15. Gilbert, 178.
16. Schneider, 66.

17. Raul Hilberg, *The Destruction of the European Jews* (New York: Holmes & Meier, 1985), 178.

18. C. Gwyn Moser, "Jewish U-Boote in Austria, 1938–1945," *Simon Wiesenthal Center Annual*, vol. 2, 1985 (New York: Kraus International Publications, 1985), 54.

19. Livia Rothkirchen, "Hungary—An Asylum for the Refugees," *Yad Vashem Studies on the European Jewish Catastrophe and Resistance* (Jerusalem: Yad Vashem, 1968), 127–128.

20. Christopher Browning, *The Final Solution and the German Foreign Office* (New York: Holmes & Meier Publishers, Inc., 1978), 130.

21. Browning, 128.

22. Hilberg, as quoted in *Last Waltz in Vienna*, by George Clare (London: Macmillan London Ltd., 1981), 249.

23. Hilberg, 232.

24. Hilberg, 954.

25. Hilberg, 957.

26. Nuremberg Trials, International Military Tribunal, Transcripts of interrogations of Oswald Pohl, chief of the SS Economic and Administrative Main Office (WVHA), on the administration of concentration camps and profiteering from the possessions and labor of inmates, June 3–7, 1946.

27. Yuri Suhl, *They Fought Back: The Story of Jewish Resistance in Nazi Europe* (New York: Schocken Books, 1967), 220.

28. Gilbert, 745.

29. Gilbert, 746.

30. Suhl, 222.

31. Gilbert, 747.

32. Shirer, 1264.

33. Lucien Steinberg, *The Jews Against Hitler* (London: Gordon & Cremonesi, 1973), 285.

34. Nuremberg Trials, International Military Tribunal, vol. 20, Proceedings July 30–August 10, 1946, 316.

35. Nuremberg Trials, International Military Tribunal, Transcripts of interrogations of Oswald Pohl, chief of the SS Economic and Administrative Main Office (WVHA), on the administration of concentration camps and profiteering from the possessions and labor of inmates, June 3–7, 1946.

36. Nuremberg Trials, International Military Tribunal, vol. 13, Proceedings May 3–15, 1946, 602.
37. Nuremberg Trials, International Military Tribunal, vol. 13, Proceedings May 3–15, 1946, 612.
38. Jochen von Lang (editor), *Eichmann Interrogated: Transcripts from the Archives of the Israeli Police* (New York: Farrar, Straus, and Giroux, 1983), 122.
39. Stuart E. Eizenstat (coordinator), "U.S. and Allied Efforts to Recover and Restore Gold and Other Assets Stolen or Hidden by Germany During World War II," U.S. Department of State, May 1997, 31.
40. Hilberg, 1137.
41. Walther Funk, president of the Reichsbank on the stand at the Nuremberg Trials, May 6, 1946, International Military Tribunal, vol. 13, 162.
42. Arthur L. Smith, Jr., *Hitler's Gold: The Story of the Nazi War Loot* (Oxford, England: Berg Publishers Limited, 1989), 27.
43. Memorandum for Herbert J. Cummings, U.S. Department of State, Subject: Interview with Dr. Landwehr, from: Jason Paige, Jr., Liaison Officer, May 27, 1946, L4-10, 829-2, National Archives, Washington.
44. Eizenstat, 7.
45. Smith, 7.
46. As quoted in Reuters, "Swiss Took Stolen Gold After Sweden Refused Document," January 30, 1997.
47. Smith, 49.
48. Memorandum from R. W. Aubern, British Embassy, Washington, to Frank Dietrich, U.S. Treasury Department, Stabilization Office, Washington, January 19, 1942, ref. WT1075/PC/2/42, National Archives, Washington.
49. Reuters, "Swiss Defend Wartime Gold Shipments to Iberia," January 13, 1997.
50. Telegram from the U.S. Department of State, December 4, 1945, to the American Legation, Bern, 800.515/12-445 CS/LE, National Archives, Washington.
51. Eizenstat, 60.
52. Nicholas Faith, *Safety in Numbers: The Mysterious World of Swiss Banking* (London: Hamish Hamilton, 1982), 102.
53. Ibid.
54. Memorandum from U.S. Department of State to Officer in Charge of

American Mission, Bern, 850.3 SH-Q, "German Assets in Switzerland," July 18, 1946, National Archives, Washington.

55. Foreign Economic Administration memorandum, January 27, 1945, RG131, 1942–60, box 457, National Archives, Washington.

56. Eizenstat, 86.

57. Ibid.

58. As quoted in Faith, 96.

59. As quoted in Reuters report, "Document Accuses Swiss of Aiding Nazi War Effort," by Arthur Spiegelman, January 9, 1997.

60. Ibid.

61. Memorandum, "Hermann Goering," from the U.S. Embassy at London, England, September 22, 1940, National Archives, Washington.

62. One of ten reports submitted to U.S. Department of State by American Embassy, London, on December 1, 1940, RG407, entry 368, box 1033, National Archives, Washington.

63. Bernard Edinger, "Goering Said He Used Criminals to Loot Jewish Art," Reuters, January 29, 1997.

64. "Memorandum to Herbert J. Cummings, U.S. Department of State, "Miscellaneous Safe Haven Items from Switzerland, February 13, 1946," National Archives, Washington.

65. Ibid.

66. As quoted in Robert S. Wistrich, *Who's Who in Nazi Germany* (London: Routledge, 1995), 4–5.

67. Ibid.

68. Memorandum to U.S. Treasury Department from the British Embassy, December 10, 1941, RG131, 1942–60, box 51, National Archives, Washington.

69. "Interim Report on Johann Wehrli & Co., Zurich, June 23, 1945," National Archives, Washington.

70. Faith, 107.

71. Memorandum to the Files, Subject: Richard Holtkott, October 30, 1945, RG84, box 39, National Archives, Washington.

72. Alfred A. Häsler, *The Lifeboat Is Full: Switzerland and the Refugees, 1933–1945* (New York: Funk & Wagnalls, 1969), 292.

73. Häsler, 98.

74. Häsler, 100–101.

75. Faith, 98.

76. Edwin Roth, "Red Cross Inhumanity, No Surprise," September 4, 1990, *The Jerusalem Post*, Internet.
77. Hilberg, 314.

THREE: DISPLACEMENTS

1. Raul Hilberg, *The Destruction of the European Jews* (New York: Holmes & Meier, 1985), 254.
2. Martin Gilbert, *The Holocaust* (London: William Collins Sons & Co., Ltd., 1986), 789.
3. Hilberg, 256.
4. Hilberg, 257.
5. Hilberg, 1140–1141.
6. As quoted in Hilberg, 1142.
7. Stuart E. Eizenstat (coordinator), "U.S. and Allied Efforts to Recover and Restore Gold and Other Assets Stolen or Hidden by Germany During World War II," U.S. Department of State, May 1997, 25.
8. As quoted in Roger J. Sandilands, *The Life and Political Economy of Lauchlin Currie* (Durham, N.C.: Duke University Press, 1990), 138.
9. Nicholas Faith, *Safety in Numbers: The Mysterious World of Swiss Banking* (London: Hamish Hamilton, 1982), 129.
10. Eizenstat, 80.
11. Eizenstat, 24.
12. Reuters, "Swiss Knew Nazi Gold Was Looted—D'Amato," February 2, 1997.
13. "Nazi Gold: Information from the British Archives," Foreign and Commonwealth Office, General Services Command, No. 11, September 1996.
14. Robert Franklin Maddox, *The Senatorial Career of Harley Martin Kilgore* (New York: Garland Publishing, Inc., 1992), 237.
15. Imre Karacs, "It Cost 4.6 Billion Pounds to Stop Swiss 'Going Soviet,'" *The Independent on Sunday*, September 15, 1996, 13.
16. As quoted in "Quest for Nazis' Loot," by David B. Ottaway, *Washington Post*, December 8, 1996, 1.

NOTES

17. Francis X. Clines, "Wartime Envoy on Nazi Gold Bristles at Hindsight," *New York Times*, Sunday, May 25, 1997, 3.
18. Eizenstat, 26.
19. Eizenstat, 27.
20. Faith, 144.
21. Eizenstat, 7.
22. Eizenstat, 28.
23. Arthur L. Smith, Jr., *Hitler's Gold: The Story of the Nazi War Loot* (Oxford, England: Berg Publishers Limited, 1989), 92.
24. Marlise Simons, "Nazi Gold and Portugal's Murky Role," *New York Times*, Friday, January 10, 1997, A10.
25. Smith, 154.
26. Ibid.
27. "T. H. McKittrick, World Financier: Head of International Bank During World War II Dies," *New York Times*, Thursday, January 22, 1970, 37.
28. Ronald C. Newton, *The "Nazi Menace" in Argentina, 1931–1947* (Stanford, Calif.: Stanford University Press, 1992), 376.
29. National Archives of Latvia, "Regarding Request for Information about the Hammersfeld Family," April 14, 1997, Riga.
30. Death Certificate, Abraham Hammersfeld, June 14, 1947, State Archives, Vienna.
31. John MacCormac, "Austria's Plight Declared Worst: UNRRA Official Says Country's Food Situation Is Most Desperate in Europe," *New York Times*, Thursday, June 27, 1946, 7.
32. As quoted in "Living with Contradictions—Jews in Vienna after 1945," by Helga Embacher, in *Vienna Today: Photographs of Contemporary Jewish Life*, by Harry Webber, edited by Werner Hanak (Vienna: Jewish Museum, 1996), 179.
33. Gertrude Schneider, *Exile and Destruction: The Fate of Austrian Jews, 1938–1945* (Westport, Conn.: Praeger Publishers, 1995), 160.
34. Albion Ross, "Austrian Receives Siberian Sentence," *New York Times*, September 13, 1946, 1.
35. Schneider, 159.
36. Schneider, 161.
37. Schneider, 162–163.

38. Frances Greenfield letter to U.S. Department of State, April 20, 1947, RG84, 1942–49, box 32, National Archives, Washington.
39. Marcel E, Malige, Attaché commercial près la Légation des Etats-Unis d'Amérique, Bern, August 13, 1947, name files, 1942–49, box 32, National Archives, Washington.
40. Memorandum from the American Legation, Bern, to U.S. Secretary of State, Washington, A-371, August 15, 1947, National Archives, Washington.
41. Hilberg, 1161–1162.
42. Hilberg, 1154.
43. Letter to Walter Stucki from Randolph Paul, Special Assistant to the President, May 21, 1946, National Archives, Washington.
44. Peter Nielsen, "Swiss Banks May Have More Holocaust Money—Volcker," Reuters, January 31, 1997.
45. Stephanie Cooke, "Digging Up the Past," *Euromoney*, August 1996, 50.

FOUR: REOPENING THE FILE

1. Edgar M. Bronfman, *The Making of a Jew* (New York: G. P. Putnam's Sons, 1996) 111.
2. Bronfman, 115.
3. Bronfman, 6.
4. Bronfman, 51.
5. Bronfman, 44.
6. Frank Bruni, "With Swiss Success, a Strong, Younger Voice for Jews Shows Its Range," *New York Times*, February 16, 1997, 4.
7. Johanna McGeary, "Echoes of the Holocaust," *Time*, February 24, 1997, 21.
8. Joshua Hammer, "Don't Cry for Him: Peron's Nazi Outreach Program," *Newsweek* (International Edition), February 3, 1997, 37.
9. Ronald C. Newton, *The "Nazi Menace" in Argentina, 1931–1947* (Stanford, Calif.: Stanford University Press, 1992), 378.
10. As quoted in Nicholas Faith, *Safety in Numbers: The Mysterious World of Swiss Banking* (London: Hamish Hamilton, 1982), 116.
11. Memorandum from Henry Morgenthau, Secretary of the Treasury, to

Joseph C. Grew, Acting U.S. Secretary of State, Washington, D.C., 800.515/2-745, February 7, 1945, Natonal Archives, Washington.

12. Memorandum from the American Embassy, Buenos Aires, to U.S. Secretary of State, Washington, April 11, 1945, no. 702, National Archives, Washington.

13. Ibid.

14. Interview with author's Argentine researcher, January 6, 1997, Buenos Aires.

15. Jorge Camarasa, "La maniobra contó con la complicidad de grandes empresas," *La Nación,* December 1, 1996, Buenos Aires.

16. Ibid.

17. Mark Aarons and John Loftus, *The Ratlines* (London: William Heinemann, Ltd., 1991), 21.

18. Newton, 378.

19 Marcus Kabel, "Swiss Bank Denies Holding Huge Sums from Holocaust Victims," Reuters, February 23. 1996.

20. Leonard Lurie, *Senator Pothole: The Unauthorized Biography of Al D'Amato* (New York: Carol Publishing Group, 1994), 534.

21. From a survey conducted in February 1997 by Mason-Dixon Political/Media Research Inc., published in *Business Week,* February 24, 1997, 49.

22. Richard S. Dunham, "Why Al, the Bankers' Pal, Could Make a Comeback," *Business Week,* February 24, 1997, 49.

23. Ronald Powers, "D'Amato Hailed or Swiss Stance," Associated Press, February 3, 1997.

24. Ibid.

25. Transcripts, Hearing of the U.S. Senate Banking, Housing, and Urban Affairs Committee, April 23, 1996, Washington, 2.

26. Ibid.

27. Senate Banking Hearings, April 23, 1996, 7.

28. Ibid.

29. Senate Banking Hearings, April 23, 1996, 8.

30. Paul Volcker, statement before the Committee of Banking and Financial Services of the U.S. House of Representatives, December 11, 1996, Washington, 66.

31. Ibid.

32. Transcripts, House of Commons debate, "Holocaust Victims (compensation)," November 12, 1996, 264.
33. International Military Tribunal—Trial of the Major War Criminals, vol. 13, Proceedings May 15, 1946, 612.
34. Arthur L. Smith, Jr., *Hitler's Gold: The Story of the Nazi War Loot* (Oxford, England: Berg Publishers Limited, 1989), 143.
35. Stuart E. Eizenstat (coordinator), "U.S. and Allied Efforts to Recover and Restore Gold and Other Assets Stolen or Hidden by Germany During World War II," U.S. State Department, May 1997, 31.
36. Carolsue Holland and Thomas Rothbart, "The Merkers and Buchenwald Treasure Troves," *After the Battle,* November 1996, no. 93, London, 22.
37. Ibid.
38. Smith, 112.
39. Letter from Malcolm Rifkind, Secretary of State, Foreign and Commonwealth Office, to the Hon. Greville Janner, MP, QC, October 25, 1996.
40. David E. Sanger, "US, UK, France Agree to Freeze Gold Looted by Nazis," *New York Times,* February 4, 1997, 1.
41. Letter from the Hon. Greville Janner, QC, MP, to Malcolm Rifkind, Secretary of State, Foreign and Commonwealth Office, September 17, 1996.
42. Complaint, United States District Court for the Eastern District of New York, *Gizella Weisshaus* vs. *the Union Bank of Switzerland, Swiss Bank Corporation,* filed October 1, 1996.
43. Charisse Jones, "Armed with Faith and Memory, Survivor Leads Fight for Holocaust Money," *New York Times,* November 12, 1996, B1.
44. Ibid.
45. "Breaking the Code," *Online NewsHour,* November 19, 1996.
46. Reuters, "Jewish Group Files Class Action Naming Swiss Banks," January 31, 1997.

FIVE: THE LETTER OF THE LAW

1. Paul Volcker, statement before the Committee on Banking and Financial Services of the U.S. House of Representatives, December 11, 1996, Washington, 31.
2. Felix Bauer, "Progress Seen in Swiss Hunt for Holocaust Accounts," Reuters, November 13, 1996.
3. Translated by the Associated Press, November 13, 1996.
4. Hanspeter Häni press conference, November 12, 1996, Zürich.
5. Ibid.
6. Ibid.
7. "The Secrets of Swiss Bankers," editorial, *New York Times,* September 25, 1996, A20.
8. Peter J. Hoets and Sara G. Zwart, "Swiss Bank Secrecy and the Marcos Affair," in *New York Law School Journal of International and Comparative Law,* vol. 9, 1988, 83.
9. As quoted in Hoets and Zwart, 83.
10. Reuters, "Union Bank Cuts Swiss Operations," November 27, 1996.
11. William Hall, "Credit Suisse First Loss Heavier Than Forecast at $1.7 Billion," *Financial Times of London,* March 6, 1997, 15.
12. Alice Ratcliffe, "Holocaust Factor Weighs Heavily on Swiss Financial Markets," Reuters, January 8, 1997.
13. Niklaus Blattner, "European Integration and the Swiss Financial Centre: A Summary of the Results," in Niklaus Blattner, *European Integration and the Swiss Financial Centre: A Summary of Results* (Zürich: Verlag Reugger, 1993), 16.
14. Transcripts, Hearing of the U.S. Senate Banking, Housing, and Urban Affairs Committee, April 23, 1996, Washington, 9.
15. Ibid.
16. Clarification statement by Bank Julius Baer, June 29, 1995, Zürich.
17. Transcripts, House Banking Committee Hearing, December 11, 1996, 9.
18. Thomas Borer is the diplomat. Excerpts from his letter to Alfonse

D'Amato were reprinted in "Swiss Hit Back at D'Amato's Holocaust Charges," Reuters, November 8, 1996.

19. Transcripts, House Banking Committee Hearing, December 11, 1996, 15.
20. Transcripts, Senate Banking Committee Hearing, April 23, 1996, 6.
21. Ibid.
22. Rob Wells, "Swiss Banks Mistreated Jews," Associated Press, October 30, 1996.
23. Ronald Powers, "D'Amato Hailed on Swiss Stance," Associated Press, February 3, 1997.
24. Michael Shields, "Swiss Suspect Foreign Agenda for Wartime Review," Reuters, October 1, 1996.
25. Ibid.
26. Transcripts, House Banking Committee Hearing, December 11, 1996, 7.
27. Letter to Caterina Nägeli from the Contact Office for the Search of Dormant Accounts Administered by Swiss Banks, November 8, 1996, Zürich.

SIX: BUYING RESPECT

1. Elif Kaban, "UN Boss Calls Swiss Row with Jews PR Disaster," Reuters, January 30, 1997.
2. Ad appeared in The Financial Times of London, September 27, 1996, 9.
3. Michael Shields, "Battered Swiss Use Churchill Ads to Polish Image," Reuters, September 27, 1996.
4. Arthur Spiegelman, "Jewish Group Demands Restitution from Swiss," Reuters, October 18, 1996.
5. Michael Shields, "Swiss Vow to Clear Up 1949 Deal on Polish Wealth," Reuters, October 19, 1996.
6. Transcripts, Hearing of the U.S. House of Representatives Banking and Financial Services Committee, December 11, 1996, Washington.
7. Michael Shields, "Swiss Jews Slam Deal on Holocaust Victims' Wealth," Reuters, October 23, 1996.

8. Balz Bruppacher, "Swiss Deny Misusing Deposits," Associated Press, October 23, 1996.
9. Ibid.
10. Alan Cowell, "Swiss Used Nazi Victims' Money for War Payments, Files Reveal," *New York Times,* October 24, 1996, 1.
11. Shields, October 23, 1996.
12. Cowell, October 24, 1996.
13. Michael Shields, "Swiss-Polish Deal Used Wartime Funds for Swiss," Reuters, October 22, 1996.
14. Carolyn Henson, "World War II Heirs Have Valid Claims," Associated Press, October 24, 1996.
15. Cowell, October 24, 1996.
16. Transcripts, House Banking Committee Hearing, December 11, 1996. 56.
17. Transcripts, House Banking and Financial Services Committee, December 11, 1996, Washington, 78.
18. Ibid.
19. Ibid.
20. The comment was made by U.S. Representative James Leach, Chairman of the House Banking and Financial Services Committee, from Transcripts, House Banking and Financial Services Committee, December 11, 1996, Washington, 2.
21. Clare Nullis, "Jews Attack Swiss Government Remarks," Associated Press, January 2, 1997.
22. Marcus Kabel, "Swiss President Calls Holocaust Claims 'Blackmail,'" Reuters, December 31, 1996.
23. Clare Nullis, "Swiss President Reaps Criticism," Associated Press, December 31, 1996.
24. Clare Nullis, January 2, 1997.
25. Clare Nullis, December 31, 1996.
26. Michael Shields, "Swiss Jews Fear Anti-Semitism Mounts in Funds Row," Reuters, January 13, 1997.
27. Ibid.
28. Ueli Haldimann, *SonntagsZeitung,* January 12, 1997, 1.
29. Shields, January 13, 1997.

30. Peter Nielsen, "Swiss Minister Regrets Offense at Blackmail Remark," Reuters, January 2, 1997.

31. Marcus Kabel, "Swiss Minister Apologises for 'Blackmail' Remark," Reuters, January 15, 1997.

32. Edmund L. Andrews, "Swiss Bank's Discarded Files Saved by Night Watchman," *New York Times*, January 17, 1997, A6.

33. Jane Kramer, "Manna from Hell," *The New Yorker*, April 28 and May 5, 1997, 78.

34. Andrews, January 17, 1997.

35. Edmund L. Andrews, "Bank Says Shredded Papers May Not Have Involved Nazis," *New York Times*, January 16, 1997, 3.

36. Ibid.

37. Andrews, January 17, 1997.

38. David E. Sanger, "Swiss 'Regret' Trying to Shred Wartime Files," *New York Times*, January 15, 1997, 1.

39. Michael Shields, "U.S. Jews Hail Swiss Bank Whistle-Blower as Hero," Reuters, January 17, 1997.

40. Alexander Higgins, "Swiss Lawyer Wants Explanation," Associated Press, January 19, 1997.

41. Reuters, "Jewish Agency Welcomes Swiss Envoy Resignation," January 27, 1997.

42. Reuters, "US Lambasts Swiss Envoy Comments on Holocaust," January 27, 1997.

43. Patrick Worsnip, "Swiss Envoy Says Nazi Victims' Claims Too High," Reuters, October 30, 1996.

44. Michael Shields, "Swiss Envoy to US Quits Over Holocaust Row," Reuters, January 27, 1997.

45. Robert Green, "Swiss Ambassador Says Memo Was Misunderstood," Reuters, January 31, 1997.

46. Clare Nullis, "Swiss Try to Restore Reputation," Associated Press, February 1, 1997.

47. Alan Cowell, "Swiss to Use Gold for a Holocaust Fund," *New York Times*, March 6, 1997, 1.

48. Louise Jury, "Swiss to Give 3 Billion Pounds to Victims of Nazis," *The Independent*, March 6, 1997, 1.

49. Cowell, March 6, 1997.

50. Blocher's quotations are from both March 6 and 7, 1997, *New York Times* articles.

SEVEN: A MORAL ACCOUNTING

1. Michael Kimmelman, "How Public Art Turns Political," *New York Times,* October 28, 1996, C15.
2. Reuters, "Swiss Gold Ad for Swatch Stirs Nazi Debate," February 19, 1997.
3. "Inter Arma Caritas: The Work of the International Committee of the Red Cross During the Second World War," International Committee of the Red Cross, Geneva, 1973, 76.
4. "Red Cross Admits 'Moral Failure' in Holocaust," *Jerusalem Post,* May 31, 1995, Internet.
5. Transcripts, Hearing of the U.S. Senate Banking, Housing and Urban Affairs Committee, April 23, 1996, Washington, 8.
6. Edgar Bronfman's quotation is taken from his address to the Canadian Club, March 17, 1997, Toronto.
7. Ibid.
8. Yossi Klein Halevi, "The Accounting," *The Jerusalem Report,* March 6, 1997, 28.
9. Halevi, 32.
10. Raul Hilberg, *The Destruction of the European Jews* (New York: Holmes & Meier, 1985), 1154.
11. Stuart E. Eizenstat (coordinator), "U.S. and Allied Efforts to Recover and Restore Gold and Other Assets Stolen or Hidden by Germany During World War II," U.S. Department of State, May 1997, 4.
12. Naomi Segal, "Some Missing Jewish Assets May Be Found in Israeli Banks," Jewish Telegraphic Agency, May 15, 1997.
13. Lance Morrow, "The Justice of the Calculator," *Time,* February 24, 1997, 25.

BIBLIOGRAPHY

MAJOR WORKS

Aarons, Mark, and Loftus, John. *The Ratlines*. London: William Heinemann, Ltd., 1991.

Arendt, Hannah. *Eichmann in Jerusalem*. New York: Penguin Books, 1994.

Astor, Gerald. *The "Last" Nazi: The Life and Times of Dr. Joseph Mengele*. New York: Donald I. Fine, Inc., 1985.

Beller, Steven. *Vienna and the Jews: 1867–1938: A Cultural History*. Cambridge, England: Cambridge University Press, 1989.

Blattner, Nicklaus. *European Integration and the Swiss Financial Center*. Zürich: Verlag Reugger, 1993.

Bronfman, Edgar M. *The Making of a Jew*. New York: G. P. Putnam's Sons, 1996.

Browning, Christopher. *The Final Solution and the German Foreign Office*. New York: Holmes & Meier Publishers, Inc., 1978.

Clare, George. *Last Waltz in Vienna: The Destruction of a Family, 1842–1942*. London: Macmillan London Ltd., 1981.

Eizenstat, Stuart E. (coordinator). "U.S. and Allied Efforts to Recover and Restore Gold and Other Assets Stolen or Hidden by Germany During World War II." U.S. Department of State, May 1997.

Faith, Nicholas. *Safety in Numbers: The Mysterious World of Swiss Banking*. London: Hamish Hamilton, 1982.

Fehrenbach, T. R. *The Swiss Banks*. New York: McGraw-Hill Book Company, 1966.

Fraenkel, Josef (editor). *The Jews of Austria: Essays on their Life, History and Destruction*. London: Vallentine, Mitchell & Co., Ltd., 1967.

Foreign & Commonwealth Office. *Nazi Gold: Information from the British Archives*. London: September 1996; revised edition, January 1997.

Gilbert, Martin. *The Holocaust*. London: William Collins Sons & Co., Ltd., 1986.

Graml, Hermann. *Anti-Semitism in the Third Reich*. Oxford, England: Blackwell Publishers, 1992.

Häsler, Alfred A. *The Lifeboat is Full: Switzerland and the Refugees, 1933–1945*. New York: Funk & Wagnalls, 1969.

Hilberg, Raul. *The Destruction of the European Jews*. New York: Holmes & Meier, 1985.

International Committee of the Red Cross. *Inter Arma Caritas: The Work of the International Committee of the Red Cross During the Second World War*. Geneva: International Committee of the Red Cross, 1973.

Levin, Nora. *The Holocaust: The Destruction of European Jewry, 1933–1945*. New York: Thomas Y. Crowell Company, 1968.

Lurie, Leonard. *Senator Pothole: The Unauthorized Biography of Al D'Amato*. New York: Carol Publishing Group, 1994.

Maddox, Robert Franklin. *The Senatorial Career of Harley Martin Kilgore*. New York: Garland Publishing, Inc., 1981.

Newton, Ronald C. *The "Nazi Menace" in Argentina, 1931–1947*. Stanford, California: Stanford University Press, 1992.

Nicholas, Lynn H. *The Rape of Europa: The Fate of Europe's Treasures in the Third Reich and the Second World War*. New York: Vintage Books, 1985.

Sandilands, Roger J. *The Life and Political Economy of Lauchlin Currie: New Dealer, Presidential Adviser, and Development Economist*. Durham, North Carolina: Duke University Press, 1990.

Schneider, Gertrude, *Exile and Destruction: The Fate of Austrian Jews, 1938–1945*. Westport, Conn.: Praeger Publishers, 1995.

Shirer, William L. *The Rise and Fall of the Third Reich: A History of Nazi Germany*. New York: Ballantine Books, 1992.

Smith, Arthur L., Jr. *Hitler's Gold: The Story of the Nazi War Loot*. Oxford, England: Berg Publishers Limited, 1989.

Steinberg, Lucien. *The Jews Against Hitler*. London: Gordon & Cremonesi, 1973.

Suhl, Yuri. *They Fought Back: The Story of Jewish Resistance in Nazi Europe*. New York: Schocken Books, 1967.

Toynbee, Arnold, and Veronica Toynbee. *Survey of International Affairs, 1939–1946: The War and the Neutrals*. Oxford, England: Oxford University Press for the Royal Institute of International Affairs, 1956.

Von Lang, Jochen, and Sibyll Claus, eds. *Eichmann Interrogated: Transcripts from the Archives of the Israeli Police,* New York: Farrar, Straus, and Giroux, 1983.

Webber, Harry. *Vienna Today: Photographs of Contemporary Jewish Life*. Vienna: Bohlau Verlag, 1996.

The Project for the Study of Anti-Semitism, Tel Aviv University. *Anti-Semitism Worldwide, 1995/96*. Tel Aviv: Tel Aviv University, 1996.

Wistrich, Robert S., *Who's Who in Nazi Germany*. London: Routledge, 1995.

INTERVIEWS

Anita Ammersfeld, October 30, 1996
Renée Appel, October 10, 1996; January 2, 1997; January 3, 1997; May
   27, 1997
Hans Baer, December 6, 1996
Brigitte Bailer, October 31, 1996
Wilhelm Becker, October 28, 1996
Renée Bellas, October 30, 1996
Ruben Beraja, August 30, 1996; January 6, 1997 (researcher)
Rolf Bloch, December 16, 1996
Thomas Borer, December 16, 1996
Beat Brenner, December 5, 1996
Edgar Bronfman, February 6, 1997; March 17, 1997
Jorge Camarasa, January 6, 1997 (researcher)
Carla del Ponte, December 11, 1996
Alessandro Delprete, December 10, 1996
Irene Etzersdorfer, October 31, 1996
Kurt Fraser, October 29, 1996

Curt Gasteyger, December 12, 1996 (telephone)

Aloisia Greisinger, November 5, 1996

Verena Grendelmeier, December 10, 1996

Paul Grosz, October 29, 1996

Daniel Guggenheim, December 13, 1996

Erich Haberer, November 15, 1996

Ueli Haldimann, December 5, 1996

Willy Halpert, January 17, 1997

Hans Hamersfeld, October 10, 1996; November 25, 1996 (telephone); November 27, 1996

Hanspeter Häni, December 5, 1996

Rafael Harpaz, December 16, 1996

Avshalom Hodik, October 31, 1996

Greville Janner, November 8, 1996

Saul Kagan, February 6, 1997 (telephone)

Aria Karas, November 19, 1996

Sergio Karas, July 30, 1996; September 26, 1996; November 19, 1996 (telephone); March 21, 1997

Frédéric Koller, December 13, 1996

Mathias-Charles Krafft, December 10, 1996

Annette Landers, October 28, 1996

Stephen Lash, October 28, 1996

Fran Laufer, October 29, 1996

Robert Liska, October 28, 1996; October 31, 1996

Janice Lopatkin, November 9, 1996

Leonard Lurie, February 20, 1997

Walter Manoschek, November 1, 1996

Antoine Maurice, December 12, 1996

Lili Nabholz, December 10, 1996

Caterina Nägeli, December 4, 1996

Jacques Picard, December 16, 1996

Lord Poltimore, October 28, 1996

Gerhart Riegner, December 12, 1996

Pierfranco Riva, December 9, 1996

Martin Rosenfeld, December 10, 1996

Hans Safrian, January 21, 1997 (telephone)

Gertrude Schneider, February 7, 1997

Israel Singer, October 29, 1996

Henry Sobel, August 22, 1996

Leopold Spira, November 3, 1996

Elan Steinberg, March 17, 1997; May 28, 1997 (telephone)

Albert Sternfeld, November 2, 1996

Herbert Stilman, February 3, 1997 (telephone); February 5, 1997;
    March 6, 1997 (telephone); March 21, 1997 (telephone)

Linus von Castelmur, December 16, 1996

Sergio Widder, December 27, 1996 (researcher)

Simon Wiesenthal, November 4, 1996

Veit Wyler, December 6, 1996

Jean Ziegler, December 10, 1996

INDEX

imprisonment of, 22
Jewish extermination plan of, 2, 22, 34,
	36–37, 77–78, 84, 94, 125–126,
	127
political rise of, 22, 37, 60
racial purity obsession of, 36–38, 95
secret bank account of, 119
Hitler's Gold (Smith), 240
Hitler's Willing Executioners (Goldhagen),
	10
Hitler Youth, 31
Hochermann, Arthur, 161
Hodik, Avshalom, 291
Hofmann, Madeleine, 231
Holocaust:
	memorials of, 5, 202, 208, 262, 290–292
	modern reexamination of, 9–18, 125–
		126, 181–182
	Polish victims of, 12
	restitution and compensation for
		survivors of, 5, 10, 145, 178
	systematic murder of six million Jews in,
		3, 4, 9, 77, 78, 90, 93–100, 125–
		126, 131, 151
*Holocaust, The: The Destruction of
	European Jews, 1933–1945*
	(Levin), 42
Holocaust Educational Trust, 202, 208
Holocaust Museum (Washington), 5, 262
Holtkott, Richard, 121–122
Holy Roman Empire, 58
Homberger, Max, 68
homosexuals, 171, 277
Höss, Rudolf, 101, 131
House in the Park (Cézanne), 118
House of Commons, British, 203
House of Representatives, U.S., 215–216,
	232, 240–241, 247
Hrdlicka, Alfred, 291
Hug, Peter, 256, 258–260
Huguenots, 60
Hull, Cordell, 117
Hungarian Army, 90
Hungary, 285
	Jewish community in, 25, 26, 89–91, 94,
		133
	in Swiss claims dispute, 14, 259

I. G. Farben, 103
Indonesia, 6, 12, 149
Inter-Allied Declaration Against the Acts of
	Dispossession Committed in
	Territories Under Enemy
	Occupation, 111–112
Inter Allied Reparations Agency (IARA),
	147
International Bank for Reconstruction and
	Development, 149
International Committee of the Red Cross
	(ICRC), 14, 64, 91–92, 93, 234

failure to act on knowledge of Holocaust
	by, 125–126, 295–297, 304
founding of, 63
Nazi escapes facilitated by, 151, 190,
	191
World War II archives of, 125–126
International Court of Justice, 144
International Monetary Fund, 149, 297
International Refugee Organization (IRO),
	142, 145, 146
Iran, 143, 287
Israel, 15, 64, 169–170, 191, 232, 305
	founding of, 168, 169, 175
Israeli Cultural Center (Zürich), 268–269
Israelitische Kultusgemeinde (Jewish
	community organization), 41–42, 72,
	86–87, 154, 161, 164, 288
Italian Mafia, 229–230
Italian Red Cross, 190
Italy, 10–11, 58, 63, 114–116, 117, 138,
	143, 147, 160, 190, 191, 228–230

Jagland, Thorbjorn, 12
Jagmetti, Carlo, 242, 273–275
Janner, Greville, 202, 203–204, 206–208,
	222, 234, 244, 255, 277
Japan, 2, 75, 85, 102
	bombing of Pearl Harbor by, 84, 310
	U.S. war with, 84, 134–135, 310
Jerusalem, 5, 273, 299
Jerusalem Report, 301
Jewish Agency, 15, 265–266, 273
Jewish Colonization Association, 186
Jewish Historical Institute (Warsaw), 276
Jewish Kommando, 87
Jewish Museum (Vienna), 287
Jewish organizations, 175
	compensation and restitution sought by,
		9, 12, 13, 14, 15, 17, 168–170
	financial aid to displaced Jews by, 41–42,
		134, 164
	see also specific organizations
Jewish refugees, 132–134
	communiqués from, 152–153
	in displaced persons camps, 133–134,
		152–154, 161, 169, 175
	hardships of, 45–47, 63–64, 89–92, 132–
		134, 151–158
	rejection of, 15, 71–72, 133
	resettlement of, 142
"Jewish Situation, The," 39–40
Jews:
	assimilation and secularization of, 5, 6,
		23, 24–25, 26–27, 30–31
	despair and suicide among, 48, 291
	Eastern European, 25, 28, 53, 63, 81,
		126, 172
	nationalist vs. religious identity of, 25,
		27, 30–31
	religious conversion of, 27

INDEX